Sports and the American Presidency

In loving memory of David Burns (1959–2022)

New Perspectives on the American Presidency
Series Editors: Michael Patrick Cullinane and Sylvia Ellis,
University of Roehampton

Published titles
Constructing Presidential Legacy: How We Remember the American President
Edited by Michael Patrick Cullinane and Sylvia Ellis

Presidential Privilege and the Freedom of Information Act
Kevin M. Baron

Donald Trump and American Populism
Richard S. Conley

Trump's America: Political Culture and National Identity
Edited by Liam Kennedy

Obama v. Trump: The Politics of Rollback
Clodagh Harrington and Alex Waddan

Obama's Fractured Presidency: Policies and Politics
Edited by François Vergniolle de Chantal

The Republican Party and the War on Poverty: 1964–1981
Mark McLay

Midterms and Mandates: Electoral Reassessment of Presidents and Parties
Edited by Patrick Andelic, Mark McLay and Robert Mason

Sports and the American Presidency: From Theodore Roosevelt to Donald Trump
Edited by Adam Burns and Rivers Gambrell

Forthcoming titles
Harry S. Truman and Higher Education
Rebecca Stone

JFK's Grand Strategy: Breaking the Cold War Mould in the Kennedy White House
James Cooper and Ian Horwood

Donald Trump and the Transformation of US Foreign Policy
Edward Ashbee and Steven Hurst

Series website: https://edinburghuniversitypress.com/
new-perspectives-on-the-american-presidency.html

SPORTS AND THE AMERICAN PRESIDENCY

From Theodore Roosevelt to Donald Trump

Edited by Adam Burns and Rivers Gambrell

EDINBURGH
University Press

Edinburgh University Press is one of the leading university presses in the UK. We publish academic books and journals in our selected subject areas across the humanities and social sciences, combining cutting-edge scholarship with high editorial and production values to produce academic works of lasting importance. For more information visit our website: edinburghuniversitypress.com

Edinburgh University Press Ltd
The Tun – Holyrood Road
12(2f) Jackson's Entry
Edinburgh EH8 8PJ

Typeset in 11/13 Adobe Sabon by
IDSUK (DataConnection) Ltd, and
printed and bound in Great Britain.

A CIP record for this book is available from the British Library

ISBN 978 1 3995 0794 3 (hardback)
ISBN 978 1 3995 0796 7 (webready PDF)
ISBN 978 1 3995 0797 4 (epub)

Contents

Contributors

About the editors

Adam Burns is Head of History and Politics at Bristol Grammar School in the UK. He earned his PhD at the University of Edinburgh and his EdD at the University of Leicester. He is the author of *American Imperialism: The Territorial Expansion of the United States, 1783–2013* (Edinburgh University Press, 2017); *The United States: Reuniting a Nation, 1865–1920* (2020); and *William Howard Taft and the Philippines: A Blueprint for Empire* (2020); as well as several peer-reviewed articles and book chapters on the late nineteenth and early twentieth century United States. His current research focuses on North American sports history and has led to recent articles in *Sport History Review* and the *European Journal of American Culture*.

Rivers Gambrell is a research fellow at the Rothermere American Institute at the University of Oxford. She is currently writing a book entitled *Pigskin Politics: How Richard Nixon Reinvented the Presidency*. She holds a doctorate in History from the University of Oxford, a Masters in Liberal Studies and Certificate in International Development Policy from Duke University, and a BA from Flagler College.

About the authors

Jesse Berrett teaches History at San Francisco University High School in California. He earned his PhD in U.S. History from the University of California, Berkeley. He is the author of *Pigskin Nation: How the NFL Reshaped American Politics* (2018), and has also written articles on the relationship between politics and American football for *Politico* and *Victory Journal*, as well as numerous pieces that have appeared in newspapers such as the *Washington Post* and the *San Francisco Chronicle*.

Chris Birkett is a Visiting Lecturer in Journalism at City, University of London. Chris has had a long and distinguished career in the media, most notably as the executive editor of Sky News between 2006 and 2013. He earned his MA in American Studies and his PhD in History at King's College London where he was a Professor Sir Richard Trainor Scholar between 2017 and 2020. His chapter in this collection represents part of the research for his current book project, titled *Bill Clinton at the Church of Baseball: The Presidency, Civil Religion, and the National Pastime in the 1990s*.

Michael L. Butterworth is the Director of the Center for Sports Communication & Media and Professor of Communication Studies at the University of Texas at Austin. He earned his PhD at Indiana University in 2006. He is the author of *Baseball and Rhetorics of Purity: The National Pastime and American Identity during the War on Terror* (2010); editor of *Sport and Militarism: Contemporary Global Perspectives* (2017), co-editor of *Sport, Rhetoric, and Political Struggle* (2019); and editor of the *Handbook of Communication and Sport* (2021). His work has also appeared in journals such as *Communication and Sport*, the *International Review for the Sociology of Sport*, and the *Journal of Sport & Social Issues*.

Robert Chiles is a Senior Lecturer at the University of Maryland, College Park, where he also earned his PhD in History in 2012. He is the author of *The Revolution of '28: Al Smith, American Progressivism, and the Coming of the New Deal* (2018), as well as various articles on early twentieth-century political history for journals such as the *Journal of the Gilded Age and Progressive Era*, *Environmental History*, and *North Dakota History*. In addition to his academic outputs, he has also contributed opinion pieces to newspapers, including the *Washington Post* and the *New York Daily News*. He is currently the co-editor of the journal *New York History*.

Russ Crawford is a Professor of History at Ohio Northern University. He earned his PhD at the University of Nebraska-Lincoln, and is the author of two monographs, *The Use of Sports to Promote the American Way of Life During the Cold War: Cultural Propaganda, 1946–1963* (2008) and *Le Football: The History of American Football in France* (2016). He has published widely on U.S. and world sports history, and contributed to several edited collections. He is also a regular contributor to the popular "Sport in American History" blog, and his women's football manuscript is forthcoming as *Women's American Football: Breaking Barriers On and Off the Gridiron*.

Heather L. Dichter is an Associate Professor at the International Centre for Sports History and Culture at De Montfort University, Leicester. She earned her PhD at the University of Toronto and is the author of the recent monograph, *Bidding for the 1968 Olympic Games: International Sport's Cold War Battle with NATO* (2021). She has published extensively on the relationship between sports and politics and has edited a number of collections on related themes, including *Soccer Diplomacy: International Relations and Football Since 1914* (2020); with Bruce Kidd, *Olympic Reform Ten Years Later* (2012); and with Andrew Johns, *Diplomatic Games: Sport, Statecraft and International Relations since 1945* (2014).

Michael Hinds is an Associate Professor of English at Dublin City University. He earned his PhD in English at Trinity College, Dublin. He is co-author with Jonathan Silverman of *Johnny Cash International: How the World Loves the Man in Black* (2020); and co-editor of *Rebound: The American Poetry Book* (2007), and *The Irish Reader: Essays for John Devitt* (2007). He has written numerous book chapters on different literary themes, in addition to writing on the subject of horse racing for the *Cambridge Companion to Horse Racing* (2013) and ABC-CLIO's *Encyclopedia of Irish–American Relations* (2007).

Dean J. Kotlowski is Professor of History at Salisbury University. He is the author of *Nixon's Civil Rights: Politics, Principle, and Policy* (2001); *Paul V. McNutt and the Age of FDR* (2015); and the editor of *The European Union: From Jean Monnet to the Euro* (2000). He has published over forty articles and book chapters on U.S. political and policy history, including in journals such as *Diplomatic History*, *Pacific Historical Review*, *Journal of Policy History*, *The Historian*, and *Business History Review*. He has served four times as a Fulbright scholar, in the Philippines (2008), Austria (2016), and Australia (2020, 2022), the last of which was a distinguished chair. He is currently working on his next book, *Toward Self-Determination: Federal Indian Policy from Truman to Clinton*.

Andrew McGregor is a Professor of History at Dallas College. He earned his PhD in History at Purdue University. He has published numerous works on U.S. sports history in peer-reviewed journals, including the *Journal of Sport History* and the *Journal of Sport and Social Issues*, as well as contributing book chapters on baseball, boxing, and Native American identity in sports, and entries to the *American National Biography Online*. He is currently working on an edited collection exploring sport and regional identity in postwar America. He has also written for a variety of media outlets, including the *Washington Post*, and he is the founder of the popular blog "Sport in American History."

Aaron J. Moore is an Associate Professor of Sports Media at Rider University. He earned his PhD from Temple University. He has written for journals, including the *Sport Journal*, and besides his academic work focusing on the sports media and the business of sports, Moore is a member of the United States Basketball Writers Association. He covers college basketball for *Basketball Times Magazine* and has written about sports for the *Philadelphia Inquirer*, *Los Angeles Times*, and the *Sporting News*. Moore is an avid golfer who resides in Lawrence, New Jersey.

Hendrik W. Ohnesorge is Managing Director of the Center for Global Studies, as well as Lecturer and Research Fellow at the Chair in International Relations at the University of Bonn, having previously held guest lectureships at Leiden University and the University of St. Andrews. He earned his doctorate from the University of Bonn in 2019, and has recently published his first monograph titled *Soft Power: The Forces of Attraction in International Relations* (2020), winner of the 2021 ifa Research Award on Foreign Cultural Policy. He has also published a number of scholarly book chapters and journal articles on the presidency and the role of personality in U.S. politics.

Elizabeth Rees is currently a doctoral candidate in History at the University of Oxford, having earned her MA in United States Studies from University College London. Her current DPhil project focuses on the role of the East Wing staff, and is provisionally titled "The Counterpart System: How Does the East Wing and the Office of First Lady Develop Within the Executive Establishment Between 1961–1980?" She is also the author of two forthcoming publications: "The Animal Envoy: Gifting Animals to the White House in Diplomatic History," for the White House Historical Association; and "Plains and Simple: The Influences of Plains, Georgia, and Ideas of the American South on Jimmy Carter's Public Persona," in *Presidents and Place*. She is also the convenor of the American History Research Seminar at the Rothermere American Institute at the University of Oxford.

Jonathan Silverman is a Professor of English and Director of American Studies at the University of Massachusetts Lowell. He is the co-author, with Michael Hinds, of *Johnny Cash International: How and Why the World Loves the Man in Black* (2020); author of *Nine Choices: Johnny Cash and American Culture* (2010); co-author of *The World Is a Text: Writing About Visual and Popular Culture* (2018); and co-editor of *Remaking the American College Campus: Essays* (2016). He served as a Roving Fulbright Scholar in American Studies in Norway and as a John H. Daniels fellow at the National Sporting Library. He is currently editing a collection, *Trash Canned: Understanding the Houston Astros Cheating Scandal*, and working on a critical study on horse racing and technology.

Shawn N. Smith earned his PhD in Communication Studies from the University of Texas at Austin. He is a scholar of race, entrepreneurship, and capitalism. He is deeply involved in a rhetorical and phronetic approach to organizational resistance in and around commercial enterprises. Smith is interested in the ways in which capital is capable of inversion, empowering the very communities it often exploits. For this reason, Smith is dedicated to building communicative organizations that serve the common good.

Ryan Swanson is an Associate Professor of History at the University of New Mexico. He earned his PhD from Georgetown University and has subsequently written and taught widely on the history of sports in the United States. He is the author of two monographs, *When Baseball Went White: Reconstruction, Reconciliation & Dreams of National Pastime* (2014), and *The Strenuous Life: Theodore Roosevelt and the Making of the American Athlete* (2019). He has also co-edited two books on sport history, *Philly Sports* and *Separate Games* (both 2016), published numerous scholarly articles, and has written on sports for the *Washington Post* and *College Football News*.

Introduction: The Sporting Presidency

Rivers Gambrell and Adam Burns

In recent years, the importance of the relationship between sports and the presidency has been easy for all to see via mainstream news outlets and all manner of social media. For example, in a 2016 edition of the *Tampa Bay Times*, columnist David Whitley wrote the following telling lines:

> Bad news, America. When it comes to sport and the presidency, both [Hillary] Clinton and Trump will make you consider moving to Canada. I realize a candidate's sporting cachet isn't as important as their plan to defeat ISIS. But it never hurts to have a vigorous, sports-savvy figure in the Oval Office. It makes them more formidable to our enemies and more relatable to the average American . . .[1]

In essence, there are two directions the media usually approaches it – first, through a president's own skills and athletic prowess, and, second, through their interest in sports as a spectator or fan. Across both Barack Obama and Donald Trump's presidencies, these sporting lenses through which to view the presidency were employed with great frequency.

During Obama's first term, the press often remarked on the president's connection to basketball.[2] For example, in early 2009 Obama played a game at the University of Chicago that was reviewed by a panel of NBA All-Stars on CNN. Hall of Famer Magic Johnson described him as "smart at the game."[3] At the same time, he became known as the nation's "basketball fan-in-chief," watching numerous games during his time in office, though

1

admittedly this habit did not go entirely without criticism.[4] Indeed, by the start of his second term, reports of a different tone were noting just how often the president was *playing* his other favorite game. CBS reporter Mark Knoller reckoned that Obama played more than one hundred games of golf during his first term.[5] For some, his sportiness and fandom was appealing, while for others it was a distraction from the business of running the country.

Donald Trump has often been compared with and most often contrasted to his predecessor, yet the sense that he also played too much golf was a theme often picked up by the press. For columnist Windsor Mann, critics of Trump were missing a trick when criticizing the president for taking to the links: "The more time he spends playing golf, the less time he has to play president."[6] As a spectator, Trump was seen at a variety of sports games, though his attendance sparked a range of responses from fellow fans. As journalist Deb Riechmann noted, his enthusiastic reception at a college football game in Alabama in 2019 contrasted markedly to more divided attitudes at a mixed martial arts event in New York, and a chorus of booing at a World Series game in Washington, DC that same year. As Riechmann rightly went on to note, "Presidents have long used sporting events to woo support, but these events also are a venue for fans to express their own political leanings."[7] Yet though such analytical lenses are commonly used in the media, academic scholarship on the combined subjects is barely out of the starting gate.

Before seeking the Democratic presidential nomination in 1968, Senator Eugene McCarthy quipped, "Being in politics is like being a football coach. You have to be smart enough to understand the game, and dumb enough to think it's important."[8] Although McCarthy's five presidential runs were ultimately unsuccessful, his colleagues who managed to reach the White House would likely agree with this assessment. Over the course of the twentieth century, sports and politics in the United States became inextricably linked, and presidents who could 'understand the game,' so to speak, often fared better than those who were either unwilling or unable to tap into the nation's most popular pastimes, whether as spectators or participants.

As this book shows, the intertwined history of athletics and the presidency is one that rivals even the most gripping sports sagas.

2

Since Theodore Roosevelt took the oath of office in 1901, Americans have witnessed narrow victories, motivational speeches, devastating health problems, and unlikely comebacks in the tumultuous political sphere that Richard Nixon, borrowing from Roosevelt, aptly dubbed 'the Arena.' Both publicly and behind the scenes, athletes, coaches, and other individuals who made their livings in real arenas and stadiums across the country played important roles in presidential campaigns and, in some cases, the White House itself.

As the nation's leading sportsmen and women became more heavily involved in politics, so too did presidents more closely align themselves with the world of athletics, both for personal and political purposes. There was a marked shift over the course of twentieth-century history from presidential attendance at seemingly benign ceremonial events (William Howard Taft first throwing out the first pitch at a baseball game in 1910) to controversial engagements with multi-billion dollar sports industries (Donald Trump's insistence that the college football season move forward during the COVID-19 pandemic in 2020). The goal of this volume is to provide the first interdisciplinary examination of the sporting presidency in the twentieth and twenty-first centuries – its origins, transformation, and importance.

Sports are a central, highly visible aspect of the human experience, and the presidency is the central, most visible feature of the American political apparatus. It is not surprising that the general public and press have taken a vested interest in a combination of the two for well over a century. Indeed, the *Brooklyn Daily Eagle* headline from 1907, "President Defends College Athletics: Is in Favor of All Kinds of Sports, But Thinks Students Should Also Study," could just as easily be found on a leading news organization's Twitter feed in 2021.[9] And yet, while presidential engagement in the sports world – and the population's interest in this engagement – is nothing new, over the years the phenomenon has taken on new dimensions that crave scholarly evaluation. Hitherto, the sporting presidency has flown under the historical radar, even as presidents have increasingly come to recognize sport as an important component of both personal and national prestige.

While there are several trade publications that touch on sports and the presidency, and at least one book penned by a former

3

president himself (Herbert Hoover's charming *Fishing for Fun*), academic scholarship still lags well behind.[10] To date, no single volume has provided a multifaceted evaluation of the various and vital connections between sport and the American presidency. John Sayle Watterson perhaps came the closest with his book *The Games Presidents Play: Sports and the Presidency*, which remains the only scholarly monograph to summarily outline the "uses (and abuses) of sports" by American presidents.[11] Focusing primarily on the mid to late twentieth century, Watterson speculates on the ways in which presidential hobbies and pastimes may have influenced individual leadership styles.

A small number of academic texts have further explored the close relationship between sport and the presidency, including recent volumes such as Curt Smith's *The President and the Pastime*, Jesse Berrett's *Pigskin Nation*, and Nicholas Evans Sarantakes' *Fan in Chief*.[12] Smith explains how the country's initial favorite pastime (baseball) personally influenced various presidents, whilst Berrett evaluates the substantial impact that football had on American politics during the 1960s and early 1970s from a more socio-cultural angle. Sarantakes, meanwhile, takes a more personal approach to Richard Nixon, describing the thirty-seventh president's intense sports fandom.

This edited collection goes beyond the aforementioned works by providing an overarching interdisciplinary analysis of the relationship between sports and the American presidency from the early twentieth century to the end of the Trump presidency in 2021. Incorporating the research of a diverse group of scholars from across academia, and stretching far beyond the confines of a single sport, pastime, or administration, *Sports and the American Presidency* offers a novel approach to the complex relationship between the nation's top office and its most popular sporting pastimes.

This book was conceived during a time when the sporting world was becoming increasingly politicized and polarizing – one need only look to the extensive resonance of the Black Lives Matter movement for evidence of this. Following American footballer Colin Kaepernick's 2016 protest, the decision by players across sports to 'take a knee' against racism has become an international, and controversial, phenomenon.[13] The broad nature of the case studies presented in this book allows readers to draw their own conclusions regarding the increasingly significant socio-political connections between sport and the presidency. This volume draws upon the expertise of scholars from the United States and further afield, and brings together historians with scholars of other disciplines, such as media and communication studies. Also, unlike Watterson's existing volume on presidents and sport, this collection does not take a president-by-president approach to the sporting presidency. Instead, the following chapters provide a cross-disciplinary exploration of the subject in three main parts: 'Presidents and Their Sports,' 'Sports and Their Presidents,' and 'Athletes and the Presidency.'

The first section features four very different presidents united by their shared belief in the importance of sport, which they viewed as integral not only to the health of the individual, but also to the nation as a whole. Each of these presidents promoted sport and physical activity passionately, and these chapters reveal the impact and consequences of their intimate involvement with the world of athletics. The section opens with Ryan Swanson's examination of the chief executive who is perhaps most often associated with personal athletic ability: Theodore Roosevelt. Swanson situates the modern sporting presidency's origins with Roosevelt, and approaches TR's renowned athleticism and sports affiliations from a new angle through a close analysis of one of his lesser known speeches. The chapter explains how the twenty-sixth president advanced the idea of sports as progress, both to his own family and to the country.

The shadow of Roosevelt's robust sporting image was cast over all his successors in office, including the youngest man to sit in the Oval Office after him: John F. Kennedy. Hendrik W. Ohnesorge's chapter considers Kennedy's promotion of physical fitness during the Cold War, and demonstrates the ways in which JFK was able to project a masculine and athletic image despite his own physical limitations. Ohnesorge also examines sport as a facet of diplomacy, and discusses how athleticism became a core component of U.S. soft power during Kennedy's thousand days in office.

The third chapter focuses on Kennedy's nemesis in the 1960 presidential election, Richard Nixon. By the time Nixon reached the White House, his love of sport was well known and highly publicized, a politically useful aspect of his otherwise awkward personality. Jesse Berrett takes a step back to consider Nixon's origins as a sports fan, demonstrating how Nixon was able to establish his role as a public authority on sport during his formative years in Congress and as Dwight Eisenhower's vice president. Berrett explains how Nixon's fandom was simultaneously authentic and performative, and concludes that the thirty-seventh president wrote the playbook for future politicians hoping to capitalize on sports spectatorship.

Bill Clinton also hoped to score political points when he involved himself in Major League Baseball's heated labor dispute during the winter of 1994–95. In the section's final chapter, Chris Birkett provides an in-depth assessment of Clinton's ill-fated decision to intervene in the conflict, and explains why presidential engagement with the world of sports does not always result in mutually beneficial outcomes. Like those before him, Clinton operated on the assumption that what was good for baseball was good for the people of the United States, and, accordingly, his poll numbers. As Birkett notes, "one of the driving forces behind his thinking was a myth that had been propagated by journalists, scholars, and politicians since the early twentieth century – that the health of the national pastime was a measure of the health and vitality of American society itself."

The health and vitality of the presidents themselves is featured prominently in the book's second section, titled Sports and Their Presidents. Organized thematically, these chapters explore the relationships of several presidents to a single sporting activity. These chapters veer away from the nation's more traditional pastimes, as they address running and jogging, golf, rugby, and horse racing, respectively. The final chapter then centers on rugby's more popular offshoot, college football.

In the section's first chapter, Elizabeth Rees argues that there is a significant link in the public consciousness between the president's ability to run physically and his ability to run the country. In order to assess presidents' 'fitness' to govern, she identifies two categories of presidential running and jogging – 'struggling' or 'striving' – and explains how the practice has had serious implications for presidents' political images since the 1970s. The chapter features four joggers-in-chief: Jimmy Carter, George H. W. Bush, Bill Clinton, and George W. Bush.

Golf is perhaps the most favored of all presidential pastimes since the start of the twentieth century, and it is another sport that has produced varied political ramifications for recent presidents. A. J. Moore demonstrates this through his thematic analysis of mainstream press coverage of golfing presidents from William Howard Taft to Donald Trump. Moore's chapter aims to determine whether or not prevailing attitudes in the media on the topic have changed since Taft took the oath of office in 1909. He argues that presidents who hit the links face a 'golf paradox,' as the sport can prove both beneficial and problematic from a public relations perspective.

Unlike golf, rugby has been virtually ignored in the existing literature on sport and the presidency. Adam Burns effectively fills this gap with his chapter on American football's predecessor, by exploring three presidents who engaged with the sport long before entering the Oval Office: Woodrow Wilson, Bill Clinton, and George W. Bush. Though Wilson's involvement began this often ignored presidential sporting relationship, it was Clinton and Bush – in the midst of the Cold War – who became active rugby players during their college years. Burns' chapter explores the latter two's involvement with the game through the lenses of class and masculinity, and considers why – despite its 'foreignness' – playing rugby helped to bolster both of their presidential images in later life.

Next out of the gates are Michael Hinds and Jonathan Silverman, who explore the long-standing yet erratic connections between horse racing and the presidency. After briefly exploring the roots of the relationship way back under the nation's first commander in chief, the authors investigate three presidents who attempted to 'harness' the political potential of the increasingly controversial sport, and consider how presidential attendance at the race track has defined various administrations. After considering the presidencies of Franklin D. Roosevelt and Richard Nixon, Hinds and Silverman conclude with an evaluation of Donald Trump's foray into the world of horse racing, which took place via social media amidst a decline in the sport's popularity.

In the section's final chapter, Andrew McGregor traces the relationship between college football and the presidency, and examines how Kennedy, Nixon, and others were able to retool the sport for political purposes during the Cold War. McGregor argues that some of college football's most prominent coaches and administrators furthered the politicization of the sport by selectively honoring presidents and using presidential rhetoric to attach political meaning to the game. Amidst the burgeoning 'Culture Wars,' college football became a partisan weapon.

Just as coaches have played instrumental roles in the convergence of sport and presidential politics, so too have their charges, and it is to them that the last section of this book is dedicated. The chapters comprising 'Athletes and the Presidency' describe the ways in which presidents and presidential candidates have courted the country's most successful sportsmen and women. Over the years, however, many of the country's most prominent athletes have not been willing to 'play ball,' and more than a few presidents struck out with the players whose political support they most desperately craved. The chapters explore how athletes – whether associated with or alienated from the White House – have been able to leverage their status as popular sports figures into positions of political significance, both on and off the field.

First to bat is Robert Chiles, whose chapter examines Babe Ruth's enthusiastic involvement in the 1928 presidential election. Ruth was an ardent supporter of the Democratic nominee, New York Governor Al Smith, the unsuccessful opponent of the eventual winner, Herbert Hoover. Ruth was one of the first celebrity athletes to publicly endorse a candidate, a decision that – as this chapter shows – met with mixed results. Yet, as Chiles explores, Ruth and other athletes' involvement in the 1928 presidential race represented a subtle and early form of identity politics, and signaled the rise of famous sports figures as potential political representatives.

Following in Ruth's political footsteps was the barrier-breaking second baseman Jackie Robinson, the first black player to enter Major League Baseball. Unlike Ruth – whose incursion into presidential politics was basically limited to a single election – Robinson was politically active for several years. Dean J. Kotlowski situates the evolution of Robinson's involvement in politics within the context of the changing Civil Rights Movement and partisan realignments of the 1960s. The chapter explains how Robinson's activism normalized the blending of sports and political advocacy, and set an important precedent for other Black athletes.

Robinson also features in Michael L. Butterworth and Shawn N. Smith's chapter on sport, merit, and respectability politics. In order to identify the limits of sport as a political metaphor, Butterworth and Smith explore the analogical associations made between Barack Obama and distinguished athletes of color – including Robinson and champion golfer Tiger Woods – during the 2008 presidential campaign. They argue that the media's common narrative of racial progress through sport served (and continues to serve) as a rhetorical means for deflecting political conflict. They conclude that athlete activism has, for the most part, been absorbed into universalist narratives that help to preserve the status quo.

The final chapter of the book touches on similar themes, as Russ Crawford explains how Donald Trump's engagement with the world of sport – and the polarized reactions that these interactions produced – elevated the politicization of athletes to an unprecedented level. Crawford's chapter explores the traditional visits of championship teams to the White House, and how this usually sedate tradition became the site of increasing partisanship and friction during his years in office, with both Trump and various athletes using their relationship (or lack of one) to make political points. Beyond this, the chapter also traces the growing role of social media in exacerbating the fractured nature of the relationship between sportspeople and the presidency by the end of Trump's term in office.

Following these three thematic sections, sports historian Heather L. Dichter provides an expert summary of how this volume adds to the existing academic landscape on sport, politics, and the presidency, and where potential avenues for future exploration lie. In this chapter she identifies how themes explored here could be expanded, as well as how further avenues for investigation – such as women's sports and international competitions – provide fertile ground for future investigations into how the U.S. presidency and sport are inextricably intertwined. As Dichter makes clear, this volume provides a starting point for re-evaluating this important connection, but there is still much for scholars to unearth to get a fuller understanding of this ongoing, symbiotic relationship.

Notes

1. David Whitley, "Candidates Fail the Presidential Sports Test," *Tampa Bay Times*, October 5, 2016, T29.
2. For more on this, see Alexander Wolff, *The Audacity of Hoop: Basketball and the Age of Obama* (Philadelphia, PA: Temple University Press, 2015).
3. *Chicago Tribune*, "Obama's Weekend: Dining Out and Hoops," *Clarion-Ledger*, February 16, 2009, 6A.
4. Tina Daunt, "Obama Keeps Eye on the Ball," *Los Angeles Times*, May 29, 2009, available at: https://www.latimes.com/archives/la-xpm-2009-may-29-et-cause29-story.html; Associated Press, "Obama Watches UNC Beat Michigan State," *Herald & Review*, November 12, 2011, B7; Frank James, "Critics Trash Talk Obama For Doing ESPN Brackets During Multiple Crises," *NPR*, March 16, 2011, available at: https://www.npr.org/sections/itsallpolitics/2011/03/19/134599376/obama-trash-talked-for-doing-espn-brackets-during-multiple-crises.
5. George Bennett, "Visit Fifth to Area in Past Year," *Palm Beach Post*, February 15, 2013, A4.
6. Windsor Mann, "The More Trump Plays Golf, the Less He Plays President," *Times Recorder*, February 21, 2017, 6A.
7. Deb Riechmann, "Trump Soaks in Deep South Cheers at College Football Matchup," *Boston Herald*, November 9, 2019, available at: https://www.bostonherald.com/2019/11/09/trump-soaks-in-deep-south-cheers-at-college-football-matchup.
8. Joseph Kraft, "The McCarthy Enigma," *Washington Post*, November 12, 1967, B7.
9. "President Defends College Athletics," *Brooklyn Daily Eagle*, February 24, 1907, 6.
10. Herbert Hoover, *Fishing for Fun and to Wash Your Soul* (New York: Random House, 1963). Examples of some of the better-known volumes include: John Durant, *The Sports of Our Presidents* (New York: Hastings House, 1964); Edmund Lindop and Joseph Jares, *White House Sportsmen* (Boston, MA: Houghton Mifflin, 1964); George Sullivan, *Presidents at Play* (New York:

Walker, 1995); Shep Campbell and Peter Landau, *Presidential Lies: The Illustrated History of White House Golf* (New York: Macmillan, 1996); William B. Mead and Paul Dickson, *Baseball: The President's Game* (Washington, D.C.: Farragut, 1997); Don Van Natta, Jr., *First Off the Tee: Presidential Hackers, Duffers, and Cheaters from Taft to Bush* (New York: PublicAffairs, 2003); Terry Frei, *Horns, Hogs, and Nixon Coming: Texas vs. Arkansas in Dixie's Last Stand* (New York: Simon & Schuster, 2002); Paul F. Boller, Jr., *Presidential Diversions: Presidents at Play from George Washington to George W. Bush* (New York: Harcourt, 2007); Catherine M. Lewis, *Don't Ask What I Shot: How Eisenhower's Love of Golf Helped Shape 1950's America* (New York: McGraw-Hill, 2007); Lars Anderson, *Carlisle versus Army: Jim Thorpe, Dwight Eisenhower, Pop Warner, and the Forgotten Story of Football's Greatest Battle* (New York: Random House, 2007); Rick Reilly, *Commander in Cheat: How Golf Explains Trump* (London: Headline, 2019).

11. John Sayle Watterson, *The Games Presidents Play: Sports and the Presidency* (Baltimore, MD: Johns Hopkins University Press, 2006), 4.

12. Curt Smith, *The President and the Pastime: The History of Baseball and the White House* (Lincoln: University of Nebraska Press, 2018); Jesse Berrett, *Pigskin Nation: How the NFL Remade American Politics* (Urbana: University of Illinois Press, 2018); Nicholas Evans Sarantakes, *Fan in Chief: Richard Nixon and American Sports, 1969–1974* (Lawrence: University Press of Kansas, 2019).

13. "What's Taking the Knee and Why is it Important," *BBC News*, October 13, 2021, available at: https://www.bbc.com/news/explainers-53098516.

Part One

Presidents and Their Sports

Theodore Roosevelt: Father of a Sporting Nation

Ryan Swanson

On February 23, 1907, President Theodore Roosevelt delivered a speech at Harvard University that once and for all summarized his opinions on what athletics *should* be in the United States. The address came as Roosevelt, a popular president in his second term in the White House, crested a wave of political power.[1] The foundation for the speech had been laid over the previous decades. For years, Americans had read stories about Roosevelt playing tennis and boxing at the White House. They had seen images of him at the Army–Navy football game. They had learned that he liked to spend his Sunday afternoons taking long, muddy point to point hikes through Rock Creek Park. More recently, they knew that the president had hosted a White House football summit in 1905, a move that thwarted those reformers who wanted to abolish football and contributed to the rise of the National Collegiate Athletic Association (NCAA).

The location and audience for this speech fit the task at hand. Athletics at the turn of the twentieth century, and for Roosevelt more specifically, were about young men. Roosevelt was a graduate of Harvard University, class of 1880. His oldest son, Ted Jr., was studying at the institution in 1907. And so, with Ted Jr. and nearly 2,000 of his classmates looking on, Roosevelt wove together in this speech a tapestry that advocated for wide participation, that positioned athletics as a form of nationalism, and that made the case for the co-mingling of sports and higher education. In a way, the speech had a Gettysburg Address quality to it. It took something big and attempted to distill it down to its core.

Roosevelt never had Abraham Lincoln's penchant for brevity, nor his discipline to hammer home only one topic during one speech. But on this day in 1907, Roosevelt tried to get at the essential elements of how athletics fit into American life.

Roosevelt drove home four main points. First, the number of Americans participating in athletics needed to grow. Roosevelt believed that more Americans, particularly boys and men, needed the sharpening that athletics could provide. Second, intercollegiate athletics not only served the athletes that participated, but also served to grow sports more generally. Roosevelt believed in America's unique blending of athletics and higher education because he saw it as a conduit to bigger changes. Third, the threat of "mollycoddle" men made sports a necessity. Yes, the mollycoddle man was a strawman of sorts, but Roosevelt feared that America was becoming softer and weaker. And, fourth, athletics must not overtake education and citizenship as national priorities. Athletics in service of the nation, TR stressed, not the other way around.

Roosevelt's words found their mark – not only with the students that crowded into the Harvard Union to hear the speech, but also with those who read the front pages of the next day's newspapers. "'No Mollycoddles,' Says Roosevelt," was how the *New York Times* summarized the speech on its front page.[2] What the headline lacked in nuance, it got right in terms of tenor. For Roosevelt, the threat of America going 'mollycoddle' always loomed just around the corner. This threat in many ways fueled Roosevelt's support for athletics. None of the four points were new for those who had been paying attention to the president across the last few years. Roosevelt had tried out these ideas in public, and instituted them in his own home, with his own children. The ideas had been present in his 'Strenuous Life' speech nearly eight years earlier.[3] But, for the purpose of codifying a Rooseveltian athletics doctrine and demonstrating just how fundamentally Roosevelt had changed the relationship between sports and the U.S. presidency, the Harvard Union speech was a tour de force.

Not surprisingly, most Roosevelt biographers fail to mention his speech at Harvard. Given the sheer number of speeches Roosevelt gave over the course of his public lifetime, and the number of causes he supported, the omission makes sense. Also, there was much going on in late 1906 and 1907 that might distract the otherwise diligent Roosevelt scholar from picking up on TR's athletic trailblazing via a Harvard parents' weekend. Roosevelt received his Nobel Peace Prize, for his work in brokering a truce between Russia and Japan, in December 1906. Late in the year, the Panic of 1907, labeled by the president's critics 'The Roosevelt Panic,' wrecked the still fragile stock market. A run on banks, in a time before the advent of federal deposit insurance, forced Roosevelt to cooperate with Wall Street tycoons in order to save the American banking system.[4]

Roosevelt also entered the New Year of 1907 with burgeoning political problems.[5] Late in 1906, Roosevelt made an impetuous decision that earned him the scorn of Black voters. At issue was the handling of the Brownsville, Texas, uprising of August 1906. For months after the conflict, the administration had haphazardly investigated the matter. The Black troops involved, understandably, had refused to break ranks and cooperate with investigators. The issue festered until, believing that he had information enough, Roosevelt issued Special Order number 266. The order dishonorably discharged all the Black enlisted men stationed in Brownsville – 167 in total. Roosevelt, who previously had strong support among Black Americans, lost his standing among the community almost overnight. And, after the deed was done, the *New York Times* and several other major U.S. newspapers rushed to the defense of the Black soldiers. Roosevelt had made a significant political, and moral, mistake.[6]

On a more personal note, 1907 found Roosevelt confronting his own physical limitations. Gone were the days of hours-long work-outs in the boxing gymnasium followed by late nights of reading whatever might catch his fancy. Roosevelt was breaking down. He was tired. His weight had swelled to more than 200 pounds. "I'm sorry to say that I have not only grown fat, but also a little gouty," Roosevelt would admit to a friend later.[7] While Roosevelt was young for a president (still not fifty at this point), he was no longer a young man. Roosevelt's long quest to live a life of strenuous activity had shifted towards maintenance and forestalling.

Increasingly, Roosevelt's views on sports and athletics were wrapped up in the experiences of his six children (Alice, Ted, Kermit, Ethel, Archie, and Quentin). His older boys had taken to the athletic

fields at Groton School and Harvard.[8] Through the experiences of
Ted Jr. especially, Roosevelt contemplated how athletics might aid
young men in becoming fully functional American citizens.

Roosevelt had always ridden his oldest son hard. When Ted
was ten years old, he had collapsed under the weight of his father's
expectations. Over a period of months in 1887 and 1888, Ted suffered from debilitating headaches and remained bedridden. A host
of physicians visited the family's home at Sagamore Hill but could
not identify the cause of the intense pain. Finally, in March 1888,
New York City physician Alexander Lambert identified Roosevelt
as the root cause of Ted's illness. Roosevelt – the nineteenth-century
equivalent of an overbearing Little League dad – was to blame.

"Dr. Lambert reported that the boy was suffering from nervous
prostration brought on by the way Teddy constantly drove him to
perfection and Ted's desire to live up to his father's expectations,"
explained a Ted Jr. biographer.[9] The diagnosis stunned Roosevelt.
"Hereafter I shall never press Ted either in body or in mind,"
Roosevelt wrote to Dr. Lambert, making a promise that he could
not keep. "The fact is that the little fellow, who is peculiarly dear
to me, had bidden fair to be all things I would like to have been
and wasn't, and it has been a great temptation to push him."[10]

Ted participated in athletics at significant cost to his health.
He did so, one might guess, in part to please his father and to fit
into the Strenuous Life paradigm. During his time on the Groton
football team, Ted suffered a broken collarbone, chipped teeth,
bruised ribs and a dislocated thumb.[11] At Harvard, Ted, though
only 5 ft 6 in. and 130 pounds, earned a position on the freshman
football squad – he started at end.

The action, against much bigger players, soon took its toll.
During the 1905 season Ted broke his thumb and suffered from
bruised ribs. In a game against Yale, Ted broke a finger and suffered what was probably a concussion. The *Boston Daily Globe*
praised Ted for showing "the grit that's in him," and described
how Ted lost his bearings on the field. "In the second half he
began to get groggy, and the Elis sent play after play at him," the
paper reported.[12] Three times during the 1905 football season Ted
appeared on the "Details of the More Serious Injuries" list kept
by the *Chicago Daily Tribune*.[13] Such injuries led to Harvard's

President, Charles Eliot, leading a movement to abolish college football altogether. And in response both to his son's injuries and Eliot's pressure, Roosevelt called the coaches of Harvard, Princeton, and Yale to the White House in October 1905. There the coaches learned first-hand of Roosevelt's passion for football as well as his concern for its future. While changes came slowly, Roosevelt's involvement eventually contributed to the adoption of more stringent rules and the establishment of a governing body – the NCAA.[14]

In the 1906 season, Ted sprained his knee and broke his ankle. Initially misdiagnosed as a sprain, the ankle never healed properly. Ted finally gave up football, just weeks before his father came to visit in 1907.[15]

Preventing a generation of mollycoddles

Roosevelt arrived on campus on a raw, bone-chilling Saturday. The high for the day was just 36°F, with a mix of snow and rain expected.[16] While the *Washington Post* characterized the trip to Massachusetts, in the midst of the Congressional session, as "purely a personal one," Roosevelt rarely wasted an opportunity to make a political point. He planned to see his son *and* make an argument for the utility of sports in America. Per the security protocol of the times, Roosevelt and his family traveled in a private railcar attached to an express train. Accompanied by his daughters Ethel, Alice, and Alice's husband, Nicholas Longworth, both Roosevelt and his wife, Edith, looked forward to visiting their oldest sons – Ted Jr. at Harvard and Kermit at Groton. Only Quentin and Archie remained in Washington, under the care of White House staff.[17]

The impetus for the trip, Ted's admission ceremony into the exclusive Porcellian Club at Harvard, was slated for 6.30 pm on Saturday evening.[18] This left plenty of time for Roosevelt to engage in activities rooted in nostalgia, parental interest, and political calculation.[19] As always, he kept a breakneck schedule. In a matter of 48 hours, Roosevelt had breakfast with a former Harvard classmate, attended the christening of the son of a fellow 'Rough Rider' from his time in Cuba, stopped in at the offices of the publisher Houghton Mifflin, took a side trip to visit Kermit at Groton, and, of course, gave a talk on athletics in America at Harvard.[20] While at Groton, Roosevelt shared a few words with Kermit and 150 of his classmates. He urged the boys to study, and "always play football fairly." Roosevelt wrapped up, somewhat oddly given the young audience, with the opinion "that intercollegiate football should by no means be abolished."[21]

By 2.30 pm, students were jammed into the Harvard Union in anticipation of Roosevelt's speech. The collective body heat made up for the biting cold outside. The Harvard Union was a relatively new building, completed in 1901 and funded through a donation from Major Henry L. Higginson. The object of the Union was to "promote comradeship among the members of the university by providing at Cambridge a suitable club for social purposes." To make sure that all Harvard men could enjoy this camaraderie, the Union leadership pledged to keep dues low.[22] If there was an 'everyman' space at Harvard – an elite institution closed off from the vast majority of Americans (and shut off to females) – the Union was that place.

In the building's large living room, "thirteen mounted heads of American game" decorated the walls. Moose, buffalo, and mountain sheep were among the trophy heads mounted. A rugged antler chandelier hung above the solid, heavy living room table.[23] Trophies commemorating Harvard's victories in lacrosse and other sports decorated the bookshelves and walls.[24] All furniture had been removed from the facility's largest room; a standing-room only crowd of about 1,900 men awaited Roosevelt. There was no man that would have inspired a bigger audience at America's preeminent university. Roosevelt sprouted at Harvard. The students claimed him as one of their own. Roosevelt had both academic and everyman qualities, along with a charisma that few politicians could equal. The crowd pushed toward the small platform – just enough to hold several chairs for honored guests and a podium for the President of the United States – ready to hear the words of the world's most prominent statesman.

"When the President arose to speak, he was greeted by a long cheer, which lasted several minutes," the *Harvard Crimson* reported.[25] Roosevelt began by praising the university: "I wish to say first a special word as one Harvard man to his fellow Harvard men." That taken care of, Roosevelt plunged into a speech that would careen from athletics first, to education, and then to broader foreign policy. "One reason why I so thoroughly believe in the athletic spirit at Harvard is because the athletic spirit is essentially democratic," Roosevelt started. In the more than 4,700 words that followed, the president expanded on this thought. Sports served to make men. Sports created opportunity. They had, Roosevelt hoped, done much to make his own sons. Roosevelt made four central points in the speech that electrified his audience and clarified what he hoped sports had become – and would continue to become – in the United States. Roosevelt spent most of his time on participation: "our concern should be most of all to widen the base, the founding in athletic sports." He followed this foundation point by advocating for the combining of education and athletics via intercollegiate sport, and by declaring pointedly that America risked a generation of "mollycoddles" if academic learning completely supplanted physical instruction.[26]

On this occasion, Roosevelt spoke both as a father *and* as a politician. Roosevelt had traveled with his wife and daughters to see his sons. The weekend celebrated Ted Jr.'s entry into his father's exclusive club. And, perhaps, Roosevelt recognized that time was growing short. Roosevelt's boys were moving rapidly toward their independence. In another year, Ted would be graduating from Harvard. "It is of far more importance that a man shall play something himself, even if he plays it badly, than that he shall go with hundreds of companions to see some one else play well," Roosevelt told the Harvard men. While Roosevelt favored boxing and tennis, he mostly required of his own children just that they play something. When, for example, Quentin took to baseball – Roosevelt's least favorite athletic activity – Roosevelt reacted with enthusiasm. The boy was playing; that is what mattered. Roosevelt's letters to his children, and his letters about his children, reflect this participatory bent. Do not watch; go play. Roosevelt saw, in fact, a level of low-grade tragedy in spectator sports.[27]

Just as Roosevelt's Harvard weekend in February 1907 involved a jumble of responsibilities, Roosevelt did not view his parenting as a task completely cut off from his presidential duties. While he protected his children, fiercely at times, from prying reporters, Roosevelt gave speeches at his children's schools. Later, he would make sure that his correspondence with his children was published. "Only a short time before he died," editor Joseph Bishop conveyed in his introduction, "he said to me, as we were going over the letters and planning this volume, which is arranged as he wished it to be: 'I would rather have this book published than anything that has ever been written about me.'"[28] The idea of parenting a child, but also considering one's example as a parent to the nation as a whole, sheds some light on Roosevelt's trip to Harvard in 1907. Roosevelt came to support Ted Jr. and to celebrate his son's accomplishments. Roosevelt recognized, perhaps, that he should visit Harvard as a father rather than as president, or even as an alum, but he could not seem to help himself. The public and the private became commingled, especially when sports were involved.

Roosevelt wrote hundreds of letters to his six children. Selected father-to-child letters have been used to compile several collections of 'Theodore Roosevelt's Letters to His Children.' The first and most significant of these collections was released in 1919, as the nation mourned Roosevelt's death. It came too, of course, as the Roosevelt children grieved over the loss of their father. It was at this point that the nation learned that Roosevelt had written to his children throughout their lives. "Whenever he was separated from them, in the Spanish War, or on a hunting trip, or because they were at school, he sent them these messages of constant thought and love, for they were never out of his mind and heart," wrote Bishop.[29] The letters reveal a fawning, intimate Roosevelt. Off at war in 1898, for example, Roosevelt wrote to his "Darling Ethel." He dipped his prose right to the six-year-old's level: "I loved your little letter. Here there are lots of funny little lizards that run about in the dusty roads . . ."[30] Scholars have been lavishly kind, for the most part, in assessing Roosevelt as a father. David McCullough, one of America's best-selling historians, viewed fatherhood as Roosevelt's ultimate role. "Incapable of doing anything by half measure, he embraced every part he ever played – scholar, suitor, soldier, cowboy and bear-hunter, husband, politician, President of the United States – but that of being a father most especially. He took on the role for his six children as if life depended on it, his and theirs."[31] It is a touching assessment. But what about Roosevelt as an early sports dad?

Roughly one-third of the letters that Roosevelt selected to include in his *Letters from Theodore Roosevelt to His Children* make mention of athletics. Roosevelt shared stories about his own athletic pursuits, and those of Quentin and Archie, with Ted and Kermit. Picking out a singular 'athletic' theme from these letters is difficult. But, as much as anything, Roosevelt urged the idea of participation. He assured his children that he did not expect athletic excellence. Roosevelt certainly supported winning and competition, but his children received regular reminders from their father that being a part of a team, being on the field, taking one's spot at the starting line – rather than outstanding achievement – were his 'requirements.'

To "Blessed Ted," Roosevelt wrote in 1901, "I am entirely satisfied with your standing, both in your studies and in athletics." He then, as he almost always did, expanded further on the topic at hand: "I want you to do well in your sports, and I want even more to have you do well with your books; but I do not expect you to stand first in either . . ." Roosevelt wanted well-roundedness, he wanted robust activity: "To have you play football as well as you do, and make a good name in boxing and wrestling, and be cox of your second crew, and stand second or third in your class in the studies is all right."[32] Two years later, in 1903, the president wrote to his oldest son again. Ted Jr., now sixteen years old and a junior at Groton, received further advice from his father on how to pursue athletics. At issue was the question of whether Ted should push to make the second team in football, rather than the third, at the risk of getting injured. In a series of letters, Roosevelt urged that Ted make decisions that would allow him to keep playing – this was the goal.[33]

"If you get mashed up now in a serious way," Roosevelt wrote to his son, "it may prevent your playing later . . . I do not in the least object to your getting smashed if it is for an object that is worth while, such as playing on the Groton team or playing on your class team when you get to Harvard." But this was not such a case: "I think it a little silly to run any imminent risk of a serious smash simply to play on the second squad instead of third." Roosevelt could not help concluding by reflecting upon his own declining athletic state: "I am judging for you as I would for myself," he wrote, before confessing that he had grown "stiff and heavy," flashing a trace of envy toward his young, virile son.[34]

A League of His Own

Roosevelt wanted education and athletics combined at virtually all age levels. "It is not healthy for either students or athletes if the terms are mutually exclusive," he told Ted Jr. and his Harvard classmates during his February visit.[35] Fortunately for Roosevelt, progress on this front was underway. Just two weeks after his speech at Harvard, New York City gave rise to a Rooseveltian league of its own. The *New York Times* announced the new league's establishment, gushing over the precedent of a sitting U.S. president allowing his name to be used for the promotion of interscholastic athletics.[36] The formerly named 'District League No. 7' of the Public Schools Athletic League (PSAL) of New York City became the Roosevelt Athletic League.[37]

Even before its name change, the New York PSAL had already shown distinctively Rooseveltian ideals. "The object of the Public Schools Athletic League is the physical development of the pupils of the public schools and the cultivation of an interest in athletic sports under correct instruction and wholesome influences," declared a 1905 statement outlining the PSAL's ideals and donors.[38] The PSAL was the brainchild of Luther Gulick, an acclaimed physical education instructor.[39] "All the boys in the city needed the physical benefits and moral and social lessons afforded by properly conducted games and sport," Gulick surmised.[40]

Roosevelt supported the PSAL right from the start, even before granting his naming rights. "It will give me the greatest pleasure to accept the office of Honorary Vice President of the Public Schools Athletic League," Roosevelt wrote in a letter to George Wingate, President of the PSAL. "I most heartily believe in your league, and I feel that in promoting athletics among the school children of New York City along the sane and healthy lines it has followed it is performing a service which is of the utmost importance."[41]

During his presidency, and as the PSAL grew, Roosevelt's own children moved through the elementary and high school ranks. Only Alice, the rebellious oldest daughter, truly experienced the bulk of her father's time in office as a near-adult or adult. The youngest three, Ethel (born 1891), Archibald (1894), and Quentin (1897), worked their ways through elementary and high school while living in the White House – not an easy task, to be sure. But Roosevelt's athletic expectations for his children remained reasonable. Archie struggled to remain healthy and Roosevelt worried about him. Just after Roosevelt's visit to Harvard in 1907, Archie came down with diphtheria. There was no ready cure for the ailment at the time, and for a few weeks, Roosevelt worried he might lose his second-youngest son.[42] Despite Archie's serious and legitimate health concerns, and the fact that Roosevelt must have remembered what it was like to be a child battling against one's own body (asthma in Roosevelt's case), he still pushed Archie to get stronger. Archie "must not be a softy," Roosevelt warned.[43]

Since the three youngest children had the run of the White House, they watched eagerly when their father invited in athletes. The children would climb the furniture and secure perches "on the top of the library bookshelves" in order to watch TR box or wrestle. Sometimes they, too, got a lesson from boxing instructor Mike Donovan or another visiting expert.[44] These exchanges could sometimes be violent; they certainly stretched the boundaries of presidential behavior. But Roosevelt liked sharing the experiences with his children. For the older boys, off at Groton and Harvard, Roosevelt passed along his athletic war stories. "I am wrestling with two Japanese wrestlers three times a week," Roosevelt informed Kermit in 1904, "I am not of the age or the build one would think to be whirled lightly over an opponent's head . . . but I have not been hurt at all." Or, at least, not too badly. Roosevelt confessed that he did have some lingering soreness in his throat because of a chokehold standoff: "Once when one of them had a strangle hold I also got hold of his windpipe and thought I could perhaps choke him off before he could choke me. However, he got ahead."[45]

From the letters that flew back and forth within the extended Roosevelt family, the interested scholar learns of Archie's football and Quentin's baseball. Both played tennis occasionally, although not nearly as well as Ethel. Quentin seemed to be the favorite. He charmed his father ("He is a funny small person if ever there was one"), while Archie caused the most parental concern.[46] One cannot help but wonder if there was a gentle urging beneath the joyous reports Roosevelt passed on of Quentin's athletic activities to Archie. "I like to see Quentin practicing baseball," Roosevelt wrote to Archie in 1908, "it gives me hopes that one of my boys will not take after his father in this respect, and will prove able to play the national game!"[47]

The older boys, Ted and Kermit, received regular advice from their father on athletics. "Pay what attention you can to athletics," Roosevelt urged fifteen-year-old Kermit, "Play hockey, for instance, and try to get into shape for the mile run . . . you may be able to try for the two miles when you go to Harvard."[48] Ted received, perhaps, his father's most philosophical letter discussing athletics. "I am delighted to have you play football. I believe in rough, manly sports," he assured Ted, "But I do not believe in them if they degenerate into the sole end of any one's existence . . . Athletic proficiency is a mighty good servant, and like so many other good servants, a mighty bad master." Finally, Roosevelt turned to ancient history for an example. "Did you ever read Pliny's letter to Trajan, in which he speaks of its being advisable to keep the Greeks absorbed in athletics, because it distracted their minds from all serious pursuits, including soldiering, and prevented their ever being dangerous to the Romans?" he asked.[49] It is difficult to imagine a son receiving this type of letter without rolling his eyes, but Roosevelt made his point.

None of the Roosevelt children distinguished themselves athletically. There were no champions in the group. At their schools, Ted, Kermit, Archie, and Quentin all became *student* athletes. Athletics never overrode academic concerns. But all the Roosevelt children, like their father, took their places at the starting line and on the field of competition – they participated.

A Vigorous Nation

As Roosevelt stood in the packed Harvard Union, he surveyed America's most promising young men. The Harvard admissions process had changed since Roosevelt's day. The university functioned, increasingly, as part of the industrial world. Earning a degree opened up opportunities that could not be otherwise accessed. And Roosevelt had come to the university in order to watch his son's admission into the exclusive Porcellian Club. Exclusivity, even within Harvard University, precipitated the president's trip. Thus, there was some irony in Roosevelt's contention that sports had "essentially democratic" roots.[50]

After emphasizing the need to widen the base of participation, Roosevelt moved on to the commingling of American higher education and sports. This debate, of course, had been ongoing for several years, particularly regarding football. Roosevelt had inserted himself into this debate many times prior. But Roosevelt added a unique twist in his advocacy for intercollegiate sport. Intercollegiate athletics would benefit not only the collegiate competitor, Roosevelt argued, but also serve to foster wider participation. As Roosevelt made this point, his tone became more aggressive: "But even having this aim [to broaden participation] in view, it seems to me we can best attain it by giving proper encouragement to the champions in the sports, and this can only be done by encouraging intercollegiate sport."

This contention, that colleges should take a leading role in encouraging athletic participation, hinted at Roosevelt's philosophy of education. For Roosevelt, moral training should always accompany subject-matter expertise. Or, to put it another way, Roosevelt hoped that multifaceted, outside-the-classroom, ethical learning would take place alongside subjects such as mathematics and literature. In a speech given later in 1907 at Michigan's Agricultural College (later to become known as Michigan State University), Roosevelt guarded against a narrow view of education and the university's role in society: "Education should not confine itself to books . . . Book learning is very important, but it is by no means everything; and we shall never get the right idea of education until we definitely understand that a man may be well trained in book learning and yet, in the proper sense of the word, and for all practical purposes, be utterly uneducated."[51] To Roosevelt, a university that only offered classes, degrees, and research might well be missing the mark. Roosevelt pushed for broader, and more nebulous, educational standards.

"As I emphatically disbelieve in seeing Harvard or any other college turn out mollycoddles instead of vigorous men, I may add that I do not in the least object to a sport because it is rough," the president stated firmly. Here, Roosevelt was resuming his long-running argument with Harvard's President Charles Eliot over football's future as a college sport.[52] Roosevelt's message struck a chord with many Americans. The nation's newspapers during the early twentieth century often highlighted Roosevelt's work in sounding the alarm on the rise of 'mollycoddleism.' The *Atlanta Constitution*, for example, noted: "The surest process for securing the decay of mental, physical, moral and spiritual manhood is to coddle the boy – the man of the future; to shield him from the trivial hurts of the playground; to deprive him of the blood and brain-making life of the open air."[53]

On football specifically, Roosevelt recognized that the game needed some reforms. But what he refused to consider was the game's abolition. "It is to my mind simple nonsense, a mere confession of weakness, to desire to abolish a game because tendencies show themselves, or practices grow up, which prove that the game ought to be reformed," Roosevelt explained. Sports had been around for decades in an organized form in the United States, but a rapidly changing sports landscape had created some pushback that Roosevelt felt compelled to address. "Take football, for instance," he noted, comparing the high school game to that played at the college level, "there is no excuse whatever for colleges failing to show the same capacity [for reform], and there is no real need for considering the question of abolition of the game."[54]

The fact that Roosevelt would not even consider abolishing the game, despite football's harrowing early twentieth-century record, should give some pause. Why would Roosevelt, a man who preached a balance of athletics and academics, and athletics as a tool for development, refuse to consider the possibility that football did more harm than good? Had Roosevelt not seen the physical toll on Ted? In the February 1907 speech, at least, Roosevelt refused to consider football's abolition because he considered reform to be so eminently possible. "If necessary, let the college authorities interfere to stop any excess or perversion . . ." he declared matter-of-factly. Athletic sports had too much promise, too much utility to Roosevelt to consider throwing them out – especially the wildly popular football. "There is no justification," the president concluded, "for stopping a thoroughly manly sport because it is sometimes abused."[55]

This idea that athletics, because of their potential and their place in society, cannot be questioned still persists to this day. Sporting institutions in the twenty-first century might consider a pull back here or there, or rule changes to prevent injury, but rarely do they contemplate truly radical changes. Should, for example, athletics be disentangled from education – both at the high school and collegiate level? Should athletics that can cause significant injury risk be banned altogether? Should the federal government significantly expand its oversight of athletics? Should boys and girls compete together until they reach physical maturity? Such big, structural changes rarely move beyond the musings stage. Roosevelt did not want them considered during the first decade of the twentieth century either.

"We can not afford to turn out college men who shrink from physical effort or from a little physical pain," Roosevelt concluded before transitioning to other topics. "Courage is a prime necessity for the average citizen if he is to be a good citizen; and he needs physical courage no less than moral courage, the courage that dares as well as the courage that endures, the courage that will fight valiantly alike against the foes of the soul and the foes of the body." Athletics beget courage, Roosevelt concluded. For a nation in need of courageous young men, the thought of relegating athletics to the trash heap of progressive change clearly frightened Roosevelt. "Athletics are good, especially in their rougher forms, because they tend to develop such courage," he urged, "They are good also because they encourage a true democratic spirit; for in the athletic field the man must be judged not with reference to the outside and accidental attributes, but to that combination of bodily vigor and moral quality which go to make up prowess."[56]

The vision articulated by Roosevelt in February 1907 crystalized many of his earlier ideas. He reiterated his belief in broad participation and a symbiotic relationship between education and sports. Indeed, his speech would hardly have surprised Ted Jr., as many of his father's letters had made very similar arguments. Certainly, it was difficult to be Ted Jr. at Harvard, as he rarely escaped the shadow of his father. Even on a weekend dedicated to celebrating Ted Jr.'s acceptance into the Porcellian Club, Roosevelt still stole the show. Ironically, it was through athletics that Ted Jr. eclipsed his father's record (Ted at least made Harvard's vaunted football squad) and created his own narrative at times.

Before moving on altogether in his speech, Roosevelt felt compelled to point out to the impressionable audience that he did not intend for athletics to supersede the more important things in life: "I trust I need not add that in defending athletics I would not for one moment be understood as excusing that perversion of athletics which would make it the end of life instead of merely a means in life." Here, one can almost see Roosevelt facing off against a debating opponent. Yes, Roosevelt wanted athletics. Yes, he believed that football should be supported whether it caused injury or not. But he was not a lunatic about the issue.

"It is first-class healthful play," Roosevelt clarified, "But play is not business, and it is very poor business indeed for a college man to learn nothing but sport." At this point, 10 minutes into his time with the Harvard men, Roosevelt began his pivot toward other topics. Athletics were, after all, always a part of Roosevelt's broader ideology and approach to life. They did not exist in a vacuum. Roosevelt wanted it all, but he had a pecking order: "Athletics are good; study is even better; and best of all is the development of the type of character for the lack of which, in an individual as in a nation, no amount of brilliancy of mind or of strength of body will atone." Roosevelt hoped this pecking order would play out at both the individual and the national level.

Then, as he was wont to do, Roosevelt pivoted. He discussed his ideas about education, and then the United States' ongoing role in the Philippines, Cuba, and Panama. Roosevelt, unsurprisingly, did not apologize for the United States' imperialist reach. "We have given a wise government to the Philippines . . . We have acquired the right to build, and are now building, the Panama Canal," he reported. In wrapping up his speech, Roosevelt called the Harvard men to action. The *Brooklyn Eagle*, which provided the entire text of the speech under the headline 'President Defends College Athletics: Is in Favor of All Kinds of Sports, But Thinks Students

Should Also Study,' positioned the president's words alongside an advertisement for Grape-Nuts cereal. As so often was the case with Roosevelt, it was a juxtaposition of the inspirational with the everyday. "In short, you college men," Roosevelt concluded, "be doers rather than critics of the deeds that others do. Stand stoutly for your ideals; but keep in mind that they can only be realized, even partially, by practical methods of achievement."[57]

For Roosevelt, sports had become one of these 'practical methods' of bettering oneself. To take to the football field, or boxing ring, or tennis court was a means of developing the strength and character necessary to be an American citizen. From the White House, Roosevelt championed the idea of sports as progress – to his own children, to the young men of Harvard, and to any other American who would listen. The presidency, and the nation, would never be the same.

Notes

1. Technically Roosevelt was in his first full term as president, having initially ascended to the position in 1901 following William McKinley's assassination and then having won in a landslide in 1904. But Roosevelt had promised (with much regret after the fact) that he would not run for re-election in 1908. He had served two terms in spirit, if not technically.
2. "No Mollycoddles, Says Roosevelt," *New York Times*, February 24, 1907, 1.
3. Theodore Roosevelt, *The Strenuous Life* (New York: PF Collier, 1900).
4. Kathleen Dalton, *Theodore Roosevelt: A Strenuous Life* (New York: Vintage, 2004), 330–331.
5. Edmund Morris, *Theodore Rex* (New York: Random House, 2001), 477.
6. "Taft Gives a Respite to Negro Soldiers," *New York Times*, November 20, 1906, 1.
7. Theodore Roosevelt to Alfred E. Pearch, July 28, 1908, Theodore Roosevelt Papers, Library of Congress, Series 1, Reel 83.
8. Groton is an elite private school in Groton, Massachusetts.
9. Robert W. Walker, *The Namesake: A Biography of Theodore Roosevelt, Jr.* (New York: Brick Tower Press), 29.
10. Walker, *The Namesake*.

11. Letter from Endicott Peabody to Theodore Roosevelt, January 11, 1902, Theodore Roosevelt Papers, Library of Congress Manuscript Division.

12. "Yale, 16 to O. Weak Game Put Up by Harvard Freshmen," *Boston Daily Globe*, November 19, 1905, 2; 'Elis' being the nickname for students from Yale.

13. "Details of the More Serious Injuries," *Chicago Sunday Tribune*, November 26, 1905, 2.

14. Ryan Swanson, *The Strenuous Life* (New York: Diversion Books, 2019), 154–159.

15. Walker, *The Namesake*, 38, 47, 49, 52.

16. "The Weather," *Boston Daily Globe*, February 2, 1907, 1.

17. "President on Journey," *Washington Post*, February 23, 1907, 9.

18. "President on Journey." The Porcellian Club was, and is, the most prestigious and selective of Harvard's final clubs. Its select members include many prominent politicians, financiers, and intellectuals. See C. Ramsey Fahs, "In Most Extensive Comments in Centuries, Porcellian Club Criticizes Final Club Scrutiny," *Harvard Crimson*, April 13, 2016, available at: https://www.thecrimson.com/article/2016/4/13/porcellian-club-criticizes-college.

19. "Pres. Roosevelt's Address," *Harvard Crimson*, February 25, 1907, available at: https://www.thecrimson.com/article/1907/2/25/pres-roosevelts-address-ptheodore-roosevelt-80.

20. "A Whirlwind Visit," *Fitchburg Sentinel*, February 25, 1907, 7.

21. "A Whirlwind Visit."

22. "Harvard's Fine New Club," *New York Tribune*, February 23, 1902, Illustrated Supplement, 2; "Roosevelt and His Alma Mater," *Bismarck Tribune*, February 24, 1907, 1.

23. "Decorations for Harvard Union," *New York Times*, January 4, 1902, 8.

24. "Bits of Athletic New Gathered from the Colleges," *Brooklyn Eagle*, January 13, 1902, 17.

25. "Pres. Roosevelt's Address," *Harvard Crimson*, February 25, 1907.

26. "President Defends College Athletics," *Brooklyn Daily Eagle*, February 24, 1907, 6.

27. See Ryan Swanson, *The Strenuous Life* (New York: Diversion Books, 2019).

28. Joseph Bucklin Bishop (ed.), *Theodore Roosevelt's Letters to His Children* (New York: Charles Scribner, 1919), 10.

29. Bishop, *Theodore Roosevelt's Letters*, 3.

30. Theodore Roosevelt to Ethel Roosevelt, May 20, 1898, in Bishop, *Theodore Roosevelt's Letters*, 16.

31. Joan Paterson Kerr, *A Bully Father: Theodore Roosevelt's Letters to His Children* (New York: Random House, 1995), xiv. Includes a forward by David McCullough.

32. Theodore Roosevelt to Theodore Roosevelt, Jr., May 7, 1901, in Bishop, *Theodore Roosevelt's Letters*, 25.

33. Theodore Roosevelt to Theodore Roosevelt, Jr., October 11, 1903, in Bishop, *Theodore Roosevelt's Letters*, 66–67.

34. Theodore Roosevelt to Theodore Roosevelt, Jr., October 11, 1903, ibid.

35. "President Defends College Athletics," *Brooklyn Daily Eagle*, February 24, 1907, 6.

36. "The Roosevelt League," *New York Times*, March 10, 1907, 12.

37. The formation of the United States' first scholastic athletic league had occurred just a few years prior, in 1903.

38. *Public Schools Athletic League of the City of New York*, August 1905, Theodore Roosevelt Papers, Library of Congress Manuscript Division.

39. Benjamin Rader, *American Sports: From the Age of Folk Games to the Age of Televised Sports*, 6th edn. (Upper Saddle River, NJ: Pearson Prentice Hall, 2009), 106.

40. Rader, *American Sports*, 110.

41. "'Roosevelt Enthuses Over School Athletics," *New York Times*, August 26, 1905, 5.

42. Dalton, *A Strenuous Life*, 326.

43. Dalton, *A Strenuous Life*, 330.

44. Kerr, *A Bully Father*, 78.

45. Theodore Roosevelt to Kermit Roosevelt, March 5, 1904, in Bishop, *Theodore Roosevelt's Letters*, 93–94.

46. Theodore Roosevelt to Kermit Roosevelt, April 22, 1906, in Bishop, *Theodore Roosevelt's Letters*, 149–160.

47. Theodore Roosevelt to Archie Roosevelt, March 8, 1908, in Bishop, *Theodore Roosevelt's Letters*, 223.

48. Theodore Roosevelt to Kermit Roosevelt, February 3, 1906, in Bishop, *Theodore Roosevelt's Letters*, 149–150.

49. Theodore Roosevelt to Theodore Roosevelt, Jr., October 4, 1903, in Bishop, *Theodore Roosevelt's Letters*, 63–64.

50. "President Defends College Athletics," *Brooklyn Daily Eagle*, February 24, 1907, 6.

51. *Roosevelt Cyclopedia*, May 31, 1907.

52. "President Lectures on Athletics Today at Harvard College," *Buffalo Enquirer*, February 23, 1907, 6.
53. "The President on 'Mollycoddles,'" *Atlanta Constitution*, February 28, 1907, 8.
54. "President Defends College Athletics," *Brooklyn Daily Eagle*, February 24, 1907, 6.
55. "President Defends College Athletics."
56. "President Defends College Athletics."
57. "President Defends College Athletics."

2

Profile in Vigor: John F. Kennedy and the Quest for Athletic Excellence

Hendrik W. Ohnesorge

On July 15, 1960, upon accepting the Democratic Party's nomination for the upcoming presidential election, John F. Kennedy introduced the metaphor of the 'New Frontier,' an image that would become emblematic of his entire presidency. In Kennedy's imagery, it signaled the turning of a new leaf in American history, with a new generation of decision-makers ready to address the challenges the nation faced. Rather than sticking to past policies, Kennedy insisted, new efforts were required, new sacrifices needed to be made for the United States to persevere in the Cold War competition with the Soviet Union. In his speech, Kennedy declared, "[T]he New Frontier of which I speak is not a set of promises – it is a set of challenges. It sums up not what I intend to offer to the American people, but what I intend to ask of them."[1]

As soon as Kennedy won the election, he made good on this pledge. In an unprecedented article in *Sports Illustrated*, which had grown into the nation's leading sports magazine with 1 million weekly readers by 1960,[2] the president-elect addressed one particular arena in which, in his view, this competition would be crucially played out: he urged the American people to change their attitude toward physical fitness. In the much-noticed article, tellingly titled "The Soft American," Kennedy proclaimed:

> [T]he Greeks prized physical excellence and athletic skills among man's great goals and among the prime foundations of a vigorous state . . . This knowledge, the knowledge that the physical well-being of the citizen is

35

an important foundation for the vigor and vitality of all the activities of the nation, is as old as Western civilization itself. But it is a knowledge which today, in America, we are in danger of forgetting ... Thus, in a very real and immediate sense, our growing softness, our increasing lack of physical fitness, is a menace to our security.[3]

With this clarion call for action, Kennedy not only linked individual physical fitness with the prowess of the state. He also reminded Americans that, in his assessment, present conditions were insufficient in view of the Cold War challenges ahead. Thus, from the outset of his presidency, Kennedy put the quest for physical fitness at the very top of his agenda. In fact, he made it a cornerstone of his 'New Frontier.'

In a striking example of how personal backgrounds and characteristics affect the political, Kennedy, born into a highly competitive family with a long tradition in athletics, thus took his ingrained love of sports and sense of competition to the White House. Not only did he reinvigorate and expand governmental programs relating to sports and fitness, but as president he was personally invested in the issue on an unprecedented scale. While in office, Kennedy, as an individual, became the focal point of his administration's effort to promote a vigorous image of the United States. This chapter, therefore, examines the origins, characteristics, and ramifications of Kennedy's personal quest for sporting excellence. It discusses in particular how Kennedy sought to project a youthful and athletic image of himself and transfer it to the nation as a whole. Since this quest not only impacted the American public at home but also the way in which the United States was perceived in the world at large, the chapter further explores the key role that sports and athleticism played for America's soft power in the early Cold War. With competition and sporting excellence central to Kennedy as a private individual and as a public persona, the chapter concludes that the Kennedy presidency can indeed be regarded as a 'Profile in Vigor.'

A Competitive Family: 'We Want Winners'

When John F. Kennedy's brother, Joseph P. 'Joe' Kennedy, Jr. (the first child of Joseph Patrick Kennedy, Sr. and Rose Fitzgerald) was

36

born, a proud grandfather John F. 'Honey Fitz' Fitzgerald did not hesitate to outline his future to the press:

> Is he going into politics? Well of course he *is* going to be President of the United States; his mother and father have already decided that he is going to Harvard, where he will play on the football and baseball teams and incidentally take all the scholastic honors. Then he's going to be a captain of industry until it's time for him to be President for two or three terms. Further than that has not been decided. He may act as Mayor of Boston and governor of Massachusetts for a while on his way to the presidential chair.[4]

While arguably the sort of good-natured, tongue-in-cheek remark the former Mayor of Boston was known for, this statement also – and on a more consequential note – set the tone for the lives of the new generation of Kennedys, characterized by the dual forces of perfectionism and competition. This striving for perfection included both the realm of the mind – for instance, Rose would famously admonish her son Edward M. 'Ted' Kennedy, by then a U.S. senator, for his poor grammar – and the body.[5] In fact, when Rose Kennedy dictated her recollections more than half a century later, she recalled, "My great ambition was to have my children morally, physically, and mentally as perfect as possible."[6]

Where Rose Kennedy was a perfectionist, Joe Sr. was fiercely competitive. Biographer David Nasaw would later write, "Joe ran the family like a football team. He was the coach, the manager, and the referee. Rose was the water boy, constantly filling the children's minds with trivia. The aim was to win at everything, no matter what."[7] In fact, Joe would inculcate his offspring – which soon included second son John F. 'Jack' Kennedy – with the intransigent mantra, "We don't want any losers around here. In this family we want winners."[8] While holding true for all activities in which the growing Kennedy clan engaged, athletic excellence was of particular importance. Eunice Kennedy later recalled, "Mother and Dad put us through rigorous training in athletics."[9] At the sprawling Kennedy compound in Hyannis Port, "[t]he children reported at 7 a.m. to their physical education instructor for calisthenics. After breakfast, they had lessons in swimming, sailing, and tennis."[10] Long-time family friends, from Katherine 'Kay' Halle to Dorothy

Tubridy to John F. Dempsey, later consistently recalled this pervasive spirit of competitiveness and activity among the Kennedy family.[11] Ted Kennedy, the youngest of ultimately nine children, would likewise remember, "We competed in every conceivable way: at touch football, at sailing, at skipping rocks, and seeing whose seashell could float the farthest out to sea. We competed at games of wit and information and debate."[12]

Practically every conceivable sporting activity featured in this family competition. When it came to the 'national game,' the Kennedys had already been actively engaged in baseball for at least two generations. Honey Fitz had been a driving force behind the 'Royal Rooters,' the Boston Red Sox's first fan club, and Joe Sr., his future son-in-law, had 'lettered' at Harvard.[13] Jack would remain interested in the sport for the rest of his life as well, frequently talking shop with close friend (and later presidential aide) Dave Powers.[14]

Swimming, too, was a staple in Jack Kennedy's youth and early adulthood. An avid swimmer all his life, Kennedy made the Harvard swimming team as a freshman.[15] Swimming, a November 26, 1963, article in the *Harvard Crimson* declared, "was Kennedy's favorite sport and the one in which he performed best," while the article further noted that his "Coach Harold Ulen remembers him as a good swimmer but not an outstanding one; he also recalls that Kennedy was frequently ill."[16] In fact, swimming would, throughout Kennedy's life, provide relief for his chronic back pain.[17] His back had been a constant source of trouble for Kennedy from an early age, and it continued to plague him throughout his life even after numerous treatments, hospitalizations, and a total of four back operations.[18] As president, swimming in the White House pool, which dated back to Franklin D. Roosevelt's time in office, and which had been renovated early in the Kennedy administration, eased his back pain and became a vital part of Kennedy's daily routine.[19]

Golf also featured prominently in the activities of the Kennedy family. It had been a life-long passion for Jack's parents, with Rose trying hard to have her daily game throughout her life.[20] While Jack self-deprecatingly reported home in a 1934 letter from Choate that at school his "golf is going good and I have a slight chance for the team because it is rather sad this year," he subsequently made the freshman team at Harvard.[21] In his later life, and during the presidency, however, as life-long friend Kirk LeMoyne 'Lem' Billings as well as White House physician Dr. George G. Burkley recalled, Kennedy had to cut back on golf for fear of reinjuring his back.[22] Billings elaborated, "This was one of the great heartaches of his life, because, after the war, he never really could play golf seriously again. He did off and on, but there was always concern as to whether he was going to reinjure his back."[23]

Additionally, Kennedy learned and loved to sail in his youth, a sport that would arguably be connected to his presidency like few others. He even competed on the water during his student days, winning the Intercollegiate Sailing Championship alongside Joe Jr. in June 1938.[24] On Kennedy's love of the sea, biographer Geoffrey Perret elaborated, "Make him a skipper of a boat in a sailing competition, and the easygoing, readily laughing Jack vanished. Sailing was the one thing he seemed to lose himself in, when he became unsmiling, demanding and completely indifferent to being cold and wet."[25] Throughout his life, Kennedy remained an avid sailor, and his 1960 *Sports Illustrated* article prominently included, under the heading "Jack Kennedy Practices the Fitness that He Preaches," a double-page picture of Kennedy aboard his sailboat, the *Victura*.[26]

If sailing became emblematic of the Kennedy family, so too did football. On the significance of football in American life, Robert J. Higgs has written, "In its early days football was viewed as a substitute for war and as a training ground for war."[27] Little wonder, therefore, that it became a central rallying point for the competitive Kennedy family. Maurice A. 'Maury' Shea, a contemporary at Choate, later recalled that though Jack wanted to play football at school, illness prohibited it.[28] At Harvard he again made the freshman football team at first, but could not continue to compete due to his back.[29] James Farrell, who was in charge of football gear at Harvard and in this position outfitted, successively, four Kennedy boys, later recalled, "Oh, yes, when Jack arrived upon the scene, he didn't look much like an athlete. He was a big, tall stringbean. You could blow him over with a good breath . . . [A]s far as his football ability was concerned, he didn't have very much physique to be able to play that particular game."[30] Torbert Macdonald, Kennedy's roommate at Harvard and later a congressman for Massachusetts, remembered likewise.[31] At home, the entire Kennedy family resorted to touch football (as opposed to the 'traditional' tackle football). As family friend and former roommate of Joe Jr. at Harvard Law School, Thomas Bilodeau, recalled, "The touch football was not a matter of strategy with the Kennedy family. It was a matter of blood and thunder."[32] James Farrell agreed: "Well, they played it the same as they played everything else. They played everything for all it was worth."[33] Lem Billings would later attest that this practice went on even after Kennedy had entered the White House, though adding, "He was terribly good, you know, because he could still pass beautifully and very accurately and he could catch, but he couldn't move terribly fast because of his back problem."[34] At the same time, however, others were less convinced of the Kennedys' actual proficiency at the game. Dave Farrell, then-managing editor of the *Boston Herald*, raised his doubts in this regard in an interview with biographer Ronald Kessler, "It always amused me, this myth about them and touch football. You would think they were the greatest in touch football. I could have picked up any six kids off the streets in Dorchester where I grew up and kicked the crap out of them. Jack, Ted, and Bobby were not good athletes. But they created this myth that they were marvelous athletes."[35] While conflicting opinions can thus be found, the importance of football for the Kennedy image stands undisputed.

The struggle for an active, vigorous life, deeply ingrained in the Kennedy family from the first by means of competition in various sports, extended beyond the playing fields of Hyannis Port and Harvard University, and continued as war broke out. Despite their father's misgivings – Joe Sr. had been a prominent proponent of appeasement in his role as U.S. ambassador at the Court of St. James' – the two eldest Kennedy sons entered the military in 1941. Once more, however, health issues threatened to thwart Jack's plans. Yet, thanks to his father's intervention, he finally passed the Navy physical, and, ultimately, was assigned to active duty as commander of a Navy patrol torpedo (PT) boat in the Pacific theater.[36] Much has been written about Lieutenant (JG) Kennedy's exploits in the South Pacific, including his role in the sinking of PT-109 by a Japanese destroyer in August 1943, but in terms of his physical condition, the assessment of Barbara Leaming perhaps summed it up best:

> Had he been a healthy man, his actions would have made for a tale of astonishing heroism. Jack suffered from an unstable back and other physical limitations that ought to have kept him out of the Navy altogether; he had spent years in and out of hospitals, often near death. In the past he had proven immensely courageous in dealing with his own poor health, but now, by risking his life repeatedly for his men, he had demonstrated courage of another order entirely.[37]

Seventeen years later, as president-elect, Kennedy did not fail to allude to the importance of physical fitness in armed conflict in general and, at least by implication, also with respect to his own war record.[38]

After the war, the 1946 congressional election provided an auspicious entry into the political arena. For Kennedy, according to biographer Robert Dallek, "on one level politics was another form of the competitive sports like football or boat racing that excited his lifelong drive to be the best," an assessment Kennedy himself confirmed in 1960, when he confided to a journalist: "The fascination about politics is that it's so competitive. There's always that exciting challenge of competition."[39] The promising newcomer's election to Congress, however, also brought increased public attention to his medical record. During a trip to Ireland and England in 1947, Kennedy had been diagnosed with Addison's disease (an insufficiency of the adrenal glands frequently causing, among other symptoms, fatigue, abdominal pain, and weight loss), with the hastily summoned London doctor telling Pamela Churchill, Winston Churchill's former daughter-in-law and a long-time family friend, "That young American friend of yours, he hasn't got a year to live."[40] In response, his congressional office, however, soon "issued a press release that attributed his hospitalization to a recurrence of malaria contracted during the war."[41] Kennedy's personal physician, Dr. Janet Travell, later recalled: "Of course this was something that he didn't wish to talk about. At the time that the diagnosis was made, which was soon after the war in England, it was practically a death sentence. About that time we began to have available the adrenal hormones which completely changed the picture."[42] Upon meeting Kennedy, by then a senator, for the first time in May 1955, she remembered, "He was thin, he was ill, his nutrition was poor, he was on crutches. There were two steps from the street into my office and he could hardly navigate these."[43] Though repeatedly confined to crutches during his years in Congress, Kennedy did survive. Also, thanks to new medications and treatments available, and after more back surgeries, his condition stabilized and improved by the late 1950s.

If anything, Kennedy's frequent bouts of illness and his close encounters with death made him all the more interested in physical fitness, and all the more restless politically. After he narrowly missed the vice presidential nomination in 1956, Kennedy was determined to aim for the nation's highest office in 1960. When he was told in the late 1950s that he might have a chance to get the vice presidential nomination this time, he remained adamant, stating: "I'm not interested in running for vice president. I'm interested in running for president."[44] In short, Kennedy had, in journalist Ambrose Bierce's terms, set his eyes on the presidency, that "greased pig in the field game of American politics."[45]

Cold War confrontations and the 'fitness gap'

Kennedy ran his 1960 presidential election campaign in the spirit of his 'New Frontier' speech cited above. The Eisenhower years, he urged time and again, while years of growing prosperity and comfort, were also years of stagnation and, in fact, regression. The 1957 'Sputnik Shock' being perhaps the most visible expression of this sentiment prevalent in Kennedy's speeches on the campaign trail.[46] Even more prominently, however, Kennedy repeatedly invoked an alleged 'missile gap,' that is, the fear that the Soviet Union would soon overtake the United States in its ballistic missile stockpiles. At the same time, Kennedy promised, if elected, to preserve the United States' position of pre-eminence, telling an audience in Detroit, Michigan, "Now let me make it clear that I believe there can only be one defense policy for the United States and that is summed up in the word 'first.' I do not mean first, *but*. I do not mean first, *when*. I do not mean first, *if*. I mean first – period."[47]

For Kennedy, this drive to be first, did not stop at military clout alone. On the contrary, as the Cold War superpowers had reached a nuclear stalemate, other arenas of competition gained in importance, chief among them the arena of sporting excellence and physical fitness.[48] While sport had long been connected to national grandeur and world domination – expressed, for example, in the alleged comment by the Duke of Wellington that the Battle of Waterloo had been won on the playing fields of Eton – during the Cold War, this mentality reached new heights in the United States. Now, sport became a vital component of national prestige and soft power, vis-à-vis the Soviet Union and third countries alike.[49] American Cold War sports scholar Thomas Michael Domer, in this very sense, quoted a revelatory September 28, 1962, remark by State Department Cultural Affairs Officer William Ackerman: "Should [chess champion] Bobby Fisher one day defeat the Russians, he will be worth at least three astronauts in propaganda value, and possibly a couple of divisions to boot."[50]

Kennedy was eminently perceptive to – and in fact fueled – such sentiments, which can be illustrated in four areas. First, he admonished, in view of a number of international benchmark tests conducted in the mid-1950s, the United States' position on this particular Cold War battlefield.[51] According to James Reed, a long-time friend from their days in the Navy and later assistant secretary of the Treasury, "he was appalled really at some of the statistics relating to physical fitness or lack of physical fitness in our American youth."[52] In his *Sports Illustrated* article, Kennedy hence warned:

> [T]he harsh fact of the matter is that there is also an increasingly large number of young Americans who are neglecting their bodies – whose physical fitness is not what it should be – who are getting soft. And such softness on the part of individual citizens can help to strip and destroy the vitality of a nation.[53]

Kennedy, in short, formulated a glaring 'fitness gap' in American society. Second, Kennedy was keenly aware of the potency of soft power, that is, of the forces of attraction in international relations.[54] In fact, Mansfield D. Sprague, Deputy Director of the United States Information Agency, argued that Kennedy was "a man who perhaps better than any other President in our history understood how foreign opinion worked, what molded it, what shaped it, and how to shape it."[55] For Kennedy, sports was a vital component in this regard.[56] Third, Kennedy promised to take action, in line with an activist philosophy of executive government espoused by his 'New Frontier.'[57] In *Sports Illustrated*, Kennedy hence declared, "This is a national problem, and requires national action."[58] Fourth, and finally, Kennedy attributed a special role to the individual in this endeavor. The 1920s had seen the rise of the first sporting superstars – Babe Ruth, Bill Tilden, and Bobby Jones, for example.[59] Now, during the Cold War, this trend continued, and, as historians Tony Shaw and Denise J. Youngblood have shown, U.S. movies also focused intensely, "even in films ostensibly about team sports, on 'star performers' (both in the screen sense and on the field of play)."[60] During his presidency, Kennedy, as will be shown below, became the ultimate 'star performer.'

All things considered, as Thomas Michael Domer has noted, "The efforts of President Kennedy individually, and his administration collectively, indicate a dramatic realization of the significancy of fitness, sports, and athletics."[61] Indeed, the next section will first look at some of the collective actions taken, before turning, in greater detail, to the role of Kennedy as an individual.

Initiatives and programs

In line with his announcements in *Sports Illustrated*, which included a four-point plan to address the 'fitness gap,' Kennedy soon reinvigorated and reorganized the President's Council on Youth Fitness, established by President Eisenhower in 1956.[62] In March 1961, Charles 'Bud' Wilkinson, legendary University of Oklahoma football coach, was brought in to preside over the reorganized council.[63] From the first, Kennedy was, as Earl H. Blaik, Athletic Director of the United States Military Academy from 1949 to 1958, recalled, "vitally interested in the physical fitness program."[64] The fact that his brother, Attorney General Robert F. Kennedy, regularly joined the council's meetings is highly indicative of this increased top-level attention and importance.[65] Accompanied by "an extensive marketing and publicity campaign to spread the council's new message emphasizing fitness as an essential component of national safety and security," the council was now conceived in a broader, more inclusive sense, and Kennedy soon expanded it into the President's Council on Physical Fitness.[66] In his 1963 progress report, Kennedy reiterated, "The fitness of our people is one of the foundation stones of our national greatness."[67]

Besides the reorganized council, physical fitness and sports also became key components in U.S. cultural and exchange diplomacy during the Kennedy years. As Nicholas Rodis, a former football teammate of Robert Kennedy's at Harvard who was appointed Special Assistant for Athletic Programs in the State Department, noted, "Sports will tie a group of people together faster than many other ennobling principles. We believe that what is good for a new or developing country is good for the peace and stability of the world."[68] Consequently, sports also featured prominently in the Peace Corps program, instigated by its first director, and Kennedy's brother-in-law, R. Sargent Shriver.[69] Additionally, when Kennedy came across a 1908 letter by Theodore Roosevelt to the commandant of the Marine Corps in which 'The Hero of San Juan' suggested that in order to prove their fitness, officers should occasionally hike for 50 miles, this discovery was grist to the mill of Kennedy's push for physical fitness.[70] Expectedly, Kennedy did not hesitate to reinstate and personally promote the hikes, which grew immensely popular around the country. The fact that Kennedy charged not only servicemen to compete in them, but Americans of all ages and especially his own administration's leading officials, is further evidence of the new vigor Kennedy sought to instill.[71]

Additionally, international sports competitions featured prominently in Kennedy's mind, a meaningful expression of the considerable premium put on the prestige to be gained – or lost – at such events. For example, after Kennedy learned that the U.S. men's hockey team had been beaten decisively by the Swedish team in March 1963, he did not hesitate to call David Hackett, close friend and Special Assistant to Robert Kennedy, to bemoan the American performance:

Dave, I noticed in the paper this morning where the Swedish team beat the American hockey team, 17 to 2 . . . Christ, who are we sending over there? Girls? . . . So obviously, we shouldn't send a team unless we send a good one. Will you find out about it and let me know?[72]

Soviet triumphs at the 1956 and 1960 Olympics had put the issue at the top of the agenda, especially as Chairman Nikita Khrushchev – predictably – did not fail to indicate the significance of these developments.[73] When U.S. Olympic Development Committee Chairman Thomas Hamilton declared in a 1961 memo to the president, "Our national prestige is at stake in the Olympics as much as in other areas now spotlighted," his words, therefore, fell on sympathetic ears.[74] Consequently, Kennedy, as well as the attorney general, actively and personally intervened in the gridlocked dispute between the National Collegiate Athletic Association (NCAA) and the Amateur Athletic Union, which threatened to thwart the United States' prospects at the 1964 Games.[75] Once more emphasizing the importance attributed to the Olympic Games in particular, Robert Kennedy confirmed in March 1963 that "the President is concerned that we have our best athletes at the Olympics."[76] As these instances showcase, various facets in the quest for U.S. excellence in international athletic competition received keen and top-level attention during the Kennedy years.

Taken together, these glimpses into programs and initiatives relating to the attested 'fitness gap' illustrate that striving for physical activity and athletic excellence loomed exceptionally large during the Kennedy years. In fact, it is generally agreed that Kennedy's personal interest in the matter bore fruit politically both at the domestic and the international levels.[77] Ultimately, no individual played a greater role in this endeavor than the president himself – and the public image he sought to establish.

The president's body and the nation's prestige

In his 1960 article in *Sports Illustrated*, Kennedy declared that "[t]he President and all departments of government must make it clearly understood that the promotion of sports participation and physical fitness is a basic and continuing policy of the United States. By providing such leadership, by keeping physical fitness in the forefront of the nation's concerns, the federal government can make a substantial contribution toward improving the health and vigor of our citizens."[78] As these remarks indicate, Kennedy ascribed particular importance to the office, and person, of the President of the United States in his quest for athletic excellence.

As explored above, this sense of perfectionism and striving for excellence can be attributed to Kennedy's upbringing as a child and education as a young man. As president, he now sought to establish and project an image that was just as perfect. Historian Mark White has suggested that, throughout his political career, Kennedy sought to foster a "dual image as both man of letters and man of action."[79] While the former provides a promising starting point for future research, the latter is of particular importance at this point. On that note, professor of English and Visual and Cultural Studies, John Michael, argued that Kennedy was eager to create a "public image as an embodiment of manly vigor and heroic courage."[80] Supporting this assertion, the December 1960 issue of *Sports Illustrated* offered, subsequent to Kennedy's own article, the following: "As the record shows, the President-elect is not only an enthusiastic helmsman but a successful one. Like the other members of his large, vigorous and fiercely competitive family, he is a savage contestant, at 43, whether sailing, swimming, skin-diving, golfing or playing touch football." The piece goes on to note that, "If it had not been for his skill as a swimmer and for a hardiness of body and toughness of spirit developed through rough-and-tumble games, he probably would not be alive today."[81]

While physical prowess and athletic excellence thus constitute vital components in the creation of the Kennedy image, this image never was an end in itself. Rather, by extension, it was to be applied to and benefit the nation as a whole. Somewhat reminiscent of the notions of the ruler's 'body natural' and 'body politic,' famously explored in Ernst Kantorowicz's seminal *The King's Two Bodies* (1957), Kennedy, it may be argued, connected, or even equated, his own self with the state.[82] Historian Robert D. Dean in this sense noted:

As a corollary to the proposition that nations and empires were like men's bodies in their life cycles of growth and decay, Kennedy held the conviction that men's bodies represented the incarnation of the state . . . As president, Kennedy identified his own body with the state . . . Kennedy always cast himself as the embodiment of a national struggle against the Soviets, who in this drama were embodied in Nikita Khrushchev.[83]

This conjunction becomes evident throughout the Kennedy presidency. An especially illuminating instance revealingly occurred in the aftermath of Kennedy's first personal encounter with Khrushchev in Vienna in June 1961. The grim schedule had put Kennedy's health to a severe test, as Barbara Leaming has detailed:

The president returned to the White House in horrible physical condition. For three weeks he had managed to conceal his back injury, but the combination of pain and stress had left him greatly in need of rest . . . Meanwhile, he limited his use of crutches to those times when he was out of public view. Since boyhood, on account of his own ill health and a favored older brother's robustness, he had been sensitive to any depiction of himself as physically weak. Now, when much depended on his ability to persuade Khrushchev of U.S. resolve, it was even more important to him not to project any hint of weakness.[84]

When his condition did not improve, however, President Kennedy was finally photographed with crutches for the first time on June 12.[85] At the height of the Berlin Crisis, this fact did not go unnoticed in the Kremlin and arguably contributed to the fact that Khrushchev famously referred to the United States as a "worn-out runner" on June 25.[86] Highly indicative that this designation struck a nerve in Washington, Kennedy, ever jealous of his own image and that of the United States, did not fail to forcefully rebuff such accusations during his next press conference a mere three days later.[87]

As this episode indicates, Kennedy took scrupulous care of his own image and, indeed, sought to portray himself as a paragon of vigor. According to one of his closest friends, Lem Billings, for example, "until the day he died, Jack was concerned about his weight."[88] The same applies to the various athletic activities that were so deeply ingrained in him by way of his upbringing. Dr. Travell recalled the lengths to which Kennedy was prepared to go: "Every spring before he went to throw out the baseball for the opening of the baseball season, he would come in and have me check his right shoulder."[89] The same holds true for Kennedy's golfing. According to biographer Richard Reeves, "One of the best kept secrets of the Kennedy campaign was that he loved golf as much as Eisenhower did. But he did not play in public because he was using Ike's golfing as a symbol of age and a passive approach to governing."[90] Kennedy thus arguably put greater emphasis on the public image he sought to create and maintain than on his private preferences, and even his health.

Arguably, this very image – deliberately nourished and frequently picked up by a mostly favorable press over the course of many years – contributed to Kennedy's lasting popularity, which is not uncommonly extended to the United States during the early 1960s. In this way, the body of the president contributed to the prestige of the nation. In June 1965, it was former-actress-turned-princess Grace Kelly who put on record:

> President Kennedy's youthfulness and vitality appealed so strongly to my husband [Rainier III, Prince of Monaco] and myself . . . We felt somehow that at last the United States had a leader who, from the point of view of age, appearance, and dynamic personality, genuinely reflected his era . . . Yes, he was almost too good to be true – he was just like the All-American boy, wasn't he, handsome, a fighter, witty, full of charm . . .[91]

As we now know, the public image that Kennedy sought to foster was indeed, in Kelly's terms, "almost too good to be true." And although the full extent of his medical record did not become public until long after his death, the first cracks in the varnish soon appeared. Eight months after the president's assassination, Lem Billings, while confessing that he would not have stated so if Kennedy had lived, noted that "Jack Kennedy lived in pain."[92] Similarly, in the foreword to the 1964 edition of *Profiles in Courage*, his brother Robert would famously admit, "At least one half of the days that he spent on this earth were days of intense physical pain."[93]

Conclusion

In a meeting with Vice Admiral Hyman Rickover on February 11, 1963, 'The Father of the Nuclear Navy,' John F. Kennedy reminisced about what may have caused him to harbor what he called a distinct "competitive desire" throughout his life: "What I think of, how drilled into my life was the necessity for participating actively and successfully in the struggle."[94]

Born into a highly competitive family that sought to rear 'perfect' children who would make meaningful contributions to society, he had indeed "participat[ed] actively and successfully in the struggle" from a very early age. Never ceasing competitions in the classrooms and on the playing fields of Choate, Harvard, and Hyannis Port became an integral part of his upbringing – and they remained so throughout Kennedy's life and career. Being elected at least in part for the energetic and vigorous image he projected – and sought to extend to the nation – it is no wonder that Kennedy put a high premium on physical fitness and athletic excellence once in office. Kennedy understood, perhaps better than any of his predecessors – and more than a few of his successors – the value of prestige in international affairs. During the Cold War, sports had become a crucial component in this quest for soft power. The immediate and top-level attention paid to the reorganization and expansion of the President's Council on Physical Fitness, as well as the minute attentiveness towards U.S. athletic representation abroad, are highly indicative in this regard. Various further initiatives and programs initiated during the Kennedy presidency, from exchange programs, to the Peace Corps, to the famous 50-mile hikes, complete the picture of a president exceptionally mindful of the role of sports and fitness for national vitality, power, and prestige.

Kennedy's image as a private person and public persona was as important as anything in this endeavor. Simultaneously seeking to evoke a "dual image as both man of letters and man of action," he was perhaps more conscious of the efficacy of his image than any other political figure at the time.[95] Again traceable to his upbringing and personality, Kennedy understood the power of appearances, and athleticism and vigor were crucial variables in this equation. While it has long been known that appearances can be deceptive, and while disclosures after Kennedy's untimely death allowed for a fuller picture in subsequent years, Kennedy, to a considerable degree, remains successful in establishing an attractive image of himself – and, by extension, the United States – to this very day. Noted presidential scholar and former Kennedy advisor, Richard E. Neustadt, argued that, "Perhaps his very vigor, family, fortune, sense of fun, his manners, taste, and sportsmanship, his evident enjoyment of his life and of the job made him the heart's desire of all sorts of people everywhere, not least among the young."[96] In the final analysis, therefore, the Kennedy years constitute a 'Profile in Vigor,' indeed.

Notes

1. John F. Kennedy, "Address Accepting the Democratic Nomination for President at the Memorial Coliseum in Los Angeles, California," July 15, 1960, available at: https://www.presidency.ucsb.edu/documents/address-accepting-the-democratic-nomination-for-president-the-memorial-coliseum-los.
2. Charlie Bevis, "Sports Illustrated," *St. James Encyclopedia of Popular Culture*, available at: https://www.encyclopedia.com/media/encyclopedias-almanacs-transcripts-and-maps/sports-illustrated.
3. John F. Kennedy, "The Soft American," *Sports Illustrated*, December 26, 1960, 15–16.
4. Quoted in Nigel Hamilton, *JFK: Reckless Youth* (New York: Random House, 1992), 25.
5. Edward M. Kennedy, *True Compass: A Memoir* (New York: Little, Brown, 2009), 30.
6. Quoted in Barbara A. Perry, *Rose Kennedy: The Life and Times of a Political Matriarch* (New York: W. W. Norton, 2013), 50.
7. Ronald Kessler, *The Sins of the Father: Joseph P. Kennedy and the Dynasty He Founded* (New York: Warner, 1996), 41.
8. Quoted in Rose Fitzgerald Kennedy, *Times to Remember: An Autobiography* (London: Collins, 1974), 136.
9. Quoted in Rose Kennedy, *Times to Remember*, 136.
10. Kessler, *The Sins of the Father*, 43.
11. Kay (Katherine Murphy) Halle, Recorded interview by William M. McHugh, February 7, 1967, 3–4; Dorothy Tubridy, Recorded interview by Joseph E. O'Connor, August 8, 1966, 4–5; John F.

Dempsey, Recorded interview by Ed Martin, June 10, 1964, 2. All recorded interviews cited are part of the John F. Kennedy Library Oral History Program.

12. Edward Kennedy, *True Compass*, 22.
13. Edward Kennedy, *True Compass*, 77; David Nasaw, *The Patriarch: The Remarkable Life and Turbulent Times of Joseph P. Kennedy* (New York: Penguin, 2012), 24; the term 'to letter' refers to having proven one's excellence in intercollegiate varsity athletics by making active contributions to one's team's success.
14. John M. Bailey, Recorded interview by Charles T. Morrissey, April 10, 1964, 26–27.
15. Geoffrey Perret, *Jack: A Life Like No Other* (New York: Random House, 2002), 49.
16. "Kennedy and Harvard: A Complicated Tie," *The Harvard Crimson*, November 26, 1963, available at: https://www.thecrimson.com/article/1963/11/26/kennedy-and-harvard-a-complicated-tie.
17. Barbara Leaming, *Jack Kennedy: The Education of a Statesman* (New York: W. W. Norton, 2006), 58.
18. T. Glenn Pait and Justin T. Dowdy, "John F. Kennedy's Back: Chronic Pain, Failed Surgeries, and the Story of Its Effects on His Life and Death," *Journal of Neurosurgery: Spine* 27(3) (2017): 247–255.
19. Janet G. Travell, Recorded interview by Theodore C. Sorensen, January 20, 1966, 18.
20. Perry, *Rose Kennedy*, 44, 122.
21. Amanda Smith (ed.), *Hostage of Fortune: The Letters of Joseph P. Kennedy* (New York: Viking, 2001), 142; Perret, *Jack*, 49.
22. Kirk LeMoyne Billings, Recorded interview by Walter D. Sohier, July 22, 1964, 482–483; George G. Burkley, Recorded interview by William McHugh, October 17, 1967, 14.
23. Billings, Recorded interview, 439.
24. Perret, *Jack*, 69.
25. Perret, *Jack*.
26. "Jack Kennedy Practices the Fitness that He Preaches," *Sports Illustrated*, December 26, 1960, 20–21.
27. Robert J. Higgs, *God in the Stadium: Sports and Religion in America* (Lexington: University of Kentucky Press, 1995), 225.
28. Maurice A. Shea, Recorded interview by Ronald J. Grele, March 22, 1966, 2.
29. Perret, *Jack*, 49.
30. James Farrell, Recorded interview by Bud Collins, May 11, 1964, 2–3.

31. Torbert H. Macdonald, Recorded interview by Charles T. Morrissey, August 11, 1965, 2–3.
32. Thomas Bilodeau, Recorded interview by James Murray, May 12, 1964, 9.
33. Farrell, Recorded interview, 3.
34. Billings, Recorded interview, 486.
35. Kessler, *The Sins of the Father*, 41–42.
36. Leaming, *Jack Kennedy*, 120–121, 132–133.
37. Leaming, *Jack Kennedy*, 139.
38. J. F. Kennedy, "The Soft American," 17.
39. Robert Dallek, *An Unfinished Life: John F. Kennedy, 1917–1963* (New York: Back Bay Books, 2004), 126–127.
40. Dallek, *An Unfinished Life*, 76, 153.
41. Leaming, *Jack Kennedy*, 191.
42. Travell, Recorded interview, 11–12.
43. Travell, Recorded interview, 1.
44. Quoted in Dallek, *An Unfinished Life*, 232.
45. Ambrose Bierce, *The Devil's Dictionary* (London: Folio Society, 2003), 248.
46. The term 'Sputnik Shock' refers to the sudden advantage the Soviet Union had gained over the United States in the wake of the 1957 launch of its first satellite, *Sputnik 1*, and its vast psychological, social, and political ramifications.
47. John F. Kennedy, "Speech of Senator John F. Kennedy, VFW Convention, Detroit, Michigan," August 26, 1960, available at: https://www.presidency.ucsb.edu/documents/speech-senator-john-f-kennedy-vfw-convention-detroit-mi-verbatim-text.
48. Thomas Michael Domer, "Sport in Cold War America, 1953–1963: The Diplomatic and Political Use of Sport in the Eisenhower and Kennedy Administrations," PhD dissertation, Marquette University, 1976, 3–4.
49. Higgs, *God in the Stadium*, 230; Domer, "Sport in Cold War America," 18–19, 293–295.
50. Domer, "Sport in Cold War America," 260.
51. Matthew T. Bowers and Thomas M. Hunt, "The President's Council on Physical Fitness and the Systematisation of Children's Play in America," *International Journal of the History of Sports* 28(11) (2011): 1497.
52. James A. Reed, Recorded interview by Robert J. Donovan, June 16, 1964, 73.
53. J. F. Kennedy, "The Soft American," 16.

54. Joseph S. Nye Jr., *Soft Power: The Means to Success in World Politics* (New York: Public Affairs, 2004); Hendrik W. Ohnesorge, *Soft Power: The Forces of Attraction in International Relations* (Cham: Springer, 2020).
55. Quoted in Domer, "Sport in Cold War America," 260.
56. Thomas M. Hunt, "American Sport Policy and the Cultural Cold War: The Lyndon B. Johnson Presidential Years," *Journal of Sport History* 33(3) (2006): 274–275.
57. Domer, "Sport in Cold War America," 220.
58. J. F. Kennedy, "The Soft American," 17.
59. Domer, "Sport in Cold War America," 13–14.
60. Tony Shaw and Denise J. Youngblood, "Cold War Sport, Film, and Propaganda: A Comparative Analysis of the Superpowers," *Journal of Cold War Studies* 19(1) (2017): 163.
61. Domer, "Sport in Cold War America," 29.
62. Domer, "Sport in Cold War America," 212.
63. John F. Kennedy, "The Vigor We Need," *Sports Illustrated*, July 16, 1962, 13.
64. Earl H. Blaik, Recorded interview by Charles T. Morrissey, December 2, 1964, 14.
65. Domer, "Sport in Cold War America," 219.
66. Bowers and Hunt, "The President's Council on Physical Fitness," 1501; Domer, "Sport in Cold War America," 219.
67. John F. Kennedy, "Progress Report by the President on Physical Fitness," August 13, 1963, available at: https://www.presidency.ucsb.edu/documents/progress-report-the-president-physical-fitness.
68. Domer, "Sport in Cold War America," 267–268.
69. Domer, "Sport in Cold War America," 284–287.
70. Pierre Salinger, *With Kennedy* (Garden City: Doubleday, 1966), 239.
71. Robert D. Dean, "Masculinity as Ideology: John F. Kennedy and the Domestic Politics of Foreign Policy," *Diplomatic History* 22(1) (1988), 47–48.
72. Quoted in Ted Widmer (ed.), *Listening In: The Secret White House Recordings of John F. Kennedy* (New York: Hyperion, 2012), 271–272.
73. Domer, "Sport in Cold War America," 20.
74. Quoted in Domer, "Sport in Cold War America," 221.
75. Domer, "Sport in Cold War America," 229–238.
76. Quoted in Domer, "Sport in Cold War America," 246.
77. Domer, "Sport in Cold War America," 258–259.
78. J. F. Kennedy, "The Soft American," 17.

79. Mark White, "Apparent Perfection: The Image of John F. Kennedy," *History* 98(2) (2013): 229.

80. John Michael, "'Profiles in Courage:' JFK's Book for Boys," *American Literary History* 24(3) (2012): 424.

81. "Salt-Water Notes for a Sportsman's Biography," *Sports Illustrated*, December 26, 1960, 23.

82. Ernst Kantorowicz, *The King's Two Bodies: A Study in Medieval Political Theology* (Princeton, NJ: Princeton University Press, 2016).

83. Dean, "Masculinity as Ideology," 46–47.

84. Leaming, *Jack Kennedy*, 317.

85. Leaming, *Jack Kennedy*, 319.

86. Leaming, *Jack Kennedy*, 322.

87. John F. Kennedy, "The President's News Conference," June 28, 1961, Washington, D.C., available at: https://www.presidency.ucsb.edu/documents/the-presidents-news-conference-208.

88. Billings, Recorded interview, 440–441.

89. Travell, Recorded interview, 19.

90. Richard Reeves, *President Kennedy: Profile in Power* (New York: Touchstone, 1994), 90n.

91. Grace de Monaco, Recorded interview by Paul Gallico, June 19, 1965, 1–2.

92. Billings, Recorded interview, 475.

93. Robert F. Kennedy, "Foreword to the Memorial Edition," in John F. Kennedy, *Profiles in Courage* (New York: Harper & Row, 1964), 9.

94. Widmer, *Listening In*, 61.

95. White, "Apparent Perfection," 229.

96. Richard E. Neustadt, *Presidential Power and the Modern Presidents: The Politics of Leadership from Roosevelt to Reagan* (New York: Free Press, 1990), 175.

3

"My Second Vocation":
How Richard Nixon Talked Football

Jesse Berrett

Until the 1960s, when American presidents referred to football, they meant the lessons learned by playing college football, a crucible that taught young men leadership and fair play by burning away laziness and self-indulgence. The backbone to brave the struggle for dominance, the readiness to accept winning and losing as a team, was what counted. Theodore Roosevelt predicted that the American boy afforded himself the best chance of becoming the "good American man" if he grew up "clean-minded and clean-lived, and able to hold his own under all circumstances . . . In life, as in a football game, the principle to follow is: Hit the line hard; don't foul and don't shirk." Football dramatized Roosevelt's Strenuous Life, demanded that a boy steel himself to do "work that counts when the time arises."[1]

Roosevelt denounced anything smacking of fandom, frowning that "it is a very bad thing if, twenty years afterward, all that can be said of [a former team captain] is that he has continued to take an interest in football." Decades later, Richard Nixon made it a habit to take an interest. Nixon had played football and often drew on lessons he learned standing on the sideline. Far more influentially, however, he was the first president to make a point of watching and thinking seriously about sports. The Rooseveltian tenor of his rhetoric remained remarkably consistent; what changed was how he balanced traditional celebrations of football's character-building qualities with his passions as a fan, and how consciously he put that fandom to use. In the 1950s, football connected him to his audience; in the 1960s, it drew lines between all-Americans who loved the sport and anti-Americans whose dislike of football signaled what he called "contempt for those elemental decencies on which a free society rests."[2]

The most valuable All-Star: Nixon learns to talk football

Nixon began to establish his public authority as a fan by the late 1950s. In 1959, he told the Football Writers' Association of America that "if I had the choice, and I had the ability, there is nothing I would rather do than write sports."[3] He was the only president ever to attend an American Football League (AFL) game, the first to attend a regular season National Football League (NFL) game, and the first to congratulate the winning Super Bowl team. When he flew to Green Bay to celebrate the quarterback Bart Starr in 1970, Nixon was able to recall the Packers game he had attended back in 1956 and even remembered that Starr had not yet cracked the starting lineup. By the early 1970s, he was so well known as a fan that he turned down an invitation from *Esquire* to cover the 1973 Super Bowl.[4] He called football "perhaps my second vocation" and noted that he would happily exchange his job for NFL commissioner Pete Rozelle's. Humor columnist Art Buchwald joked that the president regularly convened the National Strategic Football Agency, "a top-secret group of men who advise him on the options he has" for advice in this crucial area.[5]

Nixon loved hobnobbing with players and coaches, relishing details from games decades before, and dropping football metaphors into his speeches. But he, and media-savvy aides eager to sell the president via modern advertising techniques, understood that the personal could be political: being a fan endeared him to the public. Throughout his career, Nixon struggled to put himself across as relaxed, regular, typical. "There is something about this man, unfortunate for himself and more unfortunate for the country, that puts off anyone with normal human feelings," *The Nation* wrote. But as a letter from a campaign operative in the spring of 1968 observed, "when I mention Nixon's knowledge of sports, [people] immediately seem to show a great interest in him." It was less what he said than the fact that he said it. Conveying enthusiasm and knowledge about the sport's past and present – a skill on which supporters and detractors agreed – built a Jacksonian common-man connection with voters.[6]

At the same time, to Nixon's critics these gestures immediately registered as ham-handed political gestures aimed at buffing his image. "The trouble . . . isn't that he watches football," a critic for *Partisan Review* wrote, "but that he makes such an obvious and cheap political gesture of it."[7] The odor of calculation haunted him: early in 1956, political cartoonist Herbert Block drew Nixon pondering a closetful of possible costumes – a tuxedo proclaiming him a "statesman," a carnival-barker's jacket and top hat for the "political pitchman," and a megaphone and cheerleader sweater with "All-American Boy" emblazoned on the chest – the implication being that there was no real Nixon underneath.[8] Together, Nixon's performative and authentic fandom, his use of it to connect and polarize, and others' awareness of what he was up to, set the rules for Barack Obama's public unveiling of his National Collegiate Athletic Association (NCAA) tournament brackets and Donald Trump's obsession with the NFL's television ratings and attacks on kneeling players. For better and worse, Nixon normalized both the notion that the president would present himself as a fan *and* criticism of that gesture.

Though he attended sporting events throughout his first four years as Dwight Eisenhower's vice president, Nixon took his first significant steps in this direction during Ike's second term. Former Notre Dame coach Frank Leahy, seconding Eisenhower's renomination, prophesied that Ike "will, through some miracle, be the main cause for a worldwide peace . . . Should this become a reality, children all over the universe can do their running on athletic fields instead of running toward bomb shelters." In a subsequent television spot, Leahy counseled young voters to support an "experienced quarterback."[9] Already planning for 1960, Nixon understood that emphasizing his love of the sport accentuated his likeness to Eisenhower; his frequent invocations of Theodore Roosevelt's "Man in the Arena" speech underscored his broader adoption of Roosevelt's notion of sports as moral instruction. Doing so also counteracted his image as "Tricky Dick," the conniving Machiavellian smear artist famously depicted clambering out of the sewer in Block's 1954 cartoon.[10]

And so, Nixon accepted with alacrity when American Football Coaches Association executive secretary Tuss McLaughry invited the vice president to the organization's 1958 meeting in Philadelphia – "a big affair with over a thousand in attendance." The coaches typically sought nationally prominent speakers (previous guests included Truman's vice president, Alben Barkley, and William 'Wild Bill' Donovan, head of the Office of Strategic Services) whose stature emphasized the institutional and ideological affinities between football and the Cold War state. McLaughry wrote to Nixon that he had "voted Republican since my first vote in 1916 and if there is ever anything that I can do in any way to further your cause, do not hesitate to call on me." Another Nixon favorite, Ohio State coach Woody Hayes, was honored as Coach of the Year immediately after his speech, and a photograph showed Hayes offering Nixon "some pointers on passing." The excited vice president had the coaches autograph his ball.[11]

In his speech, Nixon struck a classically Rooseveltian note by linking individual fitness and American global assertiveness. He denied that the administration had fallen behind the Soviet Union militarily (as Kennedy's "missile gap" rhetoric would charge) and highlighted sports' importance in preserving American martial prowess. He encouraged his listeners to maintain that prowess by inspiring youth to get out and play: "young Americans need the fighting spirit, the determination, the teamwork, the discipline which competitive athletics inevitably instills." McLaughry congratulated him: "you won many friends who will go back to their forty-eight states singing praises of you." "No speaker ever made a more profound impression on the coaches," Zipp Newman of the *Birmingham News* wrote.[12]

In most respects, Nixon delivered a speech that any previous president could have given. Predictions like "our young men . . . won't be properly prepared for life if they have been shielded from the disappointment of failure, whether in the classroom or on the athletic field" came straight from the pages of TR's famous speech 'The Strenuous Life.'[13] The one difference was Nixon's display of

59

his interest in football as a spectator. The reaction was rapturous: "After his talk coaches by the dozen swarmed around to shake his hand," according to one journalist.[14] Nixon "fitted right in," so much so that "even some life-long Democrats were promising to vote for him when he runs for President," said another attendee. The only discordant note came from the Soviet Home Service, which failed "to see the relation of football to the U.S. economic situation."[15]

The next year, Nixon addressed the Football Writers' Association of America – something he "would very much like to do," his staff told the writers. As if responding to the Home Service, he likened Soviet Premier Nikita Khrushchev, against whom he had just defended the virtues of capitalism in the Kitchen Debate, to "a great fullback . . . [who] would charge straight ahead when he sees the slightest opening." Football had taught him not to fall for the Soviets' trap play, this time a toast calling for the removal of American bases in Europe: "my interest in sports served me well." Nixon not only revealed his desire to be a sportswriter; this time he outlined his first column, which he described in remarkable detail, proudly displaying four handwritten pages to a reporter who presumed that an aide had done the research. Again, he mixed fandom and politics: he celebrated Frank Gifford as the best all-around player he had ever seen, "and not because his father is a good California Republican," remembered his first Rose Bowl (the University of Southern California defeated Pittsburgh 35–0 in 1933), and recalled Kenny Washington's spectacular 66-yard touchdown pass to football star-turned baseball legend Jackie Robinson in a UCLA victory over Oregon in 1939.[16]

The writers gave him a standing ovation. "Believe it or don't," one onlooker wrote, "the guy got an enthusiastic response – and a few hundred potential votes – from the usually cynical scribes." Another celebrated him as "the most valuable All-Star on the premises." Even the *New York Times* was impressed, noting that Nixon "astounded his informed audience with his thorough grasp of their subject . . . with fewer actual fluffs than just about any of the attendant experts would have perpetrated." Most importantly, Bill Rives of the *Dallas Morning News* observed, the speech painted Nixon as endearingly normal and in touch: "he delighted the audience . . . Another hobby of his is winning friends and influencing people."[17]

Nixon knows pro football: fandom as polarization in the 1960s

In the 1950s, Nixon put football to traditional metaphorical uses. Standing literally and rhetorically in the shadows of Roosevelt and Eisenhower, he emphasized that football tutored players in hard work, the will to win, and the character to accept defeat. It built leaders fit to captain a confident nation, unafraid to flex its muscles on the world stage. A Sunday supplement published just before the 1960 election measured his humble acceptance of a "good seat on the fifty-yard line" against the luxuries cosseting his snooty opponent, who sat in a box. These terms seemed to be borne out by Nixon's seemingly inexorable ascent from obscurity to the House of Representatives to the vice presidency in only six years.[18]

But in the mid-1960s, which he called his 'wilderness years,' his prospects darkened – he narrowly lost the 1960 presidential election and snarled that the press would not have Nixon to "kick around anymore" after losing California's gubernatorial election in 1962. After being elected president in 1968, Nixon seasoned his earlier rhetoric with new awareness of losing: "What does this mean, this common interest in football, of Presidents, of leaders, of people generally? It means . . . the character, the drive, the pride, the teamwork, the feeling of being in a cause bigger than yourself," he told the National Football Foundation in 1969. When huddling with staff and friends just before resigning the presidency in 1974, Nixon reiterated that losing football games had taught him to "take what's coming to me." After announcing that he would resign, Nixon returned to TR: "we think that when we suffer a defeat that all is ended . . . Not true. It is only a beginning, always."[19]

As president he made his mark as the nation's number one fan, a regular guy who talked sports in ways that proved surprisingly effective, even with skeptics. Even in the 1950s, sportswriters understood Nixon's speeches as political, but few would have thought to criticize him. One columnist extolled the vice president's "amazing job" and "pleasing, charming manner" before the football writers in

61

1959.[20] Sportswriters of the 1960s and 1970s were far more inclined than their predecessors to criticize those in positions of power; Red Smith wrote, "the sportswriter whose horizons are no wider than the outfield fences is a bad sportswriter, because he has no sense of proportion and no awareness of the real world." Though no friends of Nixon, writers of this generation nonetheless marveled at, and were disarmed by, the quality of his passion. Midway through a demolition of the "overhauled 1968 model," the writer Hunter S. Thompson admitted that he expected Nixon did not know football "from pig-hustling" and kept dropping it into conversation because "his wizards had told him that it would make him seem like a regular guy. But I was wrong. Nixon *knows* pro football."[21] Sportswriter Dick Schaap noted, "In an act that was contrived yet comfortable, he spoke in sports metaphors. He was obviously trying to appear friendly, pleasant and helpful, and he was, without difficulty, succeeding." Decades later, the liberal *New York Times* sportswriter Robert Lipsyte, who detested the man, remembered that "the only time I found Nixon even vaguely sympathetic" was when he talked football at a banquet in the late 1960s: "His voice grew light and high and warm as his hands darted and turned with the memory."[22]

The period between 1969 and 1972 marked Nixon's most extensive attempt to use his enthusiasm for sports to connect with wider audiences. The context, reception, and afterlives of two speeches from this period capture Nixon's evolving merger of fandom and politics: in the fall of 1969, he made a play for the support of the 'Silent Majority' – the great mass of Americans, he said, who were not actively protesting the war in Vietnam but whose voices had been drowned out by loudmouthed radicals and elites. He made common cause with them two weeks later by pointedly ignoring hundreds of thousands of protestors in the streets and watching college football instead. In a speech at Kansas State kicking off his support for Republican congressional candidates in the 1970 midterms, he invoked football to define this group against the New Left. Using his status as a fan to make the Silent Majority heard, he aimed to bind it into a coalition that would ensure Republican electoral dominance. These invocations of sport were immediately understood as nakedly political by everyone concerned; the only thing to debate was how well they worked.[23]

Nixon's 'Silent Majority' speech on November 3, 1969, consolidated his administration's handling of dissent. When Nixon took office, he knew that voters had rejected Democrats more than they had embraced him, and that a vocal peace movement that contested his authority politically and morally was rapidly gaining mainstream support. Nixon needed to assert his authority rather than let protestors make policy in the streets, but to pull this off he needed to conjure support from unmoored voters while marginalizing the opposition. Assistant for Domestic Affairs John Ehrlichman later estimated that Nixon spent half his time managing public perception. Accordingly, the White House worked to stifle, discredit, and outshout dissidents, deploying rhetoric calculated to appeal to 'Middle Americans' and reach out to traditionally Democratic labor and white-ethnic constituencies. Whatever their disagreements with Republican policy and the continued prosecution of war in Vietnam, these groups recoiled more strongly from long-haired marchers disrupting daily life.[24]

Nixon remembered that this speech "influence[d] the course of history." His explicit call to Middle Americans resonated for decades by identifying this group as the "real America," the one whose values Nixon shared but that were disdained by elites and the counterculture. (Republican politicians like Sarah Palin and Donald Trump further weaponized the term.) Nixon claimed to respect demonstrators' right to dissent, but maintained that it "would be untrue to my oath of office if I allowed the policy of this Nation to be dictated by the minority . . . who try to impose it on the Nation by mounting demonstrations in the street." So he beseeched the Silent Majority to foment home-front harmony in order to force North Vietnam to the negotiating table. Teamwork would make America great again, disunity and protest weaken it. Dissenters were off the team.[25]

A good day to watch a football game: Nixon and the mobilization against the war

With the specter of half a million protestors converging on Washington D.C. on November 15 for the Mobilization Against the War, the administration threw its busy "propaganda mill" into action, and here football played a central symbolic role in the counterprogramming. Half-time offered an excellent opportunity to emphasize "united effort": "perhaps all games could have a red, white, and blue theme or all half-times begin with 'God Bless America' and end with 'This Land Is Your Land,'" one aide suggested. The president's assistant responded that "we *did* have a patriotic theme or event at the half-time of *every major college football game which was televised.*"[26] The White House dispatched Vice President Agnew to assail the counterculture, issued intelligence reports asserting that Communists were funding and organizing the newest wave of protest, and predicted violence from mysterious, unidentifiable conglomerations ("in most cases, it is impossible to label them by a name," the attorney general explained). November 10–16 would be 'National Unity Week,' to be celebrated with flag displays and 'pro-administration propaganda' at college and pro football games and half-time ceremonies nationwide. As November 15 approached, the 'game planning' grew to include creation of nationwide 'citizens' committees' and coordination of calls, wires, and letters.[27]

The day of the march, half a million protestors massed in Washington and 150,000 in San Francisco, the largest single-site crowds yet. "[V]ery impressive . . . Whole business is sort of unreal," Chief of Staff H. R. Haldeman commented. But White House countermeasures did their job. The Silent Majority produced pro-Nixon contingents of 85,000 in Chicago and 100,000 in Pittsburgh. The networks and newspapers seemed preoccupied by violence fomented at the Justice Department by a small crowd of militants. Were protests stuck "on a treadmill?" the *Washington Post* wondered.[28]

The president usually spent Saturdays at Camp David, but on November 15 he devoted the morning to foreign policy, then pointedly told the assembled reporters after lunch that "it was a good day to watch a football game." Ohio State walloped Purdue in what Nixon predicted would be "the best college game of the year"; one journalist described the Buckeyes' dominance as so complete that "you would have thought Woody [Hayes] had scheduled Hanoi." His press secretary said, "I don't know how I could find out" whether or not the president had at any time mustered the will to glance out of the window at the protests. Nixon boasted that he had spent his time watching "a great game" instead. He even telephoned Hayes to congratulate him on the victory.[29] To complete the theme, the next day Nixon saw the Dallas Cowboys beat the Washington Redskins, becoming the first sitting president to attend a regular season NFL game.[30]

Nixon did not directly intend to "trigger the libs," as some might put it now. But for critics, this "deliberate presidential cold-shoulder" nonetheless emblematized his cynical deployment of symbolism. The *Washington Post* mocked the clumsily-staged normality inside the White House, "the theme that the administration wanted to convey. Abnormal efforts were made to get that point across." Its angry editorial the next day raged that "for sheer piquancy, we have not heard the likes of that since Marie Antoinette."[31] Secretary of the Interior Walter Hickel worried that "there is nothing wrong with watching football . . . But when a group of people in America wants to express an opinion, and is asking to be heard, I think it is the duty and obligation of those who are the leaders . . . to hear these people out." *The Washingtonian*'s mock obituary for Nixon mourned "one of the most devoted sportswriters in the business" and recalled an occasion, "perhaps apocryphal," in which "he sat serenely in his living room watching a football game on television despite the presence of several thousand protestors who were marching outside his house." Four years later, Art Buchwald's parodic Watergate trivia quiz asked, "President Nixon has insisted from the very beginning that he never had any knowledge of Watergate until March 21, 1973. What football games did he watch while the cover-up was going on?"[32]

Nixon's performance of conspicuous indifference showcased him choosing what was *truly* popular. Rather than wasting time on malcontents whose protests did not and should not register, Nixon watched football on Saturday afternoon, like a normal American. Here he was absolutely in tune with mainstream opinion; the following May (just before the Kent State shootings) a *New York Times* poll found that 70 percent of Americans did not support the right to dissent from government policies. Nixon used football to tie his values to those of Middle America and oppose them to what protestors (who purportedly hated order, Nixon, and football) stood for. Political journalist Stewart Alsop thought that connection authentic, and effective:

> It would be a mistake to underestimate the political impact of the President's squareness. A healthy majority of the President's fellow squares want their country to remain number one in the world, and, also like the President, interest themselves passionately in football. But the President's squareness in such respects is not a political put-on ... [H]is football obsession, like his true-blue, Whittier-style patriotism, comes entirely naturally.[33]

Nixon repeatedly used this rhetoric to claim common ground over the next few years, whether he was congratulating Texas for defeating Arkansas or accepting renomination in 1972.

Trained mice couldn't have done better: Nixon at Kansas State

The repeated allusions to this story reflect how effectively Nixon's behavior stuck in liberals' craw. But from the president's perspective, his gestures had simply made common cause with supporters. In the wake of Kent State, disconnecting Nixon from the wrong audiences became as important as connecting him with the right ones. Peace marchers had not provided a sufficiently abrasive foil. Counterposing rampaging college students to football players could reap greater rewards. Here Kevin Phillips' *The Emerging Republican Majority* guided the administration's tactics. Despite public denials that the president had read the book because of its controversial advocacy of racial polarization, it became "the New Testament around the Nixon White House." Most controversially, Phillips advised that alienating the right people made political sense. Who hated whom – "that is the secret," he explained.[34]

The president's rhetoric in his fall appearances in 1970 thus regularly contrasted 'bad kids' with good kids who played America's favorite sport. After pondering at length an invitation for the president to speak at Kansas State in September, the administration adroitly used football to turn Nixon's connection with his audience into a megaphone that let the Silent Majority hear itself – and marketed an almost completely controlled speaking opportunity as a Rooseveltian demonstration of character. Both tactics would define his actions throughout the fall of 1970, during which the president repeatedly linked football and political unity by celebrating Green Bay's former quarterback Bart Starr (who campaigned for Nixon in 1968 and 1972) alongside a slate of Republican candidates and mourning the recently deceased pro football coach Vince Lombardi as "an apostle of teamwork." Struck by this approach, a reporter traveling with the campaign likened Nixon to a college coach recruiting prospective players: "It may be hard for some politicians to reduce a major political campaign to football terms, but not this one."[35]

Senator Bob Dole, who had been angling for a Nixon visit for nine months, forwarded a letter from Kansas State president James McCain assuring the White House that "if past performances are any indication the President could count on an enthusiastic response." Nixon's staff nonetheless remained leery of "an agricultural school . . . [that] has had *no* disturbance," instructing Nixon to ask the senator "if he feels [Nixon] will have a good reception and any problem with student demonstrations." (Perhaps this was due as well to simple unfamiliarity, as no president had ventured onto a major university campus since Lyndon Johnson's appearance at Johns Hopkins in 1965.[36]) Even after repeated guarantees that the campus offered him a safe harbor, Nixon's staffers worked hard to minimize opposition while simultaneously celebrating the president's brave willingness to speak the truth.[37]

The school newspaper's editor described Manhattan, Kansas, as "probably among the safest campuses in the nation, as far as presidential visits are concerned." In a less guarded moment, he admitted that Kansas State was "just like any other school – 15 years ago." By way of contrast, the University of Kansas in Lawrence had seen race riots over the spring and summer and boasted multiple alternative weeklies and a Gay Liberation Front. Members of the Weather Underground, radical militants who had broken from Students for a Democratic Society, had threatened to blow up that university's football stadium the previous October.[38]

None of these things were true at Kansas State. It was not entirely immune to wider currents: the school had observed the Moratorium the previous October and sent a busload of students to Washington for the protests in November. The *National Catholic Reporter* covered the dangers for Nixon of "soft-spoken dissent" cropping up in "cow town."[39] But the local left was clearly tiny. KSU seniors most often described themselves as "straight-laced," and were four times as likely as seniors nationwide to feel "much school spirit." "The overwhelming majority will greet him warmly and be flattered that he came," the director of the Office of Educational Research predicted. The school president expected, at worst, "some constructive dissent." Even the proprietor of a local head shop, who put up a sign warning of Nixon's visit to "promote comment," elicited no responses.[40]

Upon the president's arrival on September 16, the Kansas State band kicked things off by booming out the university's fight song. "Eat 'em up, eat 'em up, KSU!" the crowd chanted. Nixon began with his usual Rooseveltian themes: "I think of the fans of Wildcat football here today who have known what it is to lose – and then who have known what it is to win." He had dared to wear a tie in school colors, even though it clashed with his blue suit, because "I am proud to wear the purple at Kansas State." "I think, too, of some of the moments of my own career: as a football player who spent most of my time on the bench, as a candidate who knew the great satisfaction of winning – and then as a candidate to learn what it is to lose." Nixon linked these lessons to native son Alf Landon's becoming an "elder statesman" rather than wallowing in defeat after being swamped by Franklin Roosevelt in 1936. So, too, "take Kansas State and its football team."[41]

In ways both literal and symbolic, that team captured the Nixon spirit. The *Kansas State Collegian* raved that Coach Vince Gibson took "a sour grape and turn[ed] it into a potent purple giant." The program had embarked on a massive buildup of force, with an $800,000 athletic dorm known locally as the Sheraton Gibson (complete with swimming pool, sauna, and color TVs), a new stadium that seated 48,000, and an expanded coaching staff. But that very week *Look* revealed that the program was losing money, and none of the six players drafted the previous spring had graduated.

In a bit of foreshadowing that nobody could have noted, three weeks later Gibson was reprimanded for NCAA ethics, eligibility, and recruiting violations and the program was placed on probation for three years.[42]

The Wildcats had gone 8–60 over the seven seasons before hiring Gibson, but, just like Richard Nixon, Kansas State had not given up. "Losing some and winning some . . . accepting the verdict and having another chance, is fundamental to the whole structure on which our liberty rests," he observed. And this was where protestors went wrong. No one could win every time in a free society, a truth that protestors would grasp – Nixon implied – if they had ever played team sports: "whether in a campaign, or a football game, or in debate on the great issues of the day, the answer to 'losing one' is not a rush to the barricades." Antiwar activists should ponder why so few Americans rallied to their cause. Nixon called for an end to violence and continued faith in America. He did not want to diminish or demean the idealism of youth, he said, merely to channel it in productive directions.[43]

The pre-speech predictions proved to be accurate. One onlooker counted twenty-nine interruptions for applause in 35 minutes. *Time* believed that "no Brechtian genius could have staged the audience participation better."[44] The "anything-but-silent" crowd "went wild" and rewarded Nixon with five standing ovations in the first 15 minutes, drowning out the forty or so dissenters, who left grumbling. "I want to apologize to the rest of the students across the country," one of them remarked. Nixon beamed as he left the platform, telling his traveling party, "we handled everything well." "He played that noisy handful . . . like an orchestra," agreed James Pearson, the state's other senator.[45]

"It would be difficult to find much fault with the President's message," the *Lawrence Journal-World* editorialized. Nixon's speech catalyzed public distaste for radicals, reassuring the president that his course was right and popular, that Middle Americans loved him and loved what he had to say. As he had with Hunter Thompson and Dick Schaap, Nixon talked knowledgeably about football to smooth his way into the hearts of his audience. But he also used it to draw multiple culture war lines: Kansas State fans were Nixon supporters, were the Silent Majority, were patriots.

Football trained them to accept losing and winning, and through that the precepts of democracy. Because radicals did not appreciate football, they understood none of these things. During the speech, he ad-libbed on his prepared text: "the voices of the small minority have been allowed to drown out the responsible majority." Celebrating the self-assurance of this segment of the Silent Majority, he rejoiced, "that may be true in some places, but not at Kansas State!"[46]

The crowd rewarded him with a "truly deafening" roar and a "tumultuous" standing ovation. An editor of the school paper protested that "we were used – exactly as planned," pointing out that Nixon had called the school "one of the great universities" due entirely to its warm reception and its football team. The president promised that he "would not for one moment call for a dull, passive conformity," she concluded, but "he found it here . . . Trained mice couldn't have done better." The paper's radical columnist mourned that "at the end of the scrimmage Country Dick had clearly defeated the K-State dissenters by a score of 15,000 to 50."[47] National media were equally dubious. Ron Fimrite of the *San Francisco Chronicle* wrote angrily that "it's all well and good to radicalize the dean of men's office and that sort of thing, but let's make sure we have a winning season first." The *St. Louis Post-Dispatch* called the speech "not terribly useful for conveying a better understanding of the complicated tensions in society . . . Students in the audience may well have wondered if Mr. Nixon were holding out a single choice, between football and radical protest, the one exemplifying the best that a youth can aspire to, the other the worst."[48]

From the administration's perspective, Kansas State went exactly as planned. A delighted Haldeman called it a "huge success, beyond all fondest hopes! . . . *Small* group of about 25 bad guys in the audience of 15,000, and their shouts, etc., played right into P's speech." All three networks carried the speech live, and a week later Chicago insurance executive W. Clement Stone (a major Nixon contributor), *Reader's Digest*, PepsiCo. and Warner-Lambert subsidized prime-time rebroadcasts in nine important cities; the administration mailed out tens of thousands of copies; and polls revealed that 90 percent of the public deemed campus protests completely or mostly unjustified.[49] President McCain thanked Nixon for his "magnificent address" and counted more than a thousand "letters, telegrams, and long-distance telephone calls from persons in every state in the Union," the vast majority of which "stated that the program had given them a renewed faith in the youth of America." McCain especially celebrated Nixon's "forthright statements" about campus protest, which took "no little courage" to deliver.[50]

A game plan mentality: evaluating Nixon's success

By 1972, these linkages were central, expert, and almost unexamined. At the Republican National Convention in Miami Beach, Starr introduced House Minority Leader Gerald Ford, and former NFL quarterback and newly-minted Republican Congressman Jack Kemp gave an "electrifying" speech seconding the nomination of Spiro Agnew – a clue, many thought, that Kemp was being showcased for the Senate in 1974 or the vice presidency in 1976. The Nixon campaign meticulously crafted events, down to a script scheduling every "spontaneous" demonstration by the minute.[51] The Democrats, on the other hand, were in such disarray during their own convention that George McGovern accepted the nomination at three in the morning. "It was all over right then and there," the rules chair remarked.[52] The head of Nixon's advertising agency chalked up his team's smooth execution to solid game planning: "the President likes football analogies, and the relationships of field position and ball control were the essential elements of what the campaign organization tried to do." Appalled by these patterns of thought and behavior, the disgusted Ripon Society, a liberal-Republican think tank, charged Nixon's team with suffering "from a game plan mentality that led them to believe that the essence of politics was outpointing antagonists and adversaries . . . It was often unclear whether they thought they were playing on a football field or a battlefield."[53]

As the Ripon Society observed, Nixon's sports fan authenticity both helped and hurt his initiatives. Pondering the "Southernization of America" in 1974, journalist John Egerton conjectured that Nixon owed "a large measure of his electoral success to his devotion to sports." That legacy is complex: one could just as well make the case that Nixon permanently poisoned the notion of president-as-fan. From the 1950s onward, onlookers described Nixon's speeches as at once sincere and calculated, politics by other means. It was exemplary postmodern politics – the president defined not by what he does but by what he follows, how he follows it, and how he talks about how he follows it. Even as they suspected that this was exactly what Nixon connived, was *always* conniving, to do, he used this tactic to convince Hunter Thompson and Dick Schaap that he was something like them. "He's not a *conscious* phony. That complicates my story considerably," Thompson wrote to a correspondent.[54] Nixon used football during the peace marches to consolidate the notion of the Silent Majority, and again at Kansas State to help that majority see and hear itself. He believed what he said about football, *and* he knew he could use it. By merging classic Rooseveltian character-building with performative normality, he wrote the playbook, as he would doubtless have put it, for politicians ever since.

Notes

1. Jacob Riis, *Theodore Roosevelt: The Man and the Citizen* (London: Hodder & Stoughton, 1904), 21; Theodore Roosevelt, *The Strenuous Life: Essays and Addresses* (New York: Charles Scribner, 1906), 153.
2. Roosevelt, *The Strenuous Life*, 117; Richard Nixon, "Address in the Alfred M. Landon Lecture Series at Kansas State University," September 16, 1970; Online by Gerhard Peters and John T. Woolley, *The American Presidency Project*, available at: http://www.presidency.ucsb.edu/ws/?pid=2663.
3. "Special Correspondent," *Sports Illustrated*, August 24, 1959, 21.
4. Frank Church, "President Lauds Starr," *Appleton Post-Crescent*, October 18, 1970, 1; Memorandum for Pat Buchanan, October 2, 1972, folder Football 10/1/69, Nixon papers.
5. Richard M. Nixon, "Remarks at the Professional Football Hall of Fame Annual Banquet in Canton, Ohio," *Public Papers of the Presidents of the United States: Richard M. Nixon, 1971* (Washington, D.C.: Government Printing Office, 1972), 834; Art Buchwald, "Games Presidents Play," *Los Angeles Times*, January 9, 1972, H1.
6. "Answering Mr. Nixon," *The Nation*, November 17, 1969, 524; Frank Walsh to John Whitaker, May 25, 1968, Campaign 1968 Collection, Nixon papers.

7. Thomas Edwards, "The Sporting Gripe," *Partisan Review* 38(3) (1971): 331.
8. Fawn Brodie, *Richard Nixon: The Shaping of His Character* (New York: W. W. Norton, 1981), 266. Thanks to Rivers Gambrell for the reference.
9. "Excerpts of Seconding Talks for Eisenhower," *Los Angeles Times*, August 23, 1956, 13; David Haven Blake, *Liking Ike: Eisenhower, Advertising, and the Rise of Celebrity Politics* (New York: Oxford University Press, 2016), 16.
10. Michael Patrick Cullinane, *Theodore Roosevelt's Ghost: The History and Memory of an American Icon* (Baton Rouge: Louisiana State University Press, 2017), 173.
11. Tuss McLaughry to Norris Cotton, July 9, 1957; Tuss McLaughry to Richard Nixon, January 29, 1958; clipping from *Milwaukee Journal*, January 9, 1958; all in folder 1/8/58 – 35th Annual Meeting, American Football Coaches Association; Box 75; Pre-Presidential Papers, Appearances, 1948–1962 – all in Nixon papers.
12. Remarks of the Vice President of the United States before the Thirty-Fifth Annual Meeting of the American Football Coaches Association, January 8, 1958; Zipp Newman, "Nixon Has Terrific Grasp of Football," *Birmingham News*, January 9, 1958; Annual Meeting, American Football Coaches Association – all in folder, Annual Meeting, American Football Coaches Association, Nixon papers.
13. Remarks of the Vice President of the United States.
14. Tom Siler, "Nixon Makes Hit at Fete," *Knoxville News-Sentinel*, January 9, 1958, 28.
15. Newman, "Nixon Has Terrific Grasp of Football"; "Nixon Demonstrates Economic Befuddlement," *Soviet Home Service*, January 13, 1958 – both in folder, Annual Meeting, American Football Coaches Association, Nixon papers.
16. Note from RHF to WWS, April 26, 1959; Joseph Sheehan, "Nixon Regales Football Writers with his Wide Sports Coverage," *New York Times*, August 14, 1959; Leo Fischer, "Politico Nixon Shows His Ken of Grid Arena" – all in folder 8/14/59, Football Writers' Association of America: All Star Game; Box 112, Pre-Presidential Papers, Appearances, 1948–1962, Nixon papers.
17. Volney Meece, "So They Tell Me," *Oklahoma City Times*, August 15, 1959, 15; Walter Johns, "Bob Ptacek Gets Award but Nixon Does Work," *The Football News*, September 19, 1959, 5 – both in folder, Football Writers' Association meeting, Nixon papers; Bill Rives, "One of Our Best Customers," *Dallas Morning News*, August 16, 1959, 2:1.

18. Kathleen Hall Jamieson, *Packaging the Presidency: A History and Criticism of Presidential Campaign Advertising* (New York: Oxford University Press, 1984), 154.

19. Richard M. Nixon, "Remarks at the National Football Foundation and Hall of Fame Dinner in New York City, December 9, 1969," *Public Papers of the Presidents of the United States: Richard M. Nixon, 1969* (Washington, D.C.: Government Printing Office, 1971), 1017; H. R. Haldeman, *The Haldeman Diaries: Inside the Nixon White House* (New York: Berkley Books, 1995), 229; Carl Bernstein and Bob Woodward, *The Final Days* (New York: Simon & Schuster, 2005), 442; Cullinane, *Theodore Roosevelt's Ghost*, 177.

20. Smith Barrier, untitled column, *Greensboro Daily News*, August 15, 1959, B2.

21. Red Smith, foreword to Ira Berkow, *Beyond the Dream: Occasional Heroes of Sports* (New York: Athenaeum, 1975), ix–x; Hunter S. Thompson, *The Great Shark Hunt* (New York: Summit Books, 1979), 190, 191.

22. Dick Schaap, "Will Richard Nixon Trip Over Himself Again on His Way to Victory?" *New York*, June 10, 1968, 26; Robert Lipsyte, "Of Sports, Comebacks and Nixon," *New York Times*, May 1, 1994, S11.

23. For a broader consideration of Nixon's history as a fan and use of his fandom, see Jesse Berrett, *Pigskin Nation: How the NFL Remade American Politics* (Urbana: University of Illinois Press, 2018), ch. 5. For a discussion of Nixon's notorious early morning visit to the Lincoln Memorial, see Jesse Berrett, "In the Trump Era, One of Richard Nixon's Worst Moments as President Looks a Lot Better," *Washington Post*, May 9, 2018, available at: https://www.washingtonpost.com/news/made-by-history/wp/2018/05/09/in-the-trump-era-one-of-richard-nixons-worst-moments-as-president-looks-a-lot-better.

24. Robert Mason, *Richard Nixon and the Quest for a New Majority* (Chapel Hill: University of North Carolina Press, 2004), 96–99, 41.

25. Richard Nixon, *RN: The Memoirs of Richard Nixon* (New York: Grosset & Dunlap, 1978), 409; Mason, *Richard Nixon and the Quest for a New Majority*, 38; "Nixon's Silent Majority Speech," *Watergate.info*, available at: http://watergate.info/1969/11/03/nixons-silent-majority-speech.html.

26. Melvin Small, *Covering Dissent: The Media and the Anti-Vietnam War Movement* (New Brunswick, NJ: Rutgers University Press, 1994), 109, 111; Tom Wells, *The War Within: America's Battle over Vietnam* (Berkeley: University of California Press, 1994), 382–383,

385, 387; Memo from Alexander Butterfield to Dwight Chapin, November 19, 1969, folder Football 10/1/1969, Nixon papers.

27. Memo from Hugh Sloan to Haldeman, November 26, 1969, Nixon papers.

28. Small, *Covering Dissent*, 114, 116–126; Haldeman, *Haldeman Diaries*, 108.

29. "Secluded Nixon Talks Football," *San Francisco Sunday Examiner & Chronicle*, November 16, 1969, A19; Raymond Price, *With Nixon* (New York: Viking, 1977), 157; President Richard Nixon's Daily Diary, November 15, 1969, available at: http://www.nixonlibrary.gov/virtuallibrary/documents/PDD/1969/017%20November%20 1-15%201969.pdf; Stuart Loory, "Mobe Day at Capital: Why They Dissented," *Los Angeles Times*, November 16, 1969, 17; Dan Jenkins, "Ohio State: Alone at the Top," in *Woody Hayes: The Man & His Dynasty*, ed. Mike Bynum (Birmingham: Gridiron Football Properties, 1991), 72; Margaret Crimmins, "Nixon: 'A Great Game,'" *Washington Post*, 17 November 1969, D1.

30. "10 Football Facts Featuring U.S. Presidents," *Prologue: Pieces of History*, National Archives, February 2, 2014, available at: http://blogs.archives.gov/prologue/?paged=27.

31. Murray Marder, "White House: A Display of Normality," *Washington Post*, November 16, 1969, A1, A18; "No," *Washington Post*, November 18, 1969, A22.

32. Walter Hickel, *Who Owns America?* (Englewood Cliffs, NJ: Prentice-Hall, 1971), 227–228; Dan Rottenberg, "Richard M. Nixon Dead at 84; U.S. President in Early War Years," *The Washingtonian*, December 1970, 16; Art Buchwald, "Who Said, 'Why Can't Timahoe be More Like Checkers?'" *Washington Post*, March 31, 1974, L1.

33. Katherine Scott, "Nixon and Dissent," in *A Companion to Richard Nixon*, ed. Melvin Small (Chichester: Wiley-Blackwell, 2011), 325; Stewart Alsop, "Nixon and the Square Majority: Is the Fox a Lion?" *The Atlantic*, February 1972, 42.

34. Robert Mason, "Political Realignment," in *A Companion to Richard Nixon*, ed. Melvin Small (Chichester: Wiley-Blackwell, 2011), 254; Mason, *Richard Nixon and the Quest for a New Majority*, 50, 46.

35. Jules Witcover, "Nixon Campaigning Like a Head Coach," *Los Angeles Times*, October 26, 1970, 19.

36. Stephen E. Ambrose, *Nixon, vol. II: The Triumph of a Politician 1962–1972* (New York: Simon & Schuster, 1989), 375; Stephen E. Ambrose, *To America: Personal Reflections of an Historian* (New York: Simon & Schuster, 2002), 139.

37. Letter, James McCain to Bob Dole, June 24, 1970; Memo from Dwight Chapin to Hugh Sloan, August 3, 1970; Memo from Dwight Chapin to Murray Chotiner, August 21, 1970; Telephone call, August 28, 1970 – all in folder Manhattan, Kansas–Kansas State University, Ahearn Fieldhouse 9/16/1970; Box 43; White House Central Files: Subject Files: Trips, Nixon papers.
38. "Nixon: The Pursuit of Peace and Politics," *Time*, September 28, 1970, 6; Ernest V. Murphy IIII, "University Readies for Nixon Visit," *Kansas State Collegian*, September 14, 1970, 1; Mike Moffet, "KSU Meets Nixon on 'Black Wednesday,'" *Daily Kansan*, September 16, 1970, 12; Rusty Monhollon, *"This Is America?": The Sixties in Lawrence, Kansas* (New York: Palgrave, 2002), 182.
39. Tom Blackburn, "'Cow Town' Expresses Soft Spoken Dissent," *Kansas State Collegian*, November 12, 1969, 5.
40. Ed Taylor, "Research Indicates Warm Nixon Reception," *Kansas State Collegian*, September 15, 1970, 3.
41. Ralph Gage, "Manhattan or Manhattan – Purple Pride Shows," *Lawrence Daily Journal-World*, September 17, 1970, 1; Nixon, "Address in the Alfred M. Landon Lecture Series."
42. Glen Iversen, "Vince Gibson's Reign: A Long Walk Over Water," *Kansas State Collegian*, October 3, 1969, 2A; Sandy Padwe, "Big-Time College Football Is on the Skids," *Look*, September 22, 1970, 69; "Big Eight Places Kansas, Kansas State on Probation," *Joplin Globe*, October 8, 1970, C1.
43. Nixon, "Address in the Alfred M. Landon Lecture Series."
44. "Roaring Throng Hears Nixon," *Kansas State Collegian*, September 17, 1970, 1; "Nixon: The Pursuit of Peace and Politics."
45. Dick Haines, "The Day the President Came . . .," *K-Stater*, October 1970, 5; Ray Morgan, "Roar of Nixon Support Drowns Shouts of Protest," *Kansas City Times*, September 17, 1970, 1A, 12A; "Reactions Surface after Nixon Leaves," *Kansas State Collegian*, September 17, 1970, 1.
46. "Nixon's Kansas Visit," *Lawrence Journal-World*, September 17, 1970, 4; Robert Wuthnow, *Red State Religion: Faith and Politics in America's Heartland* (Princeton, NJ: Princeton University Press, 2012), 250; Thurston Clarke, *The Last Campaign: Robert F. Kennedy and 82 Days That Inspired America* (New York: Macmillan, 2008), 47.
47. Sandy Flickner, "We Were Used – Exactly as Planned," *Kansas State Collegian*, September 17, 1970, 4; Frank 'Klorox' Cleveland, "Country Dick Wins Game," *Kansas State Collegian*, September 18, 1970, 4.

48. Ron Fimrite, "First a Winning Season, Then to the Barricades," *San Francisco Chronicle*, September 17, 1970, 66; "A Pep Rally in Kansas," *Kansas State Collegian*, September 21, 1970, 2.

49. Haldeman, *Haldeman Diaries*, 193, 194; Ambrose, *Nixon: The Triumph of a Politician 1962–1972*, 377.

50. Letter from James McCain to Richard Nixon, September 22, 1970; folder Manhattan, Kansas–Kansas State University, Ahearn Field-house 9/16/1970; Box 43; White House Central Files: Subject Files: Trips, Nixon papers; Sally Brownlee, "Congratulatory Messages Pour In," *Kansas State Collegian*, September 28, 1970, 3.

51. Martin Nolan, "The Re-Selling of the President," *The Atlantic* (1972): 79–81; Neil Hickey, "Make News, Not Commercials," *TV Guide*, May 27, 1972, 8; Herbert Alexander, *Financing the 1972 Election* (Lexington, MA: Lexington Books, 1976), 78, 245–248; James Wooten, "Unexpected 'Preview' Provides a Jolt to a Hitherto Predictable Convention," *New York Times*, August 23, 1972, 26.

52. *Campaign '72: The Managers Speak*, ed. Ernest May and Janet Fraser (Cambridge, MA: Harvard University Press, 1973), 186, 172, 49, 234.

53. *Campaign '72: The Managers Speak*, 196; Ripon Society, *Jaws of Victory: The Game-Plan Politics of 1972, The Crisis of the Republican Party, and the Future of the Constitution* (Boston, MA: Little, Brown, 1972), 3, 4.

54. John Egerton, *The Americanization of Dixie: The Southernization of America* (New York: Harper's Magazine Press, 1974), 179; Hunter S. Thompson, *Fear and Loathing in America: The Brutal Odyssey of an Outlaw Journalist 1968–1976* (New York: Simon & Schuster, 2000), 41.

4

"He'd Like to be Savior of the National Pastime": Bill Clinton and the 1994–1995 Baseball Strike

Chris Birkett

In February 1995, Pamela Owens, a mother from Texas who was campaigning for better educational opportunities for her autistic son, felt compelled to write to President Bill Clinton about his misplaced priorities. She had heard on the news that the president wanted to get involved in efforts to end a six-month strike in Major League Baseball (MLB) – a dispute that had led to an abrupt end to the 1994 regular season and the cancellation of the World Series for the first time in ninety years. "I would think there are a lot of more important matters to be handled by the President of the United States than the issue of baseball," Owens wrote. Perhaps, Owens mused, she had over-valued the position of the presidency.[1]

Pamela Owens was not alone in thinking that Clinton was misguided in his efforts over the winter months of 1994–95 to broker peace in an ill-tempered argument between 750 players and 28 owners about baseball's labyrinthine labor practices and complex economic model. Some in Clinton's cabinet harbored similar doubts: Vice President Al Gore feared that Clinton was being drawn into a "scorpion fight."[2] Labor Secretary Robert Reich recalled theories championed by the political scientist Richard Neustadt about the contingency of the persuasive powers of the presidency being "frittered away on lost causes."[3] The public appeared to agree: a poll circulating among White House staffers indicated that 74 percent of people were opposed to presidential intervention.[4] Media commentators were similarly unconvinced:

in the *New York Times*, Claire Smith wondered whether the president was "the last American willing to invest emotional energy in baseball."[5]

Yet despite the caution of colleagues, public suspicion, and the skepticism of much of the press, Clinton persisted in his belief that he had a role in saving professional baseball from self-destruction: he could not afford to let the national pastime die on his watch. And one of the driving forces behind his thinking was a myth that had been propagated by journalists, scholars, and politicians since the early twentieth century – that the health of the national pastime was a measure of the health and vitality of American society itself. This familiar piece of folk wisdom underpinned President Herbert Hoover's declaration that baseball, alongside religion, was the "greatest moral influence" on the American way of life; it bolstered Franklin Delano Roosevelt's enthusiasm to see professional baseball continue through the Second World War; and it was the reason Bart Giamatti (President of Yale and Commissioner of Baseball) could insist, without a trace of irony, that "Baseball is part of America's plot, part of America's mysterious underlying design – the plot in which we all conspire and collude – the story of our national life."[6] But, in late 1994, with baseball heading toward its own existential crisis and the country's political institutions awash with partisan antagonism, this mythical connection now appeared to be double-edged. It was Ken Burns, the acclaimed historical documentary filmmaker, who made the point most succinctly: "beset by the pernicious effects of self-interest and narcissism, and an inability to find common ground . . . I could be describing the country as a whole as I describe the problems that beset baseball."[7]

Baseball as American history

Burns had chosen his moment well. As the maker of the successful Public Broadcasting Service (PBS) series *The Civil War* in 1990, Burns was arguably the most influential popular historian in the United States. He already enjoyed a relationship of mutual admiration with Clinton: when they first met in late 1992, Burns recalled Clinton displaying "more understanding and insight than any critic or reviewer ever had."[8] Since then, Burns had turned his attention to baseball, producing an eighteen-and-a-half-hour history of the game which aired on PBS in nine primetime episodes between September 18 and 28, 1994. Burns' central argument was an adaptation and expansion of that folkloric myth: baseball was a prism through which to view the entire social and cultural history of twentieth-century America. The game, said Burns, was "a constant reminder of a vast past and a precise mirror of who we are."[9] A few minutes into the first episode, the cultural critic, Gerald Early, appeared on screen to suggest that in 2,000 years America would be remembered for just three things – the Constitution, jazz, and baseball.[10]

Forty-five million viewers lapped it up, including Clinton who declared the series "magnificent."[11] Clearly, the president was captivated by the program's televisual thesis, even if, according to Burns' logic, it followed that the mess in which baseball now found itself reflected badly on the state of the country and, by association, his administration. "If our national pastime was being canceled things could not be going in the right direction," Clinton admitted.[12] Channeling this belief, Clinton became the first sitting president to become publicly involved in trying to settle a labor dispute in professional sport – a decision he presented as one of institutional obligation, if not sacred duty. Mike McCurry, one of the president's pre-eminent 'spin doctors,' recalled that moment: "I remember thinking to myself, this doesn't require spin, it's baseball. Presidents are supposed to do baseball. That's what they do. It's part of what the deal is if you're the President of the United States."[13]

Of course, McCurry was right: the deal with baseball was ingrained in the cultural architecture of the Office of the President. From the first presidential Opening Day pitch thrown by President William Howard Taft in 1910, to Richard Nixon's performances as "Fan in Chief," presidents had long engaged with the national pastime to validate their claims to national leadership – celebrating the virtues of its fabled, if largely fictitious, American creation story and harvesting the political benefits of identifying with "ordinary fans."[14] Clinton had already seized his first two opportunities: pitching on Opening Day in Baltimore in 1993 and Cleveland in 1994, assiduously practicing beforehand in the

White House grounds so anxious was he to avoid the fate which befell his immediate predecessor – the indignity and damage to masculine and presidential self-esteem of seeing his ball flop into the dirt.[15]

But Clinton's engagement with the strike was not solely motivated by a desire to fulfill ceremonial obligations – the unfavorable political landscape resulting from an unsteady first twenty months in office played a part too. Early on there had been controversy over plans to lift the ban on gays serving in the military, while increased taxes on fuel had hit the less well-off. GDP growth was steady but unspectacular: real wages were stagnant. Progress on international trade, gun-control, crime, unemployment, and the federal budget was offset by the collapse of Clinton's health care plan and by the sprawling investigation into the First Family's real estate investments on the Whitewater River in Arkansas. Other 'scandals' of varying degrees of veracity, usually adorned with the 'gate' suffix, were seized upon hungrily by the media.[16] Never before had a president experienced such consistently poor approval ratings across the first two years of an administration.[17] Even so, the scale of the punishment meted out to the Democrats in the midterm elections of 1994 surprised most observers, including Clinton, with the Republicans taking control of both houses of Congress for the first time since 1952. Focusing on cultural issues and armed with the Republican *Contract With America*, Newt Gingrich had successfully exploited the emerging alternative media, dominated by conservative talk-radio, to make the elections a referendum on the president by arguing that he was the "enemy of normal Americans" for his lack of moral leadership and support for gay rights.[18] By early 1995, Labor Secretary Reich observed that Gingrich, now the House Speaker, and Senate Majority Leader Bob Dole appeared "to have taken charge of the United States Government."[19] In short, Clinton's presidency was being dismissed as 'irrelevant.'[20]

The baseball strike offered Clinton a chance to chip away at that narrative, the opportunity for him to be an activist, and to demonstrate that he could still pull on the levers of persuasion his office provided – especially where there were potential swing-state votes at stake. By cherishing a national institution and bringing an end to conflict in the national pastime, Clinton thought he could prove that the Republicans were wrong; that he did share the values of 'normal Americans.' By advocating compromise and reconciliation in baseball, he could heal a broken game, and, by implication, a fractured nation.

The 1994–1995 strike

The immediate cause of the 1994–95 strike was the breakdown in talks over a new collective bargaining agreement between MLB owners and the Major League Baseball Players Association (MLBPA). But the dispute was situated on a longer arc – one whose trajectory was defined in 1922 when baseball was granted exemption from the nation's antitrust laws by the Supreme Court.[21] That ruling allowed clubs to maintain a monopoly of the professional game in a given regional market and to profit from the reserve clause, which tied players to their teams in perpetuity. Twice the Supreme Court revisited the antitrust exemption, in 1953 and 1972, and twice left it largely intact. But, by 1994, baseball's unique legal and commercial arrangements had become a source of instability rather than security. Strikes, or the threat of them, had become commonplace because they were the union's only viable weapon, given that franchises had little to fear from an antitrust suit.[22]

There was cultural decline as well: no longer did baseball occupy the unrivaled position in the sporting imagination as it had in the postwar years. That mantle had long been surrendered to the explosively televisual, brilliantly marketed National Football League (NFL). Enjoying Congress-approved revenue-sharing freedom, the NFL built a nationally visible league with teams competing on a broadly equal footing. By 1972, a *Gallup* poll showed that pro football had overtaken baseball as America's most popular sport.[23] In baseball, a Darwinian economic model persisted: lucrative local broadcast deals meant small-market clubs struggled to compete against the revenue-rich, big-market operations. How income should be shared among the clubs, and divided between the owners and players, was unresolved. Wage inflation associated with the rise of free agency added to commercial and labor-related uncertainty. In June 1994, with the collective bargaining agreement lapsing six months earlier, MLB owners proposed a new deal: revenue-sharing between clubs and a salary cap across the industry. The union rejected it, setting the course for a strike from August 12, fifty-two days before the scheduled end of the regular season.

As the date approached, and with negotiations stalled, Clinton was aware of the frustration of fans. During a campaign trip to Cleveland, home of the division-leading Indians, he had experienced them first-hand: "the first fifteen people I shook hands with said: 'can't you do anything about the baseball strike?'"[24] Two days later Reich took a call from Bruce Lindsey, the Deputy White House Counsel: "You guys doing anything about this baseball thing?"[25] Reich, who believed that presidential abstention from industrial disputes was usually the best course, sensed this time there was an appetite in the White House for Clinton to be seen to be saving the baseball season. "Moreover," Reich noted in his diary, "without baseball, blue-collar America will be even more depressed than it is now and blue-collar blues aren't good for the party in power in a midterm election year."[26] A few days later, Clinton remarked to William Gould IV, the newly appointed chairman of the National Labor Relations Board (NLRB): "If you guys could resolve this, they would elect me president for life."[27] For now, however, Clinton remained at arm's length, heeding advice that the negotiations should be allowed to run their course.

With the players taking their final at-bats on August 11, there were no last-minute initiatives and no fresh talks scheduled. As the strike was about to begin, Clinton's tone became more urgent, warning that both sides were treading a perilous path: "what will happen if they lose their customers?" he asked, implying that the strike had the capacity to do significant economic damage as well as further threatening baseball's cultural standing.[28] The fans' pressure group, the National Union of Fans and Families, called on Clinton to impose an emergency back-to-work order, expressing their feelings in the language of cultural exceptionalism: "Baseball is the tie that binds across towns, across the country, across generations, across time . . . You, Mr. President, of all people must appreciate the importance of this rare element in today's society."[29]

However, by the time Clinton hosted a White House reception on September 10, to mark the premiere of Burns' television series, there had been no progress and barely any direct talks. Whatever hope remained that the remnants of the season could be salvaged had almost vanished. Therefore, the scene on a balmy evening on the South Lawn made an incongruous cultural tableau, as hundreds of guests joined Clinton and Burns to party amidst the paraphernalia of baseball's better times.[30] It was an opportunity, Clinton's advisors told him, to invoke "shared memories and common purposes."[31] The *Washington Post*, however, offered a more ominous take on an event which seemed strangely out of touch with the reality of the current labor crisis. The Burns series, the newspaper suggested, was likely to be the "epitaph to baseball as Americans know it."[32] And, indeed, when the cancellation of the World Series was confirmed four days later, it appeared that the *Post* had been prescient. Embracing the theme, the *New York Times* carried a front page 'In Memoriam' notice, headlined in funereal font: "The National Pastime, which was buried yesterday, died a long time ago," after collapsing of exhaustion "towards the tail end of a century-long search for its soul."[33]

Meanwhile, as the absence of the World Series was portrayed as the death knell for the professional game, another story was playing out. This tale was one that continued to celebrate a romanticized version of baseball. It was woven through the sentimental optimism of Burns' series, with its re-assertion of the game's generational ties and its secure place in the canon of American history. This notion that baseball as a commercial enterprise operated in a different realm to the game preciously cultivated in small-town America was seized upon by public intellectuals, among them the literary scholar, George Grella. Writing in the *Los Angeles Times*, Grella argued that the presumption that the Major League embodied the soul of baseball was like "some devout worshiper imagining that God only dwells in the great cathedrals of the faith."[34] The actor-activist Ossie Davis likewise recognized the religious parallel: "I don't look [at] the game today as a game. It's business. To me baseball was an act of communion . . . like I used to feel teaching Baptist Sunday school. We were lifted out of ourselves by just being together. Baseball was a secular equivalent of that."[35] For Clinton, this was the "ultimate hazard" of the strike: "if it becomes so painfully clear that it's no longer a sport and that it's just a business, then the customers may decide to take their business elsewhere." Baseball, Clinton warned, would be played only in Little Leagues and local ballparks, "almost the way soccer is" – a comment alarming to those sporting chauvinists convinced of the innate superiority of the purer, 'made-in-America' pastime.[36]

It was into this complex cultural and commercial environment – in which the professional version of baseball embodied the sins of commercialization, yet the mythologized national pastime still shouldered a significant cultural burden – that Clinton attempted to throw the weight of his office. Baseball's rituals, ideals, and heroes had been a source of social cohesion for more than a hundred years – a symbol of national identity. Clinton's role now was to ensure that the emotional connection between baseball's two diverging histories – the commercial and the sacred – was not irreparably severed. His chosen rhetorical device was a synthesis of 'the presidency,' 'baseball,' and 'the people' through which he expressed a discourse of reconciliation and American cultural exceptionalism.

In one of his first public comments on the strike, Clinton fashioned himself as a "lifelong baseball fan" and spoke of "heart-break for the American people."[37] On the eve of the shutdown, Clinton was equally solemn, adopting a tone reminiscent of a wartime leader. He called the strike "a great event" that threatened the happiness of generations of Americans – kids and "not-so little kids."[38] When the cancellation of the World Series was confirmed, Clinton suggested that baseball's antitrust exemption was at risk "in light of what has happened to the American people."[39] Living without baseball, he argued, was "depressing the spirits of millions," inferring the very health of the nation was at stake. Indeed, even baseball's mythical values were under threat: "rancor and cynicism" were "shadowing the American ideal of baseball."[40] In an interview on NBC Nightly News, Clinton urged the players and owners to "give baseball back to the American people," an implication that they had stolen a national treasure. Clinton spoke of the "significant percentage of American people – you and I among them – who really believe baseball is something special."[41]

While this rhetoric reflected baseball's cultural status, the political imperatives driving Clinton were equally powerful, and linked by the seasonal ritual of spring training. Twenty major league teams were due to compete in spring training games in Florida, with the other eight training in Arizona. Both were states that Clinton had lost narrowly back in 1992. If the dispute dragged on beyond the winter, thousands of baseball-related jobs were at risk in these two states seemingly critical to Clinton's 1996 re-election prospects. Florida Governor Lawton Chiles and Senator Bob Graham warned Clinton that the strike could put a billion tourism dollars at risk – an economic impact "not unlike that of a natural disaster."[42] A handwritten note faxed to Clinton's deputy counsel made the point directly: "Bruce, the re-election is on your shoulders." It was attached to a cartoon from the *Miami Herald* depicting Clinton's poll ratings soaring if the strike ended.[43] The context was clear: when it came to cleaning up after hurricanes in Florida, the federal government was expected to lend a hand, and this strike was potentially as devastating. The voters would have their say if spring training was canceled. Conversely, for Clinton, there was the opportunity to secure votes in key states if his actions were viewed as successful. It seemed the political temptations for Clinton to intervene were aligned with the cultural expectations embedded in his office.

The president steps in

Clinton's first direct intervention came in mid-October when he summoned Bud Selig, MLB's acting commissioner, and Don Fehr, the MLBPA executive director, to the White House for separate meetings. Clinton wanted them to accept the appointment of a special mediator, William Usery, the Labor Secretary under Gerald Ford, who had experience settling disputes in the notoriously belligerent mining and auto industries. Selig and Fehr were told that Usery would attempt to broker a deal, and Clinton would back his recommendations.[44] Both sides agreed and the early signs were promising: four days later negotiations resumed for the first time in a month. That morning Clinton went jogging wearing a sports shirt emblazoned with the words 'Play Ball.'[45] It carried a dual message: a presidential entreaty and a claim for credit for the resumption of talks. Clinton's appeal, however, was not rewarded. Throughout

November and December each potential compromise was rejected. On New Year's Day, Anthony Lake, Clinton's National Security Advisor, appeared on NBC's *Meet the Press*: "I'm not sure ... you can make a distinction between the future of the world and the future of baseball," Lake remarked. "If baseball's in serious trouble, we're all in serious trouble."[46] Here was the man responsible for counseling the president about potential threats facing the country, framing the debate about a strike in baseball in terms of national security.

As the dispute drifted into January, there were renewed efforts by the White House to increase the pressure on the negotiators via Usery, while other ways to enforce arbitration were also explored. On Capitol Hill, sympathetic Democratic legislators drafted a series of bills which, although not directly aimed at ending the strike, were intended to draw concessions from the owners by targeting their antitrust exemption. The Justice Department let it be known that, in principle, it supported such limiting legislation, arguing that baseball players should have the same antitrust recourse that was available to other professional athletes.[47] Speechwriters drafted a section for the State of the Union address calling for "responsibility" and urging the players and owners to consider what kind of role models they were offering America's youth – though the passage was eventually cut.[48] Meanwhile, Clinton's polling strategist, Dick Morris, urged him to get more involved, partly to divert attention from an upcoming biography which made allegations about his pre-presidential private life.[49]

Another pressing problem was the possibility of an asterisk being placed against one of baseball's most hallowed records.[50] Of particular concern to the media (and so to the president), was Cal Ripken Jr.'s unbroken streak of more than 2,000 appearances for the Baltimore Orioles, which had put him within sight of the Major League record for consecutive games, held by Lou Gehrig since 1939. With the owners threatening to deploy non-union players for the approaching season, Ripken, a union member, faced seeing his run end and being robbed of a potentially historic moment. Clinton faced losing Ripken as a prime example of the American work ethic, a useful rhetorical presence in his arguments for welfare reform. As his friend, the historian Taylor Branch noted after a White House visit in which he discussed Ripken's pursuit of the record, Clinton fully understood "the symbolic stakes for national character."[51] Less urgent, though perhaps as culturally significant, was the crisis facing Arthur Shorin, chairman of the company that made the Topps baseball cards collected and traded by millions of Americans. Production had fallen to a thirty-year low, and Shorin wrote to Clinton offering to print a commemorative card of him if he could broker a deal: "how can kids celebrate or collect heroes of the diamond when there are no heroes in sight?" Clinton scribbled in the margin: "I need an answer to this."[52]

A few days later, Clinton invoked one of the greatest icons of baseball – and indeed broader twentieth-century American popular culture – Babe Ruth, to aid his cause. The larger-than-life feats of the 'Sultan of Swat' had rescued the reputation of baseball in the 1920s, restoring public confidence in the game after the damage inflicted by the Black Sox Scandal. Seventy-six years later, he was posthumously called upon to save the national pastime a second time.[53] The upcoming centenary of Ruth's birth offered an opportunity for Clinton to weave his memory into the narrative of the strike. Clinton said he identified with Ruth: "he's a little overweight and he struck out a lot – but he hit a lot of home runs because he went out to bat."[54] Clinton was batting for America: he set a deadline of 5 p.m. on February 6, the Ruth centenary. Either the owners and players would reach a deal on that symbolic date, or Clinton would instruct Usery to make recommendations, backed by the threat of legislation. Initially, the Ruthian deadline provoked activity, with revised proposals and counteroffers. But the centenary passed without an agreement. Clinton set another deadline – 3 p.m. on February 7. He would make one last effort to resolve the tensions between baseball as a commercialized business and the national pastime as quasi-religious myth.

Clinton's final pitch of reconciliation was thrown on the evening of February 7 at the White House. Events earlier in the day did not augur well. That afternoon Usery had presented a complex plan for revenue-sharing and arbitration that so enraged one MLBPA negotiator that he said it looked like the work of someone who was senile.[55] On Capitol Hill, the Republicans made it clear that they remained opposed to getting involved: "It's nice the President is trying to be helpful," commented Gingrich, but this is "not a matter of national survival."[56] Not all members of the White House press corps shared Gingrich's indifference. At a lunchtime briefing, there was talk of a "national emergency" and questions to McCurry about the powers of the president in such circumstances. McCurry again explained Clinton's strategy: "when the President looked at the question of getting involved he said, 'listen this is baseball: I am the President; it makes every sense in the world to use whatever authority I can to bring the conflict to an end.'"[57] Four hours later, McCurry hosted a second briefing: the president was "exasperated" that his 3 p.m. deadline had lapsed without progress. He had therefore decided to summon the owners and players to White House.[58]

Despite little sign that a deal was in the offing, Clinton still hoped to force a settlement. Twice McCurry had referred to "jawboning," a term that recalled Lyndon Johnson's verbal arm-twisting talents.[59] And McCurry had also hinted at the existence of an 'or else' – an implied threat of legislative action initiated by the president.[60] According to Reich, Clinton was "convinced there was a deal lying out there somewhere . . . It is simply a matter of discovering where it is." Reich wrote in his diary: "He smells a deal. He'd like to be savior of the national pastime."[61]

At 6.05 p.m., players' and owners' representatives sat down on opposite sides of the large mahogany table in the Roosevelt Room in the West Wing. The setting made a powerful statement about the institutional and emotional weight of the Office of the President. "I was humbled being there," admitted Scott Sanderson, the Chicago White Sox pitcher.[62] The group was initially addressed by Gore, Usery, and Reich: Clinton joined at 7.20 p.m. David Cone, the New York Yankees pitcher, recalled Clinton pointing to the picture of Theodore Roosevelt above the fireplace, and giving a history lesson on the "bully pulpit," the term coined to describe the agenda-setting authority of the president.[63] In invoking the "bully pulpit," and with McCurry's references to Johnson's "jawboning," Clinton was placing his initiative in an historic framework of presidential executive activism. He acknowledged there were legal limits to his powers, but resumed his emotional pitch: "There are a lot of Americans who really love baseball and I feel an obligation to them."[64] The meeting adjourned, with the parties caucusing in separate rooms. In his chief of staff's office, the president shared a sofa with Selig, an encounter colorfully described by Reich as "full intensity Clinton":

> "Now all you need to do" – B's voice becomes even softer and he moves his face closer to Selig's – "is agree to have this thing arbitrated. It's in your interest Bud." B pauses and looks deeply into Selig's eyes. "And it's also in the interest of . . . *America.*"[65]

However intense Clinton's charm offensive, the talks stuttered on with little progress. Clinton turned his attention to the players, in one break practicing his golf swing in the corridor with the Atlanta Braves pitcher Tom Glavine. "He made us feel very welcome that night. We had a lot of one-on-one time with him," recalled Glavine.[66]

After almost five hours, Gore appealed to both sides to accept binding arbitration: the players agreed but the owners said they would only arbitrate parts of the proposed settlement. The players rejected it as "cherry picking."[67] Clinton made a final proposal: the 1995 season would go ahead with unionized players while a presidential committee worked on a long-term solution. The players agreed, the owners did not. Out of options, Clinton reconvened the parties to tell them he would now press Congress to intervene: "both of you have a lot at stake, and I'm afraid you're both going to wind up losers."[68] Neither the president's attempt to instrumentalize the myth of baseball, nor the hallowed White House setting had been sufficient to sway the stakeholders in a sport caught between its fabled place in the American story and the financial ambitions of the strike's protagonists. Reich noted in his diary: "B lost big tonight."[69]

Shortly before 11 p.m. Clinton addressed reporters in the West Wing. Acknowledging his mediation had failed, Clinton said he would send legislation to Capitol Hill seeking binding arbitration. He again referred to the continuity of baseball in American history and the frustrations of the American people: "If something goes on for that long without interruption, seeing our nation through wars and dramatic social changes, it becomes more than a game, more than simply a way to pass time. It becomes part of who we are."[70] The following day, the White House sent the Major League Baseball Restoration Act to Congress, with identical co-sponsored bills introduced in the Senate and the House. Republican opposition meant neither progressed. The same fate befell a separate legislative initiative that aimed to narrow the antitrust exemption. Clinton's call for public support for his plan failed to generate enthusiasm: members of Congress reported few letters or calls. Instead, Speaker Gingrich proposed something altogether more spiritual. The best way to break the deadlock, he felt, was for the owners and players to sit down together and bond over the baseball movie, *Field of Dreams*: "They ought to . . . ask themselves, 'isn't there some spirit of cooperation here? Isn't there some spirit of caring about our national pastime?'"[71] It was not a serious proposition. The next day reality kicked-in at the White House. Lindsey warned Clinton against expending more political capital: do nothing, "certainly not in public," Lindsey counseled: "You should not expose yourself politically unless success comes closer."[72]

Back to the ballpark

Baseball's 232-day strike finally ended on April 2 – not as the result of presidential intervention or negotiated agreement, but following a ruling by the future Supreme Court justice, Sonia Sotomayor, in the U.S. District Court in Manhattan when the NLRB was granted an injunction against the owners. With the terms of the old collective bargaining agreement reinstated, the MLBPA offered unconditionally to return to work: the owners agreed not to lock them out. Clinton issued a brief statement: it was good news for baseball, its fans, and the cities whose economies had suffered.[73] A shortened season would begin on April 25.

Even with the players back at the ballpark, the intervention had been a chastening experience for Clinton – more proof after the collapse of his health care plan that the power of his office could be a blunt weapon in the absence of meaningful congressional co-operation or broad public support. And while nine decades of precedent suggested that presidential engagements with baseball usually had mutually beneficial outcomes, it was clear from the strike that this was contingent upon factors beyond presidential control, including the role of the media and the willingness of athletes and other actors to bend to presidential will.

So why, in the face of reluctant colleagues, an uneasy public, and an unsupportive press, did Clinton persist in placing the presidency at the center of a conflict that even Usery considered to be extraordinarily hostile? The answer offered by two of those inside the administration is that Clinton sensed a political opportunity and was drawn inexorably toward activism because he miscalculated the weight of the presidential voice. As McCurry recalls: "Clinton had a fair amount of hubris, and thought by force of moral suasion, using the presidency, he could make it work."[74] Reich also saw an unerring self-belief as "a super-salesman."[75] Both of these observations were characteristic of Clinton's first administration: a tendency to overestimate his own, and his office's, muscularity. By this measure, Clinton emerged from the strike with a losing record.

But we can also detect in Clinton's motives a more principled seam that sets the intervention in the wider context of his post-1994 presidency. From this viewpoint, rather than offering more evidence of Clinton's early ineptitude in government, the intervention instead marked the stirrings of a values-orientated rhetoric, with an emphasis on the components of national character with which he would revitalize presidential communication from 1995 onwards. Clinton's enthusiasm for symbols of national identity was genuine: he saw them as sources of social cohesion at a time when, in his own words, communal bonds were "frayed" by the momentum of social, cultural, and economic change.[76] Clinton observed this "fracturing" of American life, as the historian Daniel Rodgers would label it, everywhere.[77] In the hyper-partisan political arena where he was being savaged by his opponents for being un-American; in the decline in participation in civic institutions; in the country's racial divisions which surfaced in the strident debates over affirmative action and education. And he witnessed it in the broken national pastime, where fan disillusionment was summed up by Steve Wulf's excoriating words in *Sports Illustrated*: "The owners suck. The players suck. Baseball sucks. They take our money, but they take us for suckers and they take us for granted."[78]

Against this background of anxiety and discontent, Clinton's intervention in the strike for the more noble purpose of rescuing and restoring one of the foundations of American culture seemed reasonable – it was an act of leadership. As McCurry pointed out to reporters: "He is the President, and we're talking about baseball [which] plays a unique role in our history and our culture. The president thinks the American people expected [him] . . . to do what he could to try to save baseball."[79] Selig reflected on the failed summit in similar terms: "It was a very emotional day and again it proved how really important baseball is to America and society. When you have the President of the United States involved it says everything."[80]

In cherishing the national pastime in the early months of 1995, Clinton had advanced language that he would later deploy to invoke broader notions of a "national community" and the "renewal of America," recurring themes as he endeavored to re-establish his relevance in the wake of the November midterm disaster. "The whole project of '95 was to try to restore a sense of the President's connection to the whole country," Clinton's former Communications Director, Don Baer, explains, "to the extent that [the country] had been deprived of him by the Republican leadership, to make it clear that he was very much of the country and leader of the whole country."[81] Distinct from partisan issues like health care, or culturally divisive issues such as gay rights, the efforts to save baseball had ostensibly been in the service of the entire American community. In advancing a misty-eyed vision of old-time baseball, Clinton had adopted an inclusive tone which had fallen out of his speeches. "It's an interesting thing to do in the context of the time," observes Baer, "when everyone is focused on government breakdown, to connect yourself so directly, in your rhetoric or your role as leader of a nation, to something that's as fundamental as baseball."[82] From that perspective, at least, his intervention had a positive side – less damaging to his long-term authority and reputation than it appeared in the immediate, embarrassing aftermath of the White House summit.

These threads converged again on the eve of the World Series, which in 1995 resumed its traditional place on the fall calendar. In his weekly radio broadcast, Clinton revisited the theme of

"American renewal" which had been the rhetorical spine of his Inaugural Address in 1993. The return of the World Series was the "renewal of our national pastime," of a common heritage, and a shared national memory: "No matter where you go in America, sooner or later, there will be a patch of green, a path of dirt and a home plate," he said. Baseball's familiar icons and artifacts were scattered among Clinton's words – legendary players, the home run, the leather glove. So were a set of idealized American values: teamwork, tolerance, dedication, and optimism; "winning with joy and losing with dignity." Baseball, said Clinton, was "more than a Field of Dreams" – it "helps hold us together. It helps us to come together."[83] In World Series week, this was the rhetorical reconnection of the big-league game with its mythical roots – a celebration of national ideals and civic institutions that transcended cultural and partisan divisions. It was the president performing the reconsecration of baseball, blotting out the lingering bitterness of his failed intervention, and attempting to re-establish the game's sacred place in the American imagination.

Notes

1. Letter, Pamela Owens to Bill Clinton, February 6, 1995, OA/ID 9947, Folder: [Unrelated General Mail and Form Letters] [Loose] [10], Roger Goldblatt, Health Care Task Force, *Clinton Presidential Records*, Clinton Presidential Library.
2. Taylor Branch, *The Clinton Tapes; A President's Secret Diary* (London: Simon & Schuster, 2009), 241.
3. Robert B. Reich, *Locked in the Cabinet* (New York: Alfred A. Knopf, 1997), 239–240; Richard E. Neustadt, *Presidential Power and the Modern Presidents: The Politics of Leadership from Roosevelt to Reagan* (New York: Free Press, 1990).
4. Facsimile, Baker and Hostetler to Bruce Lindsey, February 8, 1995, OA/ID 24792, Folder: Baseball Strike – Letters/Comments/Polls [3], Bruce Lindsey, Counsel Office, *Clinton Presidential Records*, Clinton Presidential Library.
5. Claire Smith, "Fans Should Turn Their Backs, Too," *New York Times*, February 10, 1995, B12.
6. Amy Edwards, "Hoover on Baseball," *U.S. National Archives*, available at: https://hoover.blogs.archives.gov/2015/10/28/hoover-on-baseball; Letter, Franklin D. Roosevelt to Kenesaw Mountain

Landis, "'Green Light Letter,'" January 15, 1942, *FDR Presidential Library*, available at: http://www.fdrlibrary.marist.edu/daybyday/resource/january-1942-2; Bartlett Giamatti, *Take Time for Paradise: Americans and Their Games* (New York: Summit, 1989), 83.

7. Ken Burns, "A Grain of Sand that Reveals the Universe," *U.S. News & World Report*, September 5, 1994, 58.

8. Letter, Paul Beaucorn to Lowell Weiss, November 7, 1997, OA/ID 17192, Folder: "Lewis and Clark" 11/9/97, Lowell Weiss, Speechwriting, *Clinton Presidential Records*, Clinton Presidential Library.

9. Quoted in Richard Sandomir, "Hits, Runs and Memories," *New York Times*, September 18, 1994, 2:1.

10. Ken Burns, *Baseball: First Inning, Our Game* (PBS, 1994).

11. William J. Clinton, "Remarks at a Dinner for Governor Mario Cuomo in New York, October 19, 1994," *American Presidency Project*, University of California Santa Barbara, available at: https://www.presidency.ucsb.edu.

12. William J. Clinton, *My Life* (London: Hutchinson, 2004), 620.

13. Mike McCurry, Interview by author, Washington, D.C., November 6, 2019.

14. Curt Smith, *The Presidents and the Pastime: The History of Baseball and the White House* (Lincoln: University of Nebraska Press, 2018); Nicholas Evan Sarantakes, *Fan in Chief: Richard Nixon and American Sports 1969–74* (Lawrence: University Press of Kansas, 2019).

15. John E. Yang, "Pardon His Pitch: Bush Strikes Dirt," *Washington Post*, April 7, 1992, C5.

16. Other '-gate scandals' included: 'Nannygate,' which concerned the failed nomination of Zoe Baird as Attorney General; 'Travelgate,' which involved allegations of corruption, embezzlement and nepotism within the White House Travel Office; and 'Troopergate,' in which Arkansas state troopers allegedly procured women for Clinton during his time as governor.

17. "Presidential Approval Ratings – Bill Clinton," *Gallup*, available at: https://news.gallup.com/poll/116584/presidential-approval-ratings-bill-clinton.aspx.

18. Ken Walsh, "A Polarizing President," *U.S. News & World Report*, November 7, 1994, 37; Steven Gillon: *The Pact: Bill Clinton, Newt Gingrich and the Rivalry that Defined a Generation* (New York: Oxford University Press, 2008), 124–126.

19. Reich, *Locked in the Cabinet*, 115.

20. William J. Clinton, "The President's News Conference, April 18, 1995," *American Presidency Project*.

21. Supreme Court of the United States, 259 U.S. 200 (1922), *Federal Baseball Club of Baltimore* v. *National League*, available at: https://supreme.justia.com/cases/federal/us/259/200.
22. There had been stoppages in 1972, 1973, 1976, 1980, 1981, 1985, and 1990.
23. Lydia Saad, "Gallup Vault: Football's Rise as a U.S. Spectator Sport," *Gallup*, February 2, 2017, available at: https://news.gallup.com/vault/203270/gallup-vault-football-rise-spectator-sport.aspx.
24. William J. Clinton, "Remarks at a Reception for Joel Hyatt in Mayfield Heights, Ohio, July 30, 1994," *American Presidency Project*.
25. Reich, *Locked in the Cabinet*, 186.
26. Reich, *Locked in the Cabinet*, 186.
27. Quoted in William B. Gould IV, "The 1994–'95 Baseball Strike and the National Labor Relations Board: To the Precipice and Back Again," *West Virginia Law Review* 110 (2008): 983–997 at 990.
28. William J. Clinton, "Remarks Announcing the Appointment of Abner Mikva as White House Counsel and an Exchange With Reporters, August 11, 1994," *American Presidency Project*.
29. Letter, Fans First to Bill Clinton, September 6, 1994, OA/ID 24792, Folder: Baseball Strike – Letters/Comments/Polls [2], Bruce Lindsey, Counsel Office, *Clinton Presidential Records*, Clinton Presidential Library.
30. Ann Geracimos, "News Gives Way to Nostalgia at Picnic," *Washington Times*, September 12, 1994, C12.
31. Memorandum, Don Baer to Bill Clinton, "September Speeches," August 25, 1994, OA/ID 10993, Folder: Memos, Carolyn Curiel, Speechwriting, *Clinton Presidential Records*, Clinton Presidential Library.
32. Donnie Radcliffe, "The White House Pitches In," *Washington Post*, September 12, 1994, D1.
33. Robert Lipsyte, "In Memoriam," *New York Times*, September 15, 1994, A1.
34. George Grella, "Perspective on Baseball: A Religion That Goes to Our Roots," *Los Angeles Times*, August 11, 1994, available at: https://www.latimes.com/archives/la-xpm-1994-08-11-me-25725-story.html.
35. Quoted in Geracimos, "News Gives Way to Nostalgia at Picnic."
36. William J. Clinton, "Interview with Tony Bruno and Chuck Wilson of *ESPN* Radio, March 25, 1995," *American Presidency Project*.

37. William J. Clinton, "The President's News Conference, August 3, 1994," *American Presidency Project*.
38. Clinton, "Remarks Announcing the Appointment of Abner Mikva."
39. William J. Clinton, "Interview with Wire Service Reporters on Haiti, September 14, 1994," *American Presidency Project*.
40. William J. Clinton, "Statement on the Baseball Strike, January 26, 1995," *American Presidency Project*.
41. William J. Clinton, "Interview with Tom Brokaw of NBC Nightly News, January 26, 1995," *American Presidency Project*.
42. Letter, Lawton Chiles and Bob Graham to Bill Clinton, September 7, 1994, OA/ID 24792, Folder: Baseball Strike – Letters/Comments/Polls [3], Bruce Lindsey, Counsel Office, *Clinton Presidential Records*, Clinton Presidential Library.
43. Facsimile to Bruce Lindsey, February 3, 1995, OA/ID 24792, Folder: Baseball Strike – Letters/Comments/Polls [3], Bruce Lindsey, Counsel Office, *Clinton Presidential Records*, Clinton Presidential Library.
44. Bud Selig, *For the Good of the Game: The Inside Story of the Surprising and Dramatic Transformation of Major League Baseball* (New York: William Morrow, 2019), 165.
45. Kenneth Jennings, *Swings and Misses: Moribund Labor Relations in Professional Baseball* (Westport, CT: Praeger, 1997), 97.
46. Transcript *NBC News*, "Meet The Press," January 1, 1995, OA/ID 420, Folder: [Anthony] Lake-Transcripts, Robert Boorstin, Speechwriting, *Clinton Presidential Records*, Clinton Presidential Library.
47. Draft letter, Anne K. Bingaman to Senator Patrick Leahy, Senate Judiciary Committee, March 31, 1995, OA/ID 24792, Folder: Baseball Strike – Letters/Comments/Polls [3], Bruce Lindsey, Counsel Office, *Clinton Presidential Records*, Clinton Presidential Library.
48. Draft speech with notes, State of Union Speech 1995, January 23, 1995, OA/ID 10131, Folder: SOTU – Edits by Admin Officials [1] Draft 2, Don Baer Communications, *Clinton Presidential Records*, Clinton Presidential Library.
49. Dick Morris, *Behind the Oval Office: Getting Reelected against the Odds* (Los Angeles: Renaissance, 1999), 113–114.
50. An * (asterisk) is assigned to a record if its achievement is thought to be tainted. In this case, had baseball resumed with non-unionized players it was suggested that Ripken (who would have refused to play) could have continued his consecutive game streak once unionized players returned, albeit with an * against his record.
51. Branch, *The Clinton Tapes*, 231–232.

52. Letter, Arthur Shorin to Bill Clinton, January 31,1995, OA/ID 24792, Folder: Baseball Strike – Letters/Comments/Polls [1], Bruce Lindsey, Counsel Office, *Clinton Presidential Records*, Clinton Presidential Library.

53. In 1921, eight members of the Chicago White Sox were accused of throwing the 1919 World Series against the Cincinnati Reds at the behest of a betting syndicate. Despite some players confessing to taking bribes, all were acquitted at trial due to lack of evidence. They were nevertheless banned for life from playing organized professional baseball.

54. William J. Clinton, "Remarks to the U.S. Conference of Mayors, January 27, 1995," *American Presidency Project*.

55. Michael Bevans, "Let's Make a Deal," *Sports Illustrated*, February 20, 1995, 196.

56. Quoted in "Bad Sports," *New York Magazine*, February 20, 1995, 15.

57. William J. Clinton, "Press Briefing by Mike McCurry, 1.15 p.m. February 7, 1995," *American Presidency Project*.

58. William J. Clinton, "Press Briefing by Mike McCurry, 5:10 p.m. February 7, 1995," *American Presidency Project*.

59. Clinton, "Press Briefing by Mike McCurry, 1.15 p.m."

60. Clinton, "Press Briefing by Mike McCurry, 5:10 p.m."

61. Reich, *Locked in the Cabinet*, 238.

62. Quoted in Hal Bodley, *How Baseball Explains America* (Chicago, IL: Triumph, 2014), 54.

63. Bodley, *How Baseball Explains America*, 53–54.

64. Quoted in Jon Pessah, *The Game: Inside the Secret World of Major League Baseball's Power Brokers* (New York: Back Bay, 2015), 125.

65. Reich, *Locked in the Cabinet*, 239.

66. Quoted in Bodley, *How Baseball Explains America*, 65.

67. Jennings, *Swings and Misses*, 115.

68. Quoted in Douglas Jehl, "President Will Call on Congress to Impose Baseball Arbitration," *New York Times*, February 8, 1995, A1.

69. Reich, *Locked in the Cabinet*, 240.

70. William J. Clinton, "Remarks and Exchange with Reporters on the Major League Baseball Strike, February 7, 1995," *American Presidency Project*.

71. Quoted in Associated Press, "Not Heaven, Not Iowa, This is Newt's World," *Los Angeles Times*, February 12, 1995, available at: http://articles.latimes.com/1995-02-12/sports/sp-31189_1_newt-gingrich-movie.

72. Memorandum, Bruce Lindsey to Bill Clinton, February 13, 1995, OA/ID 24792, Folder: Baseball Strike, Letters, Comments Polls [2], Bruce Lindsey, Counsel's Office, *Clinton Presidential Records*, Clinton Presidential Library.
73. William J. Clinton, "Statement on the Major League Baseball Strike Settlement, April 2, 1995," *American Presidency Project*.
74. McCurry, Interview by author.
75. Reich, *Locked in the Cabinet*, 238.
76. William J. Clinton, "Address Before a Joint Session of Congress on the State of the Union, January 24, 1995," *American Presidency Project*.
77. Daniel T. Rodgers, *Age of Fracture* (Cambridge, MA: Belknap, 2011).
78. Steve Wulf, "Fans, Strike Back!," *Sports Illustrated*, September 26, 1994, 74.
79. William J. Clinton, "Press Briefing by Mike McCurry, February 8, 1995," *American Presidency Project*.
80. Quoted in Bodley, *How Baseball Explains America*, 54.
81. Don Baer, Interview by author, New York, April 26, 2018.
82. Baer, Interview by author.
83. William J. Clinton, "The President's Radio Address: October 21, 1995," *American Presidency Project*.

Part Two

Sports and Their Presidents

5

Fit to Govern? The Presidency, Running, and Perceptions of Strength

Elizabeth Rees

Our own history, perhaps better than the history of any other great country, vividly demonstrates the truth of the belief that physical vigor and health are essential accompaniments to the qualities of intellect and spirit on which a nation is built

President John F. Kennedy, 1962.[1]

First steps: an introduction

The kind of running being practiced in the late 1960s was, according to 1964 Boston Marathon finisher Hal Higdon, "not the Bobby Kennedy type of running, which peaks during leap years, mind you, but the running type of running which until recently was practiced mostly by school athletes."[2] Whilst both forms of running identified by Higdon in his *New York Times* segment invariably, it is fair to say, result in raised heart rates, that was not where the relationship between politics and running stopped. From Theodore Roosevelt's advocacy of the Strenuous Life, arguably even all the way back to the foot races of the Olympics of Ancient Greece, physical fitness is a quality that, throughout human history, has been indicative of personal qualities of heroism, perseverance, and mental fortitude. As President Kennedy explained in his famous article, "The Vigor We Need," published by *Sports Illustrated* in 1962, physical fitness has increasingly and explicitly been related to political strength and leadership throughout American history.

Running took off quickly in Washington D.C. in the 1960s. Likely spurred on by the efforts of the Kennedy administration to promote a more vigorous lifestyle, personal physical fitness outside organized sports was becoming a point of concern for citizens in the United States as the search for national strength intensified with the Cold War. Additionally, the growth of local running clubs, the organization of road races, and the emergence of a running-specific market for consumers meant that running became an increasingly popular hobby for many Americans. Even busy politicians and high-profile civil servants were finding time to lace up their shoes and pound the pavement, including figures such as senators Strom Thurmond and William Proxmire, and press secretary to the First Lady, Liz Carpenter.[3] A keen proponent of the new craze was Secretary of the Interior Stewart Udall, who became his own best public relations asset by jogging "two miles along the Potomac River on one of the four new jogging trails opened by the National Parks Service" in November 1967.[4] Udall had a good feeling about running: "it may well develop into a national pastime," he told Higdon in 1968.[5] Indeed, it would not be long after the running boom until a convert to the running craze was themselves ensconced in the Oval Office. In 1970s Washington, politicians were not just running *for* office, they were also running *to* the office.

Literature on modern running began with manuals in the United States in the mid- to late 1970s, with figures such as Dr. George Sheehan and James F. Fixx writing handbooks which flew off the shelves as running, or 'jogging' as the activity also became known, started to become a leisure activity for millions of ordinary Americans.[6] Such manuals became the foundation for the studies of the 1970s running boom for many sports science and history writers, such as Thor Gotaas, Jay Schulkin, and Alan Latham, all writing in the mid-2010s.[7] Largely, most scholars analyzing the cultural history of running focused on the themes of running as a direct response to the sedentary lifestyle and accompanying health issues which were being realized in consumeristic, industrialized 1960s America, or the history of the popularization of marathons in U.S. cities.[8]

However, the notion that the health of the nation was embodied in the physical 'running' of its leader is a concept that has received little scholarly attention thus far, especially in relation to the American presidency. And whilst the analysis of the history of sport and society has increased greatly since the 1970s, particularly influenced by the work of Harry Edwards, most of the historical work on sport related explicitly to team activities or organized games such as baseball or football, or Olympic sport. More individualized activities aimed merely at improving personal physical fitness, like running, were rather overlooked. Indeed, running as a phenomenon has been analyzed only by a relatively slim selection of academics and sports writers, with limited consideration by historians.

Richard Lipsky was exceptional in early secondary literature with his 1979 journal article, "'The Athleticizing of Politics: The Political Implication of Sports Symbolism," which highlighted the symbolic importance of sport in leadership in the midst of the Cold War.[9] Understandably, a huge amount of political understanding of the significance of sports in history was informed by the dynamics of competition between the United States and the Soviet Union, and therefore it is natural that a substantial literature on the political history of sport, and running specifically, did not emerge until the first two decades of the twenty-first century.[10] Furthermore, the relatively recent development of the phenomenon of running as a hobby for physical fitness itself also accounts for the fact that the historiography on the subject is also quite a recent development.

The most useful scholarship for understanding the intersection between politics and running has perhaps been where scholars have considered the philosophical prisms through which sport allows us to reflect on human nature. This was fundamentally highlighted by Edwards when he argued that "sports unavoidably reflect society, particularly with regard to the character of human and institutional relations, and the ideological foundation of those relations."[11] Sport therefore facilitated self-reflection, and when the 'self' doing the sport happens to be the president, arguably the physical embodiment of the nation, then it follows that this reflects something of the nation as well. Thus, a physically strong president might symbolically represent a politically, economically, or potentially militarily strong nation.

This chapter charts the intersection of the running boom in the late twentieth century with the presidency, and ultimately argues

105

that certain presidents adopted the hobby of running as a means of demonstrating their own physical fitness. By proxy, this was extrapolated by the press and wider public reception as a barometer of the strength of both the administration and arguably the nation. In other words, running allowed these presidents to demonstrate their fitness to govern. However, not every run went as planned, and instances where presidents were caught short of their best performance were key cases in which negative judgments of presidential fitness tied into the broader sense of weakness of an administration.

This chapter identifies two categories of presidential running and 'fitness' to govern: struggling and striving, which together indicate the possible political implications behind every step taken by the president. The case studies of Jimmy Carter and George H. W. Bush demonstrate the struggling presidents, while Bill Clinton and George W. Bush are indicative of striving presidents. As intended, this structure hints that scrutiny of politicians running transcended party lines. As we shall see, running became a key campaign activity during the 1992 presidential election. Through an analysis of contemporary press and archival material, the links between the philosophical elements of running and political life bring us across the finish line to a more complete understanding of the interrelatedness of the presidency and running during the latter half of the twentieth century.

Struggling to the finish line: Jimmy Carter and George H. W. Bush

Evangelism in the United States can be applied not only to religious fervor, but also to running as it boomed in the 1970s. The epitome of this was the work of Dr. George Sheehan, producer of one of the first running manuals published in 1975. Sheehan's account of his conversion to running reads explicitly like a religious experience, referring to his rebirth through the physical activity. For Sheehan, running was a means of physically renewing oneself in a way that had broader personal ramifications, describing it as "the development of maximum physical capabilities which in turn help us to find our maximum spiritual and intellectual potential."[12]

Perhaps it was not coincidental, then, that evangelical pastor Billy Graham had been spotted running, and that President Carter, a born-again Christian, would become such a devotee of the activity.[13] Whilst Carter was known to be 'an evangelist on running,' his exhaustion in a 6-mile race in 1979 became a public relations embarrassment which echoed the weakness of his administration. Likewise, President George H. W. Bush's health scare, triggered whilst running, was similarly perceived as indicative of an aging president with a questionable ability to govern. Together, both the examples of Carter and Bush illustrate the image of the struggling political runner.

When Carter arrived in the White House in 1977, his fondness for outdoor activities was known, and his desire to control the tennis court booking system in the grounds of the presidential mansion became anecdotal. By the latter half of his term, it was reported that, "wearing a red sweatsuit and sneakers for a twice-weekly twilight tour around the White House grounds, President Jimmy Carter has joined the ranks of millions of his jogging countrymen."[14] Though accompanied by a Secret Service escort, by partaking in an evening jog Carter was sharing in the collective experience of running, which was becoming an increasingly popular pastime. Bruce Newman at *Sports Illustrated* clearly deemed the president's jogging routine newsworthy, writing in December 1978 that "Carter is not alone out there, of course; it has been estimated that 25 million Americans have become joggers recently."[15] Presumably for these millions of Americans for whom jogging was a new-found passion, this was a point on which they could relate to the president.

It appears that the Carter administration recognized the publicity value of the president's running habit, since they agreed to an interview with Newman. Discussing how Carter would describe his sporting career, White House Communications Director Jerry Rafshoon joked that "When asked about your tennis ability and athletic prowess, break with previous policy and LIE," to which Carter rebuffed "this would not deviate from policy."[16] The interview demonstrated that Carter remained confident in his athletic abilities. Furthermore, it was an important time for Carter to appear to be a good example of physical fitness, since at the end of the year he had replaced the personnel on the Council on Physical Fitness and Sports to revitalize the program, which had lain largely dormant for the previous two years.[17]

As the Council on Physical Fitness and Sports was reinvigorated in 1979, increasing attention was paid to Carter's running habits. For instance, whilst on vacation on a riverboat, Carter took twenty-two laps of the sundeck "making two miles in 13 minutes."[18] For those who were not devotees of running, this may have been an example of the excessive virtuosity of the president, and may have been a tad irritating. Indeed, Carter did bring his evangelical fervor to his running habits, as evidenced by an aide's comments during his visit to Vienna. Upon hearing that at an evening at the opera it was customary for the audience to promenade around the house during the intermission, the aide remarked "if Jimmy hears that the promenade is oval-shaped, he'll start jogging."[19] Whilst this was obviously a joke, even on visits abroad the president would not take a rest from his running. We can see the priority given to the president's running schedule from an internal memo related to the planning for a trip to Rome, in which the Italian Government invited the Carters to stay at the Presidential Palace which "is secure, convenient to the other sites of the schedule and contains walled gardens suitable for jogging."[20]

With all this discussion of Carter's running in the press, some more critical journalists began to scrutinize his running habits for signs of weakness. Journalist Charles Peters contended that Carter was lying about his resting heart rate, after the president claimed that after three months of running it had dropped from a rate of 60 to 40 beats per minute: "as experienced runners know, your pulse might decline 10 points – but not more – after five years of steady state jogging."[21] Indeed, Peters' argument seems convincing as the average heart rate for an adult is between 60 to 100 beats per minute, making it unlikely that Carter's declined that drastically.[22] Whilst Newman had employed language in his *Sports Illustrated* article which implied the physical competence of the president, describing how "in a quiet and inconspicuous way, Jimmy Carter is proving to be a bit of an all-round sportsman in his own right," it was not long before more critical judgments were drawn about Carter's running that related the habit to his personality and style of governing more broadly. In 1978, reporter Edward Walsh commented rather acridly that "it is also predictable that the president took to running in a singularly passionless way – not, like to many others, for the joy of it, but because it is efficient."[23] Whether that may have been the case or not, it was clear that Walsh linked Carter's running to his political persona, which was not that of a passionate ideologue but rather of a cool and collected administrator.

The questioning of Carter's abilities as a runner and the real blow to Carter's image as a fit leader, however, came in September 1979 when an exhausted and drained Carter dropped out of a race near his Camp David retreat. The mere proliferation of newspaper articles covering the race was indicative of the high level of interest over the episode, with all major national news outlets running lengthy stories about the event. Sarah Pileggi at *Sports Illustrated* ran the most comprehensive story retelling the incident, and from the outset clearly linked Carter's running ability to his political situation, stating that "perhaps it was the measure of Jimmy Carter's political guts that he chose to make his debut as a road racer at this shaky juncture in his presidency."[24]

With the energy crisis in full swing – having knock-on effects on an economy that was already suffering under the effects of stagflation – Carter was indeed struggling at this point in his presidency. As Pileggi perceptively pointed out, "at worst he could look foolish, a matter of little consequence to the average middle-aged jogger, but one of some importance to a man whose future hangs on his public image," a struggle distinctive to the emerging permanent campaign style of politics.[25] This was certainly true: Carter set off too fast, fueled by his intensely competitive spirit, but around the two-thirds mark he seemed to stall and needed to be supported by his Secret Service agent. His physician, Dr. William Lukash, persuaded him to concede the race.[26] The Carter administration was quick to put on a show of strength after this debacle, with Dr. Lukash reporting that the president's full strength had been restored. He further noted that "no change is expected in the President's future running schedule, which ranges from 40 to 50 miles each week."[27] Yet the image of the collapsing Carter reproduced in the newspapers provided visual confirmation of a weak president clearly struggling with the challenges of his office at that time. Compounding this in the same year, the embarrassment caused by the surfacing of the story of the infamous so-called 'killer swamp rabbit attack,' which forced Carter, enjoying a spot of fishing, to beat back the apparently savage animal with a canoe paddle, took the president's pathetic image to new heights in the public consciousness.[28] Carter's physical struggle with running thus was explicitly linked to his struggle to govern, with one reporter claiming that it was this singular image of Carter that "convinced me I could not vote for this man a second time."[29]

Whilst Carter's struggle with running was clearly emblematic of his broader political struggle with the economy and the era of malaise, President George H. W. Bush's physical ability and thus the nation's political future was rather called into question due to his age and heart problems induced by running. The presidency was an institution increasingly occupied by aging figures, with the septuagenarian Ronald Reagan's age and health having been at the forefront of public consciousness in the prior administration. Therefore, it was to be expected that the public might have similar concerns when Bush experienced an atrial fibrillation whilst jogging in 1991. Bush had a proven athletic background, having been voted best athlete at his prep school, Andover, as well as being a college sportsman as a member of the baseball team whilst at Yale. As Reagan's vice president, Bush was already using running as part of his political image-building via staged photo opportunities. For example, he enjoyed a jog with actor and martial artist Chuck Norris around the grounds of the Naval Observatory, and was photographed out jogging at Camp David with country singer George Strait. Nearly thirty years Strait's senior, Bush's running was undoubtedly a display of defiance of age, which contributed to this consistent messaging of Bush's vitality in spite of his years lived.

Opinion seemed to be split about what Bush's running habit denoted about his personality. One American writer, commenting on Bush's jogging and fondness for tennis and hunting, proclaimed that "these are rich man's pastimes," whilst a British writer countered that the levelling activity of sport "countered the patrician, preppie background" some identified with Bush.[30] Either way, Bush was keen to show that despite his age he could still get the miles in, taking his 3-mile run on his sixty-fifth birthday at Fort McNair Army base in southwest Washington D.C. in humidity of 60 percent which made his T-shirt "soaked with presidential sweat" by the time he finished.[31] Having a president who was a proficient runner gave the impression of a competent leader, organized enough to create the time in his schedule to take care of his physical fitness. Bush gave a sense of being on top of escalating situations, explaining to reporters that he would address the issue of disputes with the Colombian government over the U.S. Naval presence in Colombia to intercept drug smugglers whilst he set off on the Chesapeake & Ohio Canal towpath in Washington for his routine Sunday run after church.[32] A president who had time to go for a run, and at the same time make a collected statement on unfolding events seemingly off the top of his head, was ostensibly a president who had the situation under control.

Despite his best efforts though, Bush's running habit would ultimately cast him as a struggling runner given the health scare that he, and by extension the nation, experienced. Whilst jogging at Camp David in early May 1991, Bush experienced chest pain and faintness, and was quickly relocated to Bethesda Naval Hospital for treatment. This prompted rife speculation over the health of the president, and by implication the stability of the executive establishment. A poll conducted during Bush's hospitalization indicated that only 19 percent of the American public would be happy with the prospect of Vice President Dan Quayle stepping into the breach.[33] One commentator pointed out that "the stamina he displayed during the course of the Persian Gulf war made most forget that he was 67 years old."[34]

The press was indeed quick to point out how Bush had clearly over-exerted himself, stating that in this instance "he jogged longer than his usual 20-minute workout."[35] Although the president's staff was equally quick to point out that medical professionals considered this bout of atrial fibrillation to be a thyroid problem rather than a heart problem, the root cause of the issue was ultimately beside the point. The damage to Bush's image as a physically fit man and a reliable political leader was already done. From here on in, Bush tried to make light of the incident and resumed his normal schedule as soon as possible, even joking at a Rose Garden reception that he thanked the attendees for coming "from the bottom of [his] fibrillated heart."[36] However, although Bush worked hard to maintain a reputation as an avid jogger and a man of great stamina, befitting the requirements of his post, the struggle against age was inescapable and ultimately reminded the public of his mortality.

Running for office: the 1992 campaign

Hot on the heels of President Bush during the 1992 presidential race was the young Democratic governor of Arkansas, Bill Clinton. This election was perhaps the apex at which jogging and the notion of fitness to govern saturated political campaigning so completely. With both leading candidates self-styled college-trained athletes at Yale and Oxford, respectively, the stakes of the physical contest between the two candidates were high in the minds of the electorate and prioritized by media outlets. Thus, 1992 was arguably the first election in which running, and in turn the notion of physical fitness, was really a feature on which the respective campaign teams sought to capitalize.

In part, this shift in focus can be attributed to the culmination of rapid advances in media technology and the changing form of news media consumption: campaign coverage in the post-Watergate era had increasingly become a "feeding frenzy," in the words of Larry Sabato, focusing on the personality of the candidate often at the sake of fair political scrutiny.[37] Journalist Howard Kurtz acknowledged the changing preferences for televised news coverage, noting the challenge this presented for print journalists since, as he noted, "much of what reporters cover is instantaneously available on CNN and C-SPAN, neither of which existed two decades ago."[38] Riffing off the 'inhalation debate,' Kurtz also pointed out that "the reporters of '92 may once have inhaled, but now the only heavy-breathing activity is jogging," signaling that hitting the track was becoming a core part of the press corps coverage of the 1992 election.[39] The dialogue of sports – and running specifically – became ingrained in such coverage. After Clinton and Gore went for a jog together in Wheeling, West Virginia, reporters commented that "they were sweaty and ready for another sort of sport: Republican-bashing."[40]

For the struggling incumbent Bush, the optics of jogging were essential to his defensive play and the projection of presidential

vigor despite his age and recent health scares. While campaigning and jogging in Branson, Missouri, reporters highlighted this as
"underscoring his assertion that he is in good health."[41] Bush also
poked fun at the unfolding contest between the two jogging candidates in his acceptance speech at the Republican National Convention in August 1992, which he opened by stating that "first, I feel
great. And I am heartened by the polls – the ones that say I look
better in my jogging shorts than the governor of Arkansas."[42] Running as a hobby also fit in with the "regular guy" image the Bush
campaign aimed to project to the electorate, and the joke about
jogging shorts injected a light-hearted pause into the campaigning
which journalists seized on, with reporter Richard L. Berke at the
New York Times commenting that "still, Mr. Bush is determined
not to lose to Mr. Clinton in the fitness race."[43]

On the Democratic ticket, running was so key to the image of
the youthful and dynamic Clinton–Gore partnership as to rapidly
become cliché. A campaign reporter for *The Guardian*, Martin
Walker, perceptively stated that a Clinton–Gore jog in the morning
would "provide the television images of youthful vigor and unity
which will be the hallmark of their campaign."[44] C-SPAN indeed
covered Clinton and Gore – who donned jogging shorts and baseball caps – on a morning jog that included a stop at McDonald's.
This became one of the lasting images of the 1992 campaign, and
was immortalized in a *Saturday Night Live* sketch that December, in which Clinton was ridiculed for his insatiable appetite for
fast-food. Furthermore, footage from the report showed photogra-
phers packed in the back of a pick-up truck, their cameras trained
on the pair as they tailed them through the streets of Little Rock,
Arkansas, indicating the extent to which a run was blatantly a
public relations exercise.

The vision of fresh, athletic leadership for the Democratic Party
offered hopeful prospects for the electorate of renewed strength
and vitality in politics, with one reporter explaining that "Democrats believe their strapping Dixie duo is just what the country
wants to see jogging down the road to the site of the broken-down
economy."[45] Thus, running and the image of vitality was a significant ingredient in presenting the Clinton–Gore ticket as the realization of baby-boomer liberalism in its full fruition, with the pair

"unabashedly offering themselves as the first Fortysomethings [sic] ticket in modern presidential history."[46] Whilst sports such as golf were "too Ivy League," running instead created the impression of "that youthful good-guy glow," an image which, in the midst of infidelity rumors, Clinton needed to cultivate in order to maintain his hold on the electorate.[47]

Marital issues were not the only cause of concern for Clinton during the 1992 campaign. One of the main reasons motivating the candidates' morning jogs was the governor's burgeoning weight. Early in 1992, Clinton was publicly regarded as somewhat insufficiently in control of his weight, having "once confessed to binge eating during times of stress."[48] Whilst this weight gain was seen by some as a character flaw denoting lack of control or self-restraint, "criticism of his weight was so scathing he soon began a rigid program of diet and regular jogging," according to journalist Natalie Angier.[49] It seemed that Clinton was particularly self-conscious about this, with aides confirming that when he first started to jog with Gore, "he became self-conscious about the long, baggy shorts he was wearing to exercise, reminiscent of the ones worn by overweight boys at camp, and has been trying to go shorter himself, if not yet quite as short as his fitter running mate."[50]

Despite this, running was overwhelmingly positive for Clinton's image in the 1992 campaign, giving the impression not only of physical fitness with a youthful competitive edge over his aging Republican rival, but also a sense of responsibility for his personal health, decisiveness, and control by shedding his excess pounds. Thus, even a casual jog taken by a candidate was loaded with meaning about their personality and their potential leadership qualities. Even the choice of T-shirts worn by candidates was an opportunity for them to make an implicit statement about their political persona, with Clinton out jogging one morning and "the T-shirt sticking to his ample frame says Rock the Vote, the slogan of the campaign by MTV and the Tower Records chain," positioning himself as in touch with the time and the younger generations of voters.[51] Clinton won the race, and the momentum generated propelled him into his administration, where the pace did not drop off.

In their stride: Bill Clinton and George W. Bush

In the aftermath of the 1992 election, the image of the striving, successful runner was far clearer with the more youthful Clinton and George W. Bush administrations. For Clinton, running successfully perpetuated his image as a down-to-earth figure whilst also increasing his informal public presence and emphasizing the sense of an inner circle of those granted access to the president via tagging along on a jog. Like his father, George W. Bush was vocal about the values he felt running encouraged in life both on and off the track, and used his personal fitness to set an example to Americans as improving health became a national priority into the early years of the twenty-first century.

Clinton continued to make jogging not just an excursion for exercise, but a full-blown public relations event when he took office, with reporters claiming that his "jogging entourage has come to resemble the New York Marathon."[52] Indeed, the presidential jog fast became part of the zeitgeist, with columnists at the *Washington Post* jibing that jogging in a Rolling Stones T-shirt was 'in,' whilst jogging in the more sensible, Bush senior style windbreaker was firmly out of fashion.[53]

Ironically, whilst a daily jog on the streets was part of Clinton's strategy in public relatability, as the entourage accompanying the president grew, Clinton's runs appeared to become more about exclusive access to the president and privileged proximity to power. This bolstered the image of the president as a person of importance, a figure so in demand that he engaged with colleagues and maximized his time by having them accompany him on a run. Running with Clinton granted unprecedented levels of informal access to the president for politicians, with some "seeking simply to borrow some Presidential prestige, others come to build good will with the president or to lobby him on particular issues," echoing the dynamics of Theodore Roosevelt's tennis cabinet or Taft's golf cabinet.[54] Jogging with Clinton became the must-have photo-op for a politician during this period, whether the politician was a runner or not. For example, Los Angeles Mayor Richard J. Riordan struggled and only ran when in sight of the cameras, and – in spite of a chronic bad back – Representative Bob Filner of San Diego also jogged with Clinton, admitting, "I thought there'd be some interesting pictures taken that I could use to talk about in a fun way with my constituents."[55] Jovial reports of a straggler van picking up those who could not keep up with Clinton heightened the sense of needing to keep up with the presidential pace.[56]

The activity of running and the sense of physical momentum surrounding the president was an easy way to plug the gaps in the continuous news cycle. Kurtz argued in the *Washington Post* that the morning jog was a simple way to fill this vacuum, noting that Clinton's "sweaty, off-the-cuff comments – 'there are a lot of very troubling signs in the economy' – generate front-page headlines."[57] Running was also a way for Clinton to attempt to lead by example as the health of the nation was increasingly at the forefront of the national consciousness. When an athletics track was installed on the White House grounds in 1993, it was funded by donations, including at least $1,000 coming from the New York Road Runners Club, which attributed the increase in their membership numbers to the president's promotion of the "healthy and democratic sport of running."[58]

Whilst Clinton did not suffer from the age-related health issues that had plagued George H. W. Bush's presidency, his attempt to combat his own weight struggles through running were something of an empty gesture with the main purpose of enhancing his own image as a striving president. Fast-food culture had become firmly established and the obesity crisis was well on its way, with McDonald's signing a $40 million sponsorship deal for the 1996 Atlanta Olympics.[59] Thus, Clinton's striving to get his "notoriously problematic" weight under control through regular running and exercise was ultimately a public relations exercise to benefit his own image, rather than being part of a serious effort to improve the nation's health.[60]

Stepping into Clinton's shoes at the turn of the century then, George W. Bush built on Clinton's use of running as a public relations tool, and particularly used jogging and his physical fitness to portray himself as a strong, striving president. In 2002, he gave an interview to the specialist magazine, *Runners World*, explaining how running enhanced his political life: "running enables me to set goals and to push myself toward those goals . . . running helps me keep that discipline."[61] Indeed, the sense of discipline was one of the key things that Bush's jogging habit came to denote in the public discourse about his physical fitness. One reporter argued that "it is iron discipline and a fierce competitive edge that keep Bush going," and that his habit of wearing a heart-rate monitor when running was not for health reasons "but as a way of keeping score."[62]

Bush explicitly related running to personal discipline and a positive strength of moral character, revisiting the evangelical tone of Carter and the original proponents of jogging by stating, "I exercise a lot because it's good for my mind and for my soul," adding that "you set priorities in life, and if exercise is one of your priorities you will find out time to do it."[63] Not only was Bush striving to promote a healthier lifestyle for Americans, but by implication a superior lifestyle, insisting "I know your life will be more complete if you exercise and serve a neighbor in need."[64] Indeed, improving physical fitness became a significant part of Bush's agenda whilst in office, firmly establishing him as a president striving for physical fitness, with May 2007 being declared Physical Fitness Month as just one example of the many events organized during the administration aimed at promoting physical fitness.

Running also became an important element in Bush's display of strength as commander-in-chief in the midst of the Iraq War and the wider 'War on Terror.' During his administration, Bush cultivated the image of an indefatigable runner of superior strength, and his short times at distance were regularly featured in the press.[65] Bush was seen as a runner specifically, rather than a jogger, having completed the Boston Marathon prior to taking office. And, since according to Wilson, "jogging indicates a lack of seriousness," in comparison with running, this serious pursuit of miles burnished his image as a strong leader.[66] Running became the photo-op of choice as he welcomed veterans home to the United States, and further played into notions of 'Muscular Christianity' – an ideology developed in relation to nineteenth-century British masculinity, theorizing that physical fitness and Christian zeal went hand in hand with the ideal embodiment of masculinity.

One of the most striking cases of this display of fitness in relation to the military was when Bush invited double amputee Staff

Sergeant Christian Bagge to run on the track with him at the White House. Bagge later wrote to Bush thanking him for his leadership and the time spent together on the run, commenting in a similar vein that "terrorists may burn out buildings, our flags, even mutilate our bodies. They will soon find they can never crush our great American spirit."[67] Whilst this letter did not appear in the press, it indicated clear links between notions of American military strength and physical prowess during the Bush administration.

Thus, while leaders in the mid-twentieth century may have pulled on their tracksuit and laced up their sneakers as a leisure activity initially, jogging rapidly transformed into a staple public relations event that could be easily staged, and usually portrayed the participant in a positive light. Leaders who have time to fit running and personal exercise regimens into their schedule were seen as being sufficiently strong and 'fit' to govern. Yet it was not always as simple as putting one foot in front of the other: Jimmy Carter and George H. W. Bush both found their Achilles' heel while running, with health scares perpetuating doubts over the strength of their administrations more broadly. Jogging ultimately had lasting negative effects on both of their images. The 1992 campaign was, however, a turning point at which running can be identified as being a key strategic activity in cultivating a strong image for prospective candidates, as manifested by both Clinton and Bush Jr. Finally, though prior presidents struggled, Clinton and Bush Jr. found their stride in their administrations as they strove to be better versions of themselves, and, in turn, encouraged Americans to create a better nation for themselves. Although a simple activity then, the practice of running has had huge implications for political image in the presidency which has previously been overlooked. In a role in which stamina is vital, running has perhaps proven to be the ultimate way in which to portray one's fitness to govern.

Notes

1. John F. Kennedy, "The Vigor We Need," *Sports Illustrated*, July 16, 1962, 12–14.
2. Hal Higdon, "Jogging is an In Sport," *New York Times*, April 14, 1968, SM36.

3. Higdon, "Jogging is an In Sport."
4. "Udall in the Jog, Opens Jog Trail," *New York Times*, November 8, 1967, 41.
5. Higdon, "Jogging is an In Sport."
6. George A. Sheehan, MD., *Dr. Sheehan on Running* (New York: Bantam, 1975); James F. Fixx, *The Complete Book of Running* (London: Chatto & Windus, 1979).
7. Thor Gotaas, *Running, A Global History* (London: Reaktion, 2009); Jay Schulkin, *Sport: A Biological, Philosophical, and Cultural Perspective* (New York: Columbia University Press, 2016); Alan Latham, "The History of a Habit: Jogging as a Palliative to Sedentariness in 1960s America," *Cultural Geographies* 22(1) (2015): 103–126.
8. Jeroen Sceerder, Koen Breedveld. and Julie Borgers (eds.), *Running across Europe: The Rise and Size of One of the Largest Sports Markets* (New York: Palgrave Macmillan, 2015); John Bryant, *The London Marathon: The History of the Greatest Race on Earth* (London: Arrow Books, 2006).
9. Richard Lipsky, "The Athleticization of Politics: The Political Implication of Sports Symbolism," *Journal of Sport and Social Issues* 3(2) (1979): 28–37.
10. Robert Edelman and Christopher Young (eds.), *The Whole World is Watching: Sport in the Cold War* (Stanford, CA: Stanford University Press, 2019).
11. Harry Edwards, "Perspectives on Olympic Sport Politics: 1968–1984," *National Black Law Journal* 9(1) (1984): 38.
12. Sheehan, *Dr. Sheehan on Running*, 18.
13. Higdon, "Jogging is an In Sport."
14. Ann Corbett, "Personalities," *Washington Post*, November 6, 1978, B3.
15. Bruce Newman, "Its Jimmy, the No. 1 Jogger," *Sports Illustrated*, December 18, 1978, 32–35.
16. Jerry Rafshoon, Memorandum, November 22, 1978, Presidential Files, Office of Staff Secretary Collection, Jimmy Carter Presidential Library.
17. "Council on Fitness Reorganized," *New York Times*, December 9, 1978, 19.
18. "Towns on Mississippi Welcome Mrs. Carter," *New York Times*, August 19, 1979, 1.
19. Craig R. Whitney, "Brezhnev Arrives in Vienna and Sees Carter for 1st Time," *New York Times*, June 16, 1979, 1.

20. Bob Dunn and Jane Fenderson, Memorandum, Presidential Files, Office of Staff Secretary Collection, Jimmy Carter Presidential Library.

21. Charles Peters, "Would Carter Ever Lie About His Pulse Rate?" *Washington Post*, June 17, 1979, B8.

22. "What Your Heart Rate is Telling You," *Harvard Health*, August 20, 2020, available at: https://www.health.harvard.edu/heart-health/what-your-heart-rate-is-telling-you.

23. Edward Walsh, "Carter's Cool Competence Leaves Him Vulnerable," *Washington Post*, December 24, 1978, D1.

24. Sarah Pileggi, "Jimmy Carter Runs Into the Wall," *Sports Illustrated*, September 24, 1979, 16–19.

25. Pileggi, "Jimmy Carter Runs Into the Wall."

26. B. Drummond Ayres Jr., "Carter, Exhausted and Pale, Drops out of 6-Mile Race," *New York Times*, September 16, 1979, 1.

27. Lawrence K. Altman, "Physician Pronounces President Fit after Near-Collapse in 6-Mile Race," *New York Times*, September 17, 1979, A1.

28. Brooks Jackson, "Bunny Goes Bugs: Rabbit Attacks President," *Washington Post*, August 30, 1979, A1.

29. Joseph Epstein, "Runners-Up," *The New Republic*, November 16, 1992, 15.

30. Christopher Corbett, "Bush Should Know Real Mainer's Don't Eat Brie," *Telegram & Gazette*, January 22, 1989, 2C; Alex Brummer, "Jogging for the Public Opinion Polls a Fact of Life for American Leaders," *The Guardian*, January 9, 1992, 7.

31. "Birthday Jog by Bush Shows '65' Can Do It," *Telegram & Gazette*, June 13, 1989, A10.

32. "'Difficulties' Hinder Ship Plan," *Telegram & Gazette*, January 8, 1990, A5.

33. Allison Kaplan, "A Heartbeat Away," *Jerusalem Post*, May 10, 1991, 9.

34. Kaplan, "A Heartbeat Away."

35. Larry Thompson and Carol Krucoff, "Exercise and the Heart," *Washington Post*, May 7, 1991, 10.

36. Michel McQueen, "Bush Medical Advisers Cite Overactivity of Thyroid Gland for Heart Condition," *Wall Street Journal*, May 8, 1991, A14.

37. Larry J. Sabato, *Feeding Frenzy: How Attack Journalism has Transformed American Politics* (New York: Free Press, 1991), 1.

38. Howard Kurtz, "Media Circus," *Washington Post*, July 12, 1992, J18.

39. The 'inhalation debate' here refers to Clinton's claims in 1992 that whilst experimenting with marijuana in his youth he did not inhale the smoke; ibid.

40. Gwen Ifill, "Democrats: Exercising Their Legs and Lips," *New York Times*, July 20, 1992, A10.

41. David Broder and Ruth Marcus, "Candidates Hit the Road and Come Out Swinging: President Plunges into Truman Role," *Washington Post*, August 22, 1992, A1.

42. "The Question Is: Who Do You Trust to Make Change Work for You?" *Washington Post*, August 21, 1992, A30.

43. Richard L. Berke, "'Plain George' Plainly Tries to be Likable," *New York Times*, August 24, 1992, A13.

44. Martin Walker, "Gore gets Prepared to Outsmart Quayle," *The Guardian*, July 11, 1992, 9.

45. Mary McGrory, "Candidate in Charge of Character," *Washington Post*, July 14, 1992, A2.

46. Dan Balz and Richard Morin, "Voters Will Decide Nation's Course at Generational Crossroads," *Washington Post*, October 21, 1992, A12.

47. Roxanne Roberts, "DC Prepares to Re-invent Itself," *The Guardian*, October 19, 1992, 11.

48. David Maraniss, "Weighty Problems Absorb Democratic Front-Runner," *Washington Post*, May 18, 1992, A10.

49. Natalie Angier, "Why So Many Ridicule the Overweight," *New York Times*, November 22, 1992, 38.

50. Maureen Dowd, "The Faces Behind the Face that Clinton's Smile Masks," *New York Times*, October 25, 1992, 1.

51. Martin Walker, "First Time Voters Tune in to Clinton," *The Guardian*, September 22, 1992, 9.

52. Elizabeth Kastor, "The Man in the Big Bubble," *Washington Post*, November 13, 1992, C1.

53. Martha Sherrill, "The List," *Washington Post*, November 4, 1992, C1A.

54. Richard L. Berke, "Politicians Find Jogging with Clinton is No Stroll in the Park," *New York Times*, July 26, 1993, A1; "The 'Kitchen Cabinet' of the President," *New York Times*, August 8, 1909, SM9.

55. Berke, "Politicians Find Jogging with Clinton is No Stroll in the Park".

56. Berke, "Politicians Find Jogging with Clinton is No Stroll in the Park."

57. Howard Kurtz, "Media: The Press's Difficult Transition," *Washington Post*, November 12, 1992, D1.

58. Gwen Ifill, "The Clinton Track," *New York Times*, February 25, 1993, A16.
59. "McDonald's to Back Games," *New York Times*, October 15, 1993, B15.
60. Peter Baker, "Bill Clinton Lightens Up," *Washington Post*, August 6, 1997, C1.
61. "Running with President George W. Bush," *Runner's World Magazine*, October 1, 2002.
62. Evan Thomas, Tamara Lipper, and Rebecca Sinderbrand, "The Road to Resolve," *Newsweek* 144(10) (2004): 32–40.
63. "Getting Physical with Bush," CBS News, YouTube, June 28, 2007, available at: https://www.youtube.com/watch?v=b_tUvFerrtk.
64. "Bush Runs in Race to Encourage a Healthier Lifestyle," AP Archive, YouTube, July 21, 2015, available at: https://www.youtube.com/watch?v=Xx0KfEJZi_E.
65. "The Running Man: But What is Bush Getting Away From?" *The Guardian*, August 24, 2002, 19.
66. Emily Wilson and George W. Bush, "Gotta Run," *The Guardian*, December 4, 2002, A2.
67. Christian Bagge, Letter, January 20, 2001, Subject Files on Recreation and Sports (Track and Field), Records of the White House Office of Records Management, George W. Bush Presidential Library.

6

The Presidential Golf Paradox

Aaron J. Moore

Golf is a sport long associated with the upper class and prestige, dating back to its origins with the Scottish and English aristocracy.[1] Due to the equipment needed, time commitment, and the relatively limited availability of play compared with other sports, golf is rarely viewed as an egalitarian pastime. This perception changed somewhat following the emergence of Tiger Woods on the national scene in the late 1990s. Woods' rise to prominence led to a boom for the golf industry in terms of merchandise sales, construction of new courses, and the introduction of the game to minorities and players of all socio-economic levels.[2] The game grew in popularity throughout the early stages of the twenty-first century until its expansion was derailed by the 2008 recession.[3]

As with many aspects of American culture, the shifting tides of popularity and the perception of golf comes with political ramifications. The sport has been a mainstay for politicians for over a century and thus created a unique paradox for the American presidents who play the game. With all the limitations and restrictions placed upon the presidency, golf is a sport that allows a president to remain physically active and, as George W. Bush noted, ". . . to be able to get outside and play golf with some of your pals is important for the president. It does give you an outlet."[4] Also, traversing the course with fellow players provides ample opportunities for the president to negotiate or strategize potential policies. According to journalist Ben Macintyre, golf is the "ideal presidential game."[5]

The other side of the paradox, of course, is the aforementioned connotation of golf being elitist. Establishing an 'every-person' persona is a fundamental element of political ideology. But if that politician is playing a sport that "may suffer from historical and accurate perceptions of a discriminatory environment," it is an association that could create unwanted criticism.[6] Still, presidents need to cling on to sports since American society has long valued those who demonstrate physical prowess as a way to stay healthy and exhibit their masculinity.[7] In essence, golf is one of the best sports a president can play, but it also has its pitfalls.

To better understand this paradox, a thematic analysis of the press coverage of golfing presidents from William Howard Taft to Donald Trump was conducted. This research examined press coverage of golf and presidents to help determine whether prevailing attitudes in the media on the topic have changed since Taft took office in 1909. This constructionist analysis was conducted by doing detailed searches of ABI/INFORM on the ProQuest database, Nexis Uni, and the *New York Times* archives. The search terms used were the presidents' names (those between Taft and Trump), and the term: golf (e.g., Richard Nixon and golf). Also, a global search using the terms 'United States president' and 'golf' was incorporated into the content gathering.

The early golfing presidency: Taft to Truman

Prior to William Howard Taft's presidency, his predecessor, Theodore Roosevelt, known as an outdoorsman, helped to create the popular opinion and the notion in the press that high-ranking politicians needed to be physically active.[8] Taft carried on this connection to sports by playing golf, a game that still had not translated into mass popularity in the United States by the start of twentieth century, largely because so few people had access to courses.[9] Thus, when Taft became known as the first golfing American president, there was a rise in popularity of the game.[10] Taft's foray into golf also created the game's political liabilities in the eyes of the press, according to golf historian John Fischer.[11]

Taft played a lot of golf, and it was a large thematic portion of his media coverage. He became an avid golfer after being introduced to

124

the game by his brother Henry in 1894. Taft's increasingly frequent play was rarely seen as an issue, even when he played in the Philippines while serving as the civil governor following the Spanish–American War. This changed, however, when his fellow Republican Roosevelt endorsed Taft to replace him in the White House in 1908.[12] Even during the infancy of photo-journalism, Roosevelt conveyed his concerns to Taft about the public seeing a politician participating in a sport with which few voters could identify. Roosevelt wrote: "It would seem incredible that anyone would care one way or the other about your playing golf, but I have received literally hundreds of letters . . . protesting about it. I myself play tennis, but that game is more familiar; besides, you never saw a photograph of me playing tennis. I'm careful about that; photographs on horseback, yes; tennis, no. And golf is fatal."[13]

Taft did not heed Roosevelt's advice, and was not shy about being seen with clubs in hand. He often played in Chevy Chase, Maryland while in the Oval Office, and had a regular group of playing partners referred to as the 'golf cabinet.' This was based on Roosevelt's similar sporting group called the 'tennis cabinet.'[14] The research indicates that the first reference in the *New York Times* about Taft and golf appeared in July 1908. Interestingly, the piece could be considered positive, as it noted how golf allowed Taft to shed nearly 5 pounds and gave him time outside the office to gather his thoughts and finalize his speech.[15] However, just a few months later in the same newspaper, the sport was mentioned with negative connotations when it was reported that Taft was going to "devote himself to golf and exercise at Hot Springs and transact as little business as possible."[16]

Another article in the *New York Times* the following summer may be the seminal moment regarding this topic. With Taft in town for a summer vacation, the article detailed how reporters and residents were disappointed that the famous visitor was not as visible and as accessible as anticipated. Alongside the article was a cartoon depicting Taft dressed in golf apparel standing large while the lowly reporters are off to one side looking disappointed. With golf still on the periphery of the American sporting scene, few journalists understood the game, and covering Taft created storylines that seemed to indicate the president had a passion with which few could identify. "Just golf, golf, golf," agreed another reporter. "That's his vacation idea. No settling wars, pitching hay. It's evil time we've fallen upon boys."[17] Here was the sort of press Roosevelt warned him about.

Taft's fondness for golf and the reporters covering him lacking a fluency in the game was clearly a main theme of the press coverage for the remainder of his tenure in the White House. Headlines in the *New York Times* during his term such as "Taft Again Plays Golf," "Taft Clings to Golf," "Taft Has a Day of Rest: Does No Official Business But Plays Golf and Visits" demonstrate that his connection to the game became a focal point of the press. Golf then played a role in the contentious re-election bid for Taft when his former colleague Roosevelt challenged him. A Roosevelt ally, Governor Walter Stubbs of Kansas, criticized Taft in a quote in the *Wichita Beacon*: Taft "preferred golf to work," and "It is said that Taft plays better golf than politics. And he generally loses at golf."[18] The resurfacing of Roosevelt helped to splinter the vote and led to a surprise win for Democrat Woodrow Wilson.

When Wilson became president, his physical condition was less than optimal, so White House physician and Taft's former doctor, Cary T. Grayson, suggested the fifty-six-year-old take up the game as a form of exercise.[19] The doctor felt golf was a good sporting activity for a president since it allowed him to be outside and have the option of doing business or creating some solitude. Wilson certainly took to the doctor's orders and played golf on an almost daily basis en route to more than 1,000 rounds during his eight years as president.[20]

From a thematic point of view, the press coverage of Wilson playing so much golf was not a detriment, it was reported to be just part of his daily routine. "The president will play golf tomorrow morning and will later consider the amendments he is to make to the navigation laws."[21] In his first term, golfing led to such positive storylines as: "Wilson Golfs in Rain: Should Belie Reports that He's in Poor Health, Says White House," and "President Cheered on Trip . . . Settles Down for a Fortnight's Golfing, Automobiling, Reading and Rest." Golf was a useful way to offset rumors of Wilson's poor health and these press mentions serve as examples of early public relations tactics coming out of the Oval

Office. Whereas the jovial Taft had an association with the game as a social outlet – possibly at the expense of being president – the reserved Wilson prospered from his relationship with golf in the press since it appeared to be correlated with his intellectual nature: "President's Quiet Day: Golfs in the Morning, Reads in the Day."[22]

Wilson's replacement in the White House, Warren G. Harding, was also an avid golfer, but lasted just two years in office before his untimely death in 1923. While there is not a large body of work to examine, the press coverage of Harding and golf was positive overall. This was likely a result of Harding's working knowledge of the press and how to create favorable coverage since he was a former newspaper reporter himself. Harding's dog Laddie Boy, known to tag along during the president's rounds, became a celebrity since he was commonly covered in the *New York Times*.

One article about Harding's action on the links stated he "returned home . . . his face flushed by the raw fall air and his spirits heightened by the tramp over the muddy golf links."[23] Perhaps having another golfing president, and the resulting press coverage, including that for Laddie Boy, played a role in the sport's rapid expansion while Harding was in office. The 29th president's remaining golf legacy is his name being attached to Harding Park, one of the country's most renowned courses located just outside San Francisco.[24]

After Harding left office, there was a notable dip in his successors' interest in golf and the resulting press coverage. Calvin Coolidge "played out of obligation" as the game was becoming more popular with his constituents, and then came Herbert Hoover who had no interest in the game at all.[25] Polio prevented Franklin Roosevelt from playing as president; however, prior to contracting it at the age of thirty-nine, he was a successful player and club champion. Harry Truman's poor eyesight did not allow him the chance to take up most sporting activities.

Cold War divisions: Eisenhower to Bush Sr.

The next period in presidential golfing history features eight leaders – two of whom were famously attached to the game. Dwight Eisenhower, like Taft, was a golfing president at a time in American history when a growing economy allowed for more free time and disposable income, two vital elements within a sporting culture. After the Second World War, the game of golf enjoyed a rise in popularity, and Ike in the White House was the perfect ambassador for the game. Golf was expanding alongside the mass media, with more radio stations and magazines to go along with the newly affordable television set. If Eisenhower was golfing, there were more cameras and journalists to cover it. More voices in the media also translated to increased commentary on all presidential subjects.

While Taft had established a connection between golf and the presidency half a century earlier, the emerging media during Eisenhower's terms amplified it to the public. Because of newsreels, television, and magazines such as *Life* and *Look*, the public was regularly able to see footage of the president on the links. His presence there helped to bring more attention to the game, as did his close relationship to emerging superstar golfer Arnold Palmer. Palmer was one of the first sports sensations to come to prominence during the early days of live televised sports, and the bond with Palmer was advantageous for the public relations-minded Ike.[26] There was, however, a downside to this type of exposure. It painted a golf flag target on the president's back for his political opponents to take aim at during his two terms.

According to historian John Sayle Watterson, the Democrats saw golf as his weakness, and started characterizing Eisenhower as "being asleep at the controls and spending too much time on the golf course."[27] The president played golf over 800 times in office and his repeated trips to Augusta National Golf Club certainly provided fodder for critics.[28] The media that provided Eisenhower the ability to be visible also played a vital role in him being characterized by the opposition as just a "golfer who wasn't doing much."[29]

When analyzing the role the press played in the narrative of a president being distracted by golf, the amount of time Eisenhower spent on the links in front of journalists played a major role. When news stories about Eisenhower were presented they often featured notes about him playing, and space was provided for the opposing political viewpoint. In late 1952, the *New York Times* ran an article on lame-duck President Harry Truman questioning Eisenhower's diplomacy with Korea. Next to the article is a large photo of Ike teeing off at a Hawaiian golf course.[30] Nowhere in the story is golf mentioned, so the editorial selection of the picture is a curious one. Here is a story about an authoritative figure questioning Eisenhower's decision-making and those reading about it see him golfing.

A tonal shift in the press coverage of Eisenhower and golf was observed in a 1954 *New York Times* article. After the newspaper had run over fifty articles mentioning the president and golf came the piece "Eisenhower and Roosevelt: A Study in Press Relations." This article compared Franklin D. Roosevelt, who had an open and positive relationship with the press, with Eisenhower who was referred to as "aloof." The piece is a direct criticism of Eisenhower by journalists who believed his staff sheltered him with trips to secluded golf venues like Augusta National and Burning Tree Country Club in Maryland. Speaking for journalists covering the president, the writer remarked that golf never dominated daily life for Roosevelt like it did for Eisenhower. The game was now bluntly referred to as a distraction.[31]

Vice President Richard Nixon had to deflect the growing criticism of Ike's time on the links as the 1954 midterm elections neared. When asked if Eisenhower was playing too much golf, Nixon responded, "If the President spent as much time playing golf as Truman played poker, then the President would be able to beat Ben Hogan," the most dominant professional golfer of his day.[32]

Towards the end of Eisenhower's presidency, he started to show signs of slowing down and had increasing health issues. A weakened Ike was even a target for his own party when fellow Republican Joe McCarthy was quoted as saying that the president played golf too much.[33] This was the general reputation Eisenhower faced in the media when he left office in 1961. However, some historians believe that it was false and diminished his presidential accomplishments.[34] While today many still connect him with golf, John Shaw writes that history has treated him well because "he is credited with keeping the American economy humming and defending the nation's international position without stumbling into a catastrophic war with the Soviet Union or China. Additionally, declassified documents from his White House years show he was a far more active, engaged and

129

sophisticated chief executive than most of his contemporaries appreciated."[35]

The next three presidents were golfers to some extent, but it was not a significant aspect of their public image. John F. Kennedy was a golfer in college and some experts believe he was the best golfing president based on athleticism and an analysis of his swing. Then came the opportunistic Lyndon Johnson who did not love the sport but used it to his advantage to negotiate with other golfing politicians. Some have even suggested that Johnson's golfing with senators was one way he was able to sway enough votes to support the 1964 Civil Rights Act.[36]

Then came Nixon who had an interesting relationship with golf, likely because of his first-hand experiences with Eisenhower and his own unique personality. Nixon did not take up the game until serving as Eisenhower's vice president and, like his boss, had plenty of positive publicity in the press during the mid-1950s by riding the sport's growing popularity.[37] Once Nixon took office in 1969, he distanced himself from the game and even had Eisenhower's White House putting green removed. Nixon's muted relationship with golf is particularly noteworthy since he was sandwiched between Eisenhower and Gerald Ford, Republicans noted for being golfing presidents. Eisenhower and Ford were both former football players who spent countless hours on the links and received plenty of media attention because of their close relationships with famous playing partners. Ford was often attached to the famous entertainer Bob Hope; though, this affiliation did not generate the same type of advantageous coverage as Ike's relationship with Arnold Palmer.

Almost from the start of his presidency, Ford's relationship with golf did not play well in the media. First, came the official announcement that Ford was to grant a full pardon for the controversial Nixon. Days later, Ford attended an event at the World Golf Hall of Fame in North Carolina and made a public statement on the decision, including an analogy of someone winning a golf tournament then shaking the hand of the runner up as an example of reconciliation. Even though Ford made articulate calls for healing the nation, the press coverage of this day displayed a juxtaposition of the lighthearted Ford making self-deprecating claims about his golfing prowess while protestors critiqued the presidential pardon.[38]

As was the case with Eisenhower, when Ford made public appearances they were often on the golf course. This led to critiques in the press on how well, or not, he looked while playing. A reporter covering Ford for the *Charlotte Observer* wrote that his tee shots were "almost always strong but usually misdirected."[39] A 1975 *Newsweek* article stated that Ford's confidants recommended that he cut back on appearances at sports banquets and golf tournaments. The president's handlers were of the impression that though this had helped Ford connect with some Americans, too much golf and "an athletic image [was] too frivolous at a time of economic crisis."[40] Another *Newsweek* article saw Ford referred to as a "devoted duffer," who was having as much trouble playing the game as he was dealing with Congress.[41]

Ford's level of play became a joke that was amplified in the press after the television show *Saturday Night Live*, a cultural phenomenon that mixed comedy with politics, became extremely popular. Millions of viewers tuned in each week and then often went to work on Monday talking about one of the more popular skits, Chevy Chase portraying Ford. Even though the president was athletically gifted, Chase gained prominence by making Ford appear clumsy and hapless. Chase made the decision not to imitate the president but instead played on the public perception that he was prone to accidents and falling down in public.[42]

This image of Ford stems in part from an infamous moment for then-Vice President Ford in 1974. While playing a round in Minnesota, an errant tee shot became front-page news. The *New York Times* ran the headline "Ford, Teeing Off Like Agnew, Hits Spectator in the Head with Golf Ball." According to author Don Van Natta, this story and other related ones made their way into the news coverage because, unlike other presidents such as Eisenhower or Kennedy, Ford often played in front of crowds.[43] If the public did not read about Ford's golfing mishaps, they were likely to hear a joke about it from Hope, his friend and television host. One of Hope's memorable quips was: "The last time I played golf with President Ford he hit a birdie. And an eagle, a moose, an elk, an aardvark."[44] When Ford passed away in 2006, his passion for golf was one of the main themes of his obituaries.

Jimmy Carter, who replaced Ford, is one of the few presidents since the early twentieth century who did not play golf or have any interest in the game.[45] The Georgian was so distanced from the sport that during a search of media coverage about him and golf, the only articles that appear are from the 1976 campaign trail when he was critical of Ford's time on the course and the possibility that the president was in violation of campaign contributions by making invitations for his friends and donors to play. Instead of golf, Carter was a former high school basketball player and avid jogger.

Perhaps the most ironic aspect of studying presidential history and golf is that the owner of a reportedly powerful swing, Ronald Reagan, rarely played while in the White House. Next to Ford hitting a spectator in 1974, Reagan was involved in one of the most publicized presidential golf moments. The front page of an October 1983 edition of the *New York Times* featured a story of a man who drove his pickup truck through the gates of Augusta National Golf course in order to 'talk' to Reagan who was on the grounds playing a round. The inebriated intruder brandished a handgun and took several hostages in an effort to speak to the president about the amount of jobs leaving the country. He never got close to the president, who was shuffled away by Secret Service agents in an armored limousine.[46]

Rounding out this era of presidential golfers was George H. W. Bush, considered one of the best golfing presidents. Like Ford and Eisenhower, the press coverage during Bush's rise through the political ranks often mentioned his athletic background, including his baseball career at Yale. Golf was on that list, but by no means tied closely to his overall persona. It might have been politically driven that Bush did not golf often during his presidency because of the Gulf War that consumed so much of his time in office. Looking back at the media coverage of Bush, the majority of golf mentions in the press were biographical notes of his father, who often played with Eisenhower.[47]

This era of golfing presidents was dominated by arguably the two most associated with the game, Eisenhower and Ford. After Ford left office, the association of golf and the presidency was still present, just not as profound as it once was. That would soon change as the next residents of the White House would elevate the relationship with golf to new levels and the media was right there to cover it.

The modern golfing presidency: Clinton to Trump

This most recent era is not only recognized for the number of golfing enthusiasts populating the White House, it is also a period when the media changed dramatically. A seismic shift occurred in the mass media landscape around the time Bill Clinton took office in 1993. The growth of cable television news helped fragment the marketplace even more when networks started to cater to niche audiences based on their political preferences instead of a larger, heterogeneous population.[48] This was followed by the dot-com boom that signaled how attention would soon shift away from traditional outlets to partisan information sources. Regular consumers alongside journalists were now in a similar position to distribute information and content. Those commenting on social media were creating content that competed for eyeballs just like the major media conglomerates were doing already. This transfer of power generated more politically charged debate into the splintered marketplace. With every president in the twenty-first century being a golfer, the focus on the game became even more intense.

Of the modern presidents, perhaps none was better at creating a favorable biographic narrative in the media than the man from Hope, Arkansas. The first reference in the national media to Clinton's love of golf came in a 1992 *New York Times* feature that helped to establish his everyman quality: "Addicted to card games of hearts, golf, and crossword puzzles, a whiz on the tenor sax, Clinton has the look and loosey-goosey enthusiasm of a high school jock perched somewhere between eternal youth and paunchy middle age."[49]

The trend continued and golf soon became a controversial topic for Clinton. It was on the campaign trail when he faced heat from those in the media and other Democratic presidential candidates for playing a round at an all-white country club.[50] Stories about where Clinton played called into question his reputation as being a new Southern candidate with a strong civil rights background. One of Clinton's Democratic competitors, former California governor Edmund Brown, used the press to call out Clinton, comparing him with Republican counterpart George H. W. Bush, as someone who plays an 'elitist' sport.[51] A similar political ploy had been used against Eisenhower decades before. This golf-related controversy saw Clinton call upon a response that he would use a number of times during his political career – admit to being wrong: "I'm going to do something unconventional for a politician – when I make a mistake, I'm going to say I made a mistake, not go into some long, labored exercise."[52] Clinton survived this controversy, but it also brought in a new storyline. From this point onward, the press openly scrutinized the membership policies of the country clubs where politicians play.

Clinton was a regular golfer and was astute at using the game to gain favor with other politicians and business leaders. It even supported the positive image of him being a restless workaholic, always doing business as the president and sometimes it was on the course.[53] However, Peter Landau and Shep Campbell's 1996 book, *Presidential Lies: The Illustrated History of White House Golf*, painted a more critical picture. It detailed how past presidents such as Eisenhower, Kennedy, and Bush were active golfers and tried different ways to get the upper hand on their playing partners. Like his predecessors, the authors noted, Clinton often took mulligans and exaggerated his scores.[54]

Such varied coverage led to more scrutiny of Clinton's golf game, including a detailed article written by *Los Angeles Times* writer Glenn Bunting, who was in a playing group right behind the president on Amelia Island, Florida. This appears to be the first time a journalist actively observed and questioned what a president did on the course. In the piece the writer tried to determine "does he really cheat?"[55] Ultimately, Bunting found that Clinton did not play a "traditional style." Rather, he played with numerous balls in play and supposed practice shots. This story was not a total condemnation of Clinton, but it did bring into question his character on the course at a time when he found himself in numerous scandals. It also validated Eisenhower's decision not to be on the course playing with journalists.

With Clinton being such an avid golfer, there was a momentum in press coverage of the topic that carried into George W. Bush's presidency. The younger Bush, too, took office while the media environment was different and content was moving faster than anyone could have predicted. Eyeballs drifting toward online sites had the traditional outlets, now even more beholden to corporate commercial interests, playing catch up. The news became even more partisan and the best way to capture attention was partisanship and controversy. From the onset of his campaign for president, Bush was portrayed in the media as a legacy candidate raised in wealth – a preppy boy in the line of previous Bushes who played golf.

The narrative changed dramatically after the September 11 attacks shook the nation and took Bush off the course for an extended period of time. It was not until July 2002 that there were reports of Bush being back on the course. This time, it was when he played with his father during a family vacation in Maine.[56] The focus was that Bush was enjoying leisure time on the course. The perception created by the media was that golf should be a leisure activity and business should be transacted off the course. Thomas Friedman, a perpetual Bush critic, made just such a point about CNN coverage of Bush later that summer: "Up to now Mr. Bush has conducted the war against terrorism with serious resolve. But he shows real contempt for the world, and a real lack of seriousness, when he says from the golf tee, as he did on another occasion: 'I call upon all nations to do everything they can to stop these terrorist killers. Thank you. Now watch this drive.'"[57] In the ensuing years, when a president failed at humor in light of a pressing issue, it became known as a 'watch this drive moment.'

Barack Obama continued the trend of presidents taking office with a recognized passion for sports – in his case, basketball. The basketball angle was regularly covered by the press and was presented as unique and 'cool' since he did a lot of business and held casual meetings on the court when compared with many other politicians who do so on the golf course.[58] However, once Obama started slowing down playing hoops, he gravitated toward golf and its different physical requirements. One of the first references to Obama and golf was a favorable *New York Times* profile in early 2007 that mentioned his background in Hawaii and how he still had connections to his high school friends, with whom he maintained a playing relationship. In this case, the press mentioning golf is seen as positive as it allowed him to stay tied to his roots. There are no references to the sport being an elite activity.[59]

For the most part, the press coverage of Obama and golf in the mainstream press, like many other aspects of his politics and personal life, was non-critical. That clearly was not the case with right-leaning Fox News, which was extremely critical of his time on the course, especially during his second term. Here golf resurfaced as a political topic. Fox News' headlines on Obama and golf created a very different image. Examples such as "President Obama's Golf Problem"[60] and "President Obama plays 200th round of golf"[61] – both in 2014 – painted him as distracted from his duties.

Just as many at Fox News regularly criticized Obama for playing golf, so did then-presidential candidate Donald Trump, who often used social media to do so. This was ironic, since Trump himself was an avid golfer and dealt heavily in the business end of the sport. His tweet in 2014: "With all of the problems and difficulties facing the US, President Obama spent the day playing golf," circulated throughout the media.

Trump's criticism of Obama during the last two years of his presidency created a noticeable shift in the media's coverage of presidents and golf. First, it was the use of social media – mostly by Trump – to continually raise this as an issue, which spurred the traditional media to then follow suit. With the press growing even more splintered and partisan, outlets such as CNN, MSNBC, the *Washington Post*, and the *New York Times* essentially defended Obama and his decision to play golf. One article in *Golf Digest* titled, "We've Crunched the Numbers, and it's Official: President Obama Played A LOT of Golf While in Office in Early 2017," found that Obama played over 300 rounds of golf while in office.[62] The article was not critical, as might be expected, but rather commended him for finding time and avoiding conservative critics in order to stay active.

The media spotlight on golf and the presidency was never brighter than just before Trump took office. The mainstream media, with which Trump was often confrontational, used golf as a point of criticism. The point made in the coverage was that he was hypocritical – first, for chiding Obama for golfing when that was one of his main areas of business, and, then, for how much he played when he took over the White House.[63] Pro-Trump news outlets were far less critical and used golf as a way of reinforcing his image as a business person, not a politician.[64] Golf and the presidency became such a popular topic that it created a new area of coverage – the 'golf meters' – that compared the time Trump spent on the course with that of Obama's time.

Besides the time spent on the links, another area not seen in media coverage of other presidents regarding golf, was the possible conflict of interest that Trump could be entering into. The *New York Times* was one of many outlets to take the stance that there was concern for the synergy between the relationship with the president and his golfing business operations.[65] A point of contention was that American taxpayers were footing the bill for all the rounds Trump played at his own venues. These conflict of interest storylines were addressed throughout the Trump presidency, but there were no articles specifically detailing situations that went from possibly unethical to illegal. The term 'potential' was often used in these types of stories.[66]

Thematically, the conservative media outlets presented Trump and golf as a package. The game and the business were a main part of his overall persona. Trump golfing as much as he did was not really seen as an issue because he was a 'golfer.' These stories took the angle that golfing allowed him a different perspective when it came to negotiations and diplomacy. Playing so much golf was also beneficial for someone in his seventies, as it allowed him to stay active.

A very different story was told in outlets such as CNN, MSNBC, the *Washington Post*, and the *New York Times*. His appearance, often wearing high white pants, was commonly described in the articles, and his true physical fitness was often questioned by columnists. There was also skepticism regarding if his reported scores were actually as low as he stated. This angle of cheating within the game, first seen with Clinton, reappeared in the media.[67]

One of the final articles that analyzed the intersection of Trump, the presidency, and golf was published in early 2021 by the *Washington Post*. This was a retrospective piece that quantified all of Trump's time on the links and how significant the sport was to his presidency. First, there was Trump's 'disdain' for Obama's golfing habits and how he pledged to be different and "would not have time for golf." But just two weeks later he did have time for golf at Mar-a-Lago, his privately owned Florida resort. The article's theme is clearly stated, Trump reneged on his promise to avoid the links, just like he did on many other promises he made during his tenure.[68]

The writer, Philip Bump, provided extensive documentation of how many times and where Trump golfed during his four years in office. This type of data was certainly not seen in the press before Trump. Among some of the items listed were that: he visited a Trump Organization property on 428 days of his presidency, or one visit every 3.4 days; he was president for 418 weekend days and visited one of his properties on 240 of those days, or on 57 percent of them. And, for a final tally between his time on the links compared with Obama, Bump reported that Trump 'probably' (his team often would not report all his time on the course) played 261 rounds of golf as president. If that number is true it is a round every 5.6 days compared with the 333 rounds of golf for Obama at a rate of once every 8.8 days.[69]

Conclusions

The research indicates there are two distinct groups of American presidents since the time William Howard Taft first played the game of golf. There are those widely known for their outward association with the game; and the other group, including Roosevelt, Hoover, Truman, and Carter who stayed away from the game and found other ways to stay active in the White House. Even the likes of Nixon, Kennedy, and Reagan, who were not often portrayed in the media as golfers, still occasionally hit the links. Considering how much golf-related media coverage the most recent presidents have received, it makes Carter look like an interesting figure. If he was president today and did not play golf, that would be a storyline.

This shows how the game has become a part of the contemporary presidency.

The overall coverage from Taft to Trump is an indication of how much the game has changed in the eyes of the media. When it started with Taft, U.S. golf was in its infancy and those in the media were still learning its nuances. Taft became a trend-setter and his play helped the game become more recognized nationally. More players took up the sport, and some even went on to become president.

By the time of Eisenhower, golf had gained even more prominence, yet some still believed it was only for the elite and not representative of all sporting Americans. Nonetheless, toward the end of the twentieth century, it seemed to be less of a problem for presidents to be so closely associated with the game. Over the years, as more courses were built and figures such as Tiger Woods helped to create a more inclusive perspective of golf, the game's popularity grew.

Clinton was elected at the age of forty-six, making him the third youngest person ever elected to the office. This facilitated an image of being an active and younger politician, far different to the likes of Bush and Reagan who preceded him. Clinton used his time on the links to garner national recognition and publicity from the media. In addition, his golfing assisted in lessening the lingering concerns that golf was just an elitist sport. Even though there were issues along the way for Clinton's time on the course, nonetheless, his strong relationship with the game reinforced the expectation in the media that the president would conduct business and periodically escape from the pressure by spending time on the links.

The Trump era, like many aspects of his political career, became a period of disruption. His bombastic style on social media and constant criticism of Obama helped to weaponize golf as a controversial political topic. The splintered and partisan media gladly took on the role of bystander to create even more content. Using golf as a political talking-point was beneficial to Trump, as well as the media. There is no reason to believe that golf will not continue to be part of the media narratives surrounding the presidency.[70]

Notes

1. Hugo Ceron-Anaya, "An Approach to the History of Golf: Business, Symbolic Capital, and Technologies of the Self," *Journal of Sport and Social Issues* 34(3) (2010): 339–358.
2. K. A. Farrell, G. V. Karels, K. W. Montfort, and C. A. McClatchy, "Celebrity Performance and Endorsement Value: The Case of Tiger Woods," *Managerial Finance* 26(7) (2000): 1–15.
3. Beatrice Garcia, "As Recession Runs its Course, Golf Industry Takes a Hit," *McClatchy News*, March 11, 2010, available at: https://www.mcclatchydc.com/news/nation-world/national/economy/article24576337.html.
4. Cliff Schrock, "Eisenhower and Nixon Would Have had Barack Obama's Back When it Comes to His Golf Habit," *Golf Digest*, September 1, 2016, available at: https://www.golfdigest.com/story/throwback-thursday-eisenhower-and-nixon-would-have-had-barack-obamas-back-when-it-comes-to-his-golf-habit.
5. Ben Macintyre, "Golf Isn't Just a Game to US Presidents," *The Times*, July 14, 2018.
6. Ewan Murphy, "Golf Fights Old Perceptions and Drop in Players to Attract New Audience," *The Guardian*, June 13, 2017, available at: https://www.theguardian.com/sport/blog/2017/jun/13/golf-fights-perceptions-drop-in-players-new-audience.
7. Aaron Moore and David Dewberry, "The Masculine Image of Presidents as Sporting Figures: A Public Relations Perspective," *Sage Open* 1(11) (2012), available at: https://journals.sagepub.com/doi/pdf/10.1177/2158244012457078.
8. Adam Burns, "Fit to be President: William Howard Taft, Sports and Athleticism," *European Journal of American Culture* 40(2) (2021): 121–134.
9. Darell Napton and Christopher Laingen, "Expansion of Golf Courses in the United States," *Geographical Review* 98(1) (2008): 24–41.
10. Pamela Grundy and Benjamin Rader, *American Sports: From the Age of Folk Games to the Age of Televised Sports* (New York: Pearson, 2014), 138.
11. John Fischer, "In Golf, President Taft Finds a National Treasure," *Morning Read*, December 9, 2019.
12. Fischer, "In Golf, President Taft Finds a National Treasure."
13. Fischer, "In Golf, President Taft Finds a National Treasure."
14. Fischer, "In Golf, President Taft Finds a National Treasure."
15. "Taft Working on His Speech," *New York Times*, July 17, 1908, 2.

16. "Taft Off to Hot Springs," *New York Times*, November 7, 1908, 2.

17. "Where is Taft? Asks Beverly, Mass in Vain?" *New York Times*, August 22, 1909, 6.

18. Matthew Algeo, "The President Who Golfed Too Much (it's not Donald Trump)," *Washington Post*, April 21, 2017, available at: https://www.washingtonpost.com/opinions/the-president-who-golfed-too-much-its-not-donald-trump/2017/04/21/f803241c-2394-11e7-bb9d-8cd6118e1409_story.html.

19. "Presidents Made Play by Doctor: Horseback Riding for 'T. R.,' Golf for Taft and Wilson Recommended by Dr. Grayson," *Hartford Courant*, March 18, 1935, 12.

20. Ben Macintyre, "Golf Isn't Just a Game," *The Times*, July 14, 2018.

21. "President Takes Auto Trip," *New York Times*, August 31, 1914, 7.

22. "President's Quiet Day: Golfs in the Morning, Reads in the Day," *New York Times*, September 2, 1913, 2.

23. Dave Shedloski, "Did you know: This U.S. President Played Golf after Voting on Election Day," *Golf Digest*, November 2, 2020.

24. John Branch, "A Memorable Golf Course Honors a Forgettable President," *Virginian-Pilot*, August 5, 2020.

25. Kevin Dunleavy, "Commanders in Golf: A Guide to the U.S. Presidents and Their Games," *GOLFPASS*, November 17, 2014.

26. Karla Gower, "Eisenhower: The Public Relations President," *American Journalism* 32(2) (2015): 245–247.

27. Alexander Bolton, "Obama's Golf Game Tees Up Image Debate," *The Hill*, June 25, 2010.

28. James Masters, "The President's Club: How Golf Took Over the White House," *CNN*, October 22, 2014, available at: http://edition.cnn.com/2014/10/20/sport/golf/golf-presidents-white-house/index.html.

29. Ben Jacobson, "Historians Say Trump's Erratic Schedule is Unusual but Not Unprecedented," *The Guardian*, January 9, 2018.

30. "Eisenhower is Irked at Truman Attack," *New York Times*, December 13, 1952, 1.

31. Felix Belair, Jr., "Eisenhower and Roosevelt: A Study in Press Relations," *New York Times*, January 3, 1954, 56.

32. W. H. Lawrence, "Nixon Tells G.O.P. it is Now Trailing in Fight for House," *New York Times*, September 2, 1954, 1.

33. "McCarthy Criticizes President on Yalta," *New York Times*, March 27, 1955, 60.

34. Evan Thomas, "The Brilliant Prudence of Dwight Eisenhower," *The Atlantic*, September, 19 2012, available at: https://www.theatlantic.

com/politics/archive/2012/09/the-brilliant-prudence-of-dwight-eisen-hower/262556.

35. John Shaw, "From Mediocre to Memorable: The Evolution of Ike's Legacy," *The Washington Diplomat*, April 1, 2015, available at: https://washdiplomat.com/from-mediocre-to-memorable-the-evolution-of-ikes-legacy.

36. Todd Kelly, "Golfers in Chief: All the U.S. Presidents Who Played Golf," *USA Today*, November 1, 2020, available at: https://golfweek. usatoday.com/lists/golfers-in-chief-all-the-u-s-presidents-who-played-golf.

37. "Palmer Selected Top Golfer of '60s," *Hartford Courant*, January 27, 1970, 23.

38. Marjorie Hunter, "Ford Uses Golf as Example in 'Reconciliation' Plea," *New York Times*, September 12, 1974, 28.

39. Scott Fowler, "Round of Golf in 1974: Gerald Ford, Billy Graham, Endangered Children, $40 Hotel," *Charlotte Observer*, May 2, 2015, available at: https://www.charlotteobserver.com/sports/spt-columns-blogs/scott-fowler/article20041815.html.

40. "Back to the Bench," *Newsweek*, January 27, 1975.

41. David Alpern, Thomas DeFrank, and Henry Hubbard, "Ford Concedes the Putt," *Newsweek*, March 10, 1975, available at: https://www. yahoo.com/news/does-playing-golf-help-presidents-183542777. html?guccounter=1.

42. Matt Fotis, "Falling Down: Gerald Ford, Chevy Chase, and the Power of a Pratfall," *Medium*, June 24, 2020, available at: https:// medium.com/satire-the-state/falling-down-gerald-ford-chevy-chase-and-the-power-of-a-pratfall-199043f288f5.

43. Don Van Natta, *First Off the Tee* (New York: PublicAffairs, 2004), 92.

44. "Bob Hope – Clown Prince of Golf Joke," Golf-Info-Guide.com, n.d., available at: https://golf-info-guide.com/funny-golf-jokes/bob-hope-clown-prince-of-golf-joke.

45. "Golfers in Chief: The Best and Worst Presidential Golfers," *Golf Magazine*, February 15, 2016, available at: https://golf.com/instruction/golfers-in-chief-the-best-and-worst-presidential-golfers.

46. Frances Clines, "Reagan Unhurt as Armed Man takes Hostages," *New York Times*, October 23, 1983, 1.

47. Maureen Dowd, "Making and Remaking a Political Identity: George Herbert Walker Bush," *New York Times*, August 20, 1992, 1.

48. Anders O. Larsson, "Diversifying Likes: Relating Reactions to Commenting and Sharing on Newspaper Facebook Pages," *Journalism Practice* 12(3) (2018): 326–343.

49. Peter Applebome, "Bill Clinton's Uncertain Journey," *New York Times*, March 8, 1992, 10.

50. Mike Royko, "Bill Clinton was Caught in the Act," *Baltimore Sun*, March 30, 1992, available at: https://www.baltimoresun.com/news/bs-xpm-1992-03-30-1992090203-story.html.

51. Elizabeth Kolbert, "TV Skirmish is Sponsored by Democrats," *New York Times*, March 29, 1992, 15.

52. Andrew Rosenthal, "Clinton Says Golfing at All-White Club was Mistake," *New York Times*, March 21, 1992, 8.

53. Jeffrey Birnbaum, "Some Say All-Work-No-Play Clinton Means Presidency Lacking Perspective," *Wall Street Journal*, August 20, 1993.

54. Peter Landau and Shep Campbell, *Presidential Lies: The Illustrated History of White House Golf* (New York: Macmillan, 1996).

55. Glenn Bunting, "This Game Fits Clinton to a Tee; U.S. President Ultra Serious About Golf," *Los Angeles Times*, November 16, 1997.

56. Mike Allen, "Before Golf, Bush Decries Latest Deaths in Mideast," *Washington Post*, August 5, 2002, available at: https://www.washingtonpost.com/archive/politics/2002/08/05/before-golf-bush-decries-latest-deaths-in-mideast/1069761f-bd77-4df4-94c7-812bf7dc0ec9.

57. Thomas Friedman, "Bush's Mideast Sand Trap," *New York Times*, August 21, 2002, 17.

58. Jodi Kantor, "One Place Where Obama Goes Elbow to Elbow," *New York Times*, June 1, 2007, available at: https://www.nytimes.com/2007/06/01/us/politics/01hoops.html.

59. Jennifer Steinhauer, "Charisma and a Search for Self in Obama's Hawaii Childhood," *New York Times*, March 17, 2007, available at: https://www.nytimes.com/2007/03/17/us/politics/17hawaii.html.

60. Greg Gutfeld, "President Obama's Golf Problem," *Fox News*, August 21, 2014, available at: https://video.foxnews.com/v/3742644566001#sp=show-clips.

61. "President Obama Plays 200th Round of Golf," *Fox News*, October 14, 2014, available at: https://video.foxnews.com/v/3838584797001#sp=show-clips.

62. Sam Weinman, "We've Crunched the Numbers, and it's Official: President Obama Played A LOT of Golf While in Office," *Golf Digest*, January 19, 2017, available at: https://www.golfdigest.com/story/weve-crunched-the-numbers-and-its-official-president-obama-played-a-lot-of-golf-while-in-office.

63. James Crump, "Trump's History of Attacking Obama for Golfing in a Crisis," *The Independent*, November 7, 2020, available at: https://www.independent.co.uk/news/world/americas/us-politics/donald-trump-golf-crisis-barack-obama-us-election-2020-b1673677.html.

64. Andrew O'Reilly, "Trump Defends Trips to Golf Courses, Says it's His 'Exercise' and He Plays 'VERY Fast,'" *Fox News*, July 12, 2020, available at: https://www.foxnews.com/politics/trump-defends-trips-to-golf-courses-says-it-his-exercise.

65. Eric Lipton and Susanne Craig, "With Trump in White House, His Golf Properties Prosper," *New York Times*, March 9, 2017, available at: https://www.nytimes.com/2017/03/09/us/politics/trump-golf-courses.html.

66. Noah Bookbinder, "G-7 at Trump's Doral Resort? The Original Sin of this Presidency is Failure to Divest," *USA Today*, September 4, 2019.

67. Rick Reilly, *Commander in Cheat: How Golf Explains Trump* (New York: Hachette, 2020), 21.

68. Philip Bump, "Trump's Presidency Ends Where So Much of it Was Spent: A Trump Organization Property," *Washington Post*, January 20, 2021.

69. Bump, "Trump's Presidency Ends Where So Much of it Was Spent."

70. I would like to thank Dr. David Dewberry of Rider University for his assistance with this chapter.

7

From Wilson to Dubya:
The Curious Case of Presidents and Rugby

Adam Burns

Rugby and the American presidency are hardly synonymous to most sports fans. Indeed, many Americans see rugby as a distinctly 'foreign' game, most clearly linked to England and the British Isles.[1] Furthermore, the history of rugby in the United States itself is very much an overlooked one. Though, at one point in the 1870s, rugby was adopted by the trend-setting sporting colleges on the East Coast (such as Harvard, Yale, Princeton, and Columbia), it was later adapted into what is now known to most as 'American football' – the national distinctiveness being clear in the name the rest of the world uses. For some scholars, this is a sign of American football's exceptionalism and 'American-ness,' but at the same time this emphasizes how rugby has been correspondingly made to seem somewhat alien.[2] Though rugby made a brief comeback in the early twentieth century on the West Coast, even seeing the United States win gold in the sport in its last two appearances as a fifteen-a-side game at the Olympics in 1920 and 1924, thereafter it has remained relatively low profile across the nation as a whole. With all this in mind, one might wonder why future presidential hopefuls such as Bill Clinton and George W. Bush took part in the game during their student days. With so many more distinctly American sports around, what was the allure of rugby – a sport with very English roots?

The origins of rugby are both well known and widely misunderstood. The most recognized story has it that Rugby School pupil William Webb Ellis picked up the ball during a game of football, and ran with it, thus inventing a game that is still played to this day. Many question the veracity of this narrative, but the game still bears the name of the school and the World Cup trophy bears the name of Webb Ellis. The power of the story, whatever its accuracy, is clear.[3] Rugby's roots are at Rugby School which, by the late nineteenth century, was recognized as one of the more prestigious and exclusive of England's 'public' schools.[4] When rugby traveled to Harvard University via Canada in the 1870s, it brought with it these elite educational roots, and implanted them in a similarly elite institution in Massachusetts.[5] Notably, all three of the presidents who are documented as having a hand in rugby did so at some of the world's most prestigious universities: Woodrow Wilson at Princeton, Clinton at Oxford, and Bush at Yale.

Wilson was a rugby coach rather than a player. Therefore, though this chapter starts by exploring Wilson's role at the very beginning of rugby in U.S. collegiate life (and its links to future presidents), the bulk of the chapter focuses on the two presidents who actually played rugby while at university: Clinton and Bush. Rather than assess them individually, the chapter is thereafter organized thematically to consider why these two future presidents chose to play such an 'un-American' game during their college years, and why it might have proved useful to their future political ambitions. To start with, the relative exclusivity of the sport of rugby union (compared with American football and/or soccer) and its related 'social' side will be explored.[6] Thereafter, the chapter will go on to explore the role of masculinity (in both sports and politics), and why rugby seemingly provided an ideal way to evoke this within their nascent political narratives. These thematic elements were certainly evident in the press coverage of the presidents' respective stints as rugby players during their later presidential careers. Though rugby may not seem a natural sport for an aspiring president, in many ways it provided an accessible and well-chosen part of a future presidential narrative.

The Victorian roots of the rugby president

Rugby football only began to take root in U.S. colleges following the second clash between Harvard and McGill University (of Montreal), which took place in Massachusetts in 1874. After-wards it was rarely referred to as 'rugby' at all (instead it was gener-ally called 'football') and, from 1880 onwards, the rules increasingly adapted and evolved away from the English game. However, in this short period during the late 1870s, when the type of football played by top colleges like Harvard, Yale, and Princeton was very clearly rugby, three future U.S. presidents were attending those colleges.[7] Moreover, during the 1870s and 1880s, these elite colleges were far more at the forefront of sporting endeavor in terms of collegiate sports than they are today.[8] In terms of the wider history of presi-dential rugby, the game's origins within the United States highlight that its strong links to elite higher education establishments were there from the very beginning.

Perhaps the most obvious paragon of presidential masculinity to be in college at this time was Theodore Roosevelt (Harvard 1880). However, Roosevelt did not join any formal college team sports, and was perhaps best noted for his forays into boxing, occasional wrestling, and his frequent use of the university gym-nasium.[9] That said, he did attend the odd rugby game as a specta-tor during his time at Harvard, and went on to become a great supporter of rugby's successor in the Ivy League, American foot-ball.[10] Meanwhile, in New Haven, a young William Howard Taft (Yale 1878) was following a similar, if less strenuous, trail. Taft also engaged in wrestling during his undergraduate years, and – if a later presidential campaign biography is to be believed – might even have dabbled in rugby (though the latter is not borne out by later biographers).[11] It was in fact the young Tommy Wilson (Princeton 1879), who would later assume his more familiar mid-dle name of Woodrow, who was the most active in team sports of this future presidential trio.[12]

Wilson is described by his foremost biographer, John Milton Cooper, Jr., as an "avid fan" of rugby at Princeton.[13] Although he did not play rugby, he was a keen baseball player. Wilson did not play baseball for Princeton, but he had played baseball for Davidson College in North Carolina, from which he transferred in 1875.[14] However, even if Wilson did not feel up to playing base-ball or rugby at Princeton, he was directly involved as a coach of the 'Tigers' rugby team during his sophomore year (1876–7).

147

According to historian Parke H. Davis, the reason for Wilson's election as a 'director' of rugby was that he was one of the few people who actually knew the rules (after all, Princeton only adopted the rugby rules in the fall of 1876). Although the first encounter at Harvard in April saw Princeton record a loss, the return leg in New Jersey on the old St. George's Cricket Ground in Hoboken saw Princeton win.[15] Historian John Sayle Watterson suggests that Wilson supplied key strategic thinking, was a stickler for the rules, and played a central role in managing the team's finances.[16] However, this was not the end of Wilson's rugby/football coaching days, and the future president later went on to coach whilst a professor at Wesleyan University in Connecticut.[17]

It was not long after Roosevelt, Taft, and Wilson graduated that the game of rugby in the elite intercollegiate environs of Harvard, Yale, and Princeton started to change markedly, and move toward some of the more American football-style traditions that one might recognize later. Even so, it would not be until Roosevelt was president that the forward pass was introduced to the game, perhaps marking the final and definitive end to its rugby characteristics. Despite this, rugby survived and prospered beyond the States, while remaining a somewhat niche activity in the United States itself after the 1920s. Notwithstanding its low profile in the United States once American football had supplanted it, Coach Wilson was not the last president to engage with the game of rugby.[18]

Rugby and class

To some extent, class is central to both the origins of rugby (in both England and the United States) and its evolving narrative across the years that have followed. As the British social historian Tony Collins points out, the great split in English rugby (into league and union) at the end of the nineteenth century had class at its center. Rugby union (the code played by Clinton and Bush) was seen widely as the middle-class version of the game, in contrast to rugby league, which was viewed by many as having core working-class roots – and this distinction was decidedly the "product of the interplay and conflict between classes."[19] Soccer, though similarly associated with England (at least more so than with the

United States), has also tended to be seen as a more working-class sport than a middle-class one. In a sociological study carried out in Leicester, England, in 2015, sociologist Stacey Pope found that these class associations among fans of soccer and rugby union were still strong in the twenty-first century.[20] Although the great rupture in the English codes had not occurred when rugby was initially adopted by Oxford and Yale, it was rugby union that survived in these universities (and other elite educational institutions) into the time of Clinton and Bush. While some might question whether it is fair to class rugby union as a middle-class sport, when it is combined with the relatively socially elite environs of 1960s Oxford and Yale (despite this being a decade of growing change), it is probably fair to say that – within these conditions – rugby was a middle-class pursuit, generally played among social 'equals.'[21]

In the late fall of 1968, Georgetown graduate Bill Clinton arrived in England for a two-year stay in Oxford. Not only was Clinton traveling to the oldest and arguably most esteemed university in the country, he was also the recipient of a prestigious Rhodes scholarship, named after the Victorian arch-imperialist Cecil Rhodes. The bicycle-strewn Oxford which Clinton entered, according to another Rhodes scholar of the time, was full of "*Brideshead Revisited* types" who saw recently landed Americans as unrefined yokels seeking refinement.[22] Clinton's own reflections recall him having a good time overall, even if he frequently socialized with other Americans – though he, too, found the obsession with class at Oxford a little much.[23]

According to his autobiography, amid the maelstrom of the 1968 U.S. presidential election campaign, the young Clinton sought to immerse himself in a "blizzard of activity," that would help him relegate thoughts of the Vietnam War and the seemingly imminent return of a Republican administration in Washington the following January.[24] Clinton enrolled in University College (or 'Univ.'), part of Oxford's collegiate system, and it was as part of the Univ. rugby squad that Clinton would engage in his first rugby game not long after arriving. Only two weeks after Republican Richard Nixon triumphed over Democrat Hubert Humphrey in the November presidential election, Clinton scored his inaugural try (which, as Clinton points out to his readers, is the rugby equivalent of a touchdown in American football).[25] If Clinton had sought to distance himself from the turbulent political arena of Washington, D.C., where he had previously studied, he had clearly found himself a different sort of tumult on the rugby fields of Oxford.

Univ. had enough students to field two college teams, and Clinton, unfamiliar with the rules and new to the game, became a regular in the Univ. 2nd XV.[26] They practiced twice a week, and played their matches on Wednesdays.[27] As with rugby teams up and down the country, the Univ. 2nd XV also indulged in some regular post-match revelry. However, as this was Oxford, though Clinton might have partaken of the odd pint at the clubhouse or local pubs, he also found himself secreted in the 'buttery' taking on the more refined option of wine and cheese (which, as English cuisine of the 1960s went, was a fairly safe and largely imported option).[28] Clinton's Oxford rugby experience was, in short, a quite typical upper-middle-class one, a form of competitive social sport, far removed from the pseudo-professional atmosphere that typically surrounded top student athletes in the United States. Indeed, Clinton's rugby experience was a far cry from the high-level pursuits of the House Minority Leader at the time, Gerald Ford, who had been a stand-out football player in both high school and at university (Michigan 1934).[29]

While Clinton was playing rugby in the sport's homeland in 1968, his contemporary George W. Bush played in the United States itself. Yale was, of course, one of the most prestigious universities in the United States. Akin to Oxford and Cambridge, Yale and Harvard harbored a keen sense of competition between them, and nowhere was this more evident than in the sporting arena. Indeed, so important was the Yale–Harvard rivalry that it is a key reason why rugby was eventually adopted by both universities and their peers in the 1870s.[30] Notwithstanding Yale's excellent reputation as a seat of learning, Bush's most often-quoted review of his time at Yale was that he had not "learned a damned thing."[31] Despite this claim, however, he certainly did learn how to play rugby.

According to a former teammate, Bush was recruited from an intramural football team to play rugby during his senior year.[32]

Whereas Clinton played for his college's 2nd XV, Bush played in Yale's 1st XV during his senior year (1967–8), though this is perhaps more a sign of the relative importance of the sport of rugby at both institutions than Bush and Clinton's relative skill at the game. Bush has described rugby as "a great game, a game of speed and hard knocks with a tradition of postgame camaraderie."[33] Unlike the more studious Clinton at Oxford, Bush was better remembered as a typical frat boy during his time at Yale, a member of the Delta Kappa Epsilon fraternity and the exclusive Skull and Bones society.[34] During the 2000 presidential election, journalist David Teel noted Bush's rugby alongside the fact he also liked to hang out at "keg parties."[35] However, the reminisces of Bush's fellow ruggers have resulted in some mixed reports on his relationship with the team.

Yale alumnus Tim Weigel recalled playing rugby with Bush, and remarked that Bush was the only player he did not like. Weigel suggests that, in social situations, Bush was preoccupied with what people's fathers did for employment and with emphasizing his own father's success and contacts.[36] Similarly, other teammates recalled Bush's fondness for "postgame festivities" that included a good deal of beer and singing, as well as providing a place for him to make best use of his well-honed ability to "schmooze."[37] Bush's rugby teammates also recall him as being either conservative for a student in the 1960s, or perhaps cautious in expressing his views, with an eye on a future in politics.[38] Indeed, Yale – like Oxford – was home to a future generation of politicians, and Bush's contemporaries there included his later 2004 presidential election opponent John Kerry.[39]

Whether or not Clinton and Bush fitted in fully with their rugby teammates at Oxford and Yale, they most certainly got involved in a sport that was decidedly niche from an American perspective, and had strong associations with class privilege from an English perspective. Though these class overtones might prove useful in presenting the presidents as clubbable old boys to the power elite in the United States, there are several aspects that still need to be addressed to explain why rugby seemed the most obvious route for them to take. The strongest among these is that rugby offered not only implications of class identification, but also a strong physical contact element, somewhat lacking in other elite sports like polo or cricket. Rugby was, after all, "a game for hooligans played by gentlemen," and where it was important that these aspiring politicians were assigned as gentlemen, they needed to also show that they were capable of being 'hooligans' when necessary.[40] In line with Theodore Roosevelt's oft-cited mantra, a successful president needed to be able to "speak softly, and carry a big stick."

Rugby and masculinity

Rugby is far from the only, or most obvious, sport in the United States in which a gentleman might want to display that he can also be a hooligan when the time calls for it – boxing and American football being examples of sports through which previous U.S. presidents had expressed their youthful vigor in a very hard-hitting arena. What distinguishes rugby, at least in the United States, is that it is not played by many, and thus is not as competitive to get into at college level. In countries where it is more competitive, there are always intramural teams to allow students to get involved. This might help explain Bush and Clinton's forays into rugby – for Bush playing for the top team at Yale, and Clinton for his college's second team at Oxford. Rugby offered an accessible route to manly combat-like sport – and, as political scientist Meredith Conroy rightly notes, in the United States "masculine traits" and expertise in masculine issues are preferred in potential candidates for political office.[41]

On the matter of combat, it is important to note that both Bush in his senior year at Yale, and Clinton in his early months at Oxford, took to the rugby field in the year 1968. This was a pivotal moment in U.S. political history, and the war in Vietnam loomed large over much of the internal disruption that shook the country. The year began with the troubling Tet Offensive, which for many historians changed the course of the war. At the end of January, 84,000 Viet Cong and North Vietnamese forces launched a series of coordinated attacks on over one hundred sites in U.S.-protected South Vietnam. Though not long-lasting in its practical effects, the symbolic impact was enormous – a war that many

Americans had been led to believe they were winning now looked far from won.[42] Tet set the tone for a year beset by seemingly endless crises, and Democrat Lyndon B. Johnson's presidency turned into widespread political firefighting for the rest of the year.[43] The war was to remain a feature of American life for several years to come, and would provide many young men of that generation with a formative life (and combat) experience.

In Oxford, a self-exiled Clinton was finding a different rugged pursuit alongside a new community of comrades. The parallels between sports and warfare are identified frequently. As historian J. A. Mangan puts it, "Heroes of the sportsfield and battlefield have much in common. They are both viewed as symbols of national prowess, quality and virtue. The warrior and the athlete are crucial to the perceived success of the state."[44] Indeed, far beyond semantic analogies, in the Victorian era sports were seen as a very practical way to maintain youthful preparedness for potential wartime battles to come. If Clinton was not to be a warrior in Vietnam, he showed he was determined to prove a warrior on the playing fields of Oxford, as rugby is often considered at least as dangerous and violent as American football (and certainly more so than soccer).[45] Furthermore, various scholars have emphasized that rugby was a core "definer of masculinity in British culture," and at the time of the intersection between the Clinton and Bush presidencies, many scholars saw sports as both "the metaphor and reality of American masculinity."[46]

Clinton was purportedly introduced to rugby in 1968 by Chris McCooey, who was then the secretary-captain of Univ.'s 2nd XV. In a later recollection, McCooey claimed to have loaned Clinton some rugby boots so that he could play, again emphasizing both the amateur and social nature of the team. McCooey felt Clinton had always shown great enthusiasm for the game, "so it didn't matter about his skills" and his relative lack of fitness.[47] Clinton ended up playing second row during his time in Oxford – a forward position, and one of two men who form the second line in the scrum.[48] Clinton felt he was perfectly suited to this role. As a larger specimen than most of his English counterparts, he was well fitted to pushing in the scrum and more generally getting in people's way.[49] Rugby, it seemed, served well as a rugged masculine outlet for Clinton during a period when many other young American men were exerting their masculinity in battle.

In both the 1992 and 1996 presidential elections, Clinton was running against veterans, albeit of an earlier generation.[50] George H. W. Bush was only eighteen when he joined the U.S. Navy, and was flying a torpedo bomber in the Second World War by the time he was nineteen.[51] Republican Senator Bob Dole, meanwhile, recounted the defining period in his life as being his time in Europe during the final months of the same conflict, during which he had suffered a life-threatening injury.[52] Contemporary news reports in their respective election years (as each faced Clinton), highlighted both candidates' war records and their social credentials. For the *Philadelphia Inquirer*, Bush was a "hero of sorts," but his comrades had always remained aware "that this upper-crust, hale fellow wasn't quite one of them."[53] The *Chicago Tribune* noted Dole's service, but also the fact he was slow to sign up and "when it looked unavoidable, Dole, a dashing 6-2, 194-pound Kappa Sigma from KU [Kansas University] joined the Army."[54] Clinton, meanwhile, had no service record. Thus, critics frequently pointed to the fact he managed to avoid service in Vietnam – even though he was formally drafted while studying in England.[55]

In the run up to the 1992 presidential election, the sports channel ESPN interviewed former presidents Ford and Nixon (both of whom had enlisted during the Second World War), as well as candidates George H. W. Bush and Clinton about their differing sporting interests.[56] Where President Bush talked about horseshoes, Clinton discussed rugby.[57] During the interview, Clinton claimed to have played one rugby game with a minor concussion, causing the show's host, Bob Ley, to comment that Clinton "doesn't think he got any brain damage."[58] Clinton recalls what is presumably the same incident in his autobiography, noting that he sustained a heavy blow to the head during a game. After informing the coach about his dizziness, he was reminded that there were no substitutes and that he had better get back on field. Clinton recollects that, despite going on to lose the game, ". . . I was glad I hadn't quit the field. As long as you don't quit, you've always got a chance."[59] If Clinton had not been a wartime fighter, rugby clearly provided him with manly anecdotes to call upon when the time came.

Though George W. Bush did not take to rugby until late in his Yale career, some reports suggest he was potentially more adept than the doughty Clinton. Following a game against the University of Pennsylvania in April 1968, Bush was highlighted in a match report as being the lynchpin of Yale's defensive effort at fullback.[60] A couple of weeks later, in a game against the First City Troop of Philadelphia – Yale's second win of that campaign – Bush again came in for praise, the reporter noting that Bush "tried a couple of dazzling runs, an[d] pulled them off successfully."[61] Many years later, the *Yale Daily News* noted that Bush was remembered by others for his "lighthearted confidence and occasional clutch play."[62] Indeed, former teammate Britt Kolar said Bush showed "running skills, tackling skills and especially kicking skills."[63] Bush might not have made the cut for the Yale football team (even though he played at the intramural level), but he was skilled enough for a spot in the university's top rugby team.

Like Clinton, George W. Bush faced two veterans during his presidential campaigns: in 2000, the Harvard alumnus and Vietnam veteran Al Gore; and in 2004, Yale alumnus and Vietnam veteran John Kerry. In both cases Bush's opponents' service records were complicated, to say the least. Gore had long campaigned against the war before signing up, and Kerry had been notably outspoken against the war after he served. More tellingly, allegations that Kerry gained military decorations by deception likely did more to harm his presidential bid than his service record did to help it.[64] Yet it was when running against Kerry in 2004 that Bush's rugby pedigree really hit the newsstands. In August of that year, as re-election was heavy on Bush's mind, the *Los Angeles Times* ran a story about Bush's rugby past that presented him as not just athletic, but potentially as a hooligan too. The piece ran alongside a picture of Bush from the *Yale Yearbook*, which seemingly showed him punching an opposition player in the face.[65] In the article, Yale-based political science lecturer Jim Sleeper suggests an image like this might well have enhanced Bush's appeal to some male voters – making him appear a relatable frat boy, who liked to get up to a bit of mischief. Indeed, Sleeper remarks that former President Clinton, also had this 'bad boy' charm.[66] The image appeared to show that Bush was a ruffian when necessary, as well as a privileged scion of a political dynasty, something that was important not just to a domestic audience, but to an international one.

In his biography of Bush, Robert Draper notes the role of the president's rugby past in international relations. He recounts a meeting in 2001 between Bush and Russian leader Vladimir Putin that took place in the Slovenian capital, Ljubljana. When Putin arrived, he mentioned he had just watched a movie about Bush's family, and noted that he gathered Bush played rugby.[67] According to the New York *Daily News*, Bush's aide Karen Hughes asked the president about this discussion with Putin, and whether the Russian leader was aware Bush had played rugby only for a single semester. Bush reportedly corrected her, suggesting that he played for a year at varsity level. That particular newspaper went on to note their research showed that there was no such thing as 'varsity rugby' at Yale in the 1960s. The *News* was misinformed. Bush played for Yale against a number of other universities in 1968, as is well documented.[68] Putin is, of course, a leader well known for presenting himself publicly in robustly masculine form akin to a latter-day Theodore Roosevelt.[69] Putin seemingly chose to point to Bush's most rugged sporting pastime, and Bush was justified in emphasizing this to his Russian counterpart. Just as Sleeper suggested a 'punchy' Bush image might appeal to the average U.S. male voter, it seemed that Bush's rugby career might have even earned some modest recognition from Vladimir Putin.

Conclusions

Though this chapter seeks to highlight the often forgotten linkage between rugby and the presidency, one should not overstate this relationship. Reports of both presidents' rugby history arise in the press from time to time, but usually along the lines of 'did you know that . . .?' – rather than as core parts of Clinton or Bush's presidential narratives. Indeed, one could just as easily write a chapter on Bush and baseball or cheerleading, or Clinton and basketball or golf. However, unlike these other sports, rugby was, and remains, a relatively 'alien' game in the United States, despite significant growth since the 1960s. Its reputation in the United States – to the extent that it has one – is seemingly a useful one for politicians to raise when the timing is right. As one Missouri newspaper put it in 1970: rugby could be described as "the world's only entirely amateur sport, and as a hell-raising release for frustrated ex-gridders."[70] For those seeking to exert masculinity within a political context, and particularly those unable to play football at a high level, rugby fits the bill in many respects.

In addition to its brute masculine qualities, the game of rugby began with, and maintains, a strong class and collegiate identity. Shortly after his election in November 1992, Clinton's penchant for rugby arose in an article in a New Jersey paper. A local businessman sent Clinton an "old-style rugby shirt" emblazoned with a 'G' (for Georgetown) shortly before the election, and then spotted the president-elect playing golf in said shirt on television, leading to a spike in interest in the shirts from Georgetown University.[71] This anecdote, though obscure, shows how even once elected to the nation's highest office, Clinton maintained a pride in his collegiate and rugby past. Four years later, in the run up to his re-election, Clinton was pictured in a number of newspapers holding a rugby ball aloft, which had been presented to him by a cadet graduating from the U.S. Coast Guard Academy in New London, Connecticut.[72] And, around the same time, Republican Speaker of the House Newt Gingrich's half-sister Candace (herself a rugby player) recalled a conversation she had with Clinton about rugby. In her words, the discussion prompted Clinton to get "this sort of faraway look in his eye" and allowed him to "step out of being the president for a minute and be a rugger again."[73] Rugby, it seems, made more of a lasting impact than one might imagine.

In 1995, while Clinton was in office and the Rugby World Cup was coming to a close in South Africa, Peter Fitzsimons, an Australian rugby international player-turned-journalist, drew up a satirical celebrity Rugby World XV for the *Sydney Morning Herald*. Clinton was made captain, ahead of Winston Churchill and Che Guevara. Interestingly, Fitzsimons also picked John F. Kennedy, noting that there was little proof he had ever played, but reasoning he would serve well as "a good-looking bloke, with the aspect of one who has never had even a glove laid on him, even after years of weaving his magical way through opposition defences."[74] While Bush was in office during 2003 and another Rugby World

Cup came around in Australia, Fitzsimons rebooted his World Rugby XV to include Bush in the team alongside Clinton (with Kennedy relegated from the side altogether).[75] Fitzsimons, in fact, opened his 2003 article noting that Bush and Clinton both played in 1968: "a heavy contact football game with no helmets or pads – a game that would stand them in good stead in their later political careers."[76] Whether he meant the hard blows of political life would be comparable with rugby, or that rugby would be a feather in both men's caps, is hard to tell. However, what is clear is that rugby – despite its foreignness and class ties – did not seem to do either candidate any harm in their markedly successful political careers.[77]

Notes

1. See, for example, Dan Roberts, "Here's Why You Don't Care About the Rugby World Cup," *Fortune*, October 27, 2015, available at: https://fortune.com/2015/10/27/rugby-world-cup; Mike Henson, "United States: Are USA the Stirring Superpower at Rugby World Cup?" *BBC Sport*, September 25, 2019, available at: https://www.bbc.co.uk/sport/rugby-union/49767208.
2. Tony Collins, "Unexceptional Exceptionalism: The Origins of American Football in a Transnational Context," *Journal of Global History* 8(2) (2013): 209–230.
3. Lincoln Allison and Rusty MacLean, "There's a Deathless Myth on the Close Tonight: Re-assessing Rugby's Place in the History of Sport," *International Journal of the History of Sport* 29(13) (2012): 1866–1884.
4. In England, the term 'public school' generally refers to fee-paying independent schools, rather than state-funded schools.
5. Adam Burns, "From the Playing Fields of Rugby and Eton: The Transnational Origins of American Rugby and the Making of American Football," *Sport History Review* 52(2) (2021): 315–331.
6. In an article written to coincide with a Wales v. South Africa game played in D.C., journalist Martin Pengelly reported that some in the United States spoke of a "rugby 'illuminati,' holding the levers of power." Among those Pengelly notes as recent rugby players in the Washington political scene are Representative Conor Lamb (PA) and Senator Chris Murphy (CN) from the Democratic Party, and Republican Alex Mooney (WV), former chair of the Congressional Rugby

Caucus. See Martin Pengelly, "It's in My Blood: How Rugby Managed to Unite America's Elite," *The Guardian*, available at: https://www.theguardian.com/sport/blog/2018/jun/01/famous-american-rugby-players-wales-v-south-africa.

7. Burns, "From the Playing Fields of Rugby and Eton."
8. Ryan Swanson, *The Strenuous Life: Theodore Roosevelt and the Making of the American Athlete* (New York: Diversion, 2019), 52.
9. Swanson, *The Strenuous Life*, 55.
10. John J. Miller, *The Big Scrum: How Teddy Roosevelt Saved Football* (New York: Harper, 2011), 4–5.
11. Oscar King Davis, *William Howard Taft: The Man of the Hour* (Originally published 1908; reprinted, Honolulu, HI: University Press of the Pacific, 2002), 40 (though referred to as 'football' rather than 'rugby'); Henry Pringle, *The Life and Times of William Howard Taft*, vol. 1 (New York: Farrar & Rinehart, 1939), 38; Adam Burns, "Fit to Be President: The American Press, William Howard Taft and Physical Fitness," *European Journal of American Culture* 40(2) (2021): 121–134.
12. Princeton itself underwent a name change near the end of the nineteenth century, and was formally called the College of New Jersey at this time. Contemporaries, including Harvard and Yale students of the time, however, generally referred to the university as Princeton (the name of the town where it is based).
13. John Milton Cooper, Jr., *Woodrow Wilson: A Biography* (New York: Vintage, 2009), 25. Cooper, as did students of the time, refers to the game as football – but I am making the distinction here between rugby football and the later American football that had not yet departed from recognizable rugby rules.
14. Cooper, *Woodrow Wilson*, 26.
15. Parke H. Davis, "Woodrow Wilson Coached Princeton's First Football Team, Says Historian," *Harvard Crimson*, November 8, 1924, n.p., available at: https://www.thecrimson.com/article/1924/11/8/woodrow-wilson-coached-princetons-first-football.
16. John Sayle Watterson, *The Games Presidents Play: Sports and the Presidency* (Baltimore, MD: Johns Hopkins University Press, 2006), 93.
17. Watterson, *The Games Presidents Play*, 94.
18. There are some indications and suggestions that John F. Kennedy might have played rugby while at Harvard. The assertion seems to rest mainly on the grounds that his brothers Joe and Ted played rugby. As a former gear manager at Harvard recounted in 1964,

in addition to his prowess in football, Joe "loved to play rugby. In those days, and it still is, an informal sport," but one which was "rough ... You can really get beat up playing it." See James Farrell, "Oral History Interview," *John F. Kennedy Oral History Collection*, John F. Kennedy Presidential Library, JFK #1, 5/11/1964 [Digital ID: JFKOH-JF-01], available at: https://www.jfklibrary. org/asset-viewer/archives/JFKOH/Farrell%2C%20James/JFKOH-JF-01/JFKOH-JF-01. Therefore, it is stated by some commentators that the young Jack played it too – though one must assume that this was recreational more than competitive, given the sparsity of references (see Charles Kenney, *John F. Kennedy: The Presidential Portfolio* (New York: Public Affairs, 2000), 12).

19. Tony Collins, *Rugby's Great Split: Class, Culture and the Origins of Rugby League Football*, 2nd edn. (London: Routledge, 2006), xv.
20. Stacey Pope, "'It's Just Such a Class Thing': Rivalry and Class Distinction between Female Fans of Men's Football and Rugby Union," *Sociological Research Online* 20(2) (2015): 145–158.
21. Joseph A. Soares, *The Power of Privilege: Yale and America's Elite Colleges* (Stanford, CA: Stanford University Press, 2007), 3; Jose Harris, "The Arts and Social Sciences, 1939–1970," in Brian Harrison (ed.), *The History of the University of Oxford, Vol. XVIII: The Twentieth Century* (Oxford: Clarendon Press, 1994), 226.
22. Thomas J. Schaeper and Kathleen Schaeper, *Rhodes Scholars, Oxford and the Creation of an American Elite* (New York: Berghahn, 2010), 186
23. Schaeper and Schaeper, *Rhodes Scholars*, 189.
24. Bill Clinton, *My Life* (London: Arrow Books, 2005), 142.
25. Clinton, *My Life*, 143. The terminology of both a 'try' and a 'touchdown' have outlived their practical relevance – and both harken back to the early days of the respective sports (when they meant what they said).
26. 'XV' is the standard terminology for a rugby union side of fifteen players.
27. David Maraniss, *First in His Class: The Biography of Bill Clinton* (New York: Touchstone, 1996), 141.
28. Maraniss, *First in His Class*, 142. The often alcohol-fueled social life associated with rugby has continued well beyond the 1960s, even in these increasingly professionalized times. Eddie Butler, "You Booze, You Lose, But Drinking Culture is Hardwired into Rugby," *The Guardian*, January 7, 2012, available at: https://www. theguardian.com/sport/blog/2012/jan/07/drinking-culture-rugby-

union; Christopher Prentice, Stephen R. Stannard, and Matthew J. Barnes, "Effects of Heavy Episodic Drinking on Physical Performance in Club Level Rugby Union Players," *Journal of Science and Medicine in Sport* 18(3) (2015) 268–271.

29. Ford was captain of his high school football team and then "star football center" for the University of Michigan, see Yanek Mieczkowski, *Gerald Ford and the Challenges of the 1970s* (Lexington: University Press of Kentucky, 2005), 73.

30. Burns, "From the Playing Fields of Rugby and Eton."

31. Nigel Hamilton, *American Caesars: Lives of the Presidents from Franklin D. Roosevelt to George W. Bush* (London: Bodley Head, 2010), 477.

32. Joe Biddle, "Doctor Sees his Ex-Teammates Compete in Presidential Race," *The Tennessean*, October 21, 2004, C7.

33. George W. Bush, *A Charge to Keep: My Journey to the White House* (New York: Perennial, 2001), 47.

34. Lois Romano and George Lardner, "Bush: So-So Student but a Campus Mover," *Washington Post*, July 27, 1999, A1.

35. David Teel, "Presidential OT Should be Settled on the Gridiron," *Daily Press*, November 9, 2000, B1.

36. Karen Brandon, Joseph T. Hallinan, and Bob Kemper, "The Son Also Rises [Candidate Aims to Emulate Dad]," *Chicago Tribune*, January 18, 2000, 10.

37. Andrew Mangino, "Bush '68: Last Line of Defense," *Yale News*, March 2, 2006, available at: https://yaledailynews.com/blog/2006/03/02/bush-68-last-line-of-defense.

38. Bill Minutaglio, *First Son: George W. Bush and the Bush Family Dynasty* (New York: Three Rivers Press, 2001), 110.

39. Minutaglio, *First Son*, 87. Oxford, long the birthplace of future British politicians, was alma mater to eleven of the fifteen British PMs since the Second World War (those who did not attend Oxford being: Winston Churchill, James Callaghan, John Major, and Gordon Brown). Yale, meanwhile, was attended by presidents William Howard Taft and George H. W. Bush (as well as his son) as undergraduates, and Ford and Clinton as law postgraduates.

40. Huw Richards, *A Game for Hooligans: The History of Rugby Union* (Edinburgh: Mainstream, 2006), 19.

41. Meredith Conroy, *Masculinity, Media, and the American Presidency* (New York: Palgrave Macmillan, 2015), 3.

42. David F. Schmitz, *The Tet Offensive: Politics, War, and Public Opinion* (Lanham, MD: Rowman & Littlefield, 2005), 83–84.

43. Kyle Longley, *LBJ's 1968: Power, Politics, and the Presidency in America's Year of Upheaval* (New York: Cambridge University Press, 2018), 8–9.

44. J. A. Mangan, "Series Editor's Forward," in J. A. Mangan (ed.), *Shaping the Superman: Fascist Body as Political Icon – Aryan Fascism* (New York: Routledge, 2013), xi–xiii at xii.

45. Chris Bodenner, "Which is More Dangerous, Rugby or Football," *The Atlantic*, October 14, 2016, available at: https://www.theatlantic.com/notes/2016/10/rugby/504143.

46. Ken Muir, Keith D. Parry, and Eric Anderson, "Masculinity and Inclusive Rugby in the United Kingdom," in Rory Magrath, Jamie Cleland, and Eric Anderson (eds.), *The Palgrave Handbook of Masculinity and Sport* (Cham: Palgrave Macmillan, 2020), 323–340 at 338; Michael Kimmel, "Series Editor's Foreword," in Jim McKay, Michael A. Messner, and Don Sabo (eds.), *Masculinities, Gender Relations, and Sport* (Thousand Oaks, CA: Sage, 2000), xiii–xiv at xiii.

47. Associated Press, "Clinton Had 'Appetite for Game' Even if Skills Were Lacking," *The News & Observer*, Raleigh, N.C., January 23, 1993, 8C. A number of accounts imply Clinton made the second team for rugby (as if this means Oxford's second team), which he actually did in the far less competitive (in England, at least) sport of basketball, see, for example, Watterson, *The Games Presidents Play*, 313; or Peter Fitzsimons, "The Ultimate World XV," *The Sydney Morning Herald*, June 24, 1995, 66, where Fitzsimmons suggests that Clinton played for the "Greyhounds," which is the nickname given to the Oxford University 2nd XV.

48. Fitzsimons, "The Ultimate World XV," 66.

49. Clinton, *My Life*, 143.

50. Incidentally, both were also quite strong sportsmen. See Chapter 5, above, for more on George H. W. Bush's sporting credentials.

51. George H.W. Bush, *All the Best, George Bush: My Life in Letters and Other Writings* (New York: Scribner, 2014), 21.

52. Bob Dole, *One Soldier's Story: A Memoir* (New York: HarperCollins, 2005), 4.

53. Gary Blonston, "George Bush: Patient Competitor . . . The Life and Times of George Bush, from Preppie to President," *Philadelphia Inquirer*, October 8, 1992, D4.

54. Ellen Warren, "Defined by war, Kansas, D.C. . . . Dole," *Chicago Tribune*, January 14, 1996, 16.

55. Jill Abramson, "Top Republicans Avoided Serving in Vietnam War," *The Charlotte Observer*, September 12, 1992, 2A.

56. George Hostetter, "Stripped of TV, Bulldogs Fans Miss Out," *The Fresno Bee*, October 27, 1992, C1.

57. Ellen Goodman, "Voters Involved in this Election," *The Pantagraph*, November 3, 1992, A9.

58. Hostetter, "Stripped of TV," C1.

59. Clinton, *My Life*, 143.

60. Tom Ronai, "Ruggers Beat Penn, 8–0," *Yale Daily News*, April 9, 1968, 4.

61. "Eli Ruggers Blank Philly Team, 14–0," *Yale Daily News*, April 23, 6.

62. Mangino, "Bush '68: Last Line of Defense."

63. Mangino, "Bush '68: Last Line of Defense."

64. For an example of the sort of attacks made on Kerry's war record, see Michael Dobbs, "Swift Boat Accounts Incomplete," *Washington Post*, August 21, 2004, A1; see also Mark Major and David J. Andersen, "Polls and Elections: Swift Boating Reconsidered: News Coverage of Negative Presidential Ads," *Presidential Studies Quarterly* 46(4) (2016): 891–910.

65. Jim Sleeper, "He's Got the Bad-Boy Vote Sewed Up," *Los Angeles Times*, August 9, 2004, B11.

66. Sleeper, "He's Got the Bad-Boy Vote Sewed Up." For discussion of how this photo contrasted to an image of John Kerry windsurfing, which surfaced around the same time, see Aaron J. Moore and David Dewberry, "The Masculine Image of Presidents as Sporting Figures: A Public Relations Perspective," *Sage Open* 2(3) (2012): 5.

67. Robert Draper, *Dead Certain: The Presidency of George W. Bush* (New York: Free Press, 2008), 131.

68. Lloyd Grove, "The Briefing: Varsity Mendacity?" *Daily News*, May 5, 2004, 24. For reference, 'varsity' generally refers to the top team at a university, and – when it came to Bush and Yale's rugby career – he played for the top team. The fact that the level at which rugby was played was hardly comparable to football, is a different matter.

69. See, for example, Valerie Sperling, *Sex, Politics, and Putin* (New York: Oxford University Press, 2015), 1.

70. David Harrison, "Participant[s] Verify That Rugby's Rough Fun Attractive," *The Kansas City Times*, April 24, 1970, 26. Rugby Union was largely amateur in England until 1995.

71. William Conroy, "Rumson Man Says He Put the Shirts on Politicians' Backs," *Asbury Park Press*, November 21, 1992, C7.

72. Picture appearing alongside the article: William Neikrik, "Clinton Assails GOP Missile Plan," *Albuquerque Journal*, May 23, 1996, A4.

73. Pengelly, "It's in My Blood."

74. Fitzsimons, "The Ultimate World XV," 66.
75. Peter Fitzsimons, "Vantage Point: From Scrum to Fields of Power: A Dream Team of Ex-Rugby Players," *International Herald Tribune*, October 13, 2003, available at: https://www.nytimes.com/2003/10/13/sports/IHT-vantage-point-from-scrum-to-fields-of-power-a-dream-team-of.html.
76. Fitzsimons, "Vantage Point."
77. Many thanks to Rhodri Jeffreys-Jones and Michael Cunningham for their feedback on earlier drafts of this chapter.

8

The Sport of Presidents?
Horse Racing, Politics, and Perception

Michael Hinds and Jonathan Silverman

The Kentucky Derby, which has run continuously since 1875, is the first and most famous leg of the American Triple Crown in horse racing. Nine U.S. presidents have attended the Derby, though only Richard Nixon did so while in office.[1] This indicates both the abiding popularity of the race, but also that it was not a matter of political urgency or expediency for presidents to attend. Indeed, when Kentucky Governor Earle Clements invited Harry Truman to the race in 1949, the president took a rain check. Although Truman recalled enjoying the race in his youth, he did not see it as something he had time for while governing.[2] While well attended across the centuries, the sport has never been popular with all of the people all of the time, and as this chapter goes on to explore, it is hard to gauge how much political capital a president might gain from association with the sport.

Though not constant, horse racing does have a longstanding connection with the presidency that can be traced all the way back to George Washington (1789–97). Washington was a meticulous gambler who regularly attended race meetings, and he was the first of many commanders-in-chief renowned for their love of the turf. In the years that followed, Andrew Jackson (1829–37) retained a keen interest in racing as a presidential racehorse owner, while Gerald Ford (1974–7) went to the Derby more than a dozen times, though not while occupying the Oval Office.

Racing was valuable for Washington in that it afforded space for both pleasure and networking, both political and social. The three presidents discussed here offer variations on that theme. Radio enabled Franklin Delano Roosevelt to benefit from the perception of an unparalleled solidarity with a racehorse in 1938; Richard Nixon went to the 1969 Kentucky Derby to meet with Southern governors and look like a man of the people; and Twitter enabled Donald Trump to use the 2019 Kentucky Derby as a way of reaffirming the anger of his base. The three presidents' interactions with racing echo each other and resonate with their own political styles. Roosevelt's engagement with a national sporting event was part of a larger effort to broadly support events that could raise people's spirits in the Great Depression. Nixon was well known for his political machinations, as were FDR and Washington; his visit to the Kentucky Derby echoed the political networking of Washington as well as the Rooseveltian impulse to connect to a mass audience. By the time of Trump's tweet, mass engagement no longer meant broad appeal; rather, it was a form of fostering outrage among supporters. If racing itself seems almost beside the point of these latter interactions, it also shows how the sport is significant of larger cultural forces. This happens with singular effect when a president takes an interest in a particular horse race and is observed to be doing so, but it also suggests how the sport of horse racing has remained relevant over time, and how it has remained a stage for a president's style and ambition.

FDR: a match race at Pimlico, 1938

In July 1941, less than five months before Pearl Harbor, in 'informal, extemporaneous remarks' to the Volunteer Participation Committee of the Office of Civilian Defense, Franklin Delano Roosevelt urged the committee to help get civilians involved in the war effort: "They honestly are ready to work. So my message to you is: Act as starters of this 'horse race.'" The reference is obviously figurative, and connects with the overwhelming sense that FDR understood that sports language was a type of inclusive rhetoric. It could drive support of his policies but, more importantly, raise the spirits of a struggling country.[3]

Jeffrey K. Tulis defines 'the rhetorical presidency' as a phenomenon based on leadership by words and symbols, where popular or mass rhetoric has become a principal tool of the presidency.[4] Modern presidents necessarily deploy such rhetoric when they engage with horse racing, whether as fans or politicians. On November 1, 1938, Roosevelt became this kind of symbolic actor through a mass-media event that centered on a match race at Pimlico racetrack in Baltimore. Yet he was a minor character compared with the protagonists in that particular drama, the 1937 Triple Crown winner War Admiral and the vastly improved Seabiscuit, a phenomenal winning machine coming out of the supposedly inferior racetracks of the West.

The race was slated to start at 4 p.m. Roosevelt's diary for the day indicates a full day of meetings, including one with the former prime minister of Belgium at 3.30 p.m., followed by a press conference half an hour later.[5] The record shows that this started 10 minutes late, and Roosevelt was quick to let the press know why: "I hope you enjoyed listening to the race as much as I did. I don't think there is any other news."[6] Given the precarity of the situation in Europe, and that it was four days before critical midterm elections, it is possible that Roosevelt was joking about 'any other news.' However, he was also acknowledging the extent to which the race at Pimlico had taken over the public imagination. In this historical moment, the attention of the people appeared to be entirely fixed on the match, whatever was happening elsewhere. As such, Roosevelt was playing the role of a fan, showing solidarity with 40 million Americans who tuned in to the wireless broadcast of the race call, as well as the 40,000 in attendance at the track. Indeed, Roosevelt's administration also coincided with a period when racing was becoming more trusted than ever before across the forty-eight states. This was especially the case when it came to gambling, as state governments increasingly moved to regulate pari-mutuel betting.

Both horses were national stars of the track by the time they clashed at Pimlico in 1938. War Admiral was the thoroughbred son of the outstanding champion Man O'War, and had won all of his fourteen races at three and four years of age on his way to the match.[7] As a son of Hard Tack (and therefore a grandson of Man O'War), Seabiscuit was a reasonably close relative. Despite his solid breeding, Seabiscuit had failed to win in his first seventeen starts and was dismissed as "lazy . . . dead lazy" by his trainer James Fitzsimmons, who allowed him to be sold at the end of his two-year-old career.[8]

By the time the match with War Admiral was set for November 1938, however, Seabiscuit had become a prolific winner for new trainer Tom Smith, ascending to races of the highest class. His rise from mediocrity was undoubtedly inspirational, and the magnitude of his achievement was indexed against his diminutive physical frame. Grantland Rice described him as "a little horse with the heart of a lion and the flying feet of a gazelle."[9] Against the "exquisitely handsome" War Admiral, however, Seabiscuit was the underdog.[10] Yet neither horse in the match was an especially imposing physical specimen in terms of size; nicknamed 'The Mighty Atom,' War Admiral was at most 15.3 hands high, around the same height as his rival.[11] The key differences between the runners were in their life experience, and how that was perceived in terms of class. By virtue of his own breeding, FDR more closely paralleled the supposed aristocrat War Admiral, but his political base, roughly constructed of the working class and/or those who fought for a more equitable country, was pure Seabiscuit, constructed around the idea that hard work would bring rewards, even if you had a rough start in life. Marjorie Garber called this the "cultural baggage" that Seabiscuit carried with him, how his name became in itself a signifier of surviving a life of hard knocks and actual handicaps.[12]

The degree to which FDR cared about such a narrative is unclear. He had expressed a love for racing before, raising the possibility that he was simply a fan, attracted to the race because of the promise of a phenomenal contest. In 1911, when he was a newly-elected state senator for New York, he came under considerable pressure from moral crusaders to eradicate gambling. Even as he listened to their case and ultimately acceded to it, he expressed a sentimental affinity with the turf: "While I am personally devoted to horses and to races I have always felt that a sport cannot be a healthy one if its existence depends on gambling."[13] By the time FDR became president in 1933, his disinclination toward gambling appeared to have diminished, at least in terms of using it to raise tax revenues. By the 1930s, state governments across the nation were playing bookie under Roosevelt's watch, and horse racing, which had been under threat during his cousin Theodore's time as president some years earlier, was in fine form.

Originally imported to the United States from France in the late nineteenth century, the adoption of *pari-mutuel* betting was a vital factor in rebuilding public trust around the sport, but it was a slow process, and it took until 1933 for many states finally to adopt it, excepting the odd holdout such as Oklahoma. Pari-mutuel odds were calculated according to the democratic principle that the horse with the most money bet on it has the lowest odds, and the horses with the highest odds have the least. From the point of view of the government, it did not matter where the money came from, nor did it matter which horse won; pari-mutuel betting was a state-run enterprise that took a percentage of every dollar bet. As the legal scholar Joan S. Howland explains, "In 1933, ten states overcame their previous scruples against the perceived evils of wagering at racing events by legalizing the pari-mutuel system."[14] Horse racing's popularity soared as betting became more thoroughly transparent and accountable than ever before.

Seabiscuit's rise to popularity also has to be understood through the lens of gambling. As well as being a good story, he acquired fans from the beginning because he was an inveterate winner and a relatively reliable investment. It also helped that he raced so frequently and so widely: "Seabiscuit made the rounds of most of the mile tracks between the oceans, and left track records at more than a few."[15] While Seabiscuit campaigned all over the map, War Admiral never raced away from the prestigious tracks of the East Coast. Yet even if Seabiscuit had acquired fans in this way, the betting also affirms that the odds were against him. He went off at 22/10, while War Admiral was a heavy favorite at 1/4.[16] The market directly reflected how many dollars had been bet on each horse. Seabiscuit had to beat both War Admiral and refute the judgment implied by that weight of money.

Pari-mutuel funds helped to finance the modernization of the sport throughout the 1930s, guaranteeing levels of prize money and allowing for the standard use of starting gates, photo-finish cameras, and saliva testing to counter doping.[17] In 1936, the Milky Way Racing Stable of the candy millionaire Ethel Mars was top money earner in thoroughbred racing, making her the first woman to become leading owner in the history of the sport in America.[18] During FDR's presidency, the ascent of racing as a professionalized form of organized leisure was further confirmed through its adoption by Hollywood as a sport of choice. It was the province of celebrities like Bing Crosby, who opened the Del Mar racecourse near San Diego in 1937, and Jack Warner of Warner Brothers, who started up the Hollywood Park racecourse in Inglewood, California the same year.[19] Hollywood invested heavily in horse racing as spectacle, investing in tracks and making films such as Jean Harlow's final picture, *Saratoga* (MGM, 1937) and *Kentucky* (20th Century Fox, 1938), which described a Romeo and Juliet story between rival stud farms in the aftermath of the Civil War, endorsing the idea of racing as a unifying pursuit for the nation. This was a perfect context for performers like Seabiscuit and War Admiral to acquire star quality. When the action of *Kentucky* shifts from the Civil War to the present day, it is signified by the front page of a newspaper announcing a match race between Seabiscuit and War Admiral.

Two days before the match race, Orson Welles had terrorized Americans with his *War of the Worlds* broadcast, a vivid demonstration of the power of the radio medium and the anxiety of the political moment. In direct contrast to his happiness at hearing the race-call from Pimlico, Roosevelt wanted no association with Welles' particular panic. Roosevelt simply replied, "I did not know about it until the next morning," when asked at the November 1 press conference whether he had tuned "into Mars" on Sunday night.[20] FDR knew all about the power of radio. He had become iconic for his radio addresses during the height of the Great Depression of the 1930s. Those so-called 'fireside chats' were, according to Daniel Michael Ryfe, "the first media events – live, pre-planned, extraordinary events that riveted the attention of the nation – in American history."[21] Roosevelt was not just a media producer, however, but a consumer as well. One of his talents was expressing a type of paternalistic empathy, expressed through his advocacy of government programs to help those affected by the depression. It was also important to be *of* the people, not only *for* them. By dismissing the *War of the Worlds* broadcast, he could reassure people that the whole affair had been unworthy of serious attention. Racing provided its own thrills through the radio, but they did not threaten to traumatize the nation. By tuning in with 40 million others to listen to Seabiscuit take on War Admiral, however, he showed a sure instinct for being where the people themselves wanted to be.[22]

The race was also highly anticipated because it had already been postponed more than once, and the business of setting the conditions for the match had been a prolonged political process in themselves. Pre-race negotiations for Pimlico had fixated on arrangements for the start, with War Admiral's connections refusing to use conventional starting gates, thereby de-modernizing the sport for the occasion. Seabiscuit's connections responded by asking for a bell to signal the start of the race and set about training him to respond to that signal. The expectation was that Seabiscuit (a slow starter in his early career) would not be able to cope with War Admiral's early speed, but in reality the race unfolded contrarily. The race was won comfortably by a fast-breaking Seabiscuit, who made all the running and thereby forced War Admiral to race a little wider the whole way round. The Triple Crown winner looked beaten even as the horses entered the final stretch. He never raced again.

Roosevelt did not reveal whether or not he had wanted either Seabiscuit or War Admiral to win, but there was no need for him to do so. War Admiral was a great and gallant champion, and there was no reason to cheer over his defeat, for all of Seabiscuit's stunning superiority. Nor was there necessarily any particular political capital to be gained by appearing partial to one horse (and its 'baggage' over another). As he had averred in 1911, horse racing was a matter of 'devotion' for him, rather than an opportunity to pick a winner. There was plenty to appreciate: the athleticism of both horses, the drama of the race-call, and the impassioned attention of the American populace. Yet the last element was the most valuable, and what Roosevelt most needed. The midterms that took place in the week after the race saw the Democrats lose seats in both the House and the Senate. If there was a feel-good factor after Seabiscuit's win, it does not appear to have benefited FDR's party in the short term. Yet it would be hard to claim that it had done him any harm. An analysis of news outlets in 1938 "revealed that the little horse had drawn more newspaper coverage in 1938 than Roosevelt, who was second."[23] War Admiral had already shown that there was no humiliation in coming second to Seabiscuit.

In one sense, FDR was just listening to a race-call, symbolizing nothing. Yet the extraordinary attention that the Pimlico race commanded was in itself a confirmation of the reputational gains that racing had enjoyed from measured governmental intervention, even as the government benefited financially. This in turn laid the ground for the extraordinary unity of interest that the race inspired among Americans. Racing was now prominent in American life to the degree that the president was unabashed about saying to the press that he had been listening to a horse race in between appointments and did so for pleasure. In this, he was only doing something that millions of others had done at the same time. If the race dramatized questions of class, it also allowed for them to be resolved through the nation doing the collective work of listening to the race, and in the company of their president.

Engaging with this part of history was part of FDR's engagement with sports and recreation more generally. As John Wong writes about the Works Progress Administration (WPA), "between July 1935 and June 1941, the WPA spent $941 million on recreational facilities and $229 million on recreation services to the communities. Among the new facilities were 5,898 athletic fields and playgrounds, 770 swimming pools, 1,667 parks, fairgrounds, and rodeo grounds, and 8,333 recreational buildings."[24] But perhaps Roosevelt is best known in terms of sports for his decision to allow baseball to continue during the Second World War. Writing to baseball commissioner Judge Kenesaw Mountain Landis, Roosevelt reasoned, "I honestly feel that it would be best for the country to keep baseball going. There will be fewer people unemployed and everybody will work longer hours and harder than ever before. And that means that they ought to have a chance for recreation and for taking their minds off their work even more than before."[25] Roosevelt's brief moment of 'sport listening' during the Great Depression thus seems more like an ethos than an aberration. In a world that was chaos and destruction, he saw sport as an oasis.

Nixon: Kentucky Derby, 1969

The race-call from Pimlico had unified Americans and indicated what racing could do in terms of harmoniously concentrating the attention of the masses. At the same time, trying to generate political capital out of horse racing does represent something of a gamble. Events of the racetrack at Pimlico could have hardly gone better from the point of view of spinning a positive American story about triumph over adversity, but a calamity on the track would have made that impossible. If something like that had happened in the race at Pimlico, FDR could at least have exercised the option of not offering a comment. Listening over the radio, rather than being there in person, gave him room to maneuver.

Richard Nixon took such a gamble when he first visited the Kentucky Derby in 1968 on the campaign trail, and when he returned as president a year later to present the trophy to the owner of Majestic Prince. He was the first, and remains the only, sitting president to attend the race at Churchill Downs, where he witnessed the race alongside future presidents Ronald Reagan, who was attending a Republican Governors Association meeting, and Gerald Ford, who gave a speech there.[26] Nicholas Evans Sarantakes suggests that Nixon might have been the first modern sports fan-president: "Nixon exposed core elements of his personality, character, and values when he was in the world of sports. Nixon and sports is the story of political theater, but the president was a real fan, and nothing about his interest was manufactured."[27] Indeed, he had already made an earlier official visit to a racetrack as vice president. In 1957, he presented the Preakness Stakes trophy at Pimlico to the winning connections of Bold Ruler, future Horse of the Year and sire of Secretariat.[28]

Nixon the "real fan" stepped into the Kentucky Derby as a member of the political class, and perhaps a type of new power class, and his visit was significant for both its political insiderism and its designs on public attention. Nixon seemed to see sports as a worthy spectacle, political opportunity, and – perhaps in the same way as FDR had – as a way of seeming *of* the people. He told the *Lexington Herald Leader* that he was "going to savor this race Kentucky style," when asked if he would be sampling a

173

mint julep. At the Derby, he met the governor of Kentucky, Louie B. Nunn, as well as congressional leaders. The Louisville *Courier-Journal* reported that he received positive reviews from the public for attending the event. An unnamed fan from California told the paper: "I think it's a great idea. It shows he's one of the people, and he has a feeling for the common man."[29]

However, as the author of the 'Southern Strategy' to gain Republican votes in the traditional Democratic stronghold of the nation and, more specifically, as a law-and-order candidate whose reputation as a racial conservative was well established, Nixon's presence in Kentucky also drew protests. The Sunday edition of the *Courier-Journal* reported how Nixon's visit was protested by the University of Louisville's Black Student Union at the main gates to the racetrack. Student leader J. Blaine Wilson issued a statement to the newspaper, indicting the race as an absurd distraction from the plurality of social problems endured by the Black community: "If people can journey across the North American continent to witness animals galloping around a track, why is it that no one will journey across town to find living proof that Black People are not figments of an insane imagination?"[30] This dissent had a recent precedent. In 1967, Martin Luther King had declared his intention to stage a protest at the Pegasus Parade on the Thursday before the race, only to withdraw, such was the toxicity of the situation, after the Ku Klux Klan had announced their willingness to provide 'security.'

So, when Hunter S. Thompson accepted a commission to cover the 1970 Derby for *Scanlan's* magazine, along with British cartoonist Ralph Steadman, recent history suggested that the race might be used to symbolize both national unity and discord simultaneously. In the hallucinatory essay that resulted, titled "The Kentucky Derby is Decadent and Depraved," Thompson suggested that the Derby actually showed discord to be the unifying factor in American life. Thompson was a Kentucky native, the self-declared 'Billy the Kid of Louisville.'[31] He was highly aware of the turmoil that had surrounded the race in recent years and reported scaring a tourist by claiming that the city was going to be invaded by "busloads of white crazies."[32]

Rolling Stone has since argued that the essay made the race "a symbol of everything that was wrong with Richard Nixon's

America."[33] Yet Nixon was not present in 1970, and it seems fac-
ile to suggest that every bad vibe in America was traceable to him
at this time. By attending the race while in office, however, Nixon
had activated the race as a direct political metaphor, the force of
which lingered a year later. Going to the Derby as president was
a symbolic action, the problem was that Nixon could not control
what it might symbolize. This was a horse race with an overabun-
dance of context.

For FDR, there was already nationwide interest in the race at
Pimlico; all he had to do was attach himself to it. The fine spectacle then presented by Seabiscuit and War Admiral created a further wave of positivity and goodwill. That race felt like it was at
the center of the universe, and the runners had stardust. The field
for the 1970 Kentucky Derby had some good horses, but they
were not remarkable enough to distract from issues elsewhere. To
show that the race reveals a kind of mania within the American
system, Thompson decides to fuel it in his essay: "The face I was
trying to find in Churchill Downs that weekend was a symbol, in
my own mind, of the whole doomed atavistic culture that makes
the Kentucky Derby what it is."[34] Nixon mostly exists as a kind
of specter in the piece, but his name appears only twice, first, to
set forth a cascade of images of both American aggression abroad
and domestic unrest, culminating with an ominous reference to
Kent State University, where antiwar protestors were fatally shot
two days after the Derby.[35] Thompson's deadline for the piece was
a full week after the race; the carnage and subsequent mayhem of
Kent State percolated into his writing.

In some ways, however, this was a distraction from what
Thompson had anticipated was the real story, "the vicious-drunk
Southern bourbon horseshit mentality that surrounds the Derby
[rather] than in the Derby itself."[36] On his reimagined race day, he
ventures to the infield (the General Admission part of the track),
"that boiling sea of people across the track from the clubhouse,"
which now "looks like a postcard from the Kentucky Derby."[37]
The anarchic crowd there is unaffected by the delusions of the
"whisky gentry" elsewhere: "Total chaos, no way to see the race,
not even the track . . . nobody cares."[38] Yet Thompson prefers this
mayhem to what he finds in the clubhouse: "a pretentious mix of

booze, failed dreams and a terminal identity crisis; the inevitable result of too much inbreeding in a closed and ignorant culture."[39] His jeremiad implies a fraternity of venality between Nixon and his fellow Americans that the Derby exposes; nobody seems to really have any money, yet all of them are playing with it: "Even Richard Nixon is hungry for it. Only a few days before the Derby he said, 'If I had any money I'd invest it in the stock market.' And the market, meanwhile, continued its grim slide."[40]

Thompson presents Nixon as just another sucker in a society that is full of them, even as elite assumptions about class and breeding are sustained. The Derby displays such hypocrisies broadly and grandly, and Thompson matches this with his own contemptuous antisocial fantasies. Thompson was shadowing Nixon in other ways as well. At the time, he was campaigning as an electoral candidate for sheriff of Pitkin County, Colorado (the location of Aspen), and he was looking to affirm his contempt for self-protective elites, the people in Louisville that had let him go to prison as a teenage delinquent, while others "were waltzing because they knew the judge, and . . . he was the poor kid on the other side of the railroad tracks with no dad": "The game was fixed."[41] His takedown of class pretensions can be cross-referenced with Nixon's own modest background and disdain for elites and anxiety over where he belonged, the infield or the clubhouse. Thompson had to balance his disdain for the cynical paranoia of Nixon's worldview with his own version of the same thing.

The seeming dissolution of American society that Nixon used as his cudgel in electoral broadcasts is on full display in Thompson's saturnalia. Both manifest a social conservatism that seems to long for more order, while conjuring up images of anarchy. In his obituary for Nixon, Thompson argued that the president's fundamental duplicity had created a demand for a necessarily new form of writing, the mode that Thompson himself had pioneered with his piece on the Derby: "He seemed so all-American . . . that he was able to slip through the cracks of Objective Journalism. You had to see Subjective to see Nixon clearly, and the shock of recognition was often painful."[42] Nixon was Thompson's gonzo muse.

Nixon was also obsessed with a different kind of elite, "those who set the terms of public debate, who manipulate the symbols, who decide whether nations or leaders will be depicted on 100 million television sets as 'good' or 'bad.'"[43] Of course, Nixon's trepidation of such power had not prevented him from trying to harness it during his campaign, as had been shown in Joe McGinniss' hit book, *The Selling of the President* (1968), which drew attention to the media strategies used in Nixon's successful campaign of that year, fueled by the medium of television.[44]

As if to prove the lapse of the turf into disrepute by the 1970s, the term 'horse race reporting' was now used to characterize negatively how media reportage had moved away from analysis into speculation, promoting spectacle over policy.[45] McGinniss' book showed how this struggle to manage perception had become the central obsession of political business, but was also resigned to the bleak implications of this new reality. After having had enough of the political horse race, McGinniss chose to immerse himself in the real thing. His next book, *The Dream Team* (1972), was a novel about a trip to Hialeah racecourse in Florida.[46] It ends with a promising horse named Joie de Vivre that breaks its leg while winning a race and has to be euthanized. The noble image of the racehorse runs up against the bleak reality of its demise, another sample of the disconnection of illusion and reality that McGinniss had witnessed in Nixon's campaign.

If George Washington's racecourse was a place of relative unity, and Seabiscuit's race-call on radio allowed for solidarity across the classes, the racetrack by Nixon's time is where things fall apart. Thompson barely manages to register who won the 1970 race, as nobody seems to care. The year after Nixon left the White House in disgrace, the brilliant filly Ruffian, fresh from dominating wins in the New York racing scene, broke down in a 1975 match race with the Kentucky Derby champion, Foolish Pleasure, in which she kept running after breaking her leg. Like the fictional Joie de Vivre, Ruffian had to be euthanized. The race was screened to a national television audience. Racing historian Allan Carter confirms that this was a moment of crisis for the sport: "It sickened the country, and they said this really is not the way to go."[47] The symbolism was inevitable, and so was the despair attached to horse racing and to the presidency a year before the nation's bicentenary.

Trump: Kentucky Derby, 2019

Even after what should have been a boom period for the sport in the 1970s – with three Triple Crown winning horses in Secretariat, Seattle Slew, and Affirmed – racing struggled to maintain its audience into the next century. The quality of horses seemed to improve (although it was hard to imagine improving on Secretariat), but increasingly sports media turned to other sports for most of the year, with the Kentucky Derby and the two other Triple Crown races, the Preakness and the Belmont Stakes, being the exceptions. The rise of professional and college football to mass popularity was fueled by the key medium of television, with which racing had a complicated relationship. Races in themselves were entertaining, but the half hour in between them was not. Racing was also in danger of alienating a public that was not prepared to endure the sight of horses getting seriously injured, a constant possibility.

It was not, however, sporting brilliance in the Derby that caught President Donald Trump's attention in 2019. For only the second time in the race's history, the winner was disqualified (the candidate Nixon had been there for the first, when Dancer's Image won in 1968, only to fail a drug test). In the second year of the Trump presidency, Country House was awarded the race after the disqualification of Maximum Security for interference on the turn for home. Trump's tweet gave an unusually lyrical description of the race itself, even as it took the opportunity to inveigh against political correctness:

> The Kentuky [sic] Derby decision was not a good one. It was a rough & tumble race on a wet and sloppy track, actually, a beautiful thing to watch. Only in these days of political correctness could such an overturn occur. The best horse did NOT win the Kentucky Derby – not even close!?[48]

Trump's tweet repeats aspects of Thompson's writing decades before. It scores points, it fulminates about decay, it is reactionary and splenetic. What he inspired was a predictable torrent of commentary, with thousands of others swarming to join the debate he catalyzed. People mocked the president's misspelling of 'Kentuky' (subsequently corrected), they punned on Maximum Security, they commented drily on other contests where the 'real winner' (as in total vote share) did not win, and others remarked archly on how only a sore loser has contempt for the rules.[49] Some of the comments directed at Trump were darker in tone: "Your parents' decision to have you is the worst in U.S. history," while others were approbative and protective: "He's human, typos happen. Have you ever had a typo in a post? Yeah I thought so."[50] The noise was intense, and – as with Thompson – it is fair to say that few really cared who had been declared the winner of the Derby.

Seabiscuit's endeavors inspired an appreciative community, but the twenty-first-century discourse centered on negative commonality, where people congregated on the discourse around the race to disagree.[51] In this moment, Trump was also as much a 'man of the people' as at any time in his presidency, another voice in the rolling event of mass participation that is online culture. Yet the disqualification also demonstrated the ongoing crisis of horse racing in the twenty-first century. For racing to maintain its increasingly tenuous hold on public attention, it has to project an image of a sport that is interested in animal welfare above all else. A *New Yorker* article of May 15, 2021, asked, "Can Horse Racing Survive?," citing the mounting calls for the banning of the sport from activist groups as a reaction to increasing fatalities at racetracks, notably Santa Anita in California. Maximum Security nearly caused a pile-up of horses in the Derby that might have led to several fatalities; in this era, a fatal accident in that race might have finished the job of marginalizing racing that the breakdown of Ruffian began.

Trump was always interested in sports, having routinely tested the waters of sports ownership, but he was most interested in football, not least because of the revenues it promised. He tried repeatedly to become a team owner in the National Football League, but as an anonymous commentator with knowledge of the discussion said, the league thought he was "classless."[52] It is probably not a coincidence that as football rose as a sport, horse racing declined: one was a highly public, modern, and accessible sport enhanced by television, while the other increasingly appeared to be a nostalgic reminder of earlier times. Racehorses also do not offer much of a guaranteed return on investment, unless you breed from them. Its appeal to Trump the businessman was limited.

That said, a *Washington Post* story in 2017 reported a brief venture by Trump into racehorse ownership during the 1980s, in which he allegedly had a horse named after himself, only to renege on the deal after a training accident led to the horse being retired without running a race.[53] It is not clear whether Trump actually ever bought the horse, but records confirm that a colt called D. J. Trump did exist, and was sold at auction in 1987.[54] Unraced, he fathered fifteen horses in a brief stud career, some of whom bore Trump-related names, including A Date with Marla and Trump Who.[55]

Trump's entrance into the world of horse racing should have been an easy move for him, because class in horse racing can be either a stylish performance or an ability to accumulate and spend assets on a large scale. Yet the indications are that Trump does not see much value in racing, reputational or otherwise. What prompted Trump's intervention on Twitter was ephemeral, the opportunity to use the Derby, a national and international event, to grab a headline; but this only works if the race itself generates controversy. Trump fed on racing's bad publicity.

Trump's presidency can be seen on Twitter as simply moving from one temporary excitement to another, a politics of constant shifts in attention. Yet it is not just presidents who covet attention, and horse racing has a lot to contend with in order to promote itself. It is hard to determine whether or not the sport's leadership wanted the kind of attention that Trump gave racing, as commentators tended to focus only on the merits of the decision in sporting terms. Race reporter Mike Battaglia said to CNN: "If you don't follow the rules you harm the integrity of the whole sport."[56] In *The Bloodhorse*, Greg Hall wrote a considered and lengthy essay in which he endorsed the result of the enquiry but indicated issues with the transparency of the entire process.[57] For some, the controversy represented an opportunity for racing to reform itself effectively. In *The Sydney Morning Herald*, Michael Cox admitted that "You know when Trump is tweeting about a result of a horse race that we have reached peak outrage"; yet he also argued that if "even Trump" could see that the best horse in the race had been disqualified, then it was time for American racing to review its rules.[58] These commentators indicated that American racing needed to create a national horse racing authority with rules and laws that were cognate with jockey clubs and administrations elsewhere in the world. This would put an end to the apparent nonsense of a horse being banned in one state and eligible to run in another, and to the rights of states like Kentucky to administer their own version of the rules of the sport. Out of the sobering chaos of the disqualification, American racing was asked to contemplate a federalist and internationalist approach to governance (one reform that the progressive 1930s had not introduced).

Outside of the domain of racing, Trump's tweet only fostered familiar controversy about the typically loud and uninformed nature of his remarks: "that the President of the United States ascribed this whole thing to the damage done by political correctness suggests a monomania that is, at minimum, very weird and, at most, deeply worrisome."[59] In another respect, it was far from weird. Trump saw the opportunity to remind followers on Twitter of his broad antagonism to political correctness (however that might be defined), and friends and enemies reacted predictably. The horse race was negligible; the tweet was everything.

After his defeat in the 2020 election, and the suspension of his Twitter account after the events at the Capitol on January 6, 2021, Trump tried to repeat the trick of using the Derby to make a kind of media comeback. On May 9, 2021, Medina Spirit, a tenacious winner of the previous weekend's Kentucky Derby, had tested positive for a banned anti-inflammatory drug, betamethasone. Trainer Bob Baffert announced that the horse was a victim of 'cancel culture,' perhaps taking his cue from Trump's denunciation of political correctness at the 2019 Derby.[60] Trump took another line on his personal website, which many media outlets (although not all) could not resist reporting:

So now even our Kentucky Derby winner, Medina Spirit, is a junky. This is emblematic of what is happening to our Country. The whole world is laughing at us as we go to hell on our Borders, our fake Presidential Election, and everywhere else![61]

181

This was rhetorical presidency (or ex-presidency) at its best, seizing upon a ready-made crisis to repeat a litany of tropes and motifs that had defined his time in office. Another Derby spoiled allowed for another show from the former president.

For Washington, racing was mainly about the horses; for many of his successors, it was everything but. FDR was able to attach himself in the public mind to a singular event in which the American public was focused entirely on a horse race. Even though the horses were bona fide stars and the attention was warranted, what really was politically significant was the mass mobilization of interest that the race represented, the proof of national unity that it suggested. FDR's model of government gave racing unprecedented levels of credibility and popularity, a context in which Seabiscuit's heroics could become the biggest news story of 1938. Nixon also understood that what was happening on track was potentially of national and public significance and became the first sitting president to attend the race. However, he did not have a Seabiscuit or a War Admiral to generate affection and awe. Nixon was the main attraction at his Derby but also a focus for disaffection and distrust. As a political cipher and a type of cultural Rorschach Blot, Nixon at the Derby took on whatever meaning its spectators and commentators wanted: networker behind the scenes, man of the people, symbol of cynicism and darkness. In the news cycles of the digital age, where even Seabiscuit's triumphs are viewed with a suspicion that they might have been fixed, racing has been most visible when it is most enmired in scandal.[62] Trump contributed to keeping that scandal in the public, only adding to the image problem that racing has haplessly acquired in the twenty-first century. In the Breeder's Cup Classic of 2007, another brilliant racehorse was fatally injured in the finishing stretch and had to be humanely destroyed. His name was George Washington.

Notes

1. "US Presidents are Fans of the Kentucky Derby," Kentucky Derby Museum Blog, available at: https://www.derbymuseum.org/Blog/Article/35/US-Presidents-are-fans-of-the-Kentucky-Derby.

2. "Letter to Governor Earle Clements," Truman Library, President's Personal File (PPF) 3550, Box 667.

3. "The President Explains Our Policy Concerning the Exportation of Oil to Japan: Informal, Extemporaneous Remarks to Volunteer Participation Committee of the Office of Civilian Defense," July 24, 1941, 277–281; Samuel I. Rosenman, *The Public Papers and Addresses of Franklin D. Roosevelt, Vol. 1941* (New York: Harper, 1950), 277–281.

4. Jeffrey K. Tulis, *The Rhetorical Presidency* (Princeton, NJ: Princeton University Press, 2017), 4.

5. "November 1st, 1938," Franklin Roosevelt Day by Day, FDR Library, available at: http://www.fdrlibrary.marist.edu/daybyday/daylog/november-1st-1938.

6. Transcript, Press Conference, November 1, 1938, FDR Library, available at: http://www.fdrlibrary.marist.edu/_resources/images/pc/pc0071.pdf, 44.

7. "War Admiral," *American Classic Pedigrees*, available at: http://www.americanclassicpedigrees.com/war-admiral.html.

8. Laura Hillenbrand, *Seabiscuit: Three Men and a Racehorse* (London: Fourth Estate, 2002), 44.

9. Lee Congdon, *Legendary Sports Writers of the Golden Age: Grantland Rice, Red Smith, Shirley Povich, and W.C. Heinz* (Lanham, MD: Rowman & Littlefield, 2017), 30.

10. Congdon, *Legendary Sports Writers of the Golden Age.*

11. "War Admiral," "Seabiscuit," *American Classic Pedigrees*, available at: http://www.americanclassicpedigrees.com/war-admiral.html.

12. Marjorie Gerber, "Heart and Hoof," *London Review of Books* 23(19) (October 4, 2001), available at: https://www.lrb.co.uk/the-paper/v23/n19/marjorie-garber/heart-and-hoof.

13. Letter to Reverend Charles Gilbert Mallery, Rhinebeck, February 17, 1911, Box 20, RP; quoted in Alfred B. Rollins, "Young F.D.R and the Young Crusaders," *New York History* 37(1) (1956): 6.

14. Joan S. Howland, "Let's Not Spit the Bit in Defense of 'The Law of the Horse': The Historical and Legal Development of American Thoroughbred Racing," *Marquette Sports Law Review* 473 (2004), available at: https://www.animallaw.info/article/lets-not-spit-bit-defense-law-horse-historical-and-legal-development-american-thoroughbred#FNF176299101460.

15. Walter Wellesley 'Red' Smith, "A Horse You Had to Like," *New York Herald Tribune*, May 20, 1947, available at: https://www.pbs.org/wgbh/americanexperience/features/seabiscuits-obituary.

16. "Seabiscuit," *Encyclopedia Britannica*, available at: https://www.britannica.com/topic/Seabiscuit.

17. Roger Longrigg, *The History of Horse Racing* (London: Macmillan, 1972), 282.

18. "Sport, Luck and Mrs. Mars," *Time*, January 4, 1937, available at: https://web.archive.org/web/20120125033852/http://www.time.com/time/magazine/article/0,9171,762342,00.html.

19. Alan Shuback, *Hollywood at the Races* (Lexington: University Press of Kentucky: 2019), 40–62, 63–78.

20. Transcript, Press Conference, November 1, 1938, FDR Library, available at: http://www.fdrlibrary.marist.edu/_resources/images/pc/pc0071.pdf.

21. David Michael Ryfe, "From Media Audience to Media Public: A Study of Letters Written in Reaction to FDR's Fireside Chats," *Media, Culture & Society* 23(6) (001): 767.

22. Roosevelt's Rural Electrification Administration itself could be credited for providing Seabiscuit with his adoring crowd, as Hillenbrand contends: "By 1935, when Seabiscuit began racing, two thirds of the nation's homes had radio." See Hillenbrand, *Seabiscuit*, 142.

23. Hillenbrand, *Seabiscuit*, 309.

24. John Wong, "FDR and the New Deal on Sport and Recreation," *Sport Review* 29(2) (1998): 182.

25. Gerald Bazer and Steven Culbertson, "When FDR Said 'Play Ball,'" *Prologue* 34(1) (2002): 34.

26. Sara Dacus, "Byroad to the Kentucky Derby: The Presidents," twinspires.com, March 3, 2020, available at: https://edge.twinspires.com/racing/byroad-to-the-kentucky-derby-the-presidents.

27. Nicholas Evans Sarantakes, *Fan in Chief: Richard Nixon and American Sports, 1969–1974* (Lawrence: University Press of Kansas, 2019), 2–3.

28. "President Richard Nixon at the Kentucky Derby," *Lexington Herald Leader*, available at: https://kyphotoarchive.com/2017/05/03/president-richard-nixon-at-the-kentucky-derby-1969.

29. Quoted in Sarantakes, *Fan in Chief*, 10–11.

30. Emily Bingham, "The Collision of the 1969 Derby, Richard Nixon and the University of Louisville Student Union," louisville.com, April 23, 2019, available at: https://archive.louisville.com/content/collision-1969-derby-richard-nixon-and-university-louisville-black-student-union. For an assessment of Nixon's policies and practices on race relations, see Hugh Davis Graham, "Richard Nixon and

Civil Rights: Explaining an Enigma," *Presidential Studies Quarterly* 26(1) (1996): 93–106.

31. Hunter S. Thompson, interview with Wayne Ewing, in *Breakfast With Hunter* (Carbondale, CO: Wayne Ewing Films, 2004).

32. Hunter S. Thompson, "The Kentucky Derby is Decadent and Depraved," in David Halbestram (ed.), *The Best American Sports Writing of the Century* (Boston, MA: Houghton Mifflin, 1999), 358.

33. Dan Epstein, "Remembering Hunter S. Thompson's Fear & Loathing at the Kentucky Derby," *Rolling Stone,* May 11, 2016, available at: https://www.rollingstone.com/tv/tv-news/remembering-hunter-s-thompsons-fear-loathing-at-the-kentucky-derby-161098.

34. Epstein, "Remembering Hunter S. Thompson's Fear & Loathing at the Kentucky Derby," 363.

35. Epstein, "Remembering Hunter S. Thompson's Fear & Loathing at the Kentucky Derby," 357.

36. Timothy Denevi, "Hunter S. Thompson, James Salter, and a Drunken Trip to Kentucky," *Lithub,* October 30, 2018, available at: https://lithub.com/hunter-s-thompson-james-salter-and-a-drunken-trip-to-kentucky.

37. Denevi, "Hunter S. Thompson, James Salter, and a Drunken Trip to Kentucky," 358.

38. Denevi, "Hunter S. Thompson, James Salter, and a Drunken Trip to Kentucky," 367–368.

39. Denevi, "Hunter S. Thompson, James Salter, and a Drunken Trip to Kentucky," 368.

40. Denevi, "Hunter S. Thompson, James Salter, and a Drunken Trip to Kentucky," 362.

41. Jann S. Wenner and Corey Seymour, *Gonzo: The Life of Hunter S. Thompson* (New York: Back Bay Books, 2008), 19–20.

42. "He was a Crook," *The Atlantic,* June 6, 1994, available at: https://www.theatlantic.com/magazine/archive/1994/07/he-was-a-crook/308699.

43. Richard Nixon, "Nixon: An Elite Without Will Threatens America's Future," *Washington Post,* April 20, 1980, available at: https://www.washingtonpost.com/archive/opinions/1980/04/20/nixon-an-elite-without-will-threatens-americas-future/36c78160-7b81-4f59-a6a7-872f8409c5b5.

44. Joe McGinniss, *The Selling of the President* (London: Penguin, 1970).

45. C. Anthony Broh, "Horse-Race Journalism: Reporting the Polls in the 1976 Presidential Election," *Public Opinion Quarterly* 44(4) (1980): 514–529.

46. Joe McGinniss, *The Dream Team* (New York: Random House, 1972).
47. Christine Jackson, "After the Finish," *Baltimore Magazine*, November 2018, available at: https://www.baltimoremagazine.com/section/historypolitics/eighty-years-ago-seabiscuit-war-admiral-gripped-nation-pimlico-race-course.
48. "Donald Trump Blames Political Correctness for Kentucky Derby Chaos," *The Guardian*, May 5, 2019, available at: https://www.theguardian.com/sport/2019/may/05/donald-trump-kentucky-derby-country-house-maximum-security.
49. Ana Navarro, Twitter post, May 4, 2019, available at: https://twitter.com/ananavarro/status/1124814643325800448?lang=en.
50. Jeffrey Guterman, Twitter post, May 5, 2019; Ian Pollard, Twitter post, May 5, 2019, both available at: https://www.thetrumparchive.com.
51. Tom Rosentiel, "How a Different America Responded to the Great Depression," Pew Research Center, December 14, 2010, available at: https://www.pewresearch.org/2010/12/14/how-a-different-america-responded-to-the-great-depression.
52. Tim Marcin, "Trump's NFL Fight Dates Back to His Failed USFL Experiment in the '80s," *Newsweek,* September 25, 2017.
53. Will Hobson, "The Sad Saga of Thoroughbred D.J. Trump, Donald Trump's Lone Foray into Horse Racing," *Washington Post*, May 17, 2019, available at: https://www.washingtonpost.com/news/sports/wp/2017/05/19/the-sad-saga-of-thoroughbred-d-j-trump-donald-trumps-lone-foray-into-horse-racing.
54. "D. J. Trump KY," *Equibase*, available at: https://www.equibase.com/profiles/Results.cfm?type=Horse&refno=1066132&registry=T&rbt=TB.
55. "A Date with Marla," *Equibase*, available at: https://www.equibase.com/profiles/Results.cfm?type=Horse&refno=1295677&registry=T; "Trump Who," *Equibase*, available at: https://www.equibase.com/profiles/Results.cfm?type=Horse&refno=1289361&registry=T.
56. Roy Hodgetts, "Kentucky Derby Controversy Swirls as President Trump Weighs in and Owner Plans Appeal," *CNN*, May 7, 2019, available at: https://edition.cnn.com/2019/05/06/sport/kentucky-derby-maximum-security-country-house-appeal-president-trump-spt-intl/index.html.
57. Greg Hall, "Kentucky Derby Opinion: Right Call, Wrong Process," *The Bloodhorse*, May 5, 2019.

58. Michael Cox, "Right Call, Wrong Rule," *Sydney Morning Herald*, May 7, 2019, available at: https://www.smh.com.au/sport/racing/right-call-wrong-rule-how-dud-derby-decision-helps-harmonisation-20190507-p51kyn.html.

59. Chris Cillizza, "Donald Trump's 'Kentucky Derby' Tweet Makes Literally No Sense," *CNN*, May 6, 2019, available at: https://www.cnn.com/2019/05/06/politics/donald-trump-kentucky-derby/index.html.

60. Tom Lutz, "Trainer: Kentucky Derby Winner Faces Disqualification Owing to 'Cancel Culture,'" *The Guardian*, May 10, 2021, available at: https://www.theguardian.com/sport/2021/may/10/bob-baffert-medina-spirit-kentucky-derby-horse-racing-cancel-culture-disqualification.

61. Mayank Agaarwal, "Trump Mocked for Bizarre Statement Calling Kentucky Derby Winning Horse a 'Junky' and Blaming Biden," *The Independent*, May 10, 2021, available at: https://www.independent.co.uk/news/world/americas/us-politics/trump-medina-spirit-kentucky-derby-b1844700.html.

62. Bill Christine, "Ending is Seen as a Real Stretch," *Los Angeles Times*, November 20, 2002, available at: https://www.latimes.com/archives/la-xpm-2002-nov-20-sp-seabiscuit20-story.html.

9

Emissaries of Toughness: How Coaches Teamed with U.S. Presidents to Politicize College Football during the Cold War

Andrew McGregor

Football became a national game unlike ever before during the 1950s and 1960s. Presidents Dwight Eisenhower, John F. Kennedy, and Richard Nixon helped to transform the game into a national obsession and its leaders into critical figures in America's international and domestic conflicts against deviant insubordination, soft youth, and leftist ideas. The game represented discipline and toughness; it taught obedience and loyalty. College football leaders also recognized their outsized influence on society. Coaches cultivated relationships with political leaders, and football organizations developed close ties with politicians to establish the sport as an essential element of Cold War culture, which would eventually give rise to the United States' deeply partisan Culture Wars in the 1970s and 1980s. In their statements, these presidents extolled the virtues of college football and its coaches, polarizing the game into an institution that stood opposite both the ills of communism and, later, the perceived excesses of liberalism.

As the scholar and former professional football player Michael Oriard has argued, college football has always been political. Countless scholars have made similar arguments, pointing to Theodore Roosevelt's efforts to preserve the game, its place in military training during the world wars, and the sport's role in assimilating ethnic minorities into American society.[1] The Cold War era, however, made college football even *more* political. "During the 1960s football became marked for the radical Left as fascist and imperialist and for the radical Right as superpatriotic," Oriard explained.[2] A number of factors account for and explain this transformation, including the emergence of the Civil Rights Movement, anticonformist groups, and the rise of the New Left. Yet college football leaders and U.S. presidents also aided in this cultural development. This chapter explores how the sport's leaders further politicized the game by selectively honoring presidents and using presidential rhetoric to attach political meaning to the game.

Between 1958 and 1975, the National Football Foundation (NFF) and the American Football Coaches Association (AFCA) presented awards to several presidents, providing them with a platform to reflect on the game's importance to American culture, particularly during the height of the Cold War. These presidents repeatedly remarked on the impact of football on domestic life and its importance in instilling physical toughness, discipline, and preparing future generations for a competitive world. From Herbert Hoover, Eisenhower, and Kennedy, to Nixon, Gerald Ford, and Ronald Reagan, the past, present, and future American presidents honored during these years saw the game as essential to the American way of life. In fact, by the late 1960s, they increasingly viewed the game as central to maintaining order amid the rise of the New Left, which opposed the war in Vietnam and advocated for a more pluralistic society that provided equal rights protections for a larger number of Americans. In short, football became a political technology of Cold War America to promote subordination amid the rising rights revolution that accompanied the birth of 'identity politics.'

Eisenhower, Kennedy, and Nixon stand apart as the fiercest proponents and defenders of football. In addition to their personal experience playing the game, they developed close relationships with college football coaches, appointed former players to important political positions, and viewed the game as central to not only leadership, but to the collective ability of American society to maintain order and defeat communists.[3] Fitness and toughness became keywords in these debates. Kennedy famously bemoaned "The Soft American" in *Sports Illustrated*, and charged Bud Wilkinson, the University of Oklahoma football coach and director of his President's Council on Physical Fitness, to interrogate

189

the "Shape of the Nation" in an episode of the Department of the Army's *Big Picture* television series.[4]

While not the only political coach, and far from the most conservative, Wilkinson helps to illustrate the politicization of the sport during the Cold War era. His success in the 1950s brought him into close contact with Eisenhower and Nixon before developing a national physical fitness program under Kennedy. In 1964, he rejoined the Republican Party and ran for the U.S. Senate, relying on Nixon and Eisenhower for endorsements. Despite losing, Wilkinson remained in politics and later joined Nixon's administration as a special consultant. His political entanglements in the 1980s have received less attention. During that decade, he supported Ronald Reagan and received appointments to several commissions and boards, including the Board of Visitors of the U.S. Air Force Academy. Wilkinson's influence as the leading college football coach of the 1950s, the face of American fitness policy in the early 1960s, and a college football commentator for ABC Sports from the 1960s through the 1980s provided him with an immense amount of cultural authority. He led coaching clinics and served in leadership positions within the AFCA and on the U.S. Commission on Olympic Sports.[5] In these roles, he helped to establish college football coaches as emissaries of toughness that complemented Cold War fitness policies and provided commentary on the vigor of America's youth. Indeed, the social commentary by Wilkinson's coaching peers – as well as presidents themselves – used the rhetoric of toughness to transform college football into an increasingly politically partisan game.

The politics of toughness: football and the 'muscle gap'

Although Oriard rightly observed that "toughness has no politics," he conceded that "it acquired political resonance in the 1950s and 1960s."[6] The creation of the President's Council on Youth Fitness (PCYF) by Eisenhower in 1956 provides one of the first indicators of political interest in the rhetoric of toughness for Cold War purposes. Established in reaction to a study by Dr. Hans Kraus and Dr. Sonja Weber that revealed American children lagged behind their European counterparts in physical ability, the council embarked on a series of public relations campaigns to promote physical fitness as a means to improve the conditioning of youth.[7] Vice President Richard Nixon initially led the council, helping to shape its early activities as alarmist rhetoric surrounding the so-called 'muscle gap' reverberated throughout the country.

At a National Collegiate Athletic Association meeting in April 1958, Nixon emphatically endorsed competitive sports for the health of the nation in a speech he delivered to football coaches. "Today our young people must face the realities of a tough and challenging world," he explained, "We need stamina of mind and body not in a few but in many."[8] For Nixon, competitive sports provided determination, teamwork, discipline, and "the fighting spirit" that young Americans needed to be successful.[9]

Concerns about youth fitness – which then included personal comportment and not just physical ability – continued and remained as a central issue for President Kennedy following his election in 1960. The behavioral component to fitness emphasized the necessity of discipline and character education, not just exercise, and established team sports as essential in developing the whole child for success in Cold War American society. As politicians and coaches became increasingly worried about the conduct of college students during the late 1960s, sports, and particularly football, served as useful tool for developing toughness and cultivating fitness.

As sport sociologist Jeffrey Montez de Oca has explained, "muscle gap anxieties were infused with assumptions regarding race, gender, and national destiny in the context of changing class relations."[10] They created the conditions for the construction of a Cold War worldview that framed American youth as lacking, confounding fears of generational change with U.S. national security. Attacks on traditional centers of authority were viewed as challenges to the American way of life. In defense of American values, U.S. presidents turned to football coaches and physical educators first to help fight the Cold War and then to stem the tide of social unrest. By the late 1960s, college football stood as a beacon of toughness. Articulating this view, Washington State University coach Jim Sweeney explained, "football and athletics are a fortress that has held the wall against radical elements."[11] To him, and others, college football provided the antidote to New

Left protests and instruction on the type of fitness essential for America to win the Cold War.

The development of a fitness policy that blended physical activity and behavioral characteristics under Eisenhower and Kennedy is only half of the story. The NFF courted the influence of presidents and provided a platform for them to further link the game with the destiny of the republic. Presidents lent their authority to the foundation and endorsed the sport as vital for America's future. As this chapter shows, the NFF, college football coaches, and U.S. presidents worked together to politicize college football.

Founded in 1947 to promote the sport of football and honor its legacy, the NFF got off to a slow start. Plans for its College Football Hall of Fame took several decades to develop. The foundation inducted its first class in 1951 before reorganizing in 1954 and adding a second class. Yet it did not have a physical building until much later. The development of the Hall of Fame required fundraising. Beginning in 1958, the NFF hosted an annual dinner where they presented a series of awards. The $50-per-plate dinner attracted media coverage and money for their efforts.[12]

The main attraction for the event was a keynote speech delivered by the recipient of their annual Gold Medal award. It served as the foundation's highest individual award. A year later, the MacArthur Bowl trophy for the country's top team and the Earl 'Red' Blaik Scholarship program for scholar-athletes joined the Gold Medal award, transforming the event into a major ceremony. These awards established the dinner as a significant event that attracted press coverage and popular discussion. This reflected the foundation's strategy to cultivate relationships with national leaders, establish their authority over college football history, and raise money.[13]

The National Football Foundation honored political and military leaders – especially those with experience connected to football – in its early events. President Eisenhower received the first Gold Medal in 1958 and spoke at the awards dinner. John Kennedy, Herbert Hoover, Richard Nixon, Ronald Reagan, and Gerald Ford all received the foundation's Gold Medal between 1960 and 1973. General Douglas MacArthur and former Army football coach Earl 'Red' Blaik were awarded the Gold Medal in 1959 and 1966, respectively. Former Vice Admiral John H. 'Babe' Brown served as the foundation's president beginning in 1954.[14] Each of these men brought respect and prestige to the organization and helped to promote the game by articulating its value to American life.

Upon his appointment as the foundation's president, Vice Admiral Brown explained its goals: "We want to strengthen and honor the sport of football and assure its rightful place in the academic and national scene. We want to build a closer alliance between football and our nation's educators."[15] Chester LaRoche, chairman of the NFF's board, further outlined the importance of the sport to America and why the foundation was necessary. "There is a crisis in our country's affairs in which football spirit and training should play a part," he said in 1956.[16] Arguing that football developed the holistic type of fitness identified by the PCYF, LaRoche continued: "Home and the church make their fundamental contributions. But football, too, is one of the principal organized training grounds of national spirit and morale."[17] Historian Kurt Kemper has further suggested that LaRoche equated critiques of football with threats to U.S. security and its future.[18] He did little to hide his concerns or his politics, openly speculating that the University of Chicago had become "overloaded with beatniks, leftists, and undesirables" in the years after the school discontinued football.[19] Through these activities and public statements, LaRoche and the NFF sought to politicize the sport and align it with Cold War values.

Eisenhower offered further reflection on the role of fitness in American life during his speech at the organization's first awards dinner in 1958. "We know that fitness is more than a healthy body," he explained, "It is more than an alert, disciplined mind. Fitness is the sum of all values which enable a man to act effectively in his nation's behalf in this great contest."[20] In this analogy, he equated the Cold War with a long contest between the United States and the Soviet Union that required every American to contribute to the team effort. Football played an essential role, he suggested, because it prepared Americans for successful careers by developing this holistic version of fitness.

Former President Hoover, who was honored with the Gold Medal two years later, continued the discussion. He suggested that the moral benefits of football extended to more than just the game's participants. "It radiates to the huge crowds at college games; it radiates to the audience at all other games," he said.[21] "From true sportsmanship radiates moral inspiration to our whole nation," he concluded.[22] Hoover's views reinforced the emerging Cold War embrace of college football and further positioned the sport as a political technology that cultivated the fitness of the nation whether Americans were participants or consumers. Montez de Oca describes the emphasis on consumption that became increasingly tied to college football during the 1950s as a means of "teaching and performing Cold War citizenship."[23] Once television emerged, it extended the pedagogical lessons to people's homes and further encouraged capitalist consumption with commercial advertisements. The spectacle of college football then created disciplined and loyal citizens, making it an integral component of the American way of life.

Hoover's insistence that watching football benefited the country required teaching Americans how to watch the game. Bud Wilkinson, the most successful coach during the 1950s, shared his expertise in the *Saturday Evening Post* as well as on his own television show.[24] In both his article and on air, he carefully explained plays as well as offensive and defensive systems by using diagrams and plain-spoken language. Wilkinson hoped to educate fans so they could enjoy the game, but conceded, "you don't have to know much about the science of football to thrill to the sight of two teams fighting their hearts out to win."[25] Like Hoover, he believed that "spirit is what makes football the exciting spectacle it is," describing it as "the vital factor that sometimes enables underdogs to win."[26] As such, football viewership cultivated a type of mental fitness in American citizens. By serving as a reminder that hard work and toughness can sometimes prevail over superior tactics or physical ability, football provided inspiration that affirmed American might.

The following year President John F. Kennedy received the foundation's Gold Medal, continuing the trend of honoring presidents. An outspoken advocate for physical fitness, a junior varsity football player at Harvard, and an occasional participant in family touch football games, Kennedy disagreed with Hoover's consumerist viewpoint. In his speech, Kennedy suggested that "we have become more and more, not a nation of athletes, but a nation of spectators."[27] Though averse to the culture of spectatorship, Kennedy, like Eisenhower, challenged citizens to view themselves as members of the American team.

Participation, both in fitness programs and in other Cold War era initiatives became a staple of his speeches. Football frequently served as metaphor, allowing him to rhetorically connect with everyday Americans. For example, Kennedy famously asked, "Why does Rice [University] play Texas?" in a speech outlining the U.S. plan to go to the moon, likening the lofty goal to that of a small team seeking out a difficult challenge.[28] Football provided not just inspiration, but also a reminder of the toughness Americans possessed in the face of obstacles.

But football also served as more than rhetoric for Kennedy. He consumed the sport like a fan, venturing to bowl games and visiting locker rooms. Shortly after his election and before being inaugurated, he attended the 1961 Orange Bowl between the University of Missouri and the Naval Academy. Clearly cheering for Navy, the president-elect displayed his loyalties with groans and encouragement. The *New York Times* report on the event included photos of him clapping and anxiously biting his fingernails, and commentary on how Kennedy compared the team's strategies with his own family's touch football exploits.[29] His enjoyment of the game reflected his own participation, but also emphasized his view of football as a key component of his fitness policy.

A week after the Orange Bowl, Robert Kennedy, who served as John's campaign manager, spoke to the AFCA at their annual awards dinner, where he further outlined his brother's vision of physical fitness that relied on football coaches to instill toughness. "You here, and those you represent, can make a major difference in the future health of America," he said.[30] As leaders of a "particularly American game," who are "respected and admired in the communities and localities of your states," he believed that coaches had the "power to exert a tremendous influence for good in this country."[31] More than simple flattery, Kennedy sought to enlist coaches as allies – emissaries of toughness – to tackle America's fitness problem and address what he described as "fearful dangers" facing the nation.[32] While he left the precise nature of those dangers up for interpretation, coaches enthusiastically joined the effort. By the late 1960s, college football coaches increasingly saw themselves as deputies charged with defending American values amid generational changes and the New Left.

The Kennedys further connected their fitness vision with football coaches when they named Bud Wilkinson as director of the reorganized President's Council on Physical Fitness (PCPF). His name immediately emerged as their top choice. In fact, according to an internal memo, likely from January 1961, Kennedy's advisors recommended "a man of the type of Bud Wilkinson."[33] They unveiled the new council at a one-day conference on Youth Fitness, hosted by the Department of Health Education and Welfare (HEW) in February. Addressing the conference, the president remained steadfast in his vision, declaring "We want a nation of participants in the vigorous life."[34] Wilkinson agreed, remarking upon his appointment that "Pure spectatorship is a vicarious thrill all right, but participation is more beneficial, win or lose."[35]

The selection of Wilkinson did more than politicize the game by solidifying the connection between football and fitness. It gave the council authority due to his notoriety and experience. Wilkinson won the AFCA 'Coach of the Year Award' in 1948 and served as the organization's president in 1958. While his Oklahoma Sooners amassed forty-seven consecutive wins from 1953 to 1957, Wilkinson launched the first televised coach's show, which inspired his own syndicated series of sports shows aimed at America's youth. He also directed annual 'Coach of the Year' clinics that brought him into close contact with high school and college football coaches. Wilkinson provided the PCPF with direct access to the coaching infrastructure that Robert Kennedy saw as essential for its success.

Like Eisenhower, Hoover, Kennedy, and his coaching peers, Wilkinson also saw football as key in developing youth and fighting the Cold War. On an episode of his television show that aired in 1958, he explained why boys should play football, emphasizing both the physical and behavioral elements of fitness needed in America: "Football is a team game. It teaches a boy to subordinate his own individual ambitions and desires in order to help the other men get the job at hand accomplished in first-rate fashion."[36] He noted that the sport prepared youth for a competitive society and military service, further justifying its utility in developing fitness.

"I believe that a game that teaches them rough and tumble physical competition is the greatest possible training that a boy can have during the years of his development," he concluded.[37] To be sure, few recognized these as political statements at the time. Until his appointment as director of the PCPF, Wilkinson and other coaches did not explicitly engage in politics. During the early 1960s, however, John and Robert Kennedy actively courted Wilkinson and enlisted the help of other football coaches. They established college football and its leaders as political actors.

The growth of partisan football

The Cold War presented an ideal crisis for the marriage of football and politics. Fitness and toughness aligned the sport with public policy for the health of the country. LaRoche and the NFF recognized this early on. Their reliance on military leaders and presidents hastened the politicization of football as the sport's leaders worried about de-emphasis, insubordination caused by generational changes, and other challenges to traditional centers of authority. While 'muscle gap' rhetoric and concerns over physical fitness nurtured these political relationships as the 1960s dragged on, behavioral fitness focused on the personal comportment of college students, and athletes increasingly took center stage. Protesting students and those who refused to conform to the rigid hierarchies of the sport led to growing concerns among college football coaches and conservative politicians.[38] Presidents even worried openly about the state of American youth and college campuses.

Compared with his predecessors, Lyndon Johnson remained largely absent from the honors, awards, and statements about football and fitness. Although the AFCA presented him with their Tuss McLaughry Award in 1966, the more conservative NFF never honored him.[39] His remarks to the AFCA followed similar patterns to those of previous presidents and echoed Robert Kennedy's focus on the role of coaches in improving society. "You are developing the leaders today on the athletic field who will be the leaders tomorrow in the world," he commented.[40] Despite these similarities, Johnson did not possess the same football bona fides as Eisenhower or Kennedy, and – while he noted his affinity for the University of

197

Texas Longhorns and his anxieties about Texas coach Darrell Royal potentially leaving for Oklahoma – he never presented himself as an enthusiastic fan.

As sports journalist Robert Lipsyte recounted in a 1968 column, Johnson struggled throughout his presidency to embrace sports and frequently offended fans with his comments and actions.[41] A comment he made to the visiting Prince of Laos in 1967 illustrates how his detached engagement with sports drew criticism. "College football is a great spectacle, but I am not sure it gives an accurate picture of America," he reportedly said.[42] He later called the comment a joke, insisting that football did not necessarily make the United States appear like a peaceful nation. However, Johnson's gaff opened him up to political attack.

Republicans increasingly saw the game as more reflective of their values than those of Democrats. Former University of Michigan lineman Gerald Ford, who then served as the House Minority Leader, took the president to task in the press. "Personally I am glad that thousands of fine young Americans can spend this Saturday afternoon 'knocking each other down' in a spirit of clean sportsmanship and keen competition instead of assaulting Pentagon soldiers or policemen with 'peace' placards and filthy words," he said.[43] Ford's comments implicitly blamed Johnson for the civil unrest and antiwar protests that were emerging as part of the New Left. He sought to position football as a game of order and discipline, making it a partisan possession of American conservatives.

Ford's criticism of Johnson reflected the changing rhetoric of Republican politicians toward football. While they continued to view football as an important tool for developing leaders, instilling discipline, and cultivating toughness, they increasingly presented football in oppositional terms to radical protestors on college campuses that they associated with New Left politics. Although he did not mention Johnson in his speech, Eisenhower pointed directly to college football as a solution to American's disruptive political problems while receiving the AFCA's Tuss McLaughry Award in 1967. "I believe the football players can take care of all these 'kooks' who get into our colleges," he said.[44]

Three years earlier, Eisenhower similarly saw Bud Wilkinson as an ideal political candidate, urging him to run for U.S. Senate. The former president believed that his track record in football uniquely qualified him for office. "Such courage and decisiveness Bud Wilkinson has so often demonstrated that we can be sure he will be a fearless voice in the senate," Eisenhower argued.[45] Coaching football further provided him with a platform that demanded attention. "Bud Wilkinson already has such stature and recognition," he explained, "When he speaks in the senate, his word will be heard and read across the land; overlooked neither by the communications media nor by the people of America."[46] While Wilkinson certainly possessed more political skill and savvy than the typical football coach, Eisenhower's endorsement reflected the Republican Party's embrace of football not only to contrast its values to an increasingly liberal Democratic Party, but also to steal votes in traditionally 'blue' states. Although Wilkinson narrowly lost his race, he spent the rest of his career lending his name and his expertise to the Republican Party, helping to further link college football and conservative politics.

The football majority

Richard Nixon benefited from Wilkinson's efforts as well as those of the NFF in his quest to instill his vision of 'Law and Order' and cultivate a political coalition of the 'Silent Majority.' Retired from coaching and no longer interested in seeking office himself, Wilkinson joined the Republican National Committee as a representative from Oklahoma in February 1968.[47] He promised to help Nixon get elected, focusing primarily on youth outreach.[48]

Following the election, the Republicans briefly considered making Wilkinson head of the party.[49] Instead, however, Nixon decided to keep him in his inner circle, hiring him as a 'special consultant.'[50] They attended the Rose Bowl together in January 1969, along with California Governor Ronald Reagan, where they watched Ohio State University defeat the University of Southern California. Historians have extensively documented Nixon's interest in sport and behavior as fan, yet his relationship with Wilkinson shows how the president embraced the insights of a former football college coach to direct policy as well.[51]

Nixon used Wilkinson in a variety of ways as a special consultant.[52] While many of his duties related to public relations and appearing with the president at sporting events, youth outreach occupied a significant amount of Wilkinson's time. Like other conservative coaches, he worried about younger Americans and hoped to redirect their frustration into involvement with government programs. "The Hippies and SDS members are less than one percent of our young people," he explained, "Our assignment here is not to put out a fire, but to find ways to involve the vast majority of idealistic young people who are willing to contribute."[53] He differed, however, in his optimism. Rather than bemoaning generational changes and protestors, he saw potential in America's youth. Building on his experience as a coach, clinic director, and organization of the PCPF under Kennedy, Wilkinson invited representatives from fifteen organizations to participate in a conference on youth affairs. He described it as an effort to "open communication with all young people—those in college, in the ghettos, and the blue collar youth."[54] Wilkinson presented a moderate approach to the problem of the New Left, illustrating what Eisenhower described as his common-sense approach to leadership in 1964. "One thing I learned as a coach," he explained, "is to never underestimate what a young person is capable of doing."[55]

While Wilkinson sought to soften Nixon's image with America's youth and create a cohesive policy on "youth involvement in government," the president continued to embrace football leaders.[56] In December 1969, he traveled to Fayetteville, Arkansas, to watch the 'Game of the Century' between the undefeated University of Texas and the University of Arkansas, which were ranked number one and number two, respectively. Nixon enjoyed the attention, and joined Wilkinson, who also worked as an ABC Sports college football commentator, and his partner Chris Schenkel for a chat at half-time. During the interview the president offered lucid and well-informed commentary on the game, predicting that Texas might comeback from its 14:0 deficit. Schenkel, impressed by his analysis, joked with Nixon, "If Bud Wilkinson, our analyst, ever falters, we at ABC may call on you to do our commentary." Nixon quickly replied, "I'm not thinking Chris of what I'm going to do when I finish my present job but there's nothing I'd like better than to have Bud's job, right with you."[57] Texas followed through on the president's prediction, narrowly beating Arkansas 15:14. Wilkinson and Nixon visited the postgame locker room, where the president famously presented Darrell Royal, who played for Wilkinson at Oklahoma, with a championship plaque.

Days later, Nixon received the NFF's Gold Medal while dodging antiwar protestors in New York.[58] Wilkinson joined him at the ceremony and gained induction to the Hall of Fame based on his coaching record. While, like previous presidents, Nixon spoke about football and American society, his speech was overshadowed in the press by his action in Arkansas. Pennsylvania State University also finished the season undefeated and had a longer unbeaten streak, yet Nixon honored Texas as that year's champion.

Still, Nixon remained unapologetic, explaining he chose the Longhorns because they had the guts to attempt a two-point conversion to win the game. "In this the one-hundredth year of football and close to the two-hundredth anniversary of our nation, I thought this was the kind of competitive spirit that characterizes our nation," he explained.[59] Nixon's remarks reflected his interest in the game as a fan first and a politician second. Unlike Hoover, Eisenhower, Kennedy, or even Ford, his rhetoric was less biting and militant. He recognized football as an important part of American culture and an important tool for his political career, but beyond his friendship with coaches and his reliance on Wilkinson, Nixon rarely positioned football as political technology linked to the Cold War or the destiny of the republic. Instead, as Oriard and Lipsyte have explained, "sportspeak entangled football in the public's mind ever more intimately with the values of the Establishment."[60] In short, he built on the foundation laid by the NFF and prior administrations to connect the game with his political base, the 'Silent Majority.'[61]

A partisan game

College football became even more political during the Nixon administration – not because he intervened with fitness policy or youth outreach, but because New Left demonstrations continued to reverberate across college campuses. In a November 1969 column, Lipsyte suggested that "the four horsemen of the college football apocalypse – Injury, Ineligibility, Fumbles, and Defeat – have gained an added starter."[62] "The Fifth Horseman is called Dissent," he explained, "and he comes costumed as an

201

antiwar demonstrator, a pot smoker, a [B]lack rights activist, a mutton chop sideburn."[63] Dissent within the sport meant that coaches saw their roles as more important than ever in maintaining discipline and order; ensuring their charges were tough and fit. They embraced Robert Kennedy's call to use their influence and authority to address the "fearful dangers" facing America.[64]

In 1970, sports editor Ira Berkow wrote a five-part syndicated series on issues facing college football. The series explored four different campuses: Penn State University, Indiana University, the University of California-Berkeley, and the University of Alabama, investigating how their coaches dealt with the changing mood of college campuses.[65] Berkeley, which had witnessed a series of antiwar, civil rights, and free speech protests throughout the late 1960s – including the violent 'Bloody Thursday' event in May 1969 – kicked off the series.[66] Like Lipsyte, Berkow wondered how dissent might influence college football. "The challenging unrest of campus life has infiltrated the sports establishment at Berkeley and may be a forecast of what to expect in college athletics in the decade of the 1970s," he suggested.[67] The situation he described worried many college football coaches and sports administrators.

Out of concern, the Big Ten Conference began pre-emptively preparing plans to prevent protests from disrupting their games in September 1970. "We have received warnings that athletics may be challenged as the symbol of the Establishment," Big Ten Commissioner William R. Reed explained.[68] Reed added that "athletics does symbolize tradition, authority, and self-discipline, but I hope that athletics are never made into a political issue."[69] Reed's fears about the politicization of college sports reflect his profound naivete. He blindly refused to take note of how the NFF, college coaches such as Bud Wilkinson, and presidents like Eisenhower, Kennedy, Nixon, and future presidents Ford and Reagan had weaponized the sport for their own political ends – first to instill toughness and fitness during the Cold War, and then later to reach out to disenchanted voters among the 'Silent Majority.' In fact, the NFF continued this work well into the 1970s.

California governor and future president Ronald Reagan built his political career on responding to campus protestors and channeling the frustration of the 'Silent Majority' to squash the dissent of the New Left.[70] He deployed the National Guard several times to the Berkeley campus, including on 'Bloody Thursday.' In a speech to the Northern California Chapter of the NFF in February 1970, he explained that football stood out as a bastion of sanity on campus against the mayhem that he described as "bully tactics of Hitlerism."[71] "By and large, men who make up our football teams have been conspicuously aloof from this new campus barbarism," he told the crowd.[72]

As governor, Reagan solidified the ties between conservative politics and college football showing how partisanship took hold. Although he toned down his rhetoric a year later when he received the NFF's Gold Medal, his views clearly aligned with the sport's leaders. In his speech, he decried the recommendations of psychiatrists to de-emphasize football. He celebrated the violence of the sport, noting that it represented American toughness. "Football is the last thing we have where man can engage in nonfatal combat and do so by literally flinging his body against an opponent," he explained.[73] Like the Cold War presidents, Reagan saw military value in sport, linking it with discipline, subordination, and a competitive spirit that he described as a "clean hatred."[74]

Throughout the Cold War era, college football served as a battle ground and gained increasing political saliency as the modern conservative movement took root. Initially promoted as an essential part of the American way of life and a political technology to instruct young men on physical and behavioral fitness, it quickly became a partisan weapon to snuff out dissent and differentiate values in the burgeoning Culture Wars. Presidents along with the NFF and coaches facilitated this transformation by using their rhetoric and public notoriety to act as emissaries of toughness against enemies real and imagined.

Notes

1. See, for example, Brad Austin, *Democratic Sports: Men's and Women's College Athletics during the Great Depression* (Fayetteville: University of Arkansas Press, 2015); Russell E. Crawford, "Consensus All-American: Sport and the Promotion of the American Way of Life during the Cold War, 1946–1965," PhD dissertation, University of Nebraska, Lincoln, 2004; Gerald Gems, *For Pride, Profit,*

and Patriarchy: Football and the Incorporation of American Cultural Values (Lanham, MD: Scarecrow Press, 2000); Kurt Kemper, *College Football and American Culture in the Cold War Era* (Urbana: University of Illinois Press, 2009); Jeffrey Montez de Oca, *Discipline and Indulgence: College Football, Media, and the American Way of Life During the Cold War* (New Brunswick, NJ: Rutgers University Press, 2013); Donald J. Mrozek, "The Cult and Ritual of Toughness in Cold War America," in Ray B. Browne (ed.) *Rituals and Ceremonies in Popular Culture* (Bowling Green, OH: Bowling Green University Press, 1980); Michael Oriard, *Bowled Over: Big-Time College Football from the Sixties to the BCS Era* (Chapel Hill: University of North Carolina Press, 2009); Randy Roberts, *A Team for America: The Army–Navy Game that Rallied a Nation* (New York: Houghton Mifflin Harcourt, 2011); Donald W. Rominger, Jr., "The Impact of the United States Government's Sports and Physical Training Policy on Organized Athletics During World War II," PhD dissertation, Oklahoma State University, 1977; Ronald A. Smith, *Sports and Freedom: The Rise of Big-Time College Athletics* (Oxford: Oxford University Press, 1988).

2. Oriard, *Bowled Over*, 54.

3. See "Outstanding Americans Who Played College Football," *Mitchell Daily Republic*, September 27, 1969, 8, for a discussion of former football players who went on to hold influential political offices or appointments.

4. John F. Kennedy, "The Soft American," *Sports Illustrated*, December 26, 1960; "Shape of the Nation," Series: Motion Picture Films from *The Big Picture* Television Program Series, *c.* 1950–*c.* 1975 Record Group 111: Records of the Office of the Chief Signal Officer, 1860–1985, National Archives, College Park, MD.

5. For a biography of Bud Wilkinson, see Jay Wilkinson and Gretchen Hirsch, *Bud Wilkinson: An Intimate Portrait of An American Legend* (Champaign, IL: Sagamore Publishing, 1994); Andrew McGregor, "Bud Wilkinson," in Susan Ware (ed.), *American National Biography Online* (Oxford: Oxford University Press, April 2015).

6. Oriard, *Bowled Over*, 36.

7. Shelley McKenzie, *Getting Physical: The Rise of Fitness Culture in America* (Lawrence: University Press of Kansas, 2013), 14–15; Rachel Louise Moran, *Governing Bodies: American Politics and the Shaping of the Modern Physique* (Philadelphia: University of Pennsylvania Press, 2018), 90–98; Montez de Oca, *Discipline and Indulgence*, 32–40.

8. Al Warden, "The Sports Highway," *Ogden Standard Examiner*, April 8, 1958, 10.

9. Warden, "The Sports Highway,".

10. Montez de Oca, *Discipline and Indulgence*, 33.

11. Neil Amdur, *The Fifth Down: Democracy and the Football Revolution* (New York: Dell Publishing, 1971), 29–30.

12. "Football Hall of Fame Dinner," *New Castle News*, October 25, 1958, 8.

13. "Football Hall of Fame Dinner"; "Candidates For National Fame Selected by Awards Committee," *Oil City Derrick*, November 13, 1954, 8.

14. "Admiral Brown Named Head of National Grid Foundation," *Tucson Daily Citizen*, July 13, 1954, 13.

15. "Admiral Brown Named Head of National Grid Foundation."

16. Bill Mayers, "Sports Talk," *Lawrence Daily Journal World*, July 27, 1956, 9.

17. Mayers, "Sports Talk."

18. Kemper, *College Football and American Culture in the Cold War Era*, 28.

19. Quoted in Kemper, *College Football and American Culture in the Cold War Era*, 28. Kemper further describes LaRoche's attempt to influence the sports media, particularly *Sports Illustrated*'s editor Sidney James.

20. "Eisenhower Received Award from Football Hall of Fame Here Before 2,000," *New York Times*, October 29, 1958, 40.

21. "Hebert Hoover Says: Sportsmanship Big Teacher of Morals," *Madison Capital Times*, December 7, 1960, 30.

22. "Hebert Hoover Says: Sportsmanship Big Teacher of Morals."

23. Montez de Oca, *Discipline and Indulgence*, 63.

24. Clips of Wilkinson's TV show can be found in the Ned Hockman Football Collection within the Oklahoma Historical Society's Film and Video Archive. Several episodes are available on YouTube at: https://www.youtube.com/watch?v=J-g_ME7pA24&list=PL73jnAi D15NDJEhEDa661eLYti6SbQtwM.

25. Charles B. (Bud) Wilkinson, "How to Watch Football," *Saturday Evening Post*, November 1, 1952, 19.

26. Wilkinson, "How to Watch Football."

27. "Text of Kennedy Speech at Football Dinner Here," *New York Times*, December 6, 1961, 61.

28. John F. Kennedy, "Address at Rice University on the Nation's Space Effort," John F. Kennedy Library and Museum, available at: https://www.jfklibrary.org/asset-viewer/archives/USG/USG-15-29-2/USG-15-29-2.

29. "Kennedy Compares Bowl Play With Family's Touch Football," *New York Times*, January 3, 1961, 37.
30. "Urges Coaches to Help, Robert Kennedy 'In Fitness' Plea," *Madison Capital Times*, January 12, 1961, 37.
31. "Urges Coaches to Help, Robert Kennedy 'In Fitness' Plea."
32. "Urges Coaches to Help, Robert Kennedy 'In Fitness' Plea."
33. This document is undated and unattributed but was likely created as a part of the Kennedy transition. Papers of John F. Kennedy. Presidential Papers. President's Office Files. Departments and Agencies. Council on Youth Fitness: Survey [undated]. John F. Kennedy Presidential Library.
34. John F. Kennedy, "Remarks on the Youth Fitness Program," February 21, 1961.
35. "Football Coach at Oklahoma U. to Frame National Fitness Plan," *New York Times*, March 24, 1961, 14.
36. "Bud Wilkinson Show," WKY KTVY KFOR Archives, Oklahoma State Historical Society, Oklahoma City. This episode can be viewed on YouTube at: https://youtu.be/DTiJe93WcqQ.
37. "Bud Wilkinson Show."
38. See, for example, Neil Amdur, "Campus Crossfire: Coaches Trapped between Dissenting Athletes and Rigid Policies," *New York Times*, December 13, 1971.
39. Johnson was the first president to win the AFCA's Tuss McLaughry Award. Eisenhower won it a year later, and Nixon earned the honors in 1969. Ronald Regan and George H. W. Bush received the award in 1983 and 1998, respectively.
40. "Pres. Johnson Gets Award by Coaches," *Madison Capital Times*, January 14, 1966, 26.
41. Robert Lipsyte, "Sports of the Times," *San Antonio Express*, October 10, 1968, 62.
42. "Rep. Ford Resents Johnson's College Football Remarks," *North Adams Transcript*, November 11, 1967, 2.
43. "Rep. Ford Resents Johnson's College Football Remarks."
44. "And What are Those Representatives For?" *Albert Lea Evening Tribune*, March 20, 1967, 4.
45. "Wilkinson Paid High Tribute in Ike Speech," *The Oklahoman*, November 1, 1964, 5.
46. "Wilkinson Paid High Tribute in Ike Speech."
47. "Bud Captures Key GOP Job," *The Oklahoman*, February 8, 1968, 37; "Bud Takes New Seat on GOP Party Board," *The Oklahoman*, February 24, 1968, 11; "Bud to Be Calling Big Plays in GOP," *The Oklahoman*, February 23, 1968, 13.

48. Wilkinson gave a series of speeches for Nixon during 1968. See, for example, "Bud Wilkinson Supports Nixon," *Lawton Constitution*, March 13, 1968, 7. For more on Nixon's effort to connect with youth, see Seth Blumenthal, *Children of the Silent Majority: Young Voters and the Rise of the Republican Party, 1968–1980* (Lawrence: University Press of Kansas, 2018).

49. "Bud's Charm Puts Him High on GOP List," *The Oklahoman*, November 26, 1968, 5.

50. "Wilkinson Reportedly Will Join Nixon's Staff," *The Oklahoman*, December 29, 1968, 21; "Close to Nixon," *The Oklahoman*, February 2, 1969, 18; "Worship Services for Nixons Under Wilkinson's Direction," *The Oklahoman*, February 21, 1969, 23.

51. See, for example, Jesse Berrett, *Pigskin Nation: How the NFL Remade American Politics* (Urbana: University of Illinois Press, 2018); Nicholas Evan Sarantakes, *Fan in Chief: Richard Nixon and American Sports, 1969–1974* (Lawrence: University Press of Kansas, 2019); John Sayle Watterson, *Games Presidents Play: Sports and the Presidency* (Baltimore, MD: Johns Hopkins University Press, 2006).

52. Some of Wilkinson's duties are described in the finding aid for his papers at the Nixon Library, available at: http://www.oac.cdlib.org/findaid/ark:/13030/c8g73fcq/entire_text.

53. Ted Knap, "Nixon Seeks to Close the Generation Gap," *Albuquerque Tribune*, February 14, 1969, 32.

54. Knap, "Nixon Seeks to Close the Generation Gap."

55. Knap, "Nixon Seeks to Close the Generation Gap."

56. Noel Grove, "Under-30s Infiltrate Government," *Ames Daily Tribune*, March 18, 1969, 4.

57. "1969 NCAA Football #1 Texas at #2 Arkansas". YouTube, February 1, 2017, available at: https://www.youtube.com/watch?v=ORAFBpWrNZ8.

58. "Demonstration Mars Nixon's N.Y. Visit," *Brainerd Daily Dispatch*, December 10, 1969, 19.

59. Quoted in Terry Frei, *Horns, Hogs, and Nixon Coming: Texas vs. Arkansas in Dixie's Last Stand* (New York: Simon & Schuster, 2002), 277.

60. Oriard, *Bowled Over*, 53.

61. This mirrors Nixon's larger strategy for reaching out to blue-collar workers. See, for example, Jefferson Cowie, "Nixon's Class Struggle: Romancing the New Right Worker," *Labor History* 43(3) (2002): 257–283.

62. Robert Lipsyte, "Sports of the Times," *New York Times*, November 15, 1969, 47.

63. Lipsyte, "Sports of the Times."
64. "Urges Coaches to Help, Robert Kennedy 'In Fitness' Plea," 37.
65. Ira Berkow, "'Football Team May be on Powder Keg,'" *Jacksonville Courier*, September 17, 1970, 14; Ira Berkow, "Coach Pont Responsive to Players or Attentive," *Cambridge Daily Jeffersonian*, September 23, 1970, 10; Ira Berkow, "Players 'Bear' Up to Win Philosophy," *Jacksonville Courier*, September 23, 1970, 17; Ira Berkow, "Paternor: Football is Still a Game," *Jacksonville Courier*, September 24, 1970, 17; Ira Berkow, "Football in '70s: 'Return To Sanity,'" *Jacksonville Courier*, September 30, 1970, 17.
66. 'Bloody Thursday' was a violent confrontation between student protestors and the National Guard at People's Park in May 1969 that resulted in thousands of arrests as well as teargas and rubber bullets volleyed upon the students. For more background on Bloody Thursday, see Jon David Cash, "People's Park: Birth and Survival," *California History* 88(1) (2010): 8–29, 53–55.
67. Berkow, "Football Team May be on Powder Keg."
68. The Big Ten Conference is a big-time athletic league whose membership includes the flagship state universities from Ohio, Michigan, Indiana, Illinois, Wisconsin, Iowa, and Minnesota. "Big Ten Prepares To Halt Protests," *Jacksonville Courier*, September 22, 1970, 9.
69. "Big Ten Prepares To Halt Protests."
70. Jeffery Kahn, "Ronald Reagan Launched Political Career Using the Berkeley Campus as a Target," *UC Berkeley News*, June 8, 2014, available at: https://www.berkeley.edu/news/media/releases/2004/06/08_reagan.shtml.
71. Kahn, "Ronald Reagan Launched Political Career Using the Berkeley Campus as a Target."
72. Ed Schoenfeld, "Sports Boosted by Reagan," *Oakland Tribune*, February 21, 1970, 12.
73. "Grid Award to Reagan," *Hutchison News*, December 9, 1971, 12.
74. "Grid Award to Reagan."

Part Three

Athletes and the Presidency

10

Brown Derby Bambino:
Babe Ruth's Celebrity Endorsement and the 1928 Presidential Campaign

Robert Chiles

The sun beamed bright and warm from the blue October sky on an 86°F afternoon at Sportsman's Park in St. Louis, Missouri.[1] With two out in the bottom of the ninth and increasingly hostile fans heckling the visiting outfielders, St. Louis Cardinals captain Frankie Frisch popped up along the left field line.[2] As the ball descended toward the box seats, New York Yankees star Babe Ruth trotted in pursuit, raised his glove, and snagged the foul at the edge of the bleachers to record the final out in game four of the 1928 World Series.[3] For the second consecutive year and the third time that decade, the Yankees were world champions.

It was fitting that Ruth, who "never lost his stride after gathering the ball in and ran to the New York bench waving the ball in the air and laughing," should snare the final fly, for he had delivered a remarkable series – setting nineteen records during the four-game affair in which he hit .625, scored nine runs, drove in four, hit three doubles and, in the final game, belted three home runs.[4] It was fitting too because Ruth – also nicknamed 'the Bambino' – was not merely the brightest star on the field; he was also among the biggest celebrities in the nation – and the champion had more than baseball on his mind as the team returned home to the Big Apple.

When the victorious Yankees' train pulled into Grand Central Terminal on October 10, Ruth led a band of teammates snaking through a cacophonous crowd of 3,000 adoring New Yorkers.

Ruth and first baseman Lou Gehrig were repeatedly "singled out for particular ovations."[5] Retreating from the exultant mayhem of the Midtown streets below, Ruth's first stop on his triumphant return to New York was political. He proceeded to the Biltmore Hotel at Madison Avenue and 43rd Street, to the campaign headquarters of Governor Alfred E. Smith, New York's four-term chief executive and the Democratic nominee for president that year. Bursting into Smith's suite, Ruth blasted his "unmistakably hearty greetings" to the governor, who beamed, "well, well, well, I'm certainly glad to see you Babe" while slapping the slugger on the back and dubbing him "the boss of the youth of America."[6] Ruth autographed the ball he had snagged to sweep the series and presented the trophy to Smith.[7] He also introduced Gehrig, as well as Yankees owner Colonel Jacob Ruppert.[8] The governor engaged in a jocular back-and-forth with the Bambino, who proclaimed that his season was all over, "except a little barnstorming." Straightening his tie and preparing to depart for a rail tour of the Midwest and the South, Smith shot back: "that's what I'm going to do too."[9] "Babe," Smith then confessed, "I wish I could get as many kids to cheer for me as cheer for you, I'd be a most happy man." "Shucks, governor," Ruth buoyantly responded, "I've got all the kids cheering for you, too."[10]

In 2019, *Los Angeles Times* columnist Julia Wick reminded readers that Ruth's support for Smith is often considered "the first noteworthy celebrity presidential endorsement"; she also derided it as inconsequential: "if you don't recognize [Smith's] name, it's because he didn't win."[11] Indeed, it is unlikely that Ruth's support for Smith swayed a significant number of voters in 1928. Yet this early mixing of sport and presidential politics did hail the onset of a rather modern phenomenon: the rise of celebrity-athletes as potential representatives of particular reference groups' aspirations, ambitions, and political attitudes. Thus, Ruth and other athletes who entered into the political arena in 1928 embarked on a subtle and early form of identity politics.

Celebrity athletes, celebrity politics

Historian William E. Leuchtenburg notes that "organized sport in America had captivated the country for decades, but it was not until the 1920s that spectator sports took on a central role in American life."[12] Babe Ruth transcended sport in a decade when sport emerged as modern, mainstream, mass-entertainment.[13] As the popular syndicated columnist and cowboy-philosopher Will Rogers remarked: "it just don't seem like we have any game in America where one man stands out so prominently, and so far ahead of all the others in his line as Ruth does in baseball. He is the most colorful athlete that we have in any branch of sport."[14] Moreover, while Ruth's emergence as a 1920s folk hero proceeded initially from his record-smashing athletic accomplishments, his mythological status was fueled just as much by the way he engaged with the public sphere in a manner that appeared to align authentically with his own humble origins – as Rogers suggested: "Kids are crazy about Ruth, and he is always doing something to keep solid with them. Raised himself in an Orphans home in Baltimore, he has always kept a keen interest and sympathy with kids."[15]

Biographer Jane Leavy notes that "Ruth was the first athlete to be as famous for what he did off the field (or what people thought he did) as he was for what he did on it," and by the late 1920s "he would become the first ballplayer to be paid as much for what he did off the field as what he did on it."[16] Indeed, "what is most striking about Ruth," notes Leavy, "is how thoroughly modern he was, not just in the way he attacked a baseball, but also in the creation, manipulation, and exploitation of his public image at the precise moment in history when mass media was re-defining what it meant to be public."[17] In short, by the time he endorsed Al Smith for president, Babe Ruth was one of the most famous figures in America.[18]

In part, then, the story of Ruth's – and other athletes' – involvement in presidential politics fits with a broader story of celebrity endorsements in 1928. When Smith secured the Democratic nomination, a flurry of congratulatory telegrams arrived at his suite in the Biltmore Hotel. Some of these cheers came from celebrities, like comedian Ed Wynn and the internationally renowned Irish tenor John McCormack. Indeed, Smith's support from the entertainment world would include some of the era's leading songwriters – notables like Irving Berlin, and such Broadway luminaries as

George M. Cohan, Jerome Kern, and George and Ira Gershwin.[19] For his part, Ruth sent a laudatory telegram extolling the Democratic Party's choice as one that "assures us that public opinion demands a good president."[20]

As Broadway and the Babe were lining up behind Smith, other entertainers, including Hollywood mogul Louis B. Mayer and director Cecil B. DeMille, celebrated Republican nominee Herbert Hoover.[21] Indeed, Hoover scored the support of perhaps the one figure whose celebrity surpassed Ruth's pre-eminence in the United States of 1928: aviator Charles Lindbergh, who had completed his solo transatlantic flight the previous year and whose endorsement of the Republican nominee inspired the pro-Hoover campaign song "If He's Good Enough for Lindy, He's Good Enough for Me."[22] Nor were the Democrats unique in recognizing the rising prominence of sports in American society and the political potential of its popularity. Tennis great Helen Wills, who won the French Championship, Wimbledon, and the U.S. National Championship that summer – the latter for the fifth time that decade – supported her fellow Californian, of whom she had "long been an ardent admirer."[23] She even took some time out of her schedule during the U.S. Championships at Forest Hills, New York, to volunteer for service with the Republican's campaign.[24] Inspired by Hoover's "ability for organization, and his wonderful powers of perseverance," as well as his desire to promote "youth's eagerness for service," Wills chaired the 'Sports Division' of the 'Women's Committee for Hoover,' signaling her "debut in politics."[25]

Hoover sagely recognized the growing national culture of celebrity in the Roaring Twenties, as well as its latent political potential. Having himself ascended to national celebrity as food administrator during the First World War (his name became a neologism – to 'Hooverize' meant to economize in the national interest), the ambitious Commerce Secretary hired a publicity agent in 1926.[26] His administration of flood relief on the Mississippi River the following year made Hoover "more than ever a celebrity," and the obvious choice for his party's presidential nomination in 1928.[27]

Hoover's party, moreover, had been applying emergent mass-cultural elements to electoral politics from the opening of the decade. In 1920, Warren G. Harding's campaign had enlisted the pioneering advertising executive Albert D. Lasker, who transformed the last of America's old-fashioned 'front porch' campaigns into a savvy public relations operation utilizing "all mediums of modern advertising."[28] Not only were staged encounters between the nominee and voters filmed and distributed as newsreels to theaters nationwide as "a way to get their front-porch candidate in front of millions of Americans," but Lasker – the majority-owner of the National League's Chicago Cubs – also utilized the growing appeal of athletics. The Republicans distributed footage of Harding golfing, and staged a baseball game in Harding's home town of Marion, Ohio, between the Cubs and the Minor League Kerrigan Tailors, capturing footage of the nominee playing catch with star pitcher Grover Cleveland Alexander.[29] More broadly, Harding's campaign harnessed the culture of celebrity, enlisting support from entertainers Al Jolson and Mary Pickford, with Jolson composing campaign songs for Harding in 1920 and Calvin Coolidge in 1924.[30] Yet since Hoover was running to maintain the conservative status quo, and since he lacked the zeal for politics that characterized his opponent, Republicans and Democrats in 1928 engaged with different components of the nation's mass culture.[31] For example, Hoover's campaign announced early in the race that their efforts would focus on radio broadcasts and moving pictures, with a limited role for personal appearances by the nominee.[32] Smith energetically sought to maintain "direct contact with the people" through a series of robust policy speeches accompanied by jubilant politicking at mass rallies and exuberant parades in cities around the country – confirming the nominee's reputation as the 'Happy Warrior.'[33] In contrast, Hoover's campaign was "much less spectacular" and included "fewer speeches" – in part because many found the technocratic nominee "colorless."[34]

Likewise, it was the Democratic campaign that did the most to leverage the growing appeal of individual celebrity-athletes, and for the most part it was the inimitable Ruth who hogged the headlines. In early September, Ruth, in the heat of a pennant race, was approached by a photographer inquiring if he would pose for a snapshot with Hoover, who had stepped away from his own race to take in the Yankees-Senators game at Griffith Stadium in Washington, D.C. "Nothing doing; I'm for Al Smith," recoiled Ruth.[35] Although Ruth later apologized for this impertinence, *New York Times* sports columnist John Kieran concluded that the episode "confirms a suspicion that the whole Yankee team went Democratic more than a month ago," mentioning with playful irony that "the persons who are doing the most to take the joy out of life for the Yankees these days are the Athletics of Philadelphia and practically all of them are Democrats."[36]

Kieran was proven prophetic on October 7, when, during the World Series, a "full team" of Yankees shared a statement endorsing their governor, signed by outfielders Earl Combes and Bob Meusel, infielders Lou Gehrig, Tony Lazzeri, Mark Koenig, and Joe Duggan, and pitchers Waite Hoyt and Benny Bengough. Although manager Miller Huggins was a rare Hoover supporter in the Yankee dugout, five other managers attended the announcement and expressed their endorsement of Smith: skippers George Moriarty of the Detroit Tigers; Wilbert Robinson of Brooklyn (for whom the team was temporarily nicknamed the 'Robins'); Donie Bush of the Pittsburgh Pirates; Joe McCarthy of the Chicago Cubs; and Jack Hendricks of the Cincinnati Reds.[37] New York Giants' manager John McGraw also signed on for Smith, along with several players from across the league.[38]

The connections between Smith and the New York Yankees were not new. He had thrown out the ceremonial first pitch to open the new Yankee Stadium in the Bronx on April 18, 1923.[39] Moreover, Yankees owner Jacob Ruppert was a former Democratic congressman from New York City, who had been supported in four successful campaigns by the Tammany Hall political machine of which Smith was a prominent member.[40] Later, Colonel Ruppert sent the governor season passes to Yankee Stadium from 1924 through 1928.[41]

Yet the Smith boom in the sporting world transcended the Yankees and even baseball. The 'Champions of Al Smith' – as they were dubbed in propaganda – grew to include champion boxers Gene Tunney, Tommy Loughran, Benny Leonard, and James J. Corbett; golf champions Johnny Farrell, 'Chick' Evans, Francis Ouimet, Leo Diegel, and Gene Sarazen; tennis champion Vincent Richards; Olympic runner Joie Ray; football stars including New York Giants back Bruce Caldwell, Harvard coach Arnold Horween, and Notre Dame coach Knute Rockne; and many others, including, of course, Babe Ruth.[42] It "reads like a blue book of professional sports, with a few topnotch amateurs mixed in the list," effused *Atlanta Constitution* sports columnist Dick Hawkins, who concluded that Smith "actually has the big figures in the sports world behind him in full force . . . If by any chance [he] should not be elected president he will have a very fine course to turn to next spring. He can organize a nice new baseball league or maybe a coaching school or he could turn golf professional."[43] Many of these 'champions' had simply signed on at the urging of their agent, Christy Walsh, whose two companies, the 'Christy Walsh Syndicate' and 'Christy Walsh Management' had helped these athletes transcend sport while propelling their sole proprietor to enviable wealth.[44]

Personal appeal

Ruth was far more engaged in the political struggle than many of these athletes, who were Smith boosters in name only. On October 19, he took to the airwaves to announce that he had "temporarily renounced the world of baseball in favor of politics" and to articulate "his political affiliations and reasons" across twenty-nine stations via a nationwide radio hookup from WJZ studios in New York City.[45] Jovially greeting "radio friends, and especially all you folks who rooted for the Yankees in that little affair at St. Louis last week," Ruth noted a new trend that had emerged within his fan mail. "I'm still opening my world series mail. So far 14,000 wires and letters have come to me since I got those three lucky home runs at Sportsman's Park. I've had lots of letters before, but there is a new angle this time. Generally, they have been on one subject only – baseball – but this time the letters and telegrams mix baseball and politics."[46]

Actually, Ruth himself had been stirring this cocktail, for "on the Yankee train coming back home from St. Louis we made stops at many cities, and I did a little speechmaking for Governor Al Smith."[47] The response, according to Ruth, had been positive:

We started checking off and found, of the first 9,000 letters and wires received, 7,000 congratulated me for my home runs and my speech for Governor Smith. Only 200 letters criticized me for talking politics. That's a nice proportion for Smith – 7,000 for him, 200 against him. I'm not in politics, I'm in baseball, but the 7,000 letters is the answer as to why I am for Al Smith. In other words, Governor Smith is the type of man who appeals not only to the baseball fan, but to all red-blooded lovers of American sport.[48]

In reality, Ruth's stumping for Smith along the rail line from St. Louis to New York often drew a frosty response from Midwestern audiences – but the Babe hardly walked back his politics. When a crowd in Terre Haute, Indiana, stared silently after the champion's remarks, Ruth reportedly bellowed "the hell with you," pivoted, and returned to the celebration aboard the Yankees' victory train.[49]

As Ruth continued his major radio address, he further invoked his common-man credentials, disavowing any political expertise and insisting that "I don't know anything about tariff and those kind of things. But whether you are a farmer, a manufacturer or a baseball player, the main thing that interests a fellow in voting is how it will affect his pocket book."[50] He awkwardly derailed the potential universal application of his message by tethering his analysis squarely to his own professional perspective: "Governor Smith's friendship for baseball has made big crowds and big salaries possible, and that is why nearly every big league baseball player is going to vote for Al Smith."[51] Sticking to income but broadening his horizons, the World Series champion lamented that "Smith, who has done more for New York than all the ball players in captivity, does not get the salary of many big league ball players." This allowed Ruth to arrive, however circuitously, at a more fundamental point: "While some men desert their old friends, their home town and their obligations to the public for great salaries, Al Smith . . . has given his life to the public."[52] As an example of Smith's service, Ruth returned to his own experiences, proclaiming, "the thing that makes him so great is the very fact that he does not personally care for baseball or boxing but is so broad and considerate of the other fellow's wishes and of the great good that all forms of athletics can do."[53] Ruth's prime example of this consideration was the fact that Smith had worked to legalize Sunday baseball games in New York, which had "helped the ball player[s] get large salaries."[54]

Nevertheless, Ruth's focus was not on Smith as a 'friend of sport' as much as a friend of the common working American – and this broader invocation of working-class identity was what mattered most about Ruth's endorsement:

> The other day I took a ride down to Oliver street in New York City just to look at the little "two by four" home that Governor Smith was born in. It reminded me of my own two by four home in Baltimore, and what a wonderful thing it is to think that whether you were raised by poor parents in Oliver street, New York, or by poor parents on the river front in Baltimore, that there is a chance for every boy to get to the top in America, whether he wants to be a president or a ball player.[55]

This key portion of Ruth's endorsement was the most meaningful and perhaps the most heartfelt. In 1924, when Smith had unsuccessfully sought the Democratic nomination, his backers had solicited Ruth's endorsement and the Yankee had obliged with a short letter of support. As historian Robert Slayton notes, Ruth's letter responding to Smith ally Franklin Roosevelt's entreaties revealed his motivation: "No poor boy can go any too high in this world to suit me."[56]

Ruth was not alone in feeling this way. Smith was a poor grandson of immigrants and his education had ended in the eighth grade. Yet he had risen from the sidewalks of the polyglot Lower East Side to become chief executive of the Empire State. The governor's biography was familiar and inspiring to millions of Americans who found themselves marginalized by the 1920s' chauvinistic march toward 'One Hundred Percent Americanism' – an ideology that excluded the urban, ethnic, working-class citizens who placed hope in Smith. Athletics appealed naturally to such 'new American' voters, for the rise of sports was part of the 1920s' countercurrent *against* nativist Protestant nationalism, and the boom in sports was propelled, in part, by a people who found themselves "freed from the Puritan ethic that equated play with sin."[57]

219

Many athletes hailed from the same world as those marginalized Americans who increasingly viewed Smith as their political champion. Ruth himself was a grandson of German immigrants, and had endured a difficult youth including a broken home, six siblings who died in childhood, and long periods living at St. Mary's Industrial School.[58] He was also, like many from that world, a Roman Catholic.[59] Smith was the first Roman Catholic nominated by a major party for president, and in the nativist 1920s his candidacy was targeted by a bombardment of bigotry. Indeed, the Ku Klux Klan protested his campaign with cross burnings, while a nationwide whispering campaign questioned the patriotism of Smith and his co-communicants.[60]

While Ruth, whose celebrity appeal was supposed to transcend any demographic niche, side-stepped such questions, some of his teammates did not – at least by implication. Yankee rookie Leo Durocher, a French-Canadian American from the industrial enclave of West Springfield, Massachusetts, campaigned for Al Smith back home in Hampden County; one of the county's French-Canadian wards where the shortstop stumped went 84 percent for Smith.[61] Similarly, Yankee Tony Lazzeri – called by historian Lawrence Baldassaro "the first major star of Italian descent in the national pastime and one of the game's first ethnic heroes" – would enter the political fray for Smith.[62] Lazzeri had drawn "large numbers of first- and second-generation Italian Americans to the ballpark for the first time," while simultaneously providing them with "a newfound sense of pride at a time when the stereotypical image of their group in the American consciousness was that of a bootleg mobster."[63] Now the second baseman joined Ruth on the radio to campaign for Smith, as did Lou Gehrig (who himself was born of German immigrants in Yorkville, Manhattan, and lost three siblings in childhood). On one occasion Lazzeri reportedly singled out Smith's popularity among Italian-American voters in a playful, edgy exchange with Ruth.[64]

Identity politics

In these and other ways the significance of identity – the identity of the potential voters and of the campaigning athletes – was important to how political athletes' messages were received, even for the more universally themed speeches of Babe Ruth. There was predictable enthusiasm for Ruth's campaigning in many quarters. The *Baltimore Sun* highlighted the portions of Ruth's speech that alluded to his Baltimore boyhood. Meanwhile, the *Boston Globe* reported on a passage that many newspapers ignored: Ruth's discussion of a Massachusetts referendum on Sunday sports. Ruth lamented:

> Up in my old home town of Boston the Red Sox and the Braves, once great ball clubs, are now nearly starving to death because they cannot get the crowds and they cannot get the money to pay good salaries. Sunday baseball is on the ballot in Boston in November and they tell me Sunday baseball is going across in good old Massachusetts, just as Al Smith put it across in New York.[65]

In Georgia, where such defiance of strict Sabbatarianism was less politically useful, the stridently Democratic *Atlanta Constitution* declared "Ruth Hits Homer in Urging Smith's Election" and ignored the portions on Sunday baseball.[66]

Still, the reviews were not universally affirmative. Smith's campaign had been working to lure rural voters in the upper Midwest away from their traditional Republicanism. Plummeting commodity prices and ballooning farm debt, widespread resentment over Hoover's antipathy toward federal agricultural relief, and Smith's embrace of some progressive farm remedies all made a counterintuitive alliance between the derby-sporting Manhattanite and struggling farmers seem suddenly plausible.[67] Yet the heterogeneous urban world conveyed by Smith's signature brown derby hat and his Roman Catholic faith made him suspect to large swaths of rural America.[68] Anti-Catholic voters, who had helped to push the Ku Klux Klan's membership to upwards of 4 million by mid-decade, found much to despise in New York's 'Happy Warrior' since they routinely projected their preoccupation with the perils of ultramontanism onto a wide complex of issues – among them immigration (Smith opposed the 1924 national origins quotas as 'discriminatory'), the growth of cities (Smith's membership in the Tammany Hall machine and intense Bowery brogue made him a uniquely urban presidential contender), and prohibition, along with Sunday 'blue laws' (Smith's opposition to prohibition was well known and much discussed).[69]

Babe Ruth was not helpful in overcoming such concerns. "Some fool put Babe Ruth on the radio the other night and he talked about Al Smith having given us Sunday baseball!" fumed a frustrated Missouri farmer who had abandoned the Republicans in favor of Smith. "All right, of course, Sunday baseball is all right, but people out this way don't think so. This part of the country believes in going to church on Sunday and Sunday school, and in Sunday observance generally, not in Sunday baseball."[70]

In fact, a more cynical historical interpretation of the enthusiasm for Smith among baseball players might zero in on Ruth's candid talk about Sunday baseball. Smith's support was well known. As a state assemblyman in 1907, he had fought against New York's proscription of Sunday games for amateurs, arguing that "we tolerate such places as Coney Island and Rockaway Beach, but when it comes to allowing an innocent game of baseball on Sunday then there is a howl."[71] As governor in 1919, he had signed the legislation legalizing Sunday games in the Empire State.[72] Equally well known was organized baseball's longing for the additional revenue from Sunday games.[73] When Sunday baseball had arrived in New York City, debuting at the Polo Grounds on May 4, 1919, the game "brought out a crowd which not only filled the spacious grandstand but crowded the outfield bleachers, which have seldom been half filled except during the world's series."[74] Simultaneously, "when legalized Sunday baseball was ushered in for fans of the borough across the bridge," that game drew an estimated 25,000 spectators, awakening "memories of Brooklyn's World Series games of 1916."[75] As Ruth and others made perfectly clear, players and owners covetously pondered the financial implications of universal Sunday baseball.[76]

But as Ruth's critic in Missouri implied, Sunday baseball was not just about money. It was also a question of culture and social class. For the urban working class it was meaningful since people who worked 48 hours or more each week in the era before night games often had *only* Sunday as an opportunity for recreation, including sports spectatorship.[77] And, of course, Sunday baseball was very much a question of ethno-cultural identity – a Catholic–Protestant, immigrant–'native' controversy that had been boiling for decades as urban America increasingly shifted toward the 'continental' dispositions of Catholic and Jewish immigrants. "As early as 1902, Chicago, St. Louis, and Cincinnati, unencumbered by the mores of a strong Puritan ethic, permitted Sunday baseball," and by the end of the First World War Sunday baseball had arrived in Washington, Detroit, and Cleveland.[78] As noted, under Smith, Sunday games began in New York in the spring of 1919.[79]

The ethno-cultural implications of sport – and of athletes' endorsements of the working-class Catholic Al Smith – went beyond baseball. For example, conspicuous support for Smith among the Catholic University of Notre Dame's football team had noteworthy implications, both on and off the gridiron. Historian Gerald R. Gems has noted how Coach Knute Rockne's approach to football at Notre Dame represented a 'Catholic' alternative to the "implicitly Protestant Warner system," and would thus transform coaching strategy, create a pipeline of Catholic football talent around Chicago, and "forced a degree of accommodation" through its "resilience" against an anti-Catholic backlash.[80] Nathan Miller put it crisply in his history of the 1920s: "Knute Rockne broke the WASP control of college football and coached a team of immigrants' sons to three national championships."[81]

As noted, a common denominator in many of these endorsements, including the 'Champions of Al Smith,' was agent Christy Walsh, whose clients included both Ruth and Rockne. Walsh was enthusiastic about Smith – writing to the governor admiringly that "your personality and courage will have swept all corners of our country," and pledging that he stood "behind Governor Smith to the last ditch."[82] Walsh sent this warm letter right before sailing to Amsterdam with Coach Rockne for the Olympics, and upon their return Rockne and other Walsh-affiliated athletes joined the Walsh-organized Smith 'Champions.'[83] Walsh's ardor for Smith was not grounded in partisanship – he was a Republican.[84] Jane Leavy suggests that the athletic impresario was motivated by ethno-cultural identity, for Walsh was "a devout Catholic and son of Ireland," keen to "help elect the Catholic governor of New York president in 1928."[85]

There were many who recognized the implications of athletic endorsements – including Ruth's – for various ethno-cultural controversies. Some, like the Missouri farmer, were outraged over the results. Other negative reviews were less dismayed by the content than they were derisive of the messenger. The *Los Angeles Times*, a staunchly Republican organ, loftily concluded that "Babe is lost in a game in which he cannot use his stick. He is not permitted to drive voters home to the polls with his ponderous slat. As a pinch hitter for the [Democrats] he is likely to strike out."[86] Ruth's identity was thus as an athlete and nothing else – he had nothing, in this view, to contribute to presidential politics.

Undeterred by such jeers, Ruth continued boosting the Democrat, on one occasion sporting a Smith-like brown derby and 'Vote for Al Smith' lapel pin for a publicity photo.[87] He then campaigned alongside failed 1924 Democratic nominee John W. Davis in Louisville, Kentucky, on October 24.[88] Inadvertently injecting an element of anarchy into an otherwise unremarkable oration by Davis, Ruth "was nearly catapulted into the press seats when his chair collapsed" as the speaker skewered the incumbent administration. Fortunately, "the ball player's 200 pounds or more were caught by a railing about the speaker's stand," and the "flushed" Ruth was then given "a more substantial chair."[89] From the scene of this debacle Ruth dispatched encouragement to the governor, wiring him of successes in Kentucky and assuring the Democrat as he prepared to deliver a crucial speech at Boston that "I know you will get the warmest reception of entire campaign, because Boston loves a fearless, hard, clear fighter."[90]

Fittingly, Ruth played the role of opening act for Smith's final rally, helping to close out the governor's campaign just as he had closed out the World Series the previous month. At Madison Square Garden in New York, the slugger provided "a stellar attraction" as he "officiated as song and cheer leader." Prior to the 8 p.m. arrival of Democratic leaders like Mayor Jimmy Walker, gubernatorial nominee Franklin Delano Roosevelt, Senator Royal Copeland, and nominee Smith, Ruth led the 22,000 attendees in a one-hour sing-along featuring "old favorites of the days when the 'Side-walks of New York' was the song of the hour, as it is now."[91] The anticipatory energy in the arena, enhanced by the ebullience of Smith's celebrity ally, erupted into thunderous applause as the ecstatic audience celebrated their political champion's homecoming.[92] Three days later, Smith lost in a landslide.

Conclusions

Despite his crushing defeat, Al Smith carried the erstwhile Republican strongholds of Massachusetts and Rhode Island, and commentators at the time noted that "many voters of French and Italian descent and many Jews who had hitherto supported Republican candidates voted for Gov Smith."[93] Subsequent scholars have confirmed the ethno-cultural dimensions of this shift, while pointing out the critical intersection of recent-immigrant voters and working-class voters in Smith's New England majorities.[94] These urban, ethnic, working-class Americans propelled Smith to historic wins in Massachusetts and Rhode Island and, in subsequent elections, would emerge as the core of a formidable new coalition that would assure Democratic dominance of these formerly Republican states starting in 1928 and enduring at least to the time of this publication.[95] A similar shift toward the Democratic candidate among America's diverse urban workers could be detected in cities nationwide.[96] Notably, those New Englanders also provided the electoral muscle behind the 1928 Massachusetts referendum vote to terminate the Bay State's prohibition on Sunday Sports.[97]

As for Babe Ruth, he largely avoided politics after 1928.[98] He still fraternized with Smith on occasion – partnering, for example, with his former political ally for a golf match in Coral Gables, Florida, in 1930.[99] And he still had some scorn reserved for Herbert Hoover. By 1930, when the United States had plummeted into the Great Depression and Ruth found himself in the midst of contract negotiations, the Bambino was reminded that President Hoover made less than the $80,000 per year that Ruth was demanding. "What the hell has Hoover got to do with it?" Ruth shot back. "Besides," he added, accurately, "I had a better year than he did."[100]

The pioneering celebrity-athlete endorsement of Babe Ruth – among others noted here – was likely of minimal consequence to the results in 1928. Instead, what matters most is that in a decade when sport had emerged as a wildly popular form of mass entertainment, some athletes chose to leverage their fame to articulate perspectives that resonated with working-class and ethnic Americans from a unique position of simultaneous privilege and authenticity. When the *Los Angeles Times* dismissed the viewpoint of Babe Ruth and suggested he return to swinging his "ponderous slat," they were essentially demanding that the ball player defer to supposedly wiser minds. Such condescension paralleled that of the high-handed mill managers of New England and industrialists nationwide who displayed Hoover posters in their workshops or included Republican propaganda in workers' pay envelopes.[101] In this instance, Ruth, and a growing number of working-class Americans, decided not to keep their heads down and go quietly back to work – whether that was in a textile mill or in the batter's box.[102]

Notes

1. "The Weather," *Washington Post*, October 10, 1928, 22; Frank Getty, "Fair Weather is Promised for Today," *Washington Post*, October 9, 1928, 13.
2. George Kirksey, "One Pitch Turned Tide of 4th Game," *Washington Post*, October 10, 1928, 1, 14; Brian Bell, "Harper Puts Back to Wall," *Washington Post*, October 10, 1928, 11, 14.
3. Bell, "Harper Puts Back to Wall," 14.
4. "Ruth Corners Most Records in '28 Series," *Atlanta Constitution*, October 14, 1928, 6B.
5. "Al Smith and New York Give Yankees Roaring Welcome," *New York Times*, October 11, 1928, 2; "Throng at Station Welcomes Yankees," *New York Times*, October 11, 1928, 29.
6. "Smith Greets Babe Ruth on Homecoming; Calls Him 'Boss of the Youth of America,'" *New York Times*, October 11, 1928, 1; "Yankees Given Great Welcome," *Boston Globe*, October 11, 1928, 1.
7. "Smith Greets Babe Ruth on Homecoming"; "Governor Smith and the World Series Heroes," *New York Times*, October 11, 1928, 2; "Smith off on Trip to Border States and South," *Chicago Tribune*, October 11, 1928, 1–2.
8. "Smith Greets Babe Ruth on Homecoming"; "Governor Smith and the World Series Heroes."

9. "Smith Greets Babe Ruth on Homecoming"; "Al Smith and New York Give Yankees Roaring Welcome."

10. "'I've Got the Kids Cheering for You Too,' Babe Tells Al," *Chicago Tribune*, October 11, 1928, 21.

11. Julia Wick, "Newsletter: Do Celebrity Political Endorsements Matter?" *Los Angeles Times*, November 7, 2019. It is critical to note that there were major celebrity endorsements earlier in the decade: in 1920, singer Al Jolson and actress Mary Pickford endorsed Republican nominee Warren G. Harding. This is discussed briefly below.

12. William E. Leuchtenburg, *The Perils of Prosperity, 1914–32* (Chicago, IL: University of Chicago Press, 1958), 195.

13. As historian Mark Dyerson concludes: "Ruth was the biggest name, and baseball the most important game, in the sporting craze of the Twenties." Mark Dyerson, "The Emergence of Consumer Culture and the Transformation of Physical Culture: American Sport in the 1920s," *Journal of Sport History* 16(3) (1989): 274.

14. Will Rogers, "Babe Ruth Way Out Ahead," *Boston Globe*, October 21, 1928, B11.

15. Will Rogers, "Babe Ruth Way Out Ahead." I say "appeared to align authentically" in the text above with intentional nuance, for as biographers, including Jane Leavy have noted, much of the Ruth story blended fact and fiction. Yet Americans at the time would have understood Ruth in the way he was presented, and for the purposes of understanding his contemporary cultural and political influence, this is key.

16. Jane Leavy, *The Big Fella: Babe Ruth and the World he Created* (New York: Harper, 2018), 59.

17. Leavy, *The Big Fella*, xxvi.

18. Leavy, *The Big Fella*, 16.

19. James O'Donnell Bennett, "Chummy Chat with Al on a Hot Afternoon," *Chicago Tribune*, July 4, 1928, 1; "Smith Forces Plan Campaign from Five Strategic Centers," *New York Times*, July 4, 1928, 1–2; Robert A. Slayton, *Empire Statesman: The Rise and Redemption of Al Smith* (New York: Free Press, 2001), 297.

20. Bennett, "Chummy Chat with Al on a Hot Afternoon"; "Smith Forces Plan Campaign from Five Strategic Centers."

21. Mayme Ober Peak, "Mayer, of Cinemaland, Says People Want Hoover," *Boston Globe*, May 11, 1928, 15.

22. Russell Baker, "Won't Sparklers Do?" *New York Times*, May 16, 1992, 23.

23. "Helen Wills Heads Hoover Committee," *Christian Science Monitor*, August 25, 1928, 1.

24. "Helen Wills Wins French Tennis Title," *Chicago Tribune*, June 5, 1928, 21; "Helen Wills Wins Wimbledon Final," *Boston Globe*, July 8, 1928, 24; Westbrook Pegler, "Helen Wills Wins Two U.S. Tennis Titles," *Washington Post*, August 28, 1928, 1.

25. "Helen Wills Helps Hoover," *Los Angeles Times*, August 27, 1928, 1; "Helen Wills to Aid in Hoover Campaign," *New York Times*, August 27, 1928, 6; "Helen Wills Enlists in Hoover's Campaign," *Baltimore Sun*, August 27, 1928, 1; John Kieran, "Sports of the Times," *New York Times*, September 4, 1928, 37.

26. William E. Leuchtenburg, *Herbert Hoover* (New York: Henry Holt, 2009), 71.

27. Leuchtenburg, *Herbert Hoover*, 35, 70.

28. Jeffrey L. Cruikshank and Arthur W. Schultz, *The Man Who Sold America: The Amazing (but true) Story of Albert D. Lasker and the Creation of the Advertising Century* (Boston, MA: Harvard Business Review Press, 2010), 184.

29. Cruikshank and Schultz, *The Man Who Sold America*, 187–189. Lasker's efforts to organize the game suffered multiple setbacks, however: several Major League teams balked at the offer to join the Cubs, notably the New York Giants, whose participation was scuttled by manager John McGraw's own political preferences. Moreover, media coverage of the event was, according to Lasker's biographers, "dry." Ibid., 188–189.

30. Craig Garthwaite and Timothy J. Moore, "Can Celebrity Endorsements Affect Political Outcomes? Evidence from the 2008 U.S. Presidential Primary," *Journal of Law, Economics, and Organization* 29(2) (2013), 355–384 at 355; J. W. McCormack, "I'm Feeling Bad about America: The Sick History of the U.S. Campaign Theme Song," *The Baffler* 42 (2018), 28–34 at 30; Todd D. Kendall, "An Empirical Analysis of Political Activity in Hollywood," *Journal of Cultural Economics* 33(1) (2009), 19–47 at 30.

31. Leuchtenburg, *Herbert Hoover*, 72.

32. Tom Lewis, "'A Godlike Presence,' The Impact of Radio on the 1920s and 1930s," *OAH Magazine of History* 6(4) (1992): 26–33 at 28.

33. Oscar Handlin, "Why the Brown Derby?" *Boston Globe*, January 28, 1958, 12.

34. Alfred E. Smith, "Address of Acceptance, Albany," in *Campaign Addresses of Governor Alfred E. Smith, Democratic Candidate*

for President 1928 (Washington, D.C.: Democratic National Committee, 1929), 1–26; Robert Chiles, *The Revolution of '28: Al Smith, American Progressivism, and the Coming of the New Deal* (Ithaca, NY: Cornell University Press, 2018), 81–82; John D. Hicks, *Republican Ascendancy: 1921–1933* (New York: Harper, 1960), 210; "Rival Political Attitudes," editorial, *New Orleans Times-Picayune*, September 30, 1928, 30.

35. Kieran, "Sports of the Times." The 'pennant race' is the colloquial term for the regular season drive to finish atop the standings in the American League or National League and win the 'pennant' for that league, therefore qualifying for the World Series. At this time, there were no divisions within the leagues; the regular season first place finisher was the league champion. 'Senators' was the popular name for the Washington baseball team, which was formally named the 'Nationals.'

36. *Washington Post* sports columnist Shirley Povich later argued that Ruth's apology had been at best half-hearted, reporting in 1948 that Ruth's manager Christy Walsh had composed the apology and that 'privately' the Babe "couldn't figure out how an Al Smith man could conscientiously pose with the Republican candidate." Shirley Povich, "This Morning," *Washington Post*, March 12, 1948, B5; Shirley Povich, "This Morning," *Washington Post*, March 1, 1935, 21; Kieran, "Sports of the Times," 37.

37. "Full Team of Yanks to Support Al Smith," *Baltimore Sun*, October 8, 1928, 11.

38. Slayton, *Empire Statesman*, 297.

39. Leigh Montville, *The Big Bam: The Life and Times of Babe Ruth* (New York: Anchor, 2006), 174.

40. "Tammany Hall's Programme," *New York Times*, October 6, 1898, 3. Ruppert had also owned a brewery, further tying his ideals to those of the antiprohibitionist Smith.

41. Ruppert to Smith, April 24, 1924; Smith to Ruppert, April 24, 1924; Ruppert to Smith, April 10, 1925; Smith to Ruppert, April 16, 1925; Smith to Ruppert, April 22, 1926; Smith to Ruppert, May 3, 1927; Smith to Ruppert, May 2, 1928, George Graves Papers, Box 63, Folder 6, New York State Archives, Albany, N.Y. The author thanks Mr. Keith Swaney of the New York State Archives for his assistance in retrieving this document, which would have been otherwise inaccessible during the COVID-19 pandemic. Regrettably, none of the Ruppert/Smith correspondences discuss politics. Moreover, a thorough review of the New York Yankees corporate archival collection,

housed at the New York Public Library, returned only routine documents like insurance, banking, and vending contracts and minutes of corporate meetings. The minutes never discussed politics. Yankee Baseball Collection, 1913–1950 (one box), New York Public Library, New York, N.Y.

42. Slayton, *Empire Statesman*, image between pp. 224 and 225; Leavy, *The Big Fella*, 65.

43. Dick Hawkins, "Hawk-eye-ing Sports," *Atlanta Constitution*, November 4, 1928, 4B.

44. Leavy, *The Big Fella*, 60–63.

45. "Babe Ruth on Radio in Support of Smith," *New York Times*, October 20, 1928, 5; "Babe Ruth Hits Homer in Urging Smith's Election," *Atlanta Constitution*, October 20, 1928, 7; "Radio Drama Based on Smith's Career," *New York Times*, October 18, 1928, 10; "Smith on Radio Tonight," *New York Times*, October 19, 1928, 8.

46. "Babe Ruth on Radio in Support of Smith."

47. "Babe Ruth on Radio in Support of Smith."

48. "Babe Ruth on Radio in Support of Smith."

49. Montville, *The Big Bam*, 279.

50. "Babe Ruth on Radio in Support of Smith."

51. "Babe Ruth on Radio in Support of Smith."

52. "Babe Ruth Lauds Smith as the Friend of Sport," *Washington Post*, October 20, 1928, 2.

53. "Babe Ruth Comes to Bat for Gov Smith over the Radio," *Boston Globe*, October 20, 1928, 6.

54. "Babe Ruth Comes to Bat for Gov Smith over the Radio."

55. "Babe Ruth Talks on Radio for Smith," *Baltimore Sun*, October 20, 1928, 1; "Babe Goes to Bat for Smith Via Radio in Political Game," *Los Angeles Times*, October 20, 1928, 4.

56. Ruth quoted in Slayton, *Empire Statesman*, 206.

57. Nathan Miller, *New World Coming: The 1920s and the Making of Modern America* (New York: Scribner, 2003), 333.

58. Leavy, *The Big Fella*, 35–55.

59. Leavy, *The Big Fella*, 26, 36, 46.

60. See Chiles, *The Revolution of '28*, 114–126.

61. Leuchtenburg, *The Perils of Prosperity, 1914–32*, 236.

62. Lawrence Baldassaro, *Tony Lazzeri: Yankees Legend and Baseball Pioneer* (Lincoln: University of Nebraska Press, 2021), xi.

63. Baldassaro, *Tony Lazzeri*, x.

64. Baldassaro, *Tony Lazzeri*, 115; Montville, *The Big Bam*, 280.

65. "Babe Ruth Comes to Bat for Gov Smith over the Radio."

66. "Babe Ruth Hits Homer in Urging Smith's Election." Historian Lizabeth Cohen has urged historians to "pay careful attention to the context in which people encountered mass culture" in order to transcend "mythical assumptions about mass culture's homogenizing powers"; in the case of Ruth – an "idol of consumption" who "made sure to treat himself as a commodity," diverse Americans could celebrate divergent interpretations of the slugger. Lizabeth Cohen, "Encountering Mass Culture at the Grassroots: The Experience of Chicago Workers in the 1920s," *American Quarterly* 41(1) (1989), 6–33 at 27; Dyerson, "The Emergence of Consumer Culture and the Transformation of Physical Culture," 274.
67. See Chiles, *The Revolution of '28*, 82–92.
68. Robert Chiles, "Courting the Farm Vote on the Northern Plains: Presidential Candidate Al Smith, Governor Walter Maddock, and the Ambivalent Politics of 1928," *North Dakota History: Journal of the Northern Plains* 81(1) (2016): 16–31.
69. Thomas R. Pegram, *One Hundred Percent American: The Rebirth and Decline of the Ku Klux Klan in the 1920s* (Chicago, IL: Ivan R. Dee, 2011), 3, 20, 26.
70. "Women will Decide How Missouri Goes," *New York Times*, October 27, 1928, 12.
71. "Sunday Baseball Bill," *New York Times*, April 16, 1907, 9.
72. "Sunday Baseball in N.Y. is Assured," *St. Louis Post-Dispatch*, April 20, 1919, B9.
73. For discussion of baseball officials' enthusiasm for expanded Sunday games in 1928, see, for example, John Drebinger, "Hail Sports Vote in Massachusetts," *New York Times*, November 9, 1928, 32.
74. "Advent of Sunday Baseball Draws 60,000 Persons to Polo Grounds and Ebbets Field," *New York Times*, May 5, 1919, 14.
75. "Robins Win before Big Sunday Throng," *New York Times*, May 5, 1919, 14.
76. President Calvin Coolidge was often invoked during debates over Sunday games in Massachusetts, where he had served as governor from 1919 to 1921. As governor, he had signed legislation legalizing amateur Sunday games but maintained his opposition to professional Sunday games. His reticence as president allowed former Boston mayor John F. Fitzgerald, a Democrat and proponent of Sunday baseball, to declare that "the president of the United States does not object to it and he's Calvinistic in his Puritanism," while the *Baltimore Sun* interpreted the president's conferring with the 'Lord's Day Alliance' to signal that he "favors strict observance of

the Sabbath." "Brings Coolidge into Sunday Ball Debate," *Boston Globe*, February 5, 1925, A14; "President Favors Stricter Observance of the Sabbath," *Baltimore Sun*, October 11, 1923, 2. During a 1927 debate, arguments over the president's position on Sunday baseball unleashed "wave after wave of verbal epithets." "Sunday Sports Bill Opponents Talk," *Boston Globe*, February 16, 1927, 9.

77. While several Minor League teams had installed lights earlier, the first Major League Baseball night game under permanent electric lights was hosted by the Cincinnati Reds at Crosley Field, May 24, 1935. Jeff Seuss, "Major League Baseball's First Night Game Held at Crosley Field 85 Years Ago," *Cincinnati Enquirer*, May 21, 2020.

78. John A. Lucas, "The Unholy Experiment: Professional Baseball's Struggle Against Pennsylvania's Sunday Blue Laws, 1926–1934," *Pennsylvania History* 38(2) (1971), 163–175 at 170.

79. Lucas, "The Unholy Experiment."

80. Gerald R. Gems, "The Prep Bowl: Football and Religious Acculturation in Chicago, 1927–1963," *Journal of Sport History* 23(3) (1996), 284–302 at 287. Gems suggests the strategies of Catholic football clubs in these years were more team-oriented and less individualistic (286). The 'Warner system' refers to the dominant offensive systems devised by Coach Glen Scobey Warner, better known as Pop Warner.

81. Miller, *New World Coming*, 333.

82. Christy Walsh to Alfred E. Smith, July 19, 1928, George Graves Papers, Box 75, Folder 9, New York State Archives, Albany, N.Y. The author thanks Mr. Keith Swaney of the New York State Archives for his assistance in retrieving this document, which would have been otherwise inaccessible during the COVID-19 pandemic.

83. Christy Walsh to Alfred E. Smith, July 19, 1928.

84. Christy Walsh to Alfred E. Smith, July 19, 1928.

85. Leavy, *The Big Fella*, 62, 196.

86. "Lost Motion," *Los Angeles Times*, October 29, 1928, A4.

87. Leavy, *The Big Fella*, 196.

88. "Ruth and Davis to Speak," *New York Times*, October 22, 1928, 10.

89. "Hoover Assailed by John W. Davis," *Atlanta Constitution*, October 25, 1928, 10; "Babe Ruth's Chair Breaks as Davis Makes Speech," *Baltimore Sun*, October 25, 1928, 1.

90. "Ruth Wires Governor," *New York Times*, October 26, 1928, 2.

91. "Smith Scores Foe's Silence Before 22,000," *Washington Post*, November 4, 1928, M1.

92. See Chiles, *The Revolution of '28*, 126.

93. John D. Merrill, "Democrats Add to Legislature Seats," *Boston Globe*, November 8, 1928, 1, 21.
94. Merrill, "Democrats Add to Legislature Seats; Chiles, *The Revolution of '28*, 133–178; J. Joseph Huthmacher, *Massachusetts People and Politics:1919–1933* (New York: Atheneum, 1973), 150–190.
95. Before 1928, no Democrat had carried a majority in either state since before the Civil War; Woodrow Wilson had carried both in 1912 due to the split between Republican William Howard Taft and Progressive Theodore Roosevelt.
96. Chiles, *The Revolution of '28*, 126–132.
97. Chiles, *The Revolution of '28*, 153.
98. Leavy, *The Big Fella*, 197.
99. "Ruth, Paired with Al Smith, Develops Cramps and Loses," *Washington Post*, January 18, 1930, 15.
100. Louis J. Pantuosco and Gary Stone, "Babe Ruth as a Free Agent: What the Old-Time Greats Would Earn in Today's Labor Market for Baseball Players," *The American Economist* 55(2) (2010): 154–161 at 154.
101. Chiles, *The Revolution of '28*, 150.
102. I am grateful to Keith Swaney of the New York State Archives, Albany, N.Y., for his invaluable assistance in obtaining materials in the midst of the pandemic, and to Adam Burns, Rivers Gambrell, David Sicilia, Tom Pegram, and Leslie Chiles for their advice, feedback, guidance, and support.

11

Jackie Robinson and His Presidents: Political Endorsements and Civil Rights Advocacy

Dean J. Kotlowski

"I'm a pressure group for civil rights," Jackie Robinson once declared.[1] He was more than that. As a member of the Brooklyn Dodgers, Jack Roosevelt 'Jackie' Robinson broke baseball's color barrier in 1947. Over a decade later, as a columnist, corporate executive, and sports icon, he broke into politics when he campaigned for Richard Nixon, as the then vice president took on Democrat John F. Kennedy in the 1960 presidential election. Robinson promoted both the fortunes of the Republicans – or the 'Grand Old Party' (GOP) – and social justice for African Americans. Partially named for one Republican president (Theodore Roosevelt), he remained devoted to the egalitarian ideals of the GOP's first president, Abraham Lincoln. He was wary of Democrats such as Kennedy and Lyndon B. Johnson, whom he deemed political shapeshifters on civil rights. But racial liberalism and GOP politics were hardly a matched set, as Robinson later acknowledged: "I am black and American before I am Republican."[2] His relations with Nixon cooled after 1960, and in 1964, Robinson opposed the candidacy of conservative Republican Senator Barry M. Goldwater of Arizona, in favor of Goldwater's liberal foe, Governor Nelson A. Rockefeller of New York. Four years later, the decline of the GOP's 'Rockefeller' wing eased Robinson's endorsement of Democrat Hubert H. Humphrey, a champion of racial equality. Nevertheless, Robinson insisted that his identification as a Republican gave Blacks a presence in both major parties.[3] Besides, he noted, baseball's integration would be "meaningless" if America's "political parties are segregated."[4]

Steeled by his idealism, pragmatism, and celebrity, Robinson eagerly interacted with presidents and those he envisioned as presidents. The choices he made, and the tactics he employed, epitomized the politics of principle. Robinson's diligence, perseverance, and talent abetted his rise from poverty, while his embrace of patriotism, self-help, and entrepreneurship led him into the Republican Party. But when the party turned right on racial issues, Robinson turned to liberal Democrats. His accomplishments on and off the baseball diamond afforded him a platform unique among civil rights leaders. At the close of Robinson's inaugural season in Brooklyn, he was placed second behind the entertainer Bing Crosby in a national popularity poll. "Among black Americans," Robinson's biographer, Arnold Rampersad, emphasized, "he was even more revered."[5] Good looks, courage, and an outspoken personality enhanced his authority. "Robinson did not merely play at center stage," the writer Roger Kahn observed, "He *was* center stage."[6] Politicians recognized as much. In 1960, a Nixon aide wrote that he had been "negotiating" with Robinson about a luncheon with the vice president.[7] Meanwhile, JFK's "concern over Negro support" in that year's election prompted an "unpublicized but highly significant" meeting between Kennedy and Robinson.[8]

Robinson's political influence ebbed and flowed, yet it set an important precedent for African American athletes. Modest political involvement during his playing career grew following his retirement in 1956, cresting in a full-throated endorsement of Nixon in 1960. After this, Robinson's clout leveled off. As racial tensions heightened, Robinson became removed from an increasingly conservative GOP and from younger African Americans, some of whom chided his politics and associations as those of an "Uncle Tom."[9] Such sneers overlooked Robinson's criticism of almost every politician with whom he dealt. Sometimes fierce but seldom unfair, these rebukes challenged the willingness of national leaders to overlook injustices, court white southerners, and urge Blacks to remain patient. And Robinson's own detractors failed to foresee later electoral endorsements and civil rights protests by African American athletes – an amalgam of politics and advocacy that the baseball legend embodied and to some extent inspired.

Playing the field: from baseball to politics, 1919–1959

Robinson's character, success, celebrity, politics, and influence intersected with each other and evolved over time. His athletic prowess led to historic breakthroughs, fame, and the ability to command attention, espouse causes, and endorse candidates. His life story, attributes, and experiences with racism forged a leader who was liberal on civil rights, while moderate or conservative on other issues. Although he led no organized group and never sought office himself, he understood the value of playing the field – of maintaining ties to both parties before making strategic endorsements. In 1960, Nixon praised Robinson for handling political matters "with the same agility which you always show on the baseball diamond."[10]

Robinson's rise from rural poverty to sports icon molded his outlook and later activism. Born in Cairo, Georgia, to a sharecropper who later deserted his wife and children, Robinson was raised in Pasadena, California, where his family had migrated in 1920. Although Pasadena was segregated by race, Robinson became a standout athlete at school and in college, where he excelled in basketball, baseball, football, and track.[11] A shy demeanor, a will to succeed, and the example of his mother – a devout Methodist who worked as a maid to support her children – kept his focus on sports. "The fact that Jack did not drink liquor or chase women, and was religious," Rampersad noted, "made him an oddball to many men" – but no doubt pleased countless Republicans who identified with his 'square' lifestyle.[12] Following a stint in the U.S. Army (1942–44), Robinson honed his baseball skills playing for the Kansas City Monarchs (1944–45) of the Negro American League, before marrying in 1946. His athleticism, poise, and faultless personal life impressed Dodgers President Branch Rickey, who brought him into the Brooklyn organization. The road ahead proved to be challenging for the first Black man to play in the Major Leagues since the 1890s. But Rickey believed that Robinson could handle the abuse "with guts enough *not* to fight back."[13]

Robinson fought racism, sometimes directly and at other times less so. The racially diverse athletic contests of his youth convinced him that racial segregation in sports or "in any other aspect of American life" had no justification.[14] The reach and tenacity of Jim Crow challenged such ideals, and Robinson developed a "quick temper in the face of injustice" which tested his self-discipline.[15] Whilst training in Kansas during the Second World War, he befriended the boxing champion Joe Louis, who noted that Robinson "wouldn't take shit from anyone."[16] Robinson was later court-martialed for insubordination – though eventually exonerated – after he refused to obey a state law requiring racial segregation on buses. While playing for the Minor League Montreal Royals (1946) and then for the Dodgers (1947–56), Robinson faced numerous indignities. In 1947, a few teammates objected to playing with him, players from other clubs taunted him, and opposing fans shouted racist slurs – yet he persevered.[17]

Robinson's success led to breakthroughs elsewhere. Other Black players followed him into the Major Leagues, including Roy Campanella and Don Newcombe, who propelled Brooklyn to its only World Series title in 1955. In 1949, Robinson was named the National League's most valuable player, and he appeared in six All-Star games before retiring in 1956. In 1962, he earned induction into baseball's Hall of Fame. Although Robinson became more assertive over time, arguing with umpires and challenging pitchers, his appeal endured.[18] Count Basie recorded a song that exalted his ability to steal home plate.[19] Robinson hosted his own television and radio shows in New York, and even starred in his own film: *The Jackie Robinson Story* (1950). At a time when a number of Black entertainers came to the forefront of American popular culture – musicians Dizzy Gillespie, Charlie Parker, and Chuck Berry, and actors Harry Belafonte and Sidney Poitier – Robinson stood out.[20] "As the most visible African American in the United States," the historian Thomas W. Zeiler has asserted, "he also became a spokesman for civil rights."[21]

Robinson's civil rights advocacy and involvement in politics began during his baseball career. He learned, he later wrote, that "a black man, even after he has proven himself on and off the playing field, will still be denied his rights."[22] He supported the Anti-Defamation League of B'nai B'rith, a Jewish service organization that fought anti-Semitism and other forms of discrimination. Yet his ties to the National Association for the Advancement of Colored People (NAACP) remained "modest" during his base-ball career.[23] And his religiosity and anticommunism placed him within the main currents of postwar politics, which he entered adroitly. Testifying before the House Committee on Un-American Activities in 1949, Robinson dismissed as "silly" the allegedly pro-Soviet utterances of the African American singer and socialist Paul Robeson. Robinson went on to deny that Blacks sought the assistance of communists. He extolled African American patrio-tism, and linked communism to such antidemocratic practices as racial discrimination.[24] It proved a bravura performance: "The committee was thoroughly impressed by his solid, reasoned, well-stated thoughts," journalist Frank McNaughton reported.[25] Zeiler reckoned that "by standing up to communism," Robinson "reciprocated" President Harry S. Truman's "efforts on behalf of civil rights."[26] In 1947, Truman's Committee on Civil Rights pro-posed a series of strikes against Jim Crow and praised baseball's recent integration.[27] A decade later, Robinson signaled his regard for Truman by inviting him to appear on a radio program, a cour-tesy that the former president declined.[28]

Robinson's early thoughts about presidents revealed an uncer-tainty about whom to trust. His brief employment at the National Youth Administration during the 1930s established a tie to Franklin D. Roosevelt that apparently withstood his experiences with racism in the army. The failure of Roosevelt or Truman to secure enact-ment of civil rights legislation did not, in Robinson's mind, dimin-ish FDR's New Deal work-relief programs or Truman's executive order to desegregate the armed services in 1948. "There can be lit-tle doubt that the Negro and other minorities have benefitted more under the Democrats," Robinson asserted in 1959, "but I wonder whether the candidates in the running [for 1960] would wave the same stick that Roosevelt and Truman waved?"[29] Two interrelated dynamics troubled him: the power of white southerners within the Democratic Party, and the willingness of some liberals to placate them. The party's adoption of a weak civil rights plank in its 1956 platform disappointed Robinson.[30]

Historical, cultural, and personal circumstances left Robinson favorable to the liberal wing of the Republican Party. Between the end of the Civil War and FDR's New Deal, most African

Americans able to vote remained loyal to the party of Lincoln. Although FDR's policies drew many Blacks into the Democratic fold, some Republicans angled to reclaim their votes. In 1940, GOP presidential nominee Wendell L. Willkie's embrace of civil rights earned him endorsements from African American newspapers and from Joe Louis, who appeared at a campaign event.[31] The first Republican president, Abraham Lincoln, a hero to many Blacks, occupied a key place in Robinson's life story. Reporters likened the ending of baseball's color line to Lincoln's Emancipation Proclamation, and Branch Rickey to Lincoln. And after Robinson joined Chock Full O'Nuts Coffee Corporation as Vice President of Personnel in 1957, he kept on his desk a wooden replica of Lincoln's hand holding the Emancipation Proclamation, a gift from Richard and Pat Nixon. Robinson later quoted Lincoln's warning against a "house divided" when he implored politicians to avoid mouthing buzzwords that inflamed racial animus.[32] But, in the 1950s, Robinson amplified his antiracism more than his party preferences. He corresponded with liberal Democrats Governor W. Averell Harriman and Senator Herbert H. Lehman, both from New York, while avowing that he was "neither a Republican nor a Democrat."[33] Yet displeasure with the Democratic platform, coupled with promising moves by President Dwight D. Eisenhower – the desegregation of public facilities in Washington, D.C., the appointment of federal judges supportive of civil rights, and the introduction of voting rights legislation – led Robinson to vote for the GOP ticket in 1956.[34]

Robinson's participation in the civil rights struggle deepened during the second term of Eisenhower, who frustrated him. While working at Chock Full O'Nuts, Robinson raised funds for the NAACP and for the African-American Students Foundation, which helped Africans attend U.S. universities – a cause also pushed by Belafonte and Poitier.[35] In 1958, he appeared with Martin Luther King, Jr. and A. Philip Randolph at a Harlem rally for racially integrated schools.[36] A year later, he testified before the U.S. Commission on Civil Rights on the lack of adequate housing for minority groups. Most importantly, Robinson shared his views with a president who both courted white southerners and employed "symbolic gestures" to express his opposition to racial discrimination.[37] To

Eisenhower, Robinson's successes provided "evidence" to over-seas audiences that American democracy was "a workable, living ideal."[38] Robinson returned the compliment, describing a meeting with the president as a "big thrill."[39] But Ike's reluctance to go fur-ther on behalf of civil rights distressed him. Robinson showed no sympathy for the president's lament about the "deep-seated emo-tional difficulties" aroused by "problems" tied to race.[40] Reject-ing the argument that "half loaf [is] better than none," he pressed Eisenhower to veto the Civil Rights Act of 1957, which Senate Democrats had weakened.[41] Ike signed the measure anyway, after fretting about laws that "go too far too fast" in "this delicate field" – an aside that left Robinson "in a muddle" about "what to do" next.[42] Although he congratulated Eisenhower on sending troops to enforce court-ordered school desegregation in Little Rock, Arkansas, he objected to the president's earlier remarks "advising patience" during the crisis.[43] Robinson raised the stakes in 1960, when he told the National Urban League that Eisenhower "hasn't said a thing as far as I'm concerned on civil rights." In that speech, he repeated a Democratic Party refrain by describing the general-turned-president as "a figurehead in Washington."[44]

Robinson's remarks signified key aspects of his emerging activ-ism. Fundraising for the NAACP had sharpened his public speak-ing. "If I had to choose between baseball's Hall of Fame and first-class citizenship," he told an NAACP audience, "I would say first-class citizenship to all of my people."[45] He also maintained that racial discrimination wasted American talent and hurt the country in its struggle against the Soviet Union. With an eye on new venues of Cold War competition, he hailed the "new nations" of Africa, to which he urged Blacks to pay attention.[46] In 1959, Robinson acquired a platform of his own when he joined the *New York Post*. Its editor, James A. Weschler, deemed Robinson a "somewhat unconventional voice" who reflected "a lot of non-organizational Negro feeling."[47] The former ballplayer's thrice-weekly column spanned sports, politics, and race. Eisenhower's civil rights record quickly became a target, as Robinson urged him to fortify his "singing words with definite, positive action."[48]

Robinson approached politics pragmatically. Knowing that campaign promises often went unfulfilled, he looked for candidates who gave "honest and sincere answers," and seemed willing to lead on matters related to race.[49] As the election of 1960 neared, he scrutinized the characters and records of presidential hopefuls rather than their party affiliation or prospects for victory. His first electoral involvement was in the contest for New York governor in 1958, when he backed Harriman over Rockefeller. The Democrat's candor impressed Robinson, who worried that an inexperienced Rockefeller would become the cat's paw of GOP conservatives.[50] Partially to offset the boxer Sugar Ray Robinson's endorsement of Rockefeller, the ex-Dodger lauded Harriman's record.[51] But supporting Harriman did not represent a turn toward the Democrats. Robinson's private praise of former governor Chester Bowles of Connecticut, a steadfast liberal, did not result in public approval of Bowles' U.S. Senate bid in 1958.[52] "Robinson," Rampersad explained, "was a Republican at heart, albeit a liberal Republican on the key matter of civil rights."[53] Such sentiments partially explain his decision to campaign for Nixon in 1960.

From peak to past prime: Robinson and liberal Republicanism, 1960–1972

The 1960 election marked the highpoint of Robinson's political influence, and a falloff followed. On the eve of his enshrinement in the Hall of Fame, venerated by African Americans, situated at the *New York Post*, and present on the airwaves, Robinson won the attention of presidential hopefuls. Nixon aide Fred Lowery urged his boss to woo the former baseball star since he "'is more or less considered sort of a God'" among Blacks.[54] Meanwhile, Bowles arranged a meeting between Robinson and JFK.[55]

True to form, Robinson gave the Democrats a hearing in 1960. The sit-ins of that year focused the public's attention on racial inequality and drew praise from Senator Hubert Humphrey of Minnesota, who had entered the national stage in 1948 by pushing Democrats to support civil rights. A candidate for the party's nomination in 1960, Humphrey departed from Eisenhower's hedged rhetoric by proclaiming the sit-ins "morally right" and "a service" to democracy. The Minnesotan earned the endorsement of Robinson, who made his priorities plain: "[Until Blacks] get

241

civil rights we can't worry too much about other things." He campaigned for Humphrey in the Wisconsin primary and attended the opening of his office in Washington, D.C. Robinson's support, Humphrey beamed, made him "the luckiest man in American politics."[56] His luck ran out when Kennedy beat him in Wisconsin and West Virginia. Although Robinson had promised to consider backing a Democrat other than Humphrey, JFK did not impress him. Kennedy's vote to weaken enforcement provisions of the Civil Rights Act of 1957 concerned Robinson, as did an endorsement from John M. Patterson, Alabama's segregationist governor.[57] A meeting between the two men yielded nothing. Robinson found JFK evasive, uncertain, and flustered by his demand for proof about "what you will do for my people."[58] He complained that Kennedy "didn't look him in the eye."[59] Robinson thus saw no reason to retract his earlier assertion that he would vote for Nixon if the Democrats did not nominate Humphrey.[60]

A cluster of circumstances drew Robinson and Nixon together. A passion for sports enabled Nixon to connect with voters and athletes, including Robinson. During their first meeting, at the Republican National Convention in 1952, Nixon congratulated the star on a recent homerun, and then reminisced about Robinson's gridiron exploits at college.[61] No other president or politician with whom Robinson dealt exuded such interest in sports – especially baseball – and the two men developed a rapport.

Nixon's early civil rights record earned Robinson's respect. As vice president, he chaired a committee to stop discrimination in companies receiving government contracts and pushed for the strongest possible civil rights bill in 1957. Nixon endorsed the Supreme Court's decision in *Brown* v. *Board of Education* (1954) and denounced efforts to thwart the desegregation of Little Rock's Central High School. Political expediency often motivated his words and deeds, and his committee posted few breakthroughs. But, in 1956, White House Press Secretary James C. Hagerty reported that the vice president had become associated "with the Negro difficulty" and that support for him had fallen in the South. Nixon engaged directly with Martin Luther King, Jr., who hailed his "intense interest in solving the civil rights problem."[62] Letters also passed between Nixon and Robinson.

One missive, drafted by the vice president's friend and adviser Robert H. Finch, outlined the moral, practical, and foreign policy reasons behind Nixon's "strong position" on civil rights.[63] Following a private luncheon in 1960, Robinson told his readers that Nixon "seems very much aware of the need for using the influence and prestige of the Presidency to advance equal rights."[64] "[Robinson] hates Kennedy," Dorothy Schiff, the *Post*'s publisher, later observed, "and loves Nixon because 'he trusts him.'"[65] Nixon's choice of the liberal Henry Cabot Lodge, Jr. for vice president further heartened Robinson, who dismissed Kennedy's selection of LBJ as another sop to the South.[66]

Robinson's support of Nixon sparked criticism, and his standing at the *New York Post* slipped as the paper's Democratic readership protested his pro-Nixon musings. "He should control his personal feelings," one man vented, while another griped that Robinson's "knowledge is sports" and "not politics."[67] It is not hard to see racial bias behind such complaints. But Robinson stirred controversy when his column exaggerated Nixon's assistance to a group of African college students when, in fact, the Kennedy family had donated money to support their education. Robert F. Kennedy, JFK's brother and campaign manager, entered the fracas by publicly questioning Robinson's integrity and by suggesting that his perch at Chock Full O'Nuts made him indifferent to the concerns of working people. Robinson responded by denouncing Bobby Kennedy's "lies, innuendoes and personal attacks."[68] Behind the scenes, JFK aide Pierre Salinger discussed the column about the African students with Weschler, the *Post*'s editor.[69] Although Robinson claimed that the newspaper allowed him to write "whatever he liked," Dorothy Schiff worried that he had become a "propagandist for the Nixon machine."[70] She warned him that "most people didn't trust Nixon" and that any politician was capable of projecting earnestness, a point Robinson conceded.[71] In the end, Robinson bowed to the *Post*'s pressure and took a leave of absence in order to campaign for his candidate.

Robinson's campaigning for Nixon involved much work and large disappointments. He defended the Republican candidate, dismissed JFK as callow, and depicted LBJ as the southern-accented voice of civil rights in a Kennedy White House.[72] At a rally in

New Jersey, Robinson appeared alongside Nixon, who vowed to go to bat for African Americans.[73] At other times, he campaigned with Rockefeller, whose "substance and backbone" surprised him, especially after the governor praised the sit-ins and quoted Martin Luther King.[74] Robinson and Rockefeller appealed to liberals and minority voters, which freed Nixon to court white moderates in the suburbs and the South (a strategy he pursued more intensively in 1968). Yet, in 1960, Nixon did not appear in Harlem, which frustrated Robinson, who later asserted that white politicians needed "to connect with African Americans" by visiting "predominately black localities."[75]

Even more disquieting to Robinson was Nixon's unsympathetic reaction to King's arrest during a sit-in in Atlanta. Robinson, Rockefeller, and other advisors prodded Nixon to telephone King, but he rejected such outreach as a "grandstand play."[76] One campaign aide, doubtless thinking of white voters, averred: "'This is too hot for us to handle."[77] In contrast, JFK called Dr. King's wife, Coretta Scott King, to express his concern, and Robert Kennedy contacted the judge in Georgia to secure King's release. Such gestures enabled JFK to rally African American voters. The Republican candidate's silence saddened Robinson, who privately, albeit presciently, fumed: "Nixon doesn't deserve to win."[78] In the end, JFK took the larger share of the Black vote and enough Southern states to capture the White House. To make matters worse, the day Nixon lost the election, Robinson lost his job at the *Post*. Robinson's decision to campaign for the vice president had frayed relations between him and the paper, as did his editorial about the African students.[79] Undaunted, Robinson spoke a month later in Montgomery, Alabama, where he attacked Blacks' "mistaken" support for President-elect Kennedy.[80]

Defiance defined Robinson's politics following the 1960 election. The endorsement of Nixon had offended a number of African Americans, including an NAACP official who publicly scolded Robinson.[81] The editor of the *Baltimore Afro-American* called the former Dodger tragically "out of step" with the nearly 70 percent of Blacks who had voted for JFK.[82] And a columnist for New York's *Amsterdam News*, another Black-owned newspaper, chastised "self-styled Negro leaders" who had been "advising Negroes on how to vote."[83] The jibe did not prevent Robinson from joining that paper as a columnist. From his new platform, he derided Kennedy's reluctance to sign a much-promised executive order outlawing racial discrimination in federally funded housing. Robinson labeled the president "a fine man," but no "Abraham Lincoln."[84] In 1962, he published an open letter imploring Kennedy to display as much interest in "the high cost of race prejudice" as he had shown recently in "the threatened high cost of steel."[85] To be sure, hints of détente surfaced. Robinson appreciated Attorney General Robert Kennedy's efforts to protect the rights of African Americans, and he applauded JFK's forceful espousal of civil rights following mass protests in Birmingham, Alabama. When Americans mourned the slain Kennedy in 1963, Robinson generously declared that he had "done more for the civil rights cause than any other President."[86] Such kind words aside, Robinson remained loyal to the GOP during the early part of the decade. Two days before JFK's inauguration, he told Nixon that "our country is the loser, not you."[87] The two men exchanged letters and gifts.[88] And when the former vice president sought the California governorship in 1962, Robinson appeared on a "celebrities-for-Nixon list."[89] He continued to back Nixon, in part because he thought himself "a good judge of character" and was too stubborn to change course.[90] After Nixon's defeat, Robinson consoled him: "You are good for politics; good for America."[91]

The election of 1964 marked a crossroads for the GOP, as it shifted rightward, and for Robinson, who proved a staunch liberal 'Rockefeller' Republican. Rockefeller's presidential ambitions crashed against a grassroots movement determined to nominate Arizona Senator Barry Goldwater. Conservatives shared the senator's distaste for federal power – a disposition that had led him to vote against the Civil Rights Act of 1964, delighting white southerners and disgusting Robinson. Goldwater's campaign, according to one party honcho, stressed "race, corruption, nostalgia, and nationalism," and the candidate "equated civil rights and civil disorder, using coded language that blamed blacks for increased crime rates."[92] In contrast, Rockefeller backed civil rights and governed liberally in his home state of New York. Robinson went all out for Rockefeller, whom he called a force for "human dignity and world peace."[93] He stumped for him in the primaries and labeled Goldwater a bigot who "inspires the lunatic fringe that is out murdering Negroes in the South."[94] He also joined GOP moderates in a desperate attempt to thwart Goldwater's nomination, which he thought an affront to any "sensible, alert member of any minority group."[95] Later, Robinson cheered Rockefeller as he struggled to address the party's convention over the catcalls of triumphant Goldwater delegates.[96]

It is worth pointing out that Robinson remained devoted to, but never uncritical of, Rockefeller. Robinson later served as the governor's assistant for community affairs, campaigned for his re-election in 1966 and 1970, and backed his bid for the Republican presidential nomination in 1968. But he was troubled by Rockefeller's violent suppression of the Attica State Prison riot in 1971.[97] Goldwater, for his part, reached out to Robinson, knowing that he remained the party's best-known Black speaker. After the election, the two men communicated directly, which allowed the Arizonan to convey his opposition to racial discrimination.[98] Looming over their interactions were the events of 1964, when Robinson vowed to "fight like hell" to inflict "a stunning defeat" on Goldwater.[99]

In 1964, Robinson set aside his distrust of LBJ and chaired the national 'Republicans for Johnson Committee.'[100] Metamorphizing from conservative Texan to liberal president, Johnson secured passage of landmark civil rights legislation, which pleased Robinson. "No American in public office has grown, as you have," he wrote to LBJ. "No President could have affected the progress in our drive for human dignity as you have done."[101] He later wondered whether JFK "would have ever done as much as Pres. John. did in race relations."[102] Robinson's anticommunism prevented him from becoming a critic of the Vietnam War – indeed, he praised Johnson's efforts to seek an "honorable solution" to the conflict.[103] Not unlike Eisenhower and Kennedy, LBJ understood Robinson's unique contribution to race relations, and he hosted him and his wife, Rachel, at the White House.[104] After Johnson appointed the first Black cabinet member (Robert Weaver) and Supreme Court justice (Thurgood Marshall), White House aide Lee White likened their pathbreaking careers to Robinson's.[105] But Robinson's ruminations, including a complaint about widening racial division, annoyed the White House, as did his continuing ties to the GOP.[106] "While it is true that Jackie Robinson supported the President [in 1964] with his right hand," observed LBJ advisor Clifford L. Alexander, "he was doing everything with his left hand to defeat a variety of [D]emocratic senatorial and congressional candidates."[107] During those elections, Robinson had split his ticket by voting for both LBJ and Republican Senator Kenneth B. Keating of New York, who lost his seat to Robert Kennedy.[108] Nevertheless, Robinson continued to enjoy a close relationship with Humphrey, Johnson's vice president, whom he endorsed over Nixon in 1968.[109]

Robinson's civil rights advocacy expanded during the 1960s. In 1963, he participated in the March on Washington, along with such celebrities as Belafonte, Poitier, Lena Horne, Ruby Dee, Paul Newman, Joanne Woodward, and Charlton Heston.[110] His columns in the *Amsterdam News* cheered Black trailblazers, such as Massachusetts Republican Edward W. Brooke III, who in 1966 became the first African American elected to the U.S. Senate since Reconstruction.[111] Robinson remained committed to integration and non-violence, but he also supported Black-run institutions and economic empowerment for African Americans. He co-founded and served as chairman of the board of the Black-owned, Harlem-based Freedom National Bank. And he later formed a construction company that built 1,600 housing units for low-income people. Within the civil rights movement, Robinson was unapologetically independent. He attacked the NAACP's leaders as stodgy and dependent on white organizations, opposed Black Muslims "because they advocate the separation of the races," and compared Black Power leaders to hate-filled Southern segregationists.[112] His actions drew criticism. Robinson's defense of Rockefeller's proposed state office building in Harlem prompted young Blacks to brand him an "Oreo" – "black outside and white underneath."[113]

Meanwhile, Nixon's campaigning for Goldwater in 1964 and his courtship of segregationist Senator Strom Thurmond of South Carolina in 1968 signaled a shift to the right that had alienated Robinson. He skipped the GOP convention that both nominated Nixon over Rockefeller and ratified Nixon's choice for vice president, Governor Spiro Agnew of Maryland, who had upbraided a group of Black leaders following racial unrest in Baltimore. Robinson ridiculed the gaff-prone Agnew as "a nice stupid guy."[114] And he told an interviewer that Nixon had "prostituted himself" to the "racist" Thurmond in order "to get the Southern vote."[115] The baseball great chastised Nixon's Black allies, including Senator Brooke, and lamented Rockefeller's support for Nixon, whom he denounced as "anti-black."[116] Robinson endorsed Democratic nominee Humphrey at an event in Harlem, and even threatened to register as a Democrat "if Nixon gets in."[117] Ultimately, though, Nixon went on to defeat Humphrey.

The 1968 election proved to be the last in which Robinson participated. Robinson was suffering from declining health as well as a sense that he was no longer a leading voice in the civil rights movement or the GOP. He warned that the incoming administration "has not given Black America any hope" and that "racial harmony" was a long way off.[118] He panned the organizational chaos of Nixon's initiative to bolster minority-owned businesses, and bemoaned "the very poor relations between black America and the present Administration."[119] In his autobiography, Robinson lamented sticking with Nixon in 1960.[120] But the president's effort to boost Black entrepreneurship, a cause dear to Robinson, suggested room for reconciliation. And notwithstanding his appeals to white southerners, Nixon amassed a record that included extension and expansion of the Voting Rights Act of 1965, desegregation of southern schools, and a strong program of affirmative action. "I believe [Nixon] does have sincerity in many areas," Robinson wrote in 1969, "but I believe his commitments are such [that] he has to be cautious."[121] The president responded through form letters and by praising Robinson's athletic feats and pathbreaking career. Robinson, in turn, paid a visit to a campaign fundraiser hosted by Nixon's African American supporters. But, by 1972, diabetes, high blood pressure, and heart trouble had taken their toll on him. "Jack was no longer even a small force in national politics," Rampersad observed, and he took no part in either party's primaries.[122] Following Robinson's death later that year, Nixon released a statement that hailed his "brilliance on the playing field," which had paved the way for an America "where black and white people work side by side."[123] Having invested so much in their relationship, Nixon and Robinson parted regretfully and somewhat reluctantly.

Retrospect

Joe Louis once admitted: "Sometimes I wish I had the fire of a Jackie Robinson to speak out and tell our story."[124] That reflection underscored Robinson's contribution to both civil rights and national politics, though he bequeathed something of a mixed record. "Robinson's political career, unlike his baseball life," Roger Kahn has asserted, "trails off into disappointments and conditional sentences."[125] Regarding his presidential preferences, he went three-for-eight: Eisenhower won re-election in 1956; Nixon took the GOP nomination in 1960; and LBJ prevailed in 1964. But Nixon lost to JFK; Humphrey failed to gain the Democratic nod in 1960 or the White House in 1968; and Republicans passed on Rockefeller in 1964 and 1968. A .375 average is stellar for a baseball batter, but less so for a political operative – a position for which, the *Baltimore Afro-American* noted, Robinson lacked training.[126] The larger story was a figure defined by courage, passion, breakthroughs, and an "unconquerable" spirit.[127] In politics, Robinson avoided easy roads, never became an unbending partisan or acolyte of frontrunners, and remained, however quixotically, a liberal Republican, devoted to free enterprise and racial equality. The decline of the GOP's Rockefeller wing coincided with other regressions: lessened support for racial integration; criticism of big state liberalism; and Robinson's own failing health and waning influence. Still, he fought on. At his last public appearance, during the 1972 World Series, Robinson pressed big-league executives to hire baseball's first Black manager.[128]

Robinson's activism set an example for other African American athletes. In the election of 1968, Elgin Baylor of the Los Angeles Lakers endorsed Humphrey while Wilt Chamberlain, his teammate, supported Nixon. Four years later, National Football League greats Gayle Sayers and Jim Brown lined up behind Nixon.[129] Decades later, National Basketball Association stars LeBron James and J. R. Smith campaigned for Hillary Clinton in 2016, while Stephen Curry of the Golden State Warriors broadcast an endorsement of

Joe Biden at the 2020 Democratic convention. In 2020, Major League baseball and basketball players staged walkouts in solidarity with Black Lives Matter demonstrators. The extent to which Robinson inspired each of these sportsmen and women is hard to ascertain. But, at the very least, the former Dodger normalized the blending of sports and political advocacy which had become commonplace by the twenty-first century. The continued involvement of U.S. athletes in politics, civil rights, and the politics of civil rights owes a great deal to the life and legacy of Jackie Robinson.

Notes

1. Roger Kahn, *The Boys of Summer* (New York: Harper, 2006), 398.
2. Arnold Rampersad, *Jackie Robinson: A Biography* (New York: Alfred A. Knopf, 1997), 426.
3. Rampersad, *Jackie Robinson*, 388.
4. Kahn, *Boys of Summer*, 398.
5. Rampersad, *Jackie Robinson*, 188.
6. Kahn, *Boys of Summer*, 393.
7. 'JDH' to Richard Nixon, April 27, 1960, folder: Jackie Robinson, box 649, series 320, Richard M. Nixon Pre-Presidential Papers, Richard Nixon Library, Yorba Linda, California (hereafter 'box 649, series 320, NPPP').
8. "Capital Chatter," *Aberdeen American-News* (South Dakota), undated, box 649, series 320, NPPP.
9. Rampersad, *Jackie Robinson*, 418.
10. Nixon to Jackie Robinson, January 16, 1960, in *First Class Citizenship: The Civil Rights Letters of Jackie Robinson*, ed. Michael G. Long (New York: Henry Holt, 2007), 84 (hereafter 'FCC').
11. Jules Tygiel, *Baseball's Great Experiment: Jackie Robinson and His Legacy* (New York: Oxford University Press, 1983), 60.
12. Rampersad, *Jackie Robinson*, 71.
13. Thomas W. Zeiler, *Jackie Robinson and Race in America: A Brief History with Documents* (Boston, MA: Bedford/St. Martin, 2014), 19.
14. Rampersad, *Jackie Robinson*, 27.
15. Rampersad, *Jackie Robinson*, 83.
16. Zeiler, *Jackie Robinson*, 13.
17. Tygiel, *Baseball's Great Experiment*, 196; "Jackie Robinson Continues to 'Pack 'Em In' at Gate," *Atlanta World*, May 27, 1947, 5, in Zeiler, *Jackie Robinson*, 95.

18. Tygiel, *Baseball's Great Experiment*, 327.
19. Buddy Johnson and Count Basie, "Did You See Jackie Robinson Hit That Ball?" in Zeiler, *Jackie Robinson*, 106.
20. Bruce J. Dierenfield, *The Civil Rights Movement: The Black Freedom Struggle in America* (New York: Routledge, 2021), 27.
21. Zeiler, *Jackie Robinson*, 28.
22. Jackie Robinson (with Alfred Duckett), *I Never Had It Made: An Autobiography* (New York: HarperCollins, 1973), 78.
23. Rampersad, *Jackie Robinson*, 220–221, 288 (quotation).
24. "Jackie Robinson, "Statement to the House Committee on Un-American Activities," July 19, 1949, in Zeiler, *Jackie Robinson*, 114.
25. Frank McNaughton to Don Bermingham, July 21, 1949, folder: July 21–31, 1949, box 18, Frank McNaughton Papers, Harry S. Truman Library, Independence, Missouri.
26. Zeiler, *Jackie Robinson*, 28.
27. *To Secure These Rights: The Report of the President's Committee on Civil Rights*, December 1947, 18, Harry S. Truman Library website, available at: https://www.trumanlibrary.gov/library/to-secure-these-rights.
28. Handwritten comment on Robinson to Harry S. Truman, February 4, 1959, folder: Radio–Television, box 34, Secretary's Office Files, Harry S. Truman Post-Presidential Papers, Truman Library.
29. Robinson to Chester Bowles, October 6, 1959, *FCC*, 74.
30. Herbert H. Lehman to Robinson, August 21, 1956, *FCC*, 17.
31. Steve Neal, *Dark Horse: A Biography of Wendell Willkie* (Lawrence: University Press of Kansas, 1984), 163; David Levering Lewis, *The Improbable Wendell Willkie* (New York: Liveright, 2018), 178.
32. Tygiel, *Baseball's Great Experiment*, 5, 74–75; Rampersad, *Jackie Robinson*, 125, 321; Robinson to Barry Goldwater, September 5, 1968, *FCC*, 283–284.
33. Robinson to Nixon, December 24, 1957, *FCC*, 43.
34. Rampersad, *Jackie Robinson*, 325; David A. Nichols, *A Matter of Justice: Eisenhower and the Beginning of the Civil Rights Revolution* (New York: Simon & Schuster, 2007), 273–281.
35. Rampersad, *Jackie Robinson*, 302–307, 314–317; Jackie Robinson, Harry Belafonte, and Sidney Poitier to Mr. King, December 15, 1959, box 649, series 320, NPPP.
36. "President Scored Over Integration," *New York Times*, September 20, 1958, 10.
37. Robert Frederick Burk, *The Eisenhower Administration and Black Civil Rights* (Knoxville: University of Tennessee Press, 1984), 257.

38. Dwight D. Eisenhower to Robinson, November 30, 1953, *FCC*, 12.
39. Robinson to Eisenhower, May 15, 1957, *FCC*, 29.
40. Eisenhower to Robinson, May 21, 1957, *FCC*, 31.
41. Robinson to Frederic Morrow, August 12, 1957, *FCC*, 36–37.
42. Robinson to Maxwell Rabb, July 19, 1957, *FCC*, 34.
43. Robinson to Eisenhower, September 13 and 25, 1957, *FCC*, 40 (quotation), 41.
44. Jackie Robinson speech before the National Urban League, September 4, 1960, folder: Editorial File, Jackie Robinson, 1959, April 20 to 1969, January 15, box 63, Dorothy Schiff Papers, New York Public Library (hereafter 'box 63, Schiff Papers').
45. Rampersad, *Jackie Robinson*, 318.
46. Robinson speech, September 4, 1960, box 63, Schiff Papers.
47. James Weschler to Dorothy Schiff, June 6, 1960, box 63, Schiff Papers.
48. Rampersad, *Jackie Robinson*, 341.
49. Robinson speech, September 4, 1960, box 63, Schiff Papers.
50. Jackie Robinson handwritten notes on politics, undated, folder 12, box 12, Jackie Robinson Papers, Library of Congress, Washington, D.C.; Robinson to Bowles, October 6, 1959, *FCC*, 74.
51. "Midtown Throng Hears Harriman," *New York Times*, October 31, 1958, 18.
52. Robinson to Bowles, January 15, 1958, May 1, 1958, August 26, 1959, *FCC*, 47, 56, 70–72.
53. Rampersad, *Jackie Robinson*, 341.
54. Dean J. Kotlowski, *Nixon's Civil Rights: Politics, Principle, and Policy* (Cambridge, MA: Harvard University Press, 2001), 164.
55. Bowles to Robinson, April 7, 1958 and Robinson to Bowles, May 1, 1958, *FCC*, 52–53, 56; Robinson handwritten notes on politics, undated, folder 12, box 12, Robinson Papers.
56. United Press International (UPI) wire report, March 9, 1960, box 649, series 320, NPPP.
57. Rampersad, *Jackie Robinson*, 344.
58. Robinson handwritten notes on politics, undated, folder 12, box 12, Robinson Papers.
59. Dorothy Schiff memorandum, August 25, 1960, box 63, Schiff Papers.
60. UPI wire report, March 9, 1960, box 649, series 320, NPPP.
61. Nicholas Evan Sarantakes, *Fan in Chief: Richard Nixon and American Sports, 1969–1974* (Lawrence: University Press of Kansas, 2019), 2–3, 167; Kotlowski, *Nixon's Civil Rights*, 163.

62. Kotlowski, *Nixon's Civil Rights*, 100 (first quotation), 24 (second quotation).
63. RHF draft of Nixon to Robinson, June 3, 1960, folder: Jackie Robinson, box 649, series 320, NPPP.
64. "Jackie Robinson," *New York Post*, May 23, 1960, 72.
65. Schiff memorandum, August 25, 1960, box 63, Schiff Papers.
66. "Jackie Robinson," *New York Post*, July 29, 1960, box 649, series 320, NPPP.
67. Morris Olden to Dorothy Schiff, August 16, 1960 and George Markowitz to Schiff, August 19, 1960, box 63, Schiff Papers.
68. Rampersad, *Jackie Robinson*, 347–348.
69. Schiff memorandum, August 17, 1960, box 63, Schiff Papers.
70. Weschler to Schiff, August 22, 1960 (first quotation) and Schiff to Robinson, August 29, 1960 (second quotation), box 63, Schiff Papers.
71. Schiff memorandum, August 25, 1960, box 63, Schiff Papers.
72. Rampersad, *Jackie Robinson*, 349.
73. "Nixon Holds Kennedy Program Will Up Food Prices," *Washington Post*, October 5, 1960, A17.
74. "Jackie Robinson," *New York Post*, July 29, 1960, box 649, series 320, NPPP (quotation); "Governor Turns to Lay Preaching," *New York Times*, October 24, 1960, 1.
75. Leah Wright Rigueur, *The Loneliness of the Black Republican: Pragmatic Politics and the Pursuit of Power* (Princeton, NJ: Princeton University Press, 2015), 43.
76. W. J. Rorabaugh, *The Real Making of the President: Kennedy, Nixon, and the 1960 Election* (Lawrence: University Press of Kansas, 2009), 166–170; Rampersad, *Jackie Robinson*, 350–351; Nixon to Robinson, November 4, 1960, FCC, 115 (quotation).
77. Kotlowski, *Nixon's Civil Rights*, 161.
78. Timothy N. Thurber, *Republicans and Race: The GOP's Frayed Relationship with African Americans, 1945–1974* (Lawrence: University Press of Kansas, 2013), 129.
79. Weschler to Schiff, October 7, 1960, box 63, Schiff Papers.
80. "Jackie's Out of Step," *Baltimore Afro-American*, December 31, 1960, 4.
81. "Robinson Rebuked for Political Note," *Washington Post*, October 9, 1960, B12.
82. "Jackie's Out of Step," *Baltimore Afro-American*, December 31, 1960, 4.
83. Rampersad, *Jackie Robinson*, 352.
84. Rampersad, *Jackie Robinson*, 362–363.

85. Robinson to John F. Kennedy, May 5, 1962, *FCC*, 146.

86. Rampersad, *Jackie Robinson*, 362, 376, 381 (quotation).

87. Robinson to Nixon, January 18, 1961, *FCC*, 123.

88. Robinson to Nixon, March 3, 1961 and May 25, 1961, *FCC*, 125–126, 130.

89. Nixon Conducts 5-Hour Telethon," *New York Times*, November 4, 1962, 58.

90. Schiff memorandum, August 25, 1960, box 63, Schiff Papers.

91. Robinson to Nixon, November 12, 1962, *FCC*, 158.

92. Nancy Beck Young, *Two Suns of the Southwest: Lyndon Johnson, Barry Goldwater and the 1964 Battle between Liberalism and Conservatism* (Lawrence: University Press of Kansas, 2019), 108 (first quotation), 60 (second quotation).

93. Alfred Duckett typescript statement, [1964], folder 2, box 13, Robinson Papers.

94. News clipping, "Robinson Modifies Statements," undated, folder 17, box 5, Robinson Papers.

95. Duckett typescript statement, [1964], folder 2, box 13, Robinson Papers.

96. Rampersad, *Jackie Robinson*, 385–387.

97. Rampersad, *Jackie Robinson*, 404–408, 426–428, 451–452.

98. Correspondence between Robinson and Goldwater is in *FCC*, 198–201, 263–264, 271–272, 274, 280–284.

99. Duckett typescript statement, [1964], folder 2, box 13, Robinson Papers.

100. "Negroes Asked by Miller Not to Abandon GOP," *Washington Post*, July 18, 1964, A8.

101. Robinson to Lyndon B. Johnson, February 4, 1965, *FCC*, 213.

102. Robinson handwritten notes on politics, undated, folder 12, box 12, Robinson Papers.

103. Robinson to LBJ, April 18, 1967, *FCC*, 253.

104. Guest list, February 2, 1965, folder 17, box 5, Robinson Papers.

105. Lee C. White Oral History with Joe B. Frantz, Interview V, November 2, 1971, 3, Lyndon B. Johnson Library, Austin, Texas.

106. Clifford L. Alexander to Robinson, April 20, 1967, *FCC*, 253–254.

107. Alexander to Bess Abell, November 22, 1965, folder 17, box 5, Robinson Papers.

108. Rigueur, *Loneliness of the Black Republican*, 60.

109. Rampersad, *Jackie Robinson*, 431.

110. Dierenfield, *Civil Rights Movement*, 105.

111. "A Man We Can Be Proud Of," *New York Amsterdam News*, November 26, 1966, 7.

112. Rampersad, *Jackie Robinson*, 392–395, 436–437, 458, 462, 389 (quotation).
113. Kahn, *Boys of Summer*, 401–402.
114. "Agnew 'Stupid,' Robinson Says," *Washington Post*, October 5, 1968, D29.
115. "Jackie Robinson Splits with G.O.P. Over Nixon Choice," *New York Times*, August 12, 1968, 1.
116. "GOP Said to Seek Low Negro Vote," October 7, 1968, *Baltimore Sun*, A2.
117. "Jackie Robinson Bids Negroes Back Rocky," *Washington Post*, June 24, 1968, A2.
118. Robinson to Schiff, January 9, 1969, box 63, Schiff Papers.
119. "Jackie Robinson Scores Nixon on Black-Capitalism Problems," *New York Times*, January 21, 1970, 27.
120. Robinson, *I Never Had It Made*, 139.
121. Kotlowski, *Nixon's Civil Rights*, 165.
122. Rampersad, *Jackie Robinson*, 454.
123. Sarantakes, *Fan in Chief*, 170.
124. Joe Louis, "Muslims, Clay Go Backward," *Washington Post*, September 26, 1964, D4.
125. Kahn, *Boys of Summer*, 398.
126. "Jackie's Out of Step," *Baltimore Afro-American*, December 31, 1960, 4.
127. "Death of an Unconquerable Man," *New York Times*, October 25, 1972, 53.
128. "Jackie Robinson," *Washington Post*, November 2, 1972, A17.
129. Arnold A. Offner, *Hubert Humphrey: The Conscience of the Country* (New Haven, CT: Yale University Press, 2018), 299; Sarantakes, *Fan in Chief*, 165–166; Kotlowski, *Nixon's Civil Rights*, 184.

12

Sport, Merit, and Respectability Politics in the Election of Barack Obama

Michael L. Butterworth and Shawn N. Smith

During the 2008 presidential election, baseball card manufacturer Upper Deck produced a series of election cards featuring candidates Barack Obama and John McCain in the exaggerated illustrations of a caricaturist. In one such card, a worried-looking Senator McCain dons the gear of a baseball catcher while attempting to block his opponent from sliding into home plate. His opponent, of course, was Senator Obama, whose attempted 'steal' of home evoked the legacy of baseball pioneer, Jackie Robinson.[1] To make the association clearer, Obama's picture on the card shows him wearing Robinson's familiar number 42 Brooklyn Dodgers jersey. Baseball fans would understand the reference immediately, as Robinson's successful steal of home against the New York Yankees in the 1955 World Series is among the game's most iconic moments.[2]

The Upper Deck card was one of the many references during the 2008 campaign that compared Barack Obama's candidacy with the baseball legend. Political cartoonist J. D. Crowe's image, 'Obama #44,' depicts the president-elect sliding just as Robinson had, right arm raised with a clenched fist, left hand trailing in the dirt, cap flying off his head. The captions – "The Jackie Robinson of Politics" and "Barack Obama Elected Nation's 44th President" – are punctuated by the jersey. Although it clearly has the familiar colors and design of a Brooklyn Dodgers jersey, the details have been changed so that 'Dodgers' is replaced by 'Obama' and the number 42 has been replaced by 44. Another cartoonist, R. J. Matson, made a similar connection by drawing an 'Obama 44' jersey next to a

256

'Robinson 42' one. In both cases, viewers are invited to approach Jackie Robinson and Barack Obama on equal terms, as rhetorical expressions of a particular kind of triumph in U.S. history.[3]

What Crowe and Matson presented in images, countless others expressed in words. From journalists to political pundits, Barack Obama's success was frequently attributed to the legacy of not only Jackie Robinson, but to athletes such as Muhammad Ali and Tiger Woods as well. As sportswriter George Vecsey declared, "There is a direct line from Jackie Robinson to Barack Obama." British sportswriter Simon Barnes agreed, concluding that, "Barack Obama owes it all to Tiger Woods. Well, some of it . . . The road that led to the election of Obama has black athletes as its milestones, but sport was also one of the bulldozers that shaped it."[4] Far from simply invoking sports for dramatic effect, these various references demonstrate faith in a mythic ideal about American political culture. In short, the election of Barack Obama to the presidency can be understood as a validation of principal national values such as democracy, equality, and justice. These values are entangled, however, with the myth of meritocracy and the constraints of respectability politics and uplift ideology, each of which factor into American sports and their implications for politics.

The eagerness to articulate the election of the nation's first Black president with the sporting pioneers of racial inclusion reflects the optimism many experienced at the prospect of an Obama presidency. Rhetorical scholars saw in Obama a figure of potential transformation, a leader who might heal the divisions that characterize political culture in the United States. Academics in other disciplines shared this optimism, as did commentators in the political media. Before even taking the oath of office, President-elect Obama could be defined through a "rhetoric of heroic expectations," exceeding the considerable burdens already placed upon any president's shoulders.[5] Most central to this triumphant rhetoric was the notion that Obama's election confirmed the nation's inclination toward justice and ushered in a legitimate 'post-racial society.' Revisiting this moment after the chaos of the Donald Trump presidency makes plain the naivete of such sentiments. Nevertheless, for a nation beleaguered by the 'War on Terror' and a struggling economy, the Obama era began with understandable optimism.

It should be clear that there was reason for skepticism from the outset. As rhetorical scholar Kristen Hoerl demonstrates, mainstream media celebrated Obama's inauguration in 2009 by acknowledging the legacy of the Civil Rights Movement while, at the same time, erasing the fraught history of dissent and struggle by Black Americans.[6] Jasmine Cobb observes that images featuring a Black president presented an ideal of an inclusive society and thus failed to reckon with "the continuation of derogatory portrayals of Blackness in popular culture."[7] This chapter argues that such portrayals are consistent with mainstream narratives about the role of sport in American culture. These references rely on mythic notions of merit and liberal progress that have long underscored the narrative of the 'American Dream.' The chapter revisits the analogical associations made between Obama and figures such as Robinson and Woods to identify the limits of sport as a political metaphor. Turning to uplift ideology and the myth of meritocracy, it contends that the common narrative of racial progress through sport serves as a rhetorical means for deflecting political conflict and celebrating the triumph of liberal democracy. As observers now reflect on the legacy of Obama's presidency, it is argued here that the rhetorical associations made between him and historical sports figures help to explain some of the challenges he faced during his eight years in office.

Uplift, the 'American Dream' and the role of sport

Rhetorical scholarship about Barack Obama emphasizes his ability to express the ideals of the nation, especially through his embodiment of the 'American Dream.' By evoking this myth in terms that emphasize Americans' shared responsibilities to one another, Obama embodied and emboldened America's democratic promise.[8] At the same time, others sought to reduce him to a caricatured exemplar of uplift ideology, an aspect of political culture that curtailed his rhetorical agency.[9] Before examining this discourse, however, it is useful to detail the socio-political work of uplift ideology itself, with particular attention to the tenets of Black respectability, individualism, and meritocracy.

Uplift ideology, or 'racial uplift,' represents one of the constitutive beliefs behind political and racial culture in the United

States. It was born at the end of the nineteenth century among Black feminists in the Women's Convention, an auxiliary to the protest group of the National Baptist Convention. These clubs were aimed at mobilizing Black folks to "uplift the entire race."[10] Stretching from and beyond Black women, racial uplift for the Black middle class was equated with normalcy and conformity to white middle-class models of behavior, gendered roles, and sexuality. Within uplift ideology, African American elites argued that 'proper' and 'respectable' behavior proved Blacks worthy of civil and political rights.[11] The belief that appropriate and respectable behavior would lead to white acceptance, political and civil power, and to a more prosperous African American community is commonly referred to as the 'politics of respectability,' also known as 'respectability politics.'[12] Respectability politics often requires the validation of white society, as whites perceive Black respectability as akin to their own middle-class values and thus as non-threatening. Accommodation, then, is a central tenet of respectability and uplift ideology.[13]

Why, though, has uplift ideology – and specifically the politics of respectability – proved to be so persuasive? Two specific, and interrelated themes are especially relevant to the analysis in this chapter: meritocracy and individualism. As Seymour Lipset demonstrates, Americans are uniquely conditioned to believe that they live in a meritocratic society. That belief is an outgrowth of US commitment to equality, which early and often in the nation's history was translated as "equal opportunity for all to rise economically and socially."[14] By the late nineteenth century, as Americans began to develop a stronger sense of national identity, stories about hard-working individuals animated the myth of meritocracy. In particular, this 'rags-to-riches' motif was symbolized by the stories of Horatio Alger, who created heroes that were "obviously American, fierce democrats, independent, eager to work hard, educate themselves, and make their way to success."[15]

Hard work and upward mobility are hallmarks of the American Dream, especially when it is defined in material terms.[16] Yet those hallmarks fail to account for the systemic barriers and exclusions that limit attainment of the dream, especially for African Americans. Too often, the struggles of Black citizens are attributed to laziness, a poor work ethic, or moral deprivation. An underlying logic in these accusations is the rhetoric of a 'color-blind society.' As Michael Omi and Howard Winant explain:

> The notion of a color-blind society where no special significance, rights, or privileges attach to one's 'race' makes for appealing ideology. Taken at face value, the concept reaffirms values of 'fair play' and 'equal opportunity' – ideals, some would argue, which constitute the very essence of our democratic way of life.[17]

What is problematic, however, is that to assert the irrelevance of race is to simultaneously default to an abstract identity that hails a liberal democratic ideal of the white, masculine subject.[18] Consequently, uplift ideology homogenizes the experiences of racial minorities, such that they "must strip off their particular histories and social positions and become abstract individuals" who represent imagined universal ideals.[19]

While the achievements of high-profile African Americans have contributed to the erosion of racial barriers and facilitated greater appreciation of diversity, too often they are used as evidence that the United States is a color-blind utopia. The massive popularity of entertainers such as Jay-Z or Oprah Winfrey, for example, too often masks the disproportionate absence of opportunity among African Americans in favor of a 'tokenistic' rhetoric that, as rhetorical scholar Dana Cloud explains, "serves the hegemony of liberal individualism in U.S. popular and political culture."[20] An even stronger connection to uplift ideology is found in sport, an institution that has frequently provided the most dramatic opportunities for African Americans to pursue the American Dream.

There is a consonance between the myth of the American Dream and the institution of sport, and it is not merely because of the rhetorical association made through the metaphor of the 'level playing field.' More than this, sport provides the American public with highly visible and often dramatic enactments of the myth's guiding principles. As sociologist Howard Nixon contends, "Sport is an appropriate vehicle for testing the ideology of the American Dream because the . . . spectacular financial success and fame of athletes from modest social origins would seem to give substance to these images and reinforce the ideology that explains them."[21] Contemporary sport does, in fact, yield some appropriate models of the American Dream. What is often most compelling about these success stories is that the individuals who come from modest or underprivileged backgrounds may use their athletic talents to achieve spectacular fame and fortune. If the American Dream is defined, at least in part, by material rewards and upward mobility, then there can be little surprise that so many subscribe to sport's meritocratic ideals.

As is the case with the American Dream more generally, its specific manifestations in the world of sport often serve to reaffirm the centrality of individual agency and obscure the structures of inequality that may prevent access or inhibit advancement. This is especially the case for African Americans, a group for whom sport has been central in the quest for the American Dream. Originally writing in 1964, Benjamin Quarles summarizes the core argument of the positive impact of sport in Black culture, stating, "The participation of the Negro in sports that attract hundreds of thousands of spectators has been a significant development in bringing him [sic] into the mainstream of American life, and thereby in the larger promotion of American democracy."[22] For the average American, this is a perfectly reasonable claim, for the major sports in the United States would be unrecognizable without the presence of Black athletes who have become some of the most beloved and marketable figures in American culture.

Because so many Black athletes have become dominant, they have increased the visibility and value given to African Americans more broadly. Yet the very nature of this success contributes to the erasure of the structural inequalities that plague so many racial minorities in the United States. Taken a step further, this erasure allows some commentators to allege that African Americans are either resorting to victimization or guilty of reverse racism when they dare to express outrage at ongoing racial discrimination. The central concern about sport as an enactment of the American Dream, then, is that it heralds the irrelevance of race and thus marginalizes resistance to actual instances of discrimination or injustice. In this way, sociologist Ben Carrington warns that "the perceived level playing field of sport can serve an ideological function by leading people to assume that western societies in particular have achieved a meritocracy that transcends the structural correlates of a racialized social order."[23] Carrington's point is important because it is less about sport in and of itself and more about the political culture that sport helps to produce. Nowhere, it is argued here, has this been more evident than in the rhetorical links made between sport and Barack Obama.

Obama as Robinson

A thorough history of Black athletic achievement in the United States would include numerous pioneers, including figures such as the boxers Jack Johnson and Joe Louis, or Olympian Jesse Owens. Each of these men, in different ways, challenged existing assumptions about race and opened dialogues that were previously stifled. Nevertheless, their triumphs did little to ameliorate a culture afflicted by Jim Crow.[24] If there is a representative moment that illustrates sport's capacity to extend the American Dream to racial minorities who follow the code of uplift ideology, then it surely is found in the narrative of Jackie Robinson. Major League Baseball (MLB) did not formally exclude Black players; rather, it relied on the 'Gentleman's Agreement' that had kept the game white since 1887.[25] The formation of the first Negro League in 1920 gave Black players an opportunity to showcase their abilities, but they remained largely out of sight in the MLB and sports media. Throughout the 1930s, the Black and Communist press both campaigned actively for the integration of the sport, and the contradiction of a nation fighting a war against a racist ideology in the Second World War while preserving racist institutions at home became increasingly untenable.[26] In 1945, three years before the U.S. armed forces were formally desegregated, Brooklyn Dodgers general manager Branch Rickey signed Robinson. After one year of play with the Dodgers' Minor League affiliate in Montreal, he made his Major League debut in 1947.

Most popular memories of baseball's integration story are content to frame it in terms of 'breaking the color barrier,' emphasizing Robinson's heroic fortitude in the face of racial discrimination and hostility. As much as Robinson is mythologized for his courage,

Rickey is mythologized for having overcome baseball's systemic racism and restoring faith in it as a vessel for carrying the American Dream. "As the Robinson story teaches us," argues historian Louis Moore, "part of the mythmaking process of democracy and meritocracy in sports is celebrating the redemption of white men, especially Southern white men."[27] Thus, baseball's 'great experiment' was possible only to the extent that whiteness itself remained unchallenged and the trailblazing player remained uncontroversial. Rickey famously chose Robinson over arguably more talented players from the Negro Leagues because of his exposure to white communities, college education, and military experience.[28] In other words, his achievement was possible only through the lens of uplift ideology and respectability politics. Indeed, public memory of Robinson's achievement most often affirms Robinson's performance of respectability "as the pivotal credential . . . in baseball's integration."[29]

When Robinson first played for the Dodgers on April 15, 1947, it was a moment that reverberated well beyond the boundaries of sport. Thus, "for many Americans, Black and White alike, the desegregation of Major League Baseball represented the most important symbolic breakthrough in race relations before the 1954 Supreme Court decision in *Brown* v. *Board of Education*."[30] There can be little dispute that the presence of a high-profile Black man in the 'national pastime' helped to reshape the racial dynamics in the United States. Upon the fiftieth anniversary of Robinson's debut, MLB Commissioner Bud Selig proclaimed, "When you look at the history of our game, Jackie Robinson coming into baseball – there's no question in my mind that April 15, 1947, was the most powerful moment in baseball history . . . It transcended baseball. It was a precursor to the civil rights movement."[31] Years earlier, Dr. Martin Luther King, Jr. seems to have agreed with Selig. Speaking to Dodgers pitcher Don Newcombe, one of the prominent African American players to follow in the steps of Robinson, King said, "You'll never know what you and Jackie and Roy [Campanella] did to make it possible to do my job."[32]

President Barack Obama later echoed such sentiments, as he traveled with Willie Mays on the way to baseball's All-Star Game in 2009. Talking with Mays aboard Air Force One, Obama confessed,

"Let me tell you, you helped us get there. If it hadn't been for folks like you and Jackie, I'm not sure that I would get elected to the White House. The spirit you put in the game, how you carried yourself, all of that really makes a difference. Changed people's attitudes."[33] No clearer expression of the rhetorical significance granted to Robinson – and the politics of respectability – could be found. As it turns out, the president was only one of many who found the connection appropriate. In particular, commentators featured two prominent themes that united Obama and Robinson.

When Michael Eric Dyson referred to Obama as "the Jackie Robinson of black politics," he did so to highlight the significance of his being "the first [Black] candidate who has a real shot to become president." Meanwhile, a CBS news report detailed multiple famous 'firsts' for African Americans, moving from "Jackie Robinson who will always be remembered as one of the greatest," to Barack Obama, whose "first is arguably the most important one of all." Invoking a more literary tone, Mike Lupica narrates a progression that begins with Robinson and ends with Obama, "It starts this way, on April 15, 1947 ... with Jack Roosevelt Robinson running out to play first base for the Dodgers against the Braves, a lifetime in America before Sen. Barack Obama could very well be rounding third and heading for home."[34]

The various references to 'firsts' allow for a logical progression that leads to the inevitable triumph of liberal democracy. The *individual* achievements of these pioneers articulate comfortably with African American uplift ideology. However, for all of the hope inspired by Obama's example, lost in this narrative was the despair of pioneers such as Robinson. Rhetorical scholars Montye Fuse and Keith Miller argue, for instance, that Branch Rickey was keenly aware of the taunts and threats that greatly distressed the lone African American player in the league. Yet "isolating Robinson enabled Rickey to employ baseball integration as a Horatio Alger-like narrative in which a lonely, ethical male of supposedly lower status struggled on to a higher social stratum with a boost from a well-established businessman."[35] Such an argument raises important questions about whose interests are being served when we celebrate mythic exemplars of the American Dream and of those who have played by the rules of respectability.

As both a candidate and president, Obama navigated similar waters. For white elites, he represented racial transcendence and the promise of a 'post-racial' society. In his study that features interviews with white business executives, communication scholar Christopher Brown observes one CEO's beliefs that Obama "did not make everything about race," was a "safe person of color," and was not "in your face" like earlier Black presidential hopefuls such as Jesse Jackson and Al Sharpton. For Brown, these comments are illustrative of a rhetorical pattern in which white Americans hinder inclusion by denying structural problems and offering well-intended platitudes about the nation's ideals. He is clear, however, that "White male elites' rhetorical choices indicate that they would abandon Obama if he were to speak openly about persisting racial disparities."[36] This shallow form of solidarity is similarly displayed in sports. In his work on Michael Jordan, for example, cultural studies scholar David Andrews argues that Black athletes must constantly renew their "membership" within the white community for whom Black deviance is seen as a threat or sign of criminality.[37]

Obama has faced less overt abuse than Robinson, but was similarly praised for maintaining grace and dignity in the face of contempt. As Robinson's daughter, Sharon, remarked after the election, "You saw parallels in strength and character . . . When he was attacked during the campaign, he handled it with dignity, remained focused, and kept his eyes on the prize."[38] Obama's "famously calm demeanor" was further linked to another baseball legend who faced harassment and abuse, Hank Aaron. But as journalist Sandy Tolan acknowledges, "For Aaron, there was a price to be paid for swallowing his anger and enduring the death threats, racist catcalls, and hundreds of thousands of hate-filled letters. 'It carved a part of me out that I will never restore, never regain,' he said."[39] Aaron's haunting words are reinforced by sportswriter William Rhoden who, pointing to a common criticism of respectability politics, suggests that the almost universal praise granted Robinson for his courage and poise misses the point. As he describes it, "This was the Jackie Robinson model of how an integration-worthy African-American behaved: taking abuse, turning the other cheek, tying oneself in knots, holding one's tongue, never showing anger, waiting for racist sensibilities to smolder and die out – if your spirit didn't die first."[40] More than noting their similarities as pioneers, therefore, associations linking Obama to Robinson also reinforced expectations for how the new president should behave in the role.

Obama as Woods

Before an infidelity scandal redefined his public image in late 2009, Tiger Woods was among the most beloved athletes in the history of U.S. sports. Beyond his athletic dominance, Woods became the face of golf, a sport that has an ugly and transparent history of racial discrimination. Whereas baseball's segregation was based on the 'Gentleman's Agreement,' the Professional Golfers Association (PGA) maintained a formal 'Caucasian only' clause in its constitution until 1961.[41] Until 1983, white professional golfers who played at golf's most prestigious event, The Masters, were forced to employ Black caddies.[42] As recently as 1990 – with the PGA Championship scheduled to take place at Shoal Creek in Birmingham, Alabama – when the club's president was asked if he would revise the club's whites-only membership requirements he replied, "That's just not done in Birmingham."[43]

Many expected Woods to deliver the final blow against golf's racist legacy through the sheer force of his talent and presence in the game. Then, when Nike introduced Woods in a 1996 advertising campaign called, "Hello World," that expectation was cemented by the commercial's provocative claim that "There are still courses in the U.S. I am not allowed to play because of the color of my skin." As rhetorical scholar Davis Houck notes, "The agenda was set: Nike, Tiger Woods . . . [was] confronting a worldwide audience with skin color, discrimination, and golf's past/present."[44] That confrontation was short-lived, however, and in subsequent years Woods earned a reputation for avoiding political controversy at all costs.

Two examples illustrate Woods' reluctance to engage with racial politics. After he won the 1997 Masters, Woods earned the right to select the menu for the following year's 'Champions Dinner,' a tradition at Augusta National Golf Club. Speaking to reporters, veteran golfer Fuzzy Zoeller said, "You pat him on the back and say congratulations and enjoy it and tell him not to serve fried chicken next year . . . Or collard greens or whatever the hell they serve."[45] Woods responded with silence, refusing to engage with the political implications of an African American dominating a historically white sport. Years later, having solidified his control over the sport, Woods was again implicated in racial politics. In 2008, Golf Channel anchor Kelly Tilghman suggested that young golfers needed to show Woods their competitive fire, and that they should "lynch him in a back alley." Once again, Woods denied that race was relevant, calling Tilghman's comments a "non-issue."[46]

These two incidents are representative of Woods' political persona. Indeed, when he was asked in 2008 about Barack Obama's electoral victory, his initial response was, "Oh, God, here we go." He eventually continued, "Well, I've seen him speak. He's extremely articulate, very thoughtful."[47] Woods' indifference did little to quell the comparisons between himself and Obama, especially those that noted the multiracial heritage of both men. More important was the suggestion that Obama was "an African American politician who doesn't talk about discrimination, thus absolving white people of guilt for the prejudices he undoubtedly faced."[48] Consequently, newspaper commentary was littered with references to Obama as "race-less," a "post-racial candidate," the "Tiger Woods of politics," or as possessing a self-image that is "not about race."[49] Writing for *Golf Digest*, Jaime Diaz made perhaps the boldest connection:

> In much the same way that light-skinned black American public figures historically have been more comfortably celebrated by white America than their darker counterparts, both Woods and Obama are often perceived as "race neutral" or even "colorless" . . . For his part, Obama has pushed back against the idea of "injecting" race into his campaign. So while each grew up an outsider, their very multiculturalism presents enough connecting points that they are uniquely equipped to play Pied Piper in their separate realms . . . This especially plays out internationally, where Woods is extremely popular and an Obama presidency would appeal to foreign countries as an embodiment of America at its inclusive best.[50]

Ironically, given Woods' refusal to address issues of race substantively, these media accounts contend that the popularity, and perceived race neutrality, of Tiger Woods helped to ease Barack Obama's journey to the White House. Thus, unlike the comparison with Jackie Robinson, which *foregrounds* the importance of race as a *historical* barrier, the comparison with Woods *diminishes* the importance of race as a *contemporary* barrier to the American Dream. With uplift ideology, the individual achievement of Barack Obama is made possible less because he is a racial pioneer and more because race has ceased to be relevant at all in American political culture.

Much as Woods' esteem diminished in the wake of scandal, Obama faced public scrutiny when he dared to deviate from the postracial playbook. When Harvard professor Henry Louis Gates, Jr. was arrested in his own home by a Cambridge police officer who mistook him for a burglar, the president responded that the police "acted stupidly."[51] Fox News commentator Glenn Beck – highly influential at the time – declared that Obama is a "racist," with a "deep-seated hatred for white people or the white culture."[52] That Beck's claim was clearly outlandish was not the point; rather, his extreme words gave voice to the moderate and more popularly held belief that the United States had reached its 'postracial' moment. For the president, who had mostly kept race on the sidelines during his campaign, to 'play the race card' could be seen as changing the rules in the middle of the game. Regrettably, Obama's concession – the White House 'beer diplomacy' meeting with the officer and Gates – signaled a return to the campaign's resistance to engaging racial discourses.

Reflections on Obama's presidency, merit, and uplift ideology

All presidencies are complicated, and much of Obama's administration can be understood through conventional analyses of policy decisions, power struggles, and international conflicts. Yet, as the only president of color in U.S. history, it is vital to attend to racial discourses when evaluating the Obama years. Of course, this does not mean that Obama was above making mistakes; however, it is clear he faced constraints no other president has seen. One of his more notable addresses, "A More Perfect Union," is illustrative of these constraints. The speech was a response to controversial comments made by his pastor, the Reverend Jeremiah Wright, who chastised ongoing racism in the United States by rejecting the platitude, 'God Bless America,' asserting instead, 'God damn America' in one of his sermons.[53] Rhetorical critics have dedicated considerable energy to evaluating the effectiveness of the speech while agreeing that, as a presidential candidate, Senator Obama had little margin for error. For example, Robert Terrill attends to this by noting the polarizing nature of racial rhetoric in the United States insists that "we either affect a naïve color blindness that denies the color-line altogether, or we naturalize the color-line as an impossibly recalcitrant barrier."[54]

Despite his best efforts, as president, Obama struggled to balance this opposition. The rhetoric of racial transcendence that he featured as a candidate invited criticism from those on the left who felt he said too little on behalf of Black citizens and failed to connect racial politics to the hegemony of neoliberalism. Admonishing him for ordering drone strikes in the Middle East and bailing out Wall Street criminals, Cornel West lamented, "What a sad legacy for our hope and change candidate – even as we warriors go down swinging in the fading names of truth and justice."[55] Meanwhile, right-wing critics such as Sean Hannity pounced on the president when he did dare to acknowledge racial politics. When the president empathized with Trayvon Martin, a seventeen-year-old Black boy killed by a neighborhood watch captain, Hannity cried reverse racism: "Is the president suggesting that if it had been a white who had been shot, that would be OK because it didn't look like him? That's just nonsense dividing this country up . . . Trying to turn it into a racial issue is fundamentally wrong."[56] The sharpness of criticism from both poles of political identity in the United States is a reflection of the limitations of respectability politics: not pushing beyond the boundaries of polite representation fails to address structural and systemic problems while, at the same time, it readies white observers to claim "everything [is] about race" when a Black president dares to mention it at all.[57]

Part of this dilemma can be understood through the analogical associations made between Obama and Black athletes. In the case of Robinson, public memory of his efforts is dominated by triumphalist narratives about breaking the 'color barrier' and remaining courageous and calm in the face of racial animosity. These overly simplified recollections have the effect of marking April 15, 1947, as the moment racism disappeared from baseball and they deny Robinson's agency and the complexity of his own political beliefs. As rhetorical scholar David Naze summarizes, "We . . . have sanitized Robinson's ideas, we have twisted his identity, we have ceded control of his image, and we have used his legacy to fulfill our oversimplified racial reconciliation fantasy."[58]

Such a fantasy was equally present in the election of the nation's first Black president, a moment apparently seen by many Americans as a confirmation that a postracial society had finally been achieved.[59] In the case of Woods, celebrations of his multiracial identity presented an illusion that race did not matter. Woods' own refusal to talk about, or even acknowledge, the politics of race lent weight to the argument that others should follow suit. After all, if a 'Cablinasian' man – the term Woods used famously to describe himself to Oprah Winfrey – can succeed on his merits alone, can't everyone?[60] None other than football Hall of Famer Jim Brown, a man known for his sense of racial pride and willingness to confront injustice, confirmed this logic when talking about the election of Obama. "I don't really look at it as a racial breakthrough," Brown said, "I look at it as confirmation that in America if you work hard, if you're smart enough, you can create miracles, and that's what happened with Obama . . . He doesn't come at it from a racial point of view."[61]

Brown's optimism might have seemed reassuring, but before concluding that the United States has reached a time of miracles, there are at least three important implications of this analysis. First, that so many commentators saw fit to compare Barack Obama with sports figures reflects the extent to which sport is embedded in the very fabric of American mythology and politics. This very book, of course, takes this assertion seriously and reminds us that, instead of thinking of sport as a mere diversion or just 'fun-and-games,' we must continue to consider its rhetorical effects. This retrospective look at the nation's first Black president, highlights the fact that sport is a constitutive site from which political culture emerges and political arguments may be generated.

Second, sport is a particularly relevant but fraught site for public discussions about race. Athletes remain many of the most visible Black individuals in American society and, historically, this has enabled some productive discussions about race and white supremacy. As this chapter has demonstrated, however, too often those discussions rely on stories of individual triumph and the realization of a 'postracial society.' The backlash over Obama's muted condemnation of the Cambridge police or his identification with Trayvon Martin are but two examples, but they reveal the limits of making race a substantive issue for Black leaders. Even as athletes of color continue to excel in sport, this cannot be seen as validation that racial inequities are an artifact of the past.

The 2008 presidential election occurred in the context of an era defined by the "demise of the activist athlete."[62] At that time, athletes such as LeBron James and Serena Williams were dominant but not politically outspoken. Colin Kaepernick was not yet a household name. A resurgence of athlete activism since 2016, in particular, might suggest that the rhetorical associations made between sport and politics can advance the nation's reckoning with racial injustice. However, despite some inspired moments, athlete activism has largely been absorbed into universalist narratives that preserve the status quo. Instead of structural change, the institution of sport asks for 'unity.'[63] Meanwhile, athletes who are seen as too disruptive find themselves marginalized. As rhetorical scholar Abraham Khan summarizes, the politics of respectability "demands performances occasioned by modes of comportment and public address fit for White scrutiny."[64] The comparisons between Barack Obama and Black athletes such as Jackie Robinson and Tiger Woods appear to have only amplified such scrutiny of his performances.

Finally, as public memory of sport celebrates moments of triumph and the presumed transcendence of conflict, we should be cautious about overstating sport's democratizing effects. Athletes such as Muhammad Ali and Billie Jean King may have advanced the causes of peace, equality, and justice, but sport is largely defined by commercialism, nationalism, and militarism. Great upsets and rags-to-riches tales make for compelling conclusions, but they most certainly do not tell the whole story. Buried beneath the surface of these individual triumphs are the structures that disenfranchise millions whose vision of the American Dream, even as they play to the tune of racial uplift's ideological song, remains a dream deferred. American political culture has indeed come a long way since Jackie Robinson took the field and stole home. But a presidential administration is not a game in the World Series, and the politics of respectability – from Robinson, to Woods, to Obama – continue to constrain the nation's democratic ideals.[65]

Notes

1. Carl Campanile, "Candidates Carded," *New York Post*, June 9, 2008, available at: https://nypost.com/2008/06/09/candidates-carded.
2. Dave Brown, "Remember Jackie Robinson Stealing Home with Yogi Berra Catching," *CBS Sports*, September 23, 2015, available at: https://www.cbssports.com/mlb/news/remember-jackie-robinson-stealing-home-with-yogi-berra-catching.
3. Crowe's cartoon is cataloged by the National Baseball Hall of Fame and Museum, available at: https://collection.baseballhall.org/PASTIME/obama-44-cartoon-2008-november-05; Matson's is available at https://politicalcartoons.com/sku/60214.
4. George Vecsey, "Timeline Stretches 62 Years, From Robinson to Obama," *New York Times*, April 16, 2009, available at: https://www.nytimes.com/2009/04/16/sports/baseball/16vecsey.html; Simon Barnes, "From Jesse Owens to Barack Obama, via Muhammad Ali and Tiger Woods," *The Times*, November 7, 2008, available at: https://www.thetimes.co.uk/article/from-jesse-owens-to-barack-obama-via-muhammad-ali-and-tiger-woods-hp9d2wxnmgj.
5. Jennifer R. Mercieca and Justin S. Vaughn, "Barack Obama and the Rhetoric of Heroic Expectations," in Justin S. Vaughn and Jennifer R. Mercieca (eds.), *The Rhetoric of Heroic Expectations: Establishing the Obama Presidency* (College Station: Texas A&M University Press, 2014), 1–29.
6. Kristen Hoerl, "Selective Amnesia and Racial Transcendence in News Coverage of President Obama's Inauguration," *Quarterly Journal of Speech* 98 (2012): 178–202.

7. Jasmine Nichole Cobb, "No, We Can't!: Postracialism and the Popular Appearance of a Rhetorical Fiction," *Communication Studies* 62 (2011): 408.

8. Robert C. Rowland and John M. Jones, "Recasting the American Dream and American Politics: Barack Obama's Keynote Address to the 2004 Democratic National Convention," *Quarterly Journal of Speech* 93 (2007): 425–448.

9. For a discussion of such constraints, see Ta-Nehisi Coates, *We Were Eight Years in Power: An American Tragedy* (New York: One World, 2017).

10. E. Francis White, *Dark Continent of our Bodies: Black Feminism and the Politics of Respectability* (Philadelphia, PA: Temple University Press, 2001), 35.

11. Evelyn Brooks Higginbotham, "African-American Women's History and the Metalanguage of Signs," *Signs* 17 (1992): 251–274.

12. See Carol Bunch Davis, *Prefiguring Postblackness: Cultural Memory, Drama, and the African American Freedom Struggle of the 1960s* (Jackson: University Press of Mississippi, 2015); Higginbotham, "African-American Women's History"; Abraham I. Khan, "Michael Sam, Jackie Robinson, and the Politics of Respectability," *Communication & Sport* 5 (2017): 331–351; White, *Dark Continent of our Bodies*; and Virginia Wolcott, *Remaking Respectability: African American Women in Interwar Detroit* (Chapel Hill: University of North Carolina Press, 2001).

13. Edmund T. Gordon, "Cultural Politics of Black Masculinity," *Transforming Anthropology* 6 (1997): 36–53.

14. Seymour Martin Lipset, *American Exceptionalism: A Double-Edged Sword* (New York: W. W. Norton, 1996), 53.

15. James O. Robertson, *American Myth, American Reality* (New York: Hill & Wang, 1980), 165.

16. For more on the distinction between 'materialistic' and 'moralistic' versions of the American Dream, see Walter R Fisher, "Reaffirmation and Subversion of the American Dream," *Quarterly Journal of Speech* 59 (1973): 160–167.

17. Michael Omi and Howard Winant, *Racial Formation in the United States: From the 1960s to the 1990s*, 2nd edn. (London: Routledge, 1994), 1.

18. See Charles W. Mills, *The Racial Contract* (Ithaca, NY: Cornell University Press, 1997).

19. Jane Flax, *The American Dream in Black & White: The Clarence Thomas Hearings* (Ithaca, NY: Cornell University Press, 1998), 15.

20. Dana L. Cloud, "Hegemony or Concordance? The Rhetoric of Tokenism in 'Oprah' Winfrey's Rags to Riches Biography," *Critical Studies in Mass Communication* 13 (1996): 117.

21. Howard L. Nixon, *Sport and the American Dream* (New York: Leisure Press, 1984), 25.

22. Benjamin Quarles, *The Negro in the Making of America*, 3rd edn. (New York: Touchstone, 1996), 289.

23. Quoted in D. Stanley Eitzen, *Fair and Foul: Beyond the Myths and Paradoxes of Sport*, 4th edn. (Lanham, MD: Rowman & Littlefield, 2009), 145.

24. For a summary of this era in U.S. history, see Jerrold M. Packard, *American Nightmare: The History of Jim Crow* (New York: St. Martin's Press, 2003).

25. Jules Tygiel, *Baseball's Great Experiment: Jackie Robinson and His Legacy* (New York: Oxford University Press, 1983), 13.

26. Tygiel, *Baseball's Great Experiment*, 30–46.

27. Louis Moore, *We Will Win the Day* (Santa Barbara, CA: Praeger, 2017), 10.

28. Benjamin G. Rader, *Baseball: A History of America's Game* (Urbana: University of Illinois Press, 2002), 166.

29. Khan, "Michael Sam," 336.

30. Patrick B. Miller and David K. Wiggins, "Introduction," in Patrick B. Miller and David K. Wiggins (eds.), *Sport and the Color Line: Black Athletes and Race Relations in Twentieth-Century America* (New York: Routledge, 2004), ix.

31. Quoted in John Kelly, "Integrating America: Jackie Robinson, Critical Events and Baseball Black and White," in Mark Dyreson and J. A. Mangan (eds.), *Sport and American Society: Exceptionalism, Insularity, and "Imperialism"* (London: Routledge, 2007), 81.

32. Peter Dreier, "Jackie Robinson's Legacy: Baseball, Race, and Politics," in Robert Elias (ed.), *Baseball and the American Dream: Race, Class, Gender and the National Pastime* (Armonk, NY: M. E. Sharpe, 2001), 48.

33. Video of this exchange can be found on YouTube at "President Obama and Willie Mays on Air Force One," *The Obama White House.* July 15, 2009, available at: https://www.youtube.com/watch?v=4pbOtfa7_ok.

34. Interview with Matt Lauer, "Michael Eric Dyson Discusses Historic Nature of this Election," *Today*, November 4, 2008; Harry Smith, "Civil Rights Pioneers Who Paved the Way for Barack Obama's Victory," *CBS Evening News*, November 5, 2008; Mike Lupica,

"Jackie Robinson's Legacy," *New York Daily News*, April 12, 2008, available at: https://www.nydailynews.com/sports/baseball/jackie-robinson-legacy-article-1.283516.

35. Montye Fuse and Keith Miller, "Jazzing the Basepaths: Jackie Robinson and African American Aesthetics," in John Bloom and Michael Nevin Willard (eds.), *Sports Matters: Race, Recreation, and Culture* (New York: New York University Press, 2002), 130.

36. Christopher B. Brown, "Barack Obama as the Great Man: Communicative Constructions of Racial Transcendence in White-Male Elite Discourses," *Communication Monographs* 78 (2011): 548, 552.

37. David L. Andrews, *Michael Jordan, Inc.: Corporate Sport, Media Culture, and Late Modern America* (Albany, NY: State University of New York Press, 2001), 128.

38. Justin George, "First Her Dad, So Now Obama," *Tampa Bay Times*, November 25, 2008, available at: https://www.tampabay.com/archive/2008/11/23/first-her-dad-so-now-obama.

39. Sandy Tolan, "What Hank Aaron and Barack Obama Have in Common," *Christian Science Monitor*, April 8, 2009, available at: https://www.csmonitor.com/Commentary/Opinion/2009/0408/p09s02-coop.html.

40. William C. Rhoden, *Forty Million Dollar Slaves: The Rise, Fall, and Redemption of the Black Athlete* (New York: Crown, 2006), 101.

41. Marvin P. Dawkins and Graham C. Kinlah, *African American Golfers During the Jim Crow Era* (Westport, CT: Praeger, 2000), 5.

42. Davis W. Houck, "Crouching Tiger, Hidden Blackness: Tiger Woods and the Disappearance of Race," in Arthur A. Raney and Jennings Bryant (eds.), *The Handbook of Sports and Media* (Mahwah, NJ: Erlbaum, 2006), 469–484.

43. John Feinstein, *A Good Walk Spoiled: Days and Nights on the PGA Tour* (Boston, MA: Little, Brown, 1995), 422.

44. Houck, "Crouching Tiger, Hidden Blackness," 475.

45. Luke Norris, "A Look Back on Fuzzy Zoeller's Incredibly Racist Comments about Tiger Woods at the 1997 Masters," *Sportscasting*, November 10, 2020, available at: https://www.sportscasting.com/a-look-back-on-fuzzy-zoellers-incredibly-racist-comments-about-tiger-woods-at-the-1997-masters.

46. Randall Mell, "Woods Taking Some Heat for Response to Comment," *South Florida Sun Sentinel*, January 20, 2008, available at: https://www.sun-sentinel.com/news/fl-xpm-2008-01-20-0801190175-story.html.

47. Lorne Rubenstein, "Woods Stays Coy on Obama," *The Globe and Mail*, November 18, 2008, available at: https://www.theglobeandmail.com/sports/woods-stays-coy-on-obama/article1066267.

48. Dan Payne, "Obama's Keys to Victory," *Boston.com*, February 21, 2008, available at: http://archive.boston.com/bostonglobe/editorial_opinion/oped/articles/2008/02/21/obamas_keys_to_victory.

49. David Ignatius, "The Obama of 'Dreams,'" *Washington Post*, January 17, 2008, available at: https://www.washingtonpost.com/wp-dyn/content/article/2008/01/16/AR2008011603446.html; George Vecsey, "The Primary Season is Embracing Sports Images," *New York Times*, March 2, 2008, available at: https://www.nytimes.com/2008/03/02/sports/02vecsey.html.

50. Jaime Diaz, "The Tiger Effect and the Obama Phenomenon," *Golf Digest*, February 24, 2008, available at: https://www.golfdigest.com/story/gw20080229diaz.

51. "Obama: Police Who Arrested Professor 'Acted Stupidly,'" *CNN.com*, July 23, 2009, available at: http://www.cnn.com/2009/US/07/22/harvard.gates.interview/index.html.

52. "Glenn Beck: Obama is a Racist," *CBS News*, July 29, 2009, available at: https://www.cbsnews.com/news/glenn-beck-obama-is-a-racist.

53. Daniel Nasaw, "Controversial Comments Made by Rev. Jeremiah Wright," *The Guardian*, March 18, 2008, available at: https://www.theguardian.com/world/2008/mar/18/barackobama.uselections20083.

54. Robert E. Terrill, "Unity and Duality in Barack Obama's 'A More Perfect Union,'" *Quarterly Journal of Speech* 95 (2009): 364.

55. Cornel West, "Pity the Sad Legacy of Barack Obama," *The Guardian*, January 9, 2017, available at: https://www.theguardian.com/commentisfree/2017/jan/09/barack-obama-legacy-presidency.

56. Aliyah Shahid, "Conservatives Blast President Obama's Remarks on Trayvon Martin: He's Race Baiting!" *New York Daily News*, March 24, 2012, available at: https://www.nydailynews.com/news/politics/conservatives-blast-president-obama-remarks-trayvon-martin-race-baiting-article-1.1050298.

57. As an example, see Robert Tracisnski, "Why Obama's Presidency Has to Be All About Race Now," *The Federalist*, April 8, 2014, available at: https://thefederalist.com/2014/04/08/why-obamas-presidency-has-to-be-all-about-race-now.

58. David Naze, *Reclaiming 42: Public Memory and the Reframing of Jackie Robinson's Radical Legacy* (Lincoln: University of Nebraska Press, 2019).

59. Rhetorical scholar Bonnie Sierlecki even suggests that Obama's successful candidacy was, at least in part, facilitated by his ability to use sport to establish identification with voters. See Bonnie Sierlecki, "'Grit and Graciousness': Sport, Rhetoric, and Race in Barack Obama's 2008 Presidential Campaign," in Barry Brummett and Andrew W. Ishak (eds.), *Sports and Identity: New Agendas in Communication* (New York: Routledge, 2014), 106–127.

60. Houck, "Crouching Tiger, Hidden Blackness," 479.

61. "NFL Legend Jim Brown Considers Obama Influence," *NPR.org*, January 22, 2009, available at: https://www.npr.org/templates/story/story.php?storyId=99745657.

62. Abraham I. Khan, *Curt Flood in the Media: Baseball, Race, and the Demise of the Activist Athlete* (Jackson: University Press of Mississippi, 2012).

63. Michael L. Butterworth, "Sport and the Quest for Unity: How the Logic of Consensus Undermines Democratic Culture," *Communication & Sport* 8 (2020): 452–472.

64. Khan, "Michael Sam," 336.

65. A much earlier version of this chapter was presented at the 2009 annual meeting of the National Communication Association. The authors thank Abraham Khan, Martin Medhurst, and Robert Terrill for their comments at various stages of the chapter's development.

13

Donald Trump versus 'Woke' Athletes: Presidential Sport in the Age of Twitter

Russ Crawford

The election of Donald J. Trump disrupted the normal course of politics in the United States. One of the casualties of that disruption was the tradition of American presidents welcoming championship teams to the White House. During the Trump presidency, this once largely benign custom became politicized, and offered an opportunity for 'woke' athletes to signal their opposition to the current resident of 1600 Pennsylvania Avenue.

Presidents of the United States began the practice of inviting athletic teams to meet with them at the White House shortly after the conclusion of the American Civil War. Since then, as sports have become increasingly central to the American experience, the custom has become almost routine for the champions of the major professional leagues. Ronald Reagan increased the frequency of such visits in the 1980s and, despite a few athletes opting out of attendance, most saw the chance to visit with the president as a signal honor. However, with the social media-driven hardening of political lines, the once pro forma events became increasingly controversial.

In an examination of Trump's 2019 Twitter battle with U.S. Women's National Team soccer player Megan Rapinoe, scholars found that Trump introduced themes of nationalism and race into his response to the star's statements about the possibility of visiting the White House that will be discussed more below. Their research also found that while sporting events are often viewed through a nationalistic lens, this is less apparent on social media platforms such as Twitter. Trump also introduced race into his response by criticizing the National Basketball Association (NBA), which he tweeted, "now refuses to call owners, owners," in response to the league's decision to move away from the term, while he pushed through Criminal Justice Reform. Trump's focus on nationalism and what he considered his good record on racial issues was not taken well by Twitter users.[1] Arguably, Twitter and other social media platforms helped to create the situation that made visiting the White House problematic, particularly for Black athletes.

During his first six months in office, Trump, who has an extensive background in sports as both an athlete and team owner, continued the tradition of inviting athletes to the White House.[2] Trump had already hosted the National Football League (NFL) champion New England Patriots, and the National Collegiate Athletic Association (NCAA) National champion Clemson Tigers.[3] While a few of the Patriots, including some African American athletes such as safety Devin McCourty, found other things to do because they objected to Trump's politics, a majority of the Patriots attended.[4]

That a handful of athletes protested a president's policies through their absence was also nothing new. During Barack Obama's administration, a few players, including Baltimore Ravens center Matt Birk, who cited political differences with Obama for his decision, declined the chance to visit the White House, and was criticized in the media.[5] Most of those invited echoed Clemson Head Coach Dabo Swinney, who told Mark Packer of *College Sports Today* that he was excited to visit the White House: "Absolutely. I don't care who's in the White House. An opportunity to visit the White House is a special privilege. Put all of the political stuff aside, this is a unique experience for everyone involved." This 2017 visit would be Swinney's second; he had also visited as an Alabama player when Bill Clinton was president.[6]

However, on September 22, 2017, when star guard Stephen Curry of the NBA's Golden State Warriors expressed his hesitation about visiting the White House during a team media day, the question of whether to attend became much more complicated for athletes and teams. Although the Warriors had not yet officially been invited, the new president quickly tweeted that "Going to the White House is considered a great honor for a championship team. Stephen Curry is hesitating, therefore invitation is withdrawn!"[7] The Curry versus Trump contretemps set the tone for the rest of the president's administration. After that, athletes faced pressure to demonstrate their fealty to an often shifting idea of social justice, and to prove that they were sufficiently 'woke.' That use of the descriptor, signaling that one was awake to racial injustice, also became a battleground as Trump supporters increasingly wielded it as a mocking insult.[8] Curry's somewhat equivocal comments, along with Trump's immediate reaction, therefore shifted the ground underneath what had been a regular bit of harmless political theater.

The history of White House visits and presidential meddling in sport

American presidents love to demonstrate their passion for sports. Perhaps Andrew Johnson hoped that hosting the Washington Nationals and the Brooklyn Athletics on August 30, 1865, would help him politically. It was more likely that he was doing a favor for his friend and former congressional page Art Gorman, who had reportedly interested then-Senator Johnson in baseball. In 1865, Gorman played third base and was also vice president of the Nationals, and used his friendship with Johnson to arrange for his Nationals and the Athletics to become the first teams to visit the president at his residence.[9]

Since Ulysses Grant – Johnson's successor – took office, presidents have also sought to bask in the reflected glory of championship teams. After watching the Cincinnati Red Stockings defeat the Nationals during their inaugural professional season in 1869, Grant proceeded to warmly congratulate the winners afterwards.[10] When the Washington Senators won the World Series in 1924, President Calvin Coolidge met with the team to congratulate them after their victory parade.[11] As mentioned above, Reagan accelerated this custom, and succeeding presidents would expand the variety of teams that shared in the celebrations. President Barack Obama became the first president to invite a women's football team to meet with him at the White House in 2014, when he invited the Women's Football Alliance champion Boston Militia to celebrate their achievement.[12]

Beginning in the twentieth century, a number of presidents also played team sports. Dwight Eisenhower, John F. Kennedy, Nixon, Gerald Ford, Reagan, and Trump all played football.[13] Trump also shared a baseball background with Jimmy Carter, George H. W. Bush, and George W. Bush.[14] Not only did Trump share a playing career with many of his predecessors, but he also, along with the younger Bush, owned a professional team. Bush was a partial owner and managing partner of the Texas Rangers of Major League Baseball (MLB), and Trump had owned the New Jersey Generals of the United States Football League (USFL).[15] As had many presidents since William Howard Taft, Trump also played golf, though frequently on courses that he owned, which was often another source of controversy.[16]

Once in office, several presidents had also expressed concern for, or interfered in, sports, depending on one's perspective. Teddy Roosevelt famously called for a 1905 meeting of the Big Three – Harvard, Yale, and Princeton – the top college football programs, to discuss the violence of the sport after eighteen players died during that season's games.[17] In 1969, Nixon attended the Texas–Arkansas game and, in a nationally televised post-game celebration in the Texas locker room, seemingly conferred the championship on the Longhorns, even before their final game.[18] In his 2004 State of the Union address, George W. Bush took time to call on "team owners, union representatives, coaches, and players" to stop the use of steroids in sports.[19] In a 2009 *60 Minutes* interview, then president-elect Obama called for a college football playoff (after Bush refused to get involved).[20] Continuing that tradition, on August 31, 2020, during the COVID-19 lockdowns, Trump urged Big Ten Commissioner Kevin Warren to restart the football season that the conference had postponed on August 11.[21]

Presidential 'interest' often resulted in reform, or at least change. Roosevelt's call for reform eventually led to the creation of the NCAA.[22] The Longhorns finished the season undefeated, thereby justifying Nixon's premature awarding of the national title.[23] Major League Baseball eventually ended their Steroids Era. The NCAA established a four-team playoff system.[24] And the Big Ten had a football season that began in October 2020.[25]

Trump versus Kaepernick (and beyond)

Trump was merely traveling down a well-worn path that other presidents had blazed. What had changed was that some athletes embraced the politicization of sport in the wake of San Francisco 49ers quarterback Colin Kaepernick's decision to remain seated during the national anthem on August 26, 2016. This athlete activism was arguably driven by the access that fans and activists had to athletes through social media.[26] In some cases, athletes were also radicalized by the aggressive nature of the man occupying the White House.

Trump announced that he was running for the Republican nomination to be president on June 16, 2015. In his speech, he discussed security on the U.S. border with Mexico, and mentioned that "When Mexico sends its people, they're not sending their best . . . They're sending people that have lots of problems, and they're bringing those problems . . . They're bringing drugs. They're bringing crime. They're rapists. And some, I assume, are good people."[27] Initially the press reacted with incredulity and amusement – the *Washington Post* labeled him the "car accident candidate. You know you shouldn't slow down to look, but you know you will."[28]

By the end of July, as Trump rose in public opinion polls, newspapers such as the *New York Times* began crafting a new narrative, that the candidate was a racist. Alexander Burns of the *Times* wrote an article that discussed Trump's criticism of the Mohawk Tribe, the Central Park Five (a group of young minority men accused of raping a white woman in Central Park), and other instances when the candidate had made racially charged comments.[29] That proved to be a powerful accusation that defined Trump for those who opposed his candidacy.

As a candidate, his comments on sport confirmed such a narrative for his detractors. After the Kaepernick story broke, the quarterback claimed he was protesting "a country that oppresses black people and people of color." He told reporters that both Hillary Clinton and Trump were part of the problem, citing Clinton's remarks that called "black kids super-predators," and added that "You have Trump who's openly racist."[30] When asked about

Kaepernick's actions, candidate Trump told a Seattle radio inter-viewer, "I think it's a terrible thing. And maybe he should find a country that works better for him, let him try. It won't happen."[31]

Trump did not directly address Kaepernick's charge that he was a racist, but on October 30, 2016, he told the audience at a Colo-rado rally that "I don't know if you know, but the NFL is way down in their ratings. And you know why? Two reasons. Number one is, this politics they're finding is a rougher game than football, and more exciting. Honestly, we've taken a lot of people away from the NFL. And the other reason is Kaepernick. Kaepernick." When Trump mentioned the player's name, the crowd erupted in boos, indicating that the candidate had found an issue that reso-nated with voters. *Sports Illustrated* reported Trump's remarks and noted that "*Monday Night Football* ratings are down 24% from this time last year. *Sunday Night Football* is down 19% and Thursday night is down 18%."[32]

The NFL and many in the media argued that the ratings slide was due to the presidential campaign keeping viewers from watch-ing games.[33] However, as more players joined Kaepernick's protests, fans began calling for a boycott of the league, employing Twitter handles such as *@TurnOffFootball* and *@righttoboucott1*.[34] Although neither Twitter account had many followers, their sen-timents were echoed by millions of fans who did not post their disdain.[35] The narrative that NFL players were disrespecting the military was successfully inserted into the debate by critics, who defined the protestors' actions for a large segment of football fans.[36] Trump fed that movement, advancing the idea during his stump speeches that NFL players were disrespecting the American mili-tary, the flag, and the country. The actions of those who called for boycotts were amplified by Trump, and had an observable conse-quence. Television ratings for NFL games fell, dropping 10 percent for the season, which caused advertising revenue for networks that televised games to drop 19 percent for the season, giving credence to the effort begun by the lonely Twitter feeds.[37] By 2017, opinion polling had found that protests during the national anthem were causing as many as 41 percent to respond that such protests were the most important factor encouraging them to watch less profes-sional football.[38]

There are many things that influence a person's vote for president, but a 2018 *NBC/Wall Street Journal* poll found that 88 percent of Republicans and 57 percent of Independent voters disapproved of the anthem protests.[39] What those numbers had been earlier and what impact they might have had on the 2016 election, which was supposed to be an easy win for Clinton, is difficult to determine.[40] However, it may have had a crucial effect in some closely fought swing states such as Michigan, Wisconsin, and Pennsylvania where Trump won a narrow victory.

During the campaign, former NBA star Kareem Abdul-Jabbar became one of the first athletes to speak out against Trump. In a September 2015 opinion essay published in the *Washington Post* and reprinted in the *Chicago Tribune*, the former Laker center compared the leadership style of Trump to that of Democratic primary hopeful Bernie Sanders and, demonstrating the hyperbole that routinely marked reactions to Trump, concluded that "The biggest enemy to the principles of the Constitution right now is Trump."[41]

Both candidates had several athletes who backed their candidacy. Clinton had supporters such as current basketball stars LeBron James and Curry, and former greats Magic Johnson and Abdul-Jabbar. Former coaches Mike Ditka (football), Bobby Knight (basketball), and Lou Holtz (football) backed Trump, as did former NFL running back Herschel Walker, retired boxer Mike Tyson, and Ultimate Fighting Championship President Dana White.[42]

One momentary press and social media controversy broke out in September 2015, when a photo of New England Patriots quarterback Tom Brady's locker showed a hat with Trump's 'Make America Great Again' (MAGA) campaign slogan resting on the shelf. Brady told a Boston reporter that he had been friends with Trump since 2002, and that Trump had sent the hat to him through Robert Kraft, the team's owner. The quarterback generally avoids politics, and skipped visiting the White House during both the Obama and Trump administrations. When asked about the hat though, Brady mentioned that "I mean it's pretty amazing what he's able to accomplish. He obviously appeals to a lot of people, and he's a hell of a lot of fun to play golf with."[43]

That Brady even had to address the hat question with his rather tepid statement indicated the intense pressure that athletes would be under when they dealt with Trump. In May 2021, Brady was still receiving angry tweets directed at him because of this episode. For instance, when news broke on May 19, 2021 that the quarterback was working on a reality show, one Twitter user tweeted that "I heard on radio today that a non-scripted TV show is being developed about Tom Brady. No thank you. I won't be watching. I do not support the Maga [sic] Trump cult."[44] Another user reacted to Brady's tweet praising Phil Mickelson for winning the 2021 Professional Golfers Association championship victory by tweeting "I haven't been this heated after a sports game since Donald Trump's boyfriend Tom Brady won the super bowl."[45]

A possible back-story to Trump's relationship with Brady and Kraft broke in late May 2021. According to Shanin Specter, the son of former U.S. Senator Arlen Specter, when his father was investigating the 2008 Spygate scandal (the Patriots were disciplined by the league for inappropriately videotaping opposing coaches' defensive signals), he was approached by someone who offered him "a lot of money in Palm Beach," if he "laid off the Patriots." The younger Specter alleged to an ESPN reporter that the man who offered the cash was Trump, and he further alleged that the then-businessman and reality TV star had contacted his father at Kraft's behest.[46] Trump had also defended Brady when the NFL suspended the quarterback for four games for using deflated footballs in a 2015 playoff game.[47]

Twitter pressure, along with Trump's continuing comments against protesting athletes, finally caused Brady to back away from his support for the president. By 2017, Kaepernick was no longer playing in the NFL, but other players, such as his former teammate Eric Reid, continued to kneel during the national anthem. In a rally that year in Huntsville, Alabama, Trump told the crowd, "Wouldn't you love to see one of the NFL owners, when someone disrespects our flag to say, 'get that son of a bitch off the field right now. Out. He's fired. He's fired.'"[48] Trump's comment led to massive protests across the entire league. Some teams remained standing with linked arms to show support against what they saw as an attack on their fellow players. Other teams knelt en masse. Brady told Boston radio hosts *Kirk & Callahan* that "Yeah, I certainly disagree with what he said. I thought it was just divisive. Like I said, I just want to support my teammates."[49]

Gatekeeping at the White House

The fallout from Trump's comments continued throughout the season. The Philadelphia Eagles defeated the Patriots to win Super Bowl LII, and were invited to the White House. When "five or fewer" players actually committed to attending the ceremony, and several of the African American players turned down the invitation, the president announced that the event was called off. Trump issued a statement that said "The Philadelphia Eagles are unable to come to the White House with their full team to be celebrated tomorrow. They disagree with their president because he insists that they proudly stand for the national anthem, hand on heart, in honor of the great men and women of our military and the people of our country."[50]

In May 2018, the NFL acknowledged that Trump's criticisms, along with the individual actions of fans switching channels rather than watching games, had finally forced them to address the situation. League commissioner Roger Goodell issued a statement that set out the new policy: "This season, all league personnel shall stand and show respect for the flag and the anthem. Personnel who choose not to stand for the anthem may stay in the locker room until after the anthem has been performed." Goodell added that "It was unfortunate that on-field protests created a false perception among many that thousands of NFL players were unpatriotic. This is not and was never the case." The revised rule not only required players on the field to stand for the national anthem, but it also contained provisions for teams to be fined if their players did not comply.[51] This was met with immediate criticism, and by the time the season started, the league and the NFL Players Association had agreed to pause enforcement of the policy. By then, a relatively small number of players protested, and television networks had stopped featuring the protests on their broadcasts, so the issue had faded into the background for many.[52]

This seemed to extend to White House visits. The Patriots won Super Bowl LIII, and had planned to meet with the president, but scheduling conflicts – one from the team and one from the White House – meant that the visit never happened.[53] When the Kansas City Chiefs won Super Bowl LIV, players and coaches, including wide receiver Tyreek Hill, were invited and enthusiastic about making the trip. Hill, an African American, told reporters, "That would be great to go to the White House. I've never been to D.C., so that would be great."[54] However, the visit never happened as the reaction to COVID-19 put paid to those plans.

Meanwhile, outside the NFL and NBA, other teams were regularly visiting the White House with little notice or controversy. In November 2017, Trump hosted a number of college championship teams from various non-revenue sports, including Penn State wrestling, Oklahoma softball, Florida baseball, Ohio State's men's volleyball, Penn State's women's rugby, Washington's women's rowing, Maryland's women's and men's lacrosse, and the Utah women's ski team.[55] These teams were from sports that were not known for significant social media presences, and were largely made up of white athletes, and so the pressure on them to skip was likely much less severe. They could effectively fly below the Twitter radar.

Likewise, in 2017, the National Hockey League champion Pittsburgh Penguins visited, as did the 2017 World Series champion Houston Astros, the NCAA football champion Alabama Crimson Tide, and NASCAR champion Martin Truex, Jr. In 2018, the MLB champion Boston Red Sox, the NHL Washington Capitals, NCAA football champion Clemson, the NCAA's Football Championship Subdivision North Dakota State Bisons, NASCAR champion Joey Logano, and the NCAA women's basketball champion Baylor Bears also visited.

Clemson's 2019 trip occurred during a government shutdown. Part of the White House visit includes being fed by the president, but since non-essential government workers were temporarily furloughed, the president ordered a fast-food feast from Burger King, McDonald's, Wendy's, and Domino's Pizza.[56] Although the government was back to work by the time Baylor's Lady Bears visited the Trump White House, the Clemson players' reaction to being served fast food was positive enough that it became something of a tradition for college teams, and the athletes from Baylor were offered a similar menu.[57]

While many in the media depicted the event humorously, some linked his actions and words to the master narrative that Trump was racist, and – in this case – classist. Prior to the Clemson visit, Trump remarked that "I would think that's their favorite food," which *Vox* reporter Rebecca Jennings noted "rang as classist or racist" for some Twitter users. She wrote that, for some of the president's critics, "It's not much of a leap to assume that Trump guessed that many of the Clemson Tigers are black or come from working-class backgrounds, and thus presumed they prefer cheap, fatty foods over anything the White House would typically serve for guests in the State Dining Room."[58]

Lindsay Gibbs of *ThinkProgress*, in writing about the Lady Bears' White House visit, demonstrated the kind of pressure that coaches and athletes faced when visiting Trump, particularly in sports with high percentages of African Americans. The title of the article sent an unambiguous message that "The Baylor women's basketball team should not have accepted the White House invitation." The author argued that "the most questionable moment" of the visit was when Baylor coach Kim Mulkey thanked the president for inviting her and the team to the White House. After providing a summary of the various teams who had declined invitations, or who were not issued one, Gibbs declared that the only reason the team had received the invitation "is because Mulkey telegraphed her eagerness to accept the invite soon after the national championship win." The coach had told the *Associated Press* that "I've been every time for every president. It's an honor to go to the White House. I want everyone to say they went to the White House. Not many people can say this." Gibbs reasoning was that:

> The policies coming out of Trump's White House are racist, sexist, and homophobic. Basketball – and particularly women's basketball – is a sport dominated by black women, with a prominent queer community. These are some of the groups most marginalized by the Trump administration. By choosing to accept Trump's invitation, Mulkey was sending a clear message that in the face of that sort of disrespect, the proper thing to do is to bite one's tongue, shake hands, and smile for the photo op.[59]

Gibbs went on to criticize the three-time national champion coach for not speaking out about sexual assault at Baylor, encouraging former Baylor player Brittney Griner to not talk about her sexuality, and for promoting 'lady-like' dress and action for her players.[60]

Social media, amplified by more traditional media sources, put a great deal of pressure on teams and players who were considering whether to attend the Trump White House. Those who chose to do so were critiqued by individual tweeters, whose voices were magnified by the left-leaning press. This created a difficult choice for athletes and coaches. To visit the White House meant leaving one's career, and personal life, open to censure. Coach Mulkey's previous actions painted her in the same light as the president. On April 25, 2021, LSU Women's Basketball tweeted that Mulkey had accepted the head coach position at Louisiana State University. The first reply on the thread from 'Thomas' told "LSU Women's players . . . you deserve better than this Trump supporter, Covid denier!!"[61] By the time that Mulkey took the LSU job, Trump had been out of office for several months, but Twitter has a long memory.

Over time, Trump became more careful about who he invited to the White House. If coaches such as Mulkey signaled interest in a visit, they would receive the invitation. If players or coaches were likely to use an invitation to signal their opposition to the president, they were effectively ignored. That is likely the reason why no teams from women's professional basketball in the U.S., a league that the *New York Times* identified as the most socially progressive, or 'woke,' were invited.[62] After winning the 2018 Women's National Basketball Association (WNBA) championship, Seattle Storm players made it clear they had no intention of attending. According to four-time champion player Sue Bird, "At this point, does that even need to be discussed?"[63]

Likewise, the president became more careful in selecting sporting events to visit, after he was lustily booed when he attended game 5 of the 2019 World Series between the hometown Washington Nationals and the Astros. A sizeable number in the crowd went so far as to chant "lock him up!" and others displayed a large banner displaying the words "impeach him." Writing about the event for *The Guardian*, Tom Lutz did mention that Trump was not alone, and that several other presidents, including Jimmy Carter, Reagan, Nixon, and both of the Bushes, had been booed at MLB games.[64]

Like Nixon, Trump was on firmer ground in front of football crowds. A couple of months after his negative World Series experience, the president performed the coin toss for the Army–Navy game. In his third appearance at the annual match, the crowd welcomed him with enthusiastic applause, and chants of "Commander in Chief," "Trump we love you," and "Four more years!"[65] He received a similar rousing welcome at the NCAA National Championship game that pitted Clemson versus LSU in January, with chants of "USA, USA!" and "Four more years!"[66] In the *Washington Post*, historian Andrew McGregor called college football "a safe space" for conservatives, and that seemed to be borne out by Trump's reception at those events.[67]

The last major quarrel before COVID rendered the possibility of visiting the White House moot occurred when Megan Rapinoe of the U.S. women's national soccer team told an interviewer that if her team won the World Cup, she was "not going to the fucking White House."[68] Trump characteristically responded quickly, and tweeted that "I am a big fan of the American Team, and Women's Soccer, but Megan should WIN first before she TALKS! Finish the job!"[69] Team USA did finish the job by winning the World Cup in 2019, and the president reportedly sent a "private invitation" to the team to visit the White House, but the team did not attend.[70]

During Trump's term as president, what had been a largely apolitical tradition of championship teams visiting the White House became a scene of partisan confrontation. Athletes and teams faced tremendous pressure generated by social media to refuse to legitimize the Trump White House through their attendance. How this affected Trump's loss to Joe Biden in the 2020 election is impossible to ascertain, but it is unlikely that Trump lost much support among his Republican base by engaging in public battles with athletes that he successfully, for his base, depicted as disrespecting the military, flag, and country.

The Trump presidency: a long-term change, or momentary aberration?

Presidents love their sports, but, increasingly, some athletes do not love their presidents. The trend of athletes deciding to skip White House visits began long before Trump's presidency. A large group of athletes were, and still are, angry at Carter's decision to boycott the 1980 Moscow Olympics.[71] Small numbers of individual athletes declined, for sometimes personal and sometimes political reasons, to visit the Reagan, George H. W. Bush, Clinton, George W. Bush, and Obama White Houses. The frequency and scope of those refusals certainly increased during the Trump administration. This was no doubt largely due to the nature of Trump himself, which could be charitably called combative, or less charitably, to quote his 2016 rival Clinton, "deplorable."

Another significant reason why the relationship between presidents and athletes has become more complicated is the increasing number of athletes who have become politically active. This perhaps started, in American sports, with Tommie Smith and John Carlos raising their fists in the Black Power salute at the 1968 Mexico City Olympics. The modern iteration, however, began with Kaepernick's decision to sit during the national anthem, and since that coincided with the 2016 presidential campaign, it helped to fuel a debate about the meaning of his action that broke largely along partisan lines.

A final factor in the growing controversy surrounding presidential visits has been the increasing influence of social media, Twitter in particular. The platform offers unprecedented access to athletes, professional and collegiate alike. That access has had the effect of magnifying voices that were largely critical of Trump. According to a *Pew Research* study published in 2019, "63% of Twitter users ages 18 to 49 identify as Democrats."[72] That meant that athletes in the age of Trump were more likely to have fans tweeting anti-Trump messages at them, and encouraging them to not visit the White House, or shaming them if they did.

Curry addressed that in commenting on his 2017 decision: "I decided to speak out on me not wanting to go to the White House last year. And every team that has won a championship since then has gone through that ... So many people want to chime in ... How, I guess, social media is used today, the conversation can get out of control with so many different voices."[73] When those voices come largely from the left side of the political spectrum, and when the current resident of the White House used the platform to conduct political fights, that meant that even apolitical athletes were under enormous pressure.[74]

In Trump's case, Twitter also gave him a channel outside of the largely hostile mainstream media to instantly respond to his critics, and to generate counternarratives. Although his rapid-fire responses often gave his critics even more ammunition, they also routinely gave him the ability to shape the news cycle. When the NFL moved to allow more 'woke' messaging in the wake of the death of George Floyd, Trump told interviewer Clay Travis that he was concerned about the league's political plans, and was hopeful that the league would open during the pandemic: "(NFL officials) want to open badly and they've been working with the government. I would say this: If they don't stand for the national anthem, I hope they don't open."[75]

Twitter, along with his combative nature, helped Trump win the presidency, and conceivably helped him lose it as well. Perhaps now that he is no longer president, and banned from the platform, it will be safe for athletes to once again visit the White House. When the NFL champion Tampa Bay Buccaneers visited the Biden White House in July 2021, Brady did attend, and seemingly mocked Trump when he told Biden that "I think 40% of the people still don't think we [Tampa Bay] won." Biden responded, "I understand that." However, several comments on Twitter reminded users that Brady once had the MAGA hat in his locker.[76] It will be interesting to see what the future holds for the American Fan-in-Chief, particularly when his political affiliation does not align with that of the majority of social media users. Without a doubt, however, attend or decline, athletes should be warned that Twitter will be watching and waiting to see what they do.

Notes

1. Evan L. Frederick, Ann Pegoraro, and Samuel Schmidt, "'I'm Not Going to the F***ing White House:' Twitter Users React to

Donald Trump and Megan Rapinoe," *Communication and Sport*, August 28, 2020, available at: https://journals.sagepub.com/doi/full/10.1177/2167479520950778.

2. Brian Kilmeade, *The Games Do Count: America's Best and Brightest on the Power of Sports* (New York: Reagan Books, 2004), 297.

3. Nik DeCosta-Klipa, "Here's a First Glimpse of all the Patriots Players Visiting the White House," *Boston.com*, April 19, 2017, available at: https://www.boston.com/sports/new-england-patriots/2017/04/19/heres-a-first-glimpse-of-all-the-patriots-players-visiting-the-white-house; John Bat, "NCAA champion Clemson Tigers visit Trump at White House," *CBS News*, June 12, 2017, available at: https://www.cbsnews.com/news/ncaa-champion-clemson-tigers-visit-trump-at-white-house.

4. DeCosta-Klipa, "Here's a First Glimpse of all the Patriots Players Visiting the White House."

5. Mary Margaret Olohan, "Here's a List of the Famous Athletes Who Skipped Visiting Obama in the White House and How the Media Treated Them," *The Daily Caller*, November 4, 2019, available at: https://dailycaller.com/2019/11/04/athletes-obama-white-house-trump-media.

6. Mark Heim, "Dabo Swinney said Nick Saban Paid National Title Bet, 'Fired Up' for Clemson's White House trip," *AL.com*, January 13, 2019, available at: https://www.al.com/sports/2017/04/dabo_swinney_said_nick_saban_p.html.

7. Associated Press, "Steph Curry Doesn't Want to Visit the White House, and Trump, in a Tweet, Withdraws the Invitation," September 23, 2017, available at: https://www.latimes.com/sports/sports-now/la-sp-curry-trump-20170923-story.html.

8. Harriet Marsden, "Wither 'Woke': What Does the Future Hold for Word that Became a Weapon?" *The New European*, November 25, 2019, available at: https://www.theneweuropean.co.uk/brexit-news/future-for-woke-word-became-a-weapon-62988.

9. Jefferson Morely, "Politicians and Baseball: How a Dubious 150-Year-Old Tradition Was Born," *The Atlantic*, March 31, 2011, available at: https://www.theatlantic.com/entertainment/archive/2011/03/politicians-and-baseball-how-a-dubious-150-year-old-tradition-was-born/73187.

10. Joseph S. Stern, Jr., *The Team that Couldn't Be Beat: The Red Stockings of 1869* (Boston, MA: Oliver Ditson, 1969), 34, available at: http://library.cincymuseum.org/topics/b/files/baseball/chsbull-v27-n1-tea-025.pdf.

11. C. Norman Willis, *Washington Senators' All Time Greats* (Blooming-ton, IN: Xlibris, 2003), 15.

12. Angelique Fiske, "Adrienne Smith's Mission to Empower, Inspire the Next Generation of Women in Football," *Patriots.com*, March 10, 2021, available at: https://www.patriots.com/news/boston-renegade-adrienne-smith-s-mission-to-empower-inspire-the-next-generation.

13. "Presidents Who Played Football," *Pro Football Hall of Fame*, February 17, 2020, available at: https://www.profootballhof.com/presidents-who-played-football.

14. Patrick J. Kiger, "Oval Office Athletes: Presidents and the Sports They Played," *History.com*, February 9, 2019, available at: https://www.history.com/news/us-presidents-athletes.

15. John Sayle Watterson, *The Games Presidents Play: Sports and the Presidency* (Baltimore, MD: Johns Hopkins Press, 2006), 324; Jeff Pearlman, *Football For a Buck: The Crazy Rise and Crazier Demise of the USFL* (Boston, MA: Houghton Mifflin Harcourt, 2018), 120–121.

16. Rick Reilly, *Commander in Cheat: How Golf Explains Trump* (New York: Hachette, 2019), 5.

17. John Sayle Watterson, "The Gridiron Crisis of 1905: Was it Really a Crisis?" *Journal of Sport History* 17(2) (2000): 291.

18. Terry Frei, *Horns, Hogs, and Nixon Coming: Texas vs. Arkansas in Dixie's Last Stand* (New York: Simon & Schuster, 2002), 168.

19. David Stout, "Bush Says He Hopes 'Steroid Era' Ends Soon," *New York Times*, December 14, 2007, available at: https://www.nytimes.com/2007/12/14/sports/baseball/14cnd-bush.html.

20. "President-elect Obama Makes Another Play for College Football Playoff," *ESPN*, November 15, 2008, available at: https://www.espn.com/college-football/news/story?id=3704864.

21. Caitlin Oprysko, "Trump Lauds 'Very Productive Talk' with Big Ten Commissioner on 'Immediately' Resuming Football," *Politico*, September 1, 2020, available at: https://www.politico.com/news/2020/09/01/trump-talk-big-ten-football-406976.

22. Ronald A. Smith, *Pay For Play: A History of Big-Time College Athletic Reform* (Urbana: University of Illinois Press, 2011), 48.

23. Frei, *Horns, Hogs, and Nixon Coming*, 282.

24. J. B. Wogan, "A New Playoff is Coming," *Politifact*, June 27, 2012, available at: https://www.politifact.com/truth-o-meter/promises/obameter/promise/306/push-for-a-college-football-playoff-system.

25. Juan Perez, Jr., "Big Ten Revives Football Season in Trump-backed Turnaround," *Politico*, September 16, 2020, https://www.politico.

com/news/2020/09/16/big-ten-revives-football-season-in-trump-backed-turnaround-415870.

26. Jaime E. Settle, *Frenemies: How Social Media Polarizes America* (Cambridge: Cambridge University Press, 2018), 3.

27. Mike Jones, "Mike Jones: Let's Take a Swing at that Piñata," *Tulsa World*, July 5, 2015, available at: https://tulsaworld.com/archive/mike-jones-lets-take-a-swing-at-that-pinata/article_bda37396-fb0c-5072-8b28-dab01e02c0ca.html.

28. Chris Cillizza, "Donald Trump's Presidential Candidacy is Great Entertainment. It's Terrible for Politics," *Washington Post*, June 16, 2015, available at: https://www.washingtonpost.com/news/the-fix/wp/2015/06/16/donald-trumps-presidential-candidate-is-great-entertainment-its-terrible-for-politics.

29. Alexander Burns, "Donald Trump's Instinct for Racially Charged Rhetoric, Before His Presidential Bid," *New York Times*, July 31, 2015, available at: https://www.nytimes.com/2015/08/01/nyregion/trumps-instinct-for-racially-charged-rhetoric-before-his-presiden-tial-bid.html?searchResultPosition=1.

30. Tim Kawakami, "Colin Kaepernick on his Anthem Protest, and Much, Much More: 'This is Because I'm Seeing Things Happen to People That Don't Have a Voice,'" *Mercury News*, August 28, 2016, available at: http://blogs.mercurynews.com/kawakami/2016/08/28/colin-kaepernick-anthem-protest-much-much.

31. John Breech, "Donald Trump Fires Back at Colin Kaepernick after QB Calls Him Racist," *CBS Sports*, August 29, 2016, available at: https://www.cbssports.com/nfl/news/donald-trump-fires-back-at-colin-kaepernick-after-qb-calls-him-a-racist.

32. "Donald Trump: NFL's Ratings are Down Because of Colin Kaepernick," *Sports Illustrated*, October 30, 2016, available at: https://www.si.com/nfl/2016/10/30/donald-trump-nfl-ratings-down-colin-kaepernick.

33. Darren Rovell, Twitter post, October 7, 2016, available at: https://twitter.com/darrenrovell/status/784428496089182208/photo/2.

34. Boycott the NFL (@TurnOffFootball) and Boycott the NFL (@right-toboycott1) joined Twitter in September 2016. See at: https://twitter.com/TurnOffFootball; https://twitter.com/righttoboycott1?lang=en.

35. Jesse Washington, "The NFL is Being Squeezed by Boycotts from Both Sides Over Anthem Protests," *The Undefeated*, September 13, 2017, available at: https://theundefeated.com/features/nfl-boycotts-from-both-sides-over-anthem-protests.

36. Melissa Jacobs, "Week Under Review: Don't Take Kaepernick's Protest as Disrespect for the Military," *Sports Illustrated*, August

29, 2016, available at: https://www.si.com/nfl/2016/08/29/colin-kaepernick-national-anthem-protest-49ers.

37. Gerry Smith, "NFL Advertising Revenue Falls Sharply Despite Higher TV Ratings," *Bloomberg*, November 30, 2018, available at: https://www.bloombergquint.com/business/nfl-advertising-revenue-falls-sharply-despite-higher-tv-ratings.

38. Daniel Kaplan, "NFL Concedes that National Anthem Protests are Hurting Business," *Sports Business Journal*, October 24, 2017, available at: https://www.bizjournals.com/newyork/news/2017/10/24/nfl-concedes-that-national-anthem-protests-hurt.html.

39. Carrie Dan, "NBC/WSJ Poll: Majority Say Kneeling During Anthem 'Not Appropriate,'" *NBC News*, August 31, 2018, available at: https://www.nbcnews.com/politics/first-read/nbc-wsj-poll-majority-say-kneeling-during-anthem-not-appropriate-n904891.

40. "Who Will Win the Presidency?" *FiveThirtyEight*, November 8, 2016, available at: https://projects.fivethirtyeight.com/2016-election-forecast.

41. Kareem Abdul-Jabbar, "Kareem Abdul-Jabbar Op-Ed: The Difference Between Donald Trump and Bernie Sanders," *Chicago Tribune*, September 2, 2015, available at: https://www.chicagotribune.com/opinion/commentary/ct-kareem-abdul-jabbar-sanders-trump-20150902-story.html.

42. Ryan Fish, Andrew Vailliencourt, Jesse Kramer, and Eve Wulf, "Which Sports Figures are Supporting Hillary Clinton, Donald Trump, and Gary Johnson?" *Sports Illustrated*, September 26, 2016, available at: https://www.si.com/more-sports/2016/09/26/athlete-presidential-endorsements-donald-trump-hillary-clinton-gary-johnson.

43. Tanya Basu, "Tom Brady Explains the Donald Trump Hat in His Locker," *Time*, September 8, 2015, available at: https://time.com/4025262/tom-brady-trump-hat.

44. Twitter post, May 19, 2021, available at: https://twitter.com/DBreath2021/status/1395037939592093699.

45. Twitter post, May 20, 2021, available at: https://twitter.com/StephCurry21MVP/status/1395239532199612417.

46. Don Van Natta, Jr. and Seth Wickersham, "Son, Ghostwriter of Late Senator Say Trump Intervened to Stop Probe of Patriots' Spygate Scandal," *ESPN*, May 26, 2021, available at: https://www.espn.com/nfl/story/_/id/31484993/son-ghostwriter-late-senator-say-trump-intervened-stop-probe-patriots-spygate-scandal.

47. Cindy Boren, "Donald Trump says Tom Brady is 'Totally Innocent' in Deflategate," *Washington Post*, November 21, 2016, available at:

https://www.washingtonpost.com/news/early-lead/wp/2016/11/21/donald-trump-says-tom-brady-is-totally-innocent-in-deflategate.

48. "Presented by the 49ers," *NBC Sports*, September 22, 2017, available at: https://www.nbcsports.com/bayarea/49ers/trump-anthem-protesters-get-son-b-field.

49. Rachel Kraus, "Tom Brady Breaks His Silence, Criticizes 'Friend' Trump's NFL Comments," *Mashable*, September 25, 2017, available at: https://mashable.com/2017/09/25/tom-brady-president-trump-comments-divisive.

50. Michael D. Shear, "Trump Abruptly Calls Off Philadelphia Eagles Visit to White House," *New York Times*, June 4, 2018, available at: https://www.nytimes.com/2018/06/04/sports/philadelphia-eagles-white-house.html.

51. "Roger Goodell's Statement on the National Anthem Policy," *NFL.com*, May 23, 2018, available at: https://www.nfl.com/news/roger-goodell-s-statement-on-national-anthem-policy-0ap3000000933962.

52. Jenny Vrentas, "The NFL is Beginning the 2018 Season With No New National Anthem Policy," *Sports Illustrated*, September 9, 2018, available at: https://www.si.com/nfl/2018/09/09/national-anthem-policy-hold-2018-nfl-season.

53. Nik DeCosta-Klipa, "The Patriots Had Plans to Visit the White House this Offseason. Now, it Looks Unlikely," *Boston.com*, July 25, 2019, available at: https://www.boston.com/sports/new-england-patriots/2019/07/25/patriots-white-house-visit-2019-super-bowl.

54. Herbie Teope, "'It's Quite an Honor.' Chiefs Open to Visiting White House After Winning Super Bowl," *Kansas City Star*, February 3, 2020, available at: https://www.kansascity.com/sports/nfl/kansas-city-chiefs/article239891148.html.

55. Tyler Lauletta, "Trump Hosted 18 NCAA Championship Winning Teams to Celebrate Their Titles – and the Photos Were Great," *Business Insider*, November 18, 2017, available at: https://www.businessinsider.com/trump-hosts-18-ncaa-championship-winning-teams-at-the-white-house-2017-11.

56. Rebecca Jennings, "The Controversy Around Trump's Fast-food Football Feast, Explained," *Vox*, January 30, 2019, available at: https://www.vox.com/the-goods/2019/1/15/18183617/trump-clemson-mcdonalds-burger-king-wendys-dominos.

57. Michael Shapiro, "Baylor Served Fast Food at White House After National Championship," *Sports Illustrated*, April 29, 2019, available at: https://www.si.com/college/2019/04/29/baylor-white-house-fast-food-donald-trump-national-championship.

58. Jennings, "The Controversy Around Trump's Fast-food Football Feast, Explained."

59. Lindsay Gibbs, "The Baylor Women's Basketball Team Should Not Have Accepted the White House Invitation," *ThinkProgress*, April 29, 2019, available at: https://archive.thinkprogress.org/baylor-womens-basketball-team-white-house-invitation-bca098a939e0/.

60. Gibbs, "The Baylor Women's Basketball Team Should Not Have Accepted the White House Invitation."

61. Twitter post, April 26, 2021, available at: https://twitter.com/Thomas73798577/status/1386544227765522435.

62. Jonathan Abrams and Natalie Weiner, "How the Most Socially Progressive Pro League Got That Way," *New York Times*, October 16, 2020, available at: https://www.nytimes.com/2020/10/16/sports/basketball/wnba-loeffler-protest-kneeling.html.

63. Percy Allen, "Storm Not Expecting a White House Invitation, and it Won't Go Even if One is Extended," *Seattle Times*, September 14, 2018, available at: https://www.seattletimes.com/sports/storm/the-storm-is-not-expecting-a-white-house-invitation-and-they-wont-go-even-if-one-is-extended.

64. Tom Lutz, "Donald Trump Booed and Greeted With 'Lock Him Up' Chants at World Series," *The Guardian*, October 27, 2019, available at: https://www.theguardian.com/sport/2019/oct/27/donald-trump-booed-world-series-lock-him-up-chants-baseball.

65. Tommy Deas, "President Trump Receives Rousing Welcome From Crowd at 120th Army–Navy Game," *USA Today*, December 14, 2019, available at: https://www.usatoday.com/story/sports/ncaaf/2019/12/14/president-donald-trump-received-rousing-ovation-army-navy-game/2649259001.

66. Meagan Vazquez, "Trump Cheered at College Football Championship Game," *CNN*, January 14, 2020, https://www.cnn.com/2020/01/14/politics/donald-trump-lsu-clemson-cheers/index.html.

67. Andrew McGregor, "College Football Gives Conservatives Their Own Safe Space on Campus," *Washington Post*, September 1, 2017, available at: https://www.washingtonpost.com/news/made-by-history/wp/2017/09/01/college-football-gives-conservatives-their-own-safe-space-on-campus.

68. Charlotte Carroll, "Megan Rapinoe on Trump Tweets: I Held Up My End of the Bargain," *Sports Illustrated*, July 9 2019, available at: https://www.si.com/soccer/2019/07/09/megan-rapinoe-donald-trump-uswnt-womens-world-cup-win.

69. Andrew Keh, "Trump Criticizes Megan Rapinoe Over Refusal to Visit White House," *New York Times*, June 26, 2019, available at: https://www.nytimes.com/2019/06/26/sports/trump-megan-rapinoe-tweet.html.

70. Jenna West, "USWNT Received Private Invite From White House to Visit After World Cup," *Sports Illustrated*, December 9, 2019, available at: https://www.si.com/soccer/2019/12/09/uswnt-white-house-visit-invite-megan-rapinoe.

71. Rick Maese, "U.S. Boycott of 1980 Moscow Olympics Still Rankles Athletes," *Washington Post*, July 16, 2020, available at: https://www.washingtonpost.com/graphics/2020/sports/1980-usa-olympic-boycott-team-carter.

72. "Sizing Up Twitter Users," *Pew Research Center*, April 24, 2019, available at: https://www.pewresearch.org/internet/2019/04/24/sizing-up-twitter-users.

73. Marc J. Spears, "LeBron James, Stephen Curry Agree That Next NBA Champs Won't Visit White House," *ESPN*, June 5, 2018, available at: https://abc7news.com/sports/lebron-james-stephen-curry-agree-that-next-nba-champs-wont-visit-white-house/3565058.

74. Evette Alexander, "Polarization in the Twittersphere: What 86 Million Tweets Reveal About the Political Makeup of American Twitter Users and How They Engage with News," *Knight Foundation*, December 17, 2019, available at: https://knightfoundation.org/articles/polarization-in-the-twittersphere-what-86-million-tweets-reveal-about-the-political-makeup-of-american-twitter-users-and-how-they-engage-with-news.

75. Kyle Dalton, "President Trump Just Sent Scary Message to NFL and Players About Kneeling in 2020," August 11, 2020, available at: https://www.sportscasting.com/president-trump-just-sent-scary-message-to-nfl-and-players-about-kneeling-in-2020.

76. Twitter post, July 20, 2021, available at: https://twitter.com/TPostMillennial/status/1417518656586616833.

Afterword: The State of Presidential Sport

Heather L. Dichter

For over a century, as the chapters in this volume edited by Adam Burns and Rivers Gambrell demonstrate, sport has been a part of the presidency – both the men holding the highest elected office in the United States and those individuals who have run for and lost these elections. These individuals played a variety of sports during their youth and during their time as the occupant of the White House, with those activities shaping their outlook and approach. They have used sporting metaphors themselves or have had comparisons with sport applied to their presidencies. They have sought athlete and coach endorsements of their candidacies and used appearances at sporting events as well as championship team visits to the White House to their advantage, conveying a specific message to the public. These experiences shaped the presidents' views regarding sport and physical fitness, which they promoted in their speeches, writings, and, in some cases, within policies.

In many ways, this book is about the media, sport, and the presidency, as most of the ways the public has known about the presidents and their participation in or views on sport has been presented through the media. Sport and the media have long had a symbiotic relationship, with sport helping each new media form (newspapers, radio, television, internet) gain popularity, while that same media coverage of sport has helped to further popularize and bring new audiences to sport.[1] With an entire Washington, D.C.-based press corps to cover politics, much is known about the lives of presidents, including their sporting preferences. The growth of mass media, particularly the 24/7 coverage by the end of the twentieth century with television channels devoted entirely to politics or sport, has meant that the public knows even more about more recent presidents than their predecessors.[2] Through news stories and social media posts, scholars can even examine a president's relationship with sport less than a year after that term ended, as Russ Crawford has done for Donald Trump.

Sport has therefore played a significant role in the public relations of presidents, on the campaign trail, during their time in the White House, and afterwards. Theodore Roosevelt's speeches were quoted at length in newspapers, and he carefully curated his letters for publication as books after his presidency to convey specific ideas. Franklin Roosevelt skillfully used radio to convey his messages directly to the public with his fireside chats, and the postwar expansion of television brought the president live, in picture, into Americans' homes.[3] The entire country could see the president attend a sporting event or throw the Opening Day pitch during the nationally televised broadcast, and by the end of the twentieth century see that image repeated every hour on ESPN's SportsCenter. Social media has allowed the president to convey their thoughts at any time of day directly to the public without even requiring the presence of the press corps and their cameras.[4]

That so many of the nation's leaders had a strong interest in sport and often used sport metaphors in their public speeches is not surprising because of the role of sport within education and the military. Several of the presidents in the twentieth and twenty-first centuries attended private schools, where sport has particularly played a central role, as seen in the lives of Kennedy and both Bush presidents. Presidents with a military background (Theodore Roosevelt, George H. W. Bush, Kennedy, and Eisenhower – the latter of whom became the first military governor of the U.S. zone during the early months of the occupation of Germany when the Allies finalized a control directive on sport) also understood the importance of sport.[5] Their personal sporting preferences differed, as seen by the wide range of sports covered in this volume – from Richard Nixon's affinity for football, which Jesse Berrett examines, to the multiple White House occupants who spent time running or jogging, as Elizabeth Rees demonstrates. Of course, similar experiences growing up and, especially, while at university, have led to many of these presidents playing the same sports in their youth – particularly college football and baseball, but also the less commonly played sport (at least in the United States) of rugby, which Adam Burns has explored. Golf, a sport played by people with greater income and time, but also one that people can play throughout their lives, not surprisingly has perhaps been the sport played most frequently by presidents during their time in the White House, which Aaron Moore has demonstrated.

This edited volume covers more than a century of presidents and numerous sports. This compilation of diverse historical material is valuable in considering the many ways sport and the presidency have intersected. The ideas contained in the chapters provide an excellent starting point for future explorations of the relationship between sport and the occupants of the White House. The examples from the thirteen main chapters can be used in broader considerations of how sport and the American presidency are intertwined, from additional segments of American society to comparisons with foreign leaders.

The wealth of sources available to scholars from the explosion of media coverage and the creation of presidential libraries, which began with Franklin D. Roosevelt, should not preclude earlier examinations of the relationship between sport and the presidency. Media played a central role in the commercialization and growth of sport in the twentieth century, but sport did not begin with Theodore Roosevelt, who is most remembered as the 'Father of a Sporting Nation,' as Ryan Swanson has shown.[6] Sport underwent a modernization process in the second half of the nineteenth century, and in the 1860s alone, for instance, the sport of baseball spread as a result of the Civil War and also saw the first fully professional team appear with the 1869 Cincinnati Red Stockings.[7] What, then, were the relationships of the presidents from Abraham Lincoln to William McKinley with sport? Michael Hinds and Jonathan Silverman note that the country's first president, George Washington, as well as Andrew Jackson, were involved with horse racing, a sport that goes back to Antiquity and was one of the earlier sports in colonial America. While the modern version of the sport with parimutuel betting was a late nineteenth-century import, horse racing was long a sport of large landowners – which many early presidents were.

With almost two and a half centuries of American presidents all being men, and almost all of the candidates for the highest elected position also being men, it is not surprising that the chapters within this volume demonstrate a very masculine view of sport. Additionally, the role of sport within education and the military has long been framed as a way to develop men, a view that Theodore Roosevelt clearly took with his sons. Throughout the entire period covered by the chapters in this volume women have been participating in sport, yet women's sport is almost entirely missing from this examination of the presidency. What advice regarding sport and physical activity did Roosevelt impart to his daughters? What sports did they play, either among the family or at school, and how did Roosevelt frame those activities in terms of health, femininity, or otherwise? These questions would provide another facet to understanding Theodore Roosevelt's views on sport as well as early twentieth-century women's sport.

Just like the brief mentions of Roosevelt's daughters, women athletes play a peripheral role within the book. Some women's teams are included in Russ Crawford's examination of championship teams visiting (or not) the White House, but the media coverage of these events are viewed similarly to men's teams. The President's Physical Fitness Tests were for both boys and girls in school (which many readers of this book likely remember), but the program is largely framed – both here and in other scholarship – within the context of ensuring men would be physically in shape should they be required for military service during the Cold War.[8] Yet, when it comes to international relations, women have played a significant role within U.S. efforts to use sport to foster goodwill.[9] The State Department sent both male and female athletes overseas as part of public diplomacy efforts during the Cold War. In 2002, the State Department established SportsUnited, a division within the Bureau of Educational and Cultural Affairs, to use sport within its diplomatic efforts. One program, Empowering Women and Girls through Sport, aimed to expand the message of equality and opportunity for women across the world through sport. The creation of this program coincided with the fortieth anniversary of the passing of Title IX, and the website makes clear this program began during George W. Bush's presidency.[10] How involved was

Bush in the creation of this program? Had raising two daughters who had ample opportunities to participate in sport as children in the 1980s and 1990s influenced Bush's views? Although a program that is still relatively young and for which the archival record will remain closed for a few decades, oral history can nonetheless enable an early history of this division and its programs, including the president's role within its development.

Athletes have, at least since Babe Ruth, supported presidential candidates, and again here the role of women within this process, as well as women appearing on the presidential ticket, has been neglected from previous studies. The 2020 election alone provides many such avenues for research. Kamala Harris' place alongside Joseph Biden (as his vice president) surely deserves as much treatment, as the first woman elected to the vice presidency, as the presidents themselves. Harris' inauguration involved several individuals from sport: basketball legend Kareem Abdul-Jabbar; Miami Marlins general manager, and the first woman to serve as a general manager in baseball, Kim Ng; and Sarah Fuller, the first woman to score a point in a major college football game.[11] In addition, Harris' hometown NBA team, the Golden State Warriors, gifted her a jersey with the number 49 (as she was the country's 49th vice president) and Madame VP on the back, signed by the team's star Stephen Curry.[12] The role of the Women's National Basketball Association (WNBA), a league dominated by Black women and with a sizeable queer representation among its players, also deserves attention. The Seattle Storm, the 2020 WNBA champions, as a team endorsed Biden and Harris and encouraged their fans to support the Democratic ticket.[13] In addition, the Atlanta Dream carefully considered Senate candidates before putting their weight behind Raphael Warnock to unseat the team's co-owner, Senator Kelly Loeffler.[14]

Just as Bill Clinton became involved in trying to end the Major League Baseball (MLB) strike in 1994, perhaps a future president will become involved in labor disputes within sport. Clinton's decision to get involved in trying to end the MLB strike, as Chris Birkett's chapter shows, was in part because Clinton overestimated the power of the office of the president but also because he saw the value in using the symbols of national identity – including

America's pastime. The U.S. Women's National Team (USWNT) has been involved in a lengthy pay dispute with U.S. Soccer.[15] As the most successful women's soccer program in the world – and far more successful than the U.S. men's national soccer team – will a future president get involved in this labor dispute? The USWNT has visited the White House numerous times after its World Cup and Olympic championships (although not after the 2019 World Cup victory), so it is not inconceivable that a future president could become involved in this dispute with one of the country's most successful and most watched teams.

Race factors into three chapters within the final section of the book, about athletes and their support of (or lack thereof) presidents and their candidacies. Jackie Robinson, who broke Major League Baseball's color line in 1947, provides a fascinating case study in Dean J. Kotlowski's chapter. What about other Black athletes supporting presidential candidates? While other candidates before him may not have sought athlete endorsements as actively as Richard Nixon, how much support did presidential nominees receive from athletes in the African American press? Robert Chiles showed an earlier twentieth-century celebrity athlete endorsement with Babe Ruth's support of Alfred E. Smith's 1928 presidential campaign, so the idea of athletes publicly supporting and campaigning for presidents is not a recent phenomenon. The inability of Gerald Ford's close football teammate at the University of Michigan to play in a game at Georgia Tech in 1934 shaped Ford's views on civil rights for the rest of his life, but what about other presidents and their experiences?[16] Robinson appears again in Michael L. Butterworth and Shawn N. Smith's chapter on Barack Obama, with the country's first Black president frequently compared with the baseball icon. The emergence of Black Lives Matter and symbolic protests during the playing of the national anthem during sporting events during Trump's term brought the racial issues to the fore, particularly in the era of Twitter and other social media forms. Earlier considerations of race, as well as other nonwhite minority groups in the United States, are still needed. Sport was frequently used in the Euro-American efforts to remove indigenous culture from Native Americans; how did various presidents consider this aspect within their policies?[17]

While this book is about sport and the American presidency, many of the ideas contained within the chapters are not specific to the United States. Sport history is often written with a singular country focus. However, the arguments about sport and the American presidency can – and should – be considered within a broader, international context. Many developments within sport have taken place within the United States, but the country's sport history should not be examined in isolation. In fact, Theodore Roosevelt's emphasis in his writings to his children and within public speeches that participation was more important than both winning and spectating aligns with the sentiment from Pierre de Coubertin, the founder of the modern Olympic Games. Born just five years apart, both men came of age in the second half of the nineteenth century. What global forces or personal experiences shaped both men's views that they both developed a strong sense that taking part in the sporting event was the most important?

The belief among several presidents in the importance of sport, as seen in the first section, is an idea shared by political leaders across the globe in the twentieth and twenty-first centuries. While Theodore Roosevelt spoke about the value of playing sport for the good of the country, it was the postwar presidents who implemented and modified national physical fitness programs for the nation's youth. Several presidents even brought prominent football coaches on board to help to promote these ideas within the Cold War context, as Andrew McGregor has shown. Yet how do the approaches to physical fitness and health taken by various American presidents compare with the actions taken in other countries across the world? At the same time that the "fitness gap" troubled John F. Kennedy, which Hendrik Ohnesorge examined, north of the border Prime Minister John Diefenbaker had the same concerns regarding the Canadian population, leading him to sign the Fitness and Amateur Sport Act in 1961.[18] The idea of "sport for all" and programs that promoted sporting activity broadly (in contrast to elite sport) became a prominent feature of the 1970s and 1980s across Europe, including the Federal Republic of Germany, Austria, and most of communist eastern Europe.[19] The People's Republic of China has developed its sport for all policies "in lockstep with the changing ideology of the central government."[20] Considering American policies regarding sport and physical fitness within broader global actions will provide a greater understanding of American sport, as well as how international forces have shaped presidential views regarding sport and their ensuing domestic policies.

In addition, the images of the presidents themselves should be considered more broadly and not solely as shaping the national view of the occupant of the White House. Theodore Roosevelt participated in several sporting activities, with Americans frequently reading about his athleticism in newspapers. This same idea – a strong, athletic leader of the nation – has been repeated many times since Roosevelt. Benito Mussolini ensured his activities, whether on the beach or the snow, or participating in boxing, tennis, gymnastics, horseback riding, swimming, or fencing, were all captured in photographs and newsreels. Italian Fascism exalted the virile body, and as Gigliola Gori has demonstrated, Mussolini "embodied the ideal model of virile beauty in the eyes of most Italians who, spellbound by his magnetic charm, wanted to imitate both his physical appearance and his behaviour."[21] More recently, the numerous photographs of Russian president Vladimir Putin officially released by the Kremlin often portray him shirtless and participating in a variety of sporting activities. Andrew Foxall argues that these images demonstrate "frontier masculinity," an idea that is clearly reminiscent of Theodore Roosevelt.[22]

Delving into the photographs would provide another avenue for understanding sport and the American presidency. Many of the chapters in this volume comment on images of the presidents photographed at sporting events and how the presidents used those events to promote a specific image of themselves to the public. As public events, though, the presidents knew they would be photographed by professionals hired to cover the president and/or the sporting event. The personal photographs, either of the presidents themselves participating in sporting activities (before, during, or after their time in the White House) or the photographs they took, possibly of family sporting activities or at games they attended, would provide an even greater understanding of sport and the presidency. Cara A. Finnegan's recent work on *Photographic Presidents* considers how presidents have actively participated in that technology's development.[23] Applying photographic history methods to the sporting images of the presidency and its office holders throughout their lives would open up new avenues of inquiry in relation to the visual culture of sport and the presidency. How have presidents themselves prioritized images of themselves or family members participating in sporting activities? Have the presidents who prepared for their ceremonial Opening Day pitch kept the photographs of themselves on the pitcher's mound? Examining more than just the image itself, but the context in which photographs are taken, preserved and circulated, would further elucidate the role of sport and the presidency.

The images of presidents at sporting events are symbolic, often bestowing importance on the sporting event itself. Yet the lack of presidential attendance at sporting events is equally important for conveying messages to a broad public. The decision by Joe Biden to lead a diplomatic boycott of the 2022 Olympic Winter Games in Beijing was a clear decision to embarrass the Chinese government.[24] World leaders or their representatives (sometimes their spouses, children, or second in command) often attend the opening ceremonies and important events at the Olympic Games or FIFA World Cup. Having other world leaders attend provides the host country and its leader with an opportunity to benefit from the public diplomacy of having the world's media focused on their country. By not sending any diplomatic representation, the United States (along with the other countries that also agreed to a diplomatic boycott of the Beijing Olympics) diminished the Chinese efforts to gain positive media attention.

In a similar vein, the United States has hosted the Olympic Games more times than any other country, and it has also hosted the FIFA World Cup and Women's World Cup. The chapters in this volume have focused on domestic sporting events such as the Kentucky Derby, college football games, and baseball's Opening Day and World Series. Yet the world's media has focused its attention on the United States for sport mega-events more often than any other country. State leaders across the world have supported their country's bids to host mega-events, and particularly welcomed the opportunity to be highly visible during the events when their country won the right to host them.[25] These mega-events have served as public diplomacy opportunities because the world's media is focused on that city and/or country for two weeks (for the Olympics) to an entire month for the FIFA World Cup or Women's World Cup. With so many Olympic Games and three FIFA events having been hosted in the United States (the 1994 men's tournament and the women's tournaments in 1999 and 2003), and the upcoming 2026 FIFA World Cup and 2028 Olympic Games also being held in the country, this is an area which demands further attention.

The fact that the Summer Olympics occur during presidential election years, and, since 1994, the Winter Games during midterm election years, provides ample opportunity to explore how presidents have used the Olympics – either when opening and attending the games or how candidates used them on the campaign trail. In 1932, Herbert Hoover broke the tradition of the head of state opening the Olympic Games. For the Summer Olympics in Los Angeles this meant his vice president, Charles Curtis, officially opened the games. Hoover had also declined to open the Winter Olympics in Lake Placid earlier that year, leaving the governor of New York – Franklin Roosevelt – to open them. Roosevelt used the Olympics as an opportunity to campaign for the presidency, with his comments broadcast on two of the country's radio networks.[26] The closest connection between the Olympics and the campaign for the presidency perhaps came in 2012 when the Republican candidate was Mitt Romney, the former governor of Massachusetts but also the former head of the Salt Lake Olympic Organizing Committee. From the first Olympics in the United States (St. Louis in 1904) through the upcoming 2028 Games, which Los Angeles will host for the third time, there are numerous opportunities (including 1960 Squaw Valley, 1980 Lake Placid, 1984 Los Angeles, and 1996 Atlanta) to explore the relationship of the Olympics and the presidency.

Other American cities hoping to win the Olympic Games have also drawn on the power of the presidency, and that support also deserves to be examined. Detroit is perhaps the biggest loser when it comes to Olympic bids, having tried to bring the games to the Motor City each time from 1944 through 1972. For the city's 1968 bid, John F. Kennedy spoke on the color video which the bid committee played during its presentation at the International Olympic Committee (IOC) meeting in Baden-Baden, Germany, in October 1963.[27] Barack Obama went all in for his former hometown of Chicago's bid for the 2016 Olympics, flying to Copenhagen for only a few hours to speak during the city's presentation.[28] Of course, these efforts are not always as successful as hoped. Whereas journalists felt Detroit's video was slick and made all the other candidate cities' presentations really dull, the IOC president in the 1960s, the American Avery Brundage, felt Kennedy's comments in the candidature film were "pompous and misplaced."[29] (Brundage did not support the Democratic president or his policies.) Obama's brief visit to Denmark kept the IOC members waiting before they met him, and some political commentators in the United States criticized Obama and said Chicago's poor results in the vote would have consequences for the president.[30]

Sports have, thus, been a clear part of the presidency. The activities in which these individuals participated from their youth through their time in the White House has ranged widely, from team sports to the lifelong pursuits of golf and running or jogging. Sport has informed both domestic and foreign policies, being incorporated into a range of programs. While the United States is an anomaly as one of the only countries in the world where the government does not fund its elite athletes who compete on the international stage, the country is not exceptional in its head of state being concerned with sport, both personally and for the country. Adam Burns and Rivers Gambrell have, through chapters brought together in this volume, demonstrated that sport and the American presidency are, indeed, intertwined.

Notes

1. Tony Mason, "Sporting News, 1860–1914," in Michael Harris and Alan Lee (eds.), *The Press in English Society from the Seventeenth to Nineteenth Centuries* (London: Associated University Presses, 1986), 168–186; Andrew Walker, "Reporting Play: The Local Newspaper and Sports Journalism, c. 1870–1914," *Journalism Studies* 7(3) (2006): 452–462; Philippe Gaboriau, "The Tour de France and Cycling's Belle Epoque," *International Journal of the History of*

Sport 20(2) (2003): 57–78; James R. Walker, "The Baseball-Radio War, 1931–1935," *NINE: A Journal of Baseball History and Culture* 19(2) (2011): 53–60; Mike Huggins, "BBC Radio and Sport 1922–39," *Contemporary British History* 21(4) (2007): 491–515; Gary Whannel, "Television and the Transformation of Sport," *ANNALS of the American Academy of Political and Social Science* 625 (2009): 205–218; Richard Haynes, "A Pageant of Sound and Vision: Football's Relationship with Television, 1936–60," *International Journal of the History of Sport* 15(1) (1998): 211–226; Michael Real, "Sports Online: The Newest Player in Mediasport," in Arthur A. Raney, and Jennings Bryant (eds.), *Handbook of Sports and Media* (Abingdon: Routledge, 2006), 183–197.

2. Donald A. Ritchie, *Reporting from Washington: The History of the Washington Press Corps* (New York: Oxford University Press, 2006); Stephen Ponder, *Managing the Press: Origins of the Media Presidency, 1897–1933* (New York: St. Martin's Press, 1999); Matthew Eshbaugh-Soha, "Presidents and Mass Media," in Lori Cox Han (ed.), *New Directions in the American Presidency* (New York: Routledge, 2018), 78–101; Susan J. Douglas, "Presidents and the Media," in Brian Balogh (ed.), *Recapturing the Oval Office: New Historical Approaches to the American Presidency* (Ithaca, NY: Cornell University Press, 2015), 143–161; Travis Vogan, *ESPN: The Making of a Sports Media Empire* (Champaign: University of Illinois Press, 2015).

3. David Greenberg, *Republic of Spin: An Inside History of the American Presidency* (New York: W. W. Norton, 2016).

4. Sam A. Fontaine and Daniel M. Gomez, "Going Social: A Comparative Analysis of Presidents' Official and Social Media Messages," *Presidential Studies Quarterly* 50(3) (2020): 507–538.

5. Heather L. Dichter, "'Strict Measures Must be Taken': Wartime Planning and the Allied Control of Sport in Occupied Germany," *Stadion* 34(2) (2008): 193–217.

6. Dale L. Cressman and Lisa Swenson, "The Pigskin and the Picture Tube: The National Football League's First Full Season on the CBS," *Television Network, Journal of Broadcasting & Electronic Media* 51(3) (2007): 479–497; Travis Vogan, *ABC Sports: The Rise and Fall of Network Sports Television* (Oakland: University of California Press, 2018); Robert K. Barney, Stephen R. Wenn, and Scott G. Martyn, *Selling the Five Rings: The International Olympic Committee and the Rise of Olympic Commercialism* (Salt Lake City: University of Utah Press, 2004).

7. Larry Bowman, "Soldiers at Play: Baseball on the American Frontier," *NINE: A Journal of Baseball History and Culture* 9(1/2) (2000/1): 35–49.

8. Matthew T. Bowers and Thomas M. Hunt, "The President's Council on Physical Fitness and the Systematisation of Children's Play in America," *International Journal of the History of Sport* 28(11) (2011): 1496–1511.

9. Ashley Brown, "Swinging for the State Department: American Women Tennis Players in Diplomatic Goodwill Tours, 1941–59," *Journal of Sport History* 42(3) (2015): 289–309.

10. This program now falls under the broader Global Sports Mentoring programs within the Special Initiatives and Projects. "Our History," Global Sports Mentoring Program, available at: https://globalsportsmentoring.org/our-history.

11. Nick Selbe, "Sarah Fuller, Kareem Abdul-Jabbar, and Kim Ng Take Part in Inauguration Ceremony," *SI.com*, January 20, 2021, available at: https://www.si.com/sports/2021/01/21/sarah-fuller-introduces-kamala-harris-inauguration.

12. "'Oakland Forever': Golden State Warriors Gift Kamala Harris with Custom Jersey for Her Office," *ABC News*, January 21, 2021, available at: https://abc7news.com/golden-state-warriors-kamala-harris-jersey-oakland-forever/9841595.

13. Tom Schad, "WNBA Champion Seattle Storm Urge Fans to Support Democrats Joe Biden and Kamala Harris," *USA Today*, October 20, 2021, available at: https://eu.usatoday.com/story/sports/wnba/storm/2020/10/21/joe-biden-kamala-harris-get-support-wnba-champion-seattle-storm/3722503001.

14. Elizabeth Williams, "How the WNBA Helped Flip Georgia Blue," *Vox*, January 11, 2021, available at: https://www.vox.com/first-person/22221250/georgia-election-results-senate-warnock-ossoff-wnba-elizabeth-williams.

15. Molly Hensley-Clancy, "U.S. Soccer Argues It Paid Women's Team More than Men in Appeal Brief for Equal Pay Lawsuit," *Washington Post*, September 22, 2021, available at: https://www.washingtonpost.com/sports/2021/09/22/uswnt-equal-pay-lawsuit-appeal.

16. Joey Nowak, "Future President Gerald R. Ford Stood Up for Teammate against Racist Policy," *MLive.com*, April 3, 2019, available at: https://www.mlive.com/wolverines/2011/02/future_president_gerald_r_ford.html.

17. C. Richard King (ed.), *Native Athletes in Sport and Society: A Reader* (Lincoln: University of Nebraska Press, 2006).

18. Donald McIntosh, with Tom Bedecki and C. E. S. Franks, *Sport and Politics in Canada: Federal Government Involvement since 1961* (Kingston, ON: McGill-Queens University Press, 1987).

19. Rudolf Müllner, "Self-Improvement In and Through Sports: Cultural-Historical Perspectives," *International Journal of the History of Sport* 33(14) (2016): 1592–1605; Peter Bankov, "A Sport for All Project in Eastern Europe: 1979–89," *International Journal of the History of Sport* 21(5) (2004): 780–795.

20. Xiaolin Zhang and John Saunders, "An Historical Review of Mass Sports Policy Development in China, 1949–2009," *International Journal of the History of Sport* 36(15/16) (2019): 1408.

21. Gigliola Gori, "Model of Masculinity: Mussolini, the 'New Italian' of the Fascist Era," *International Journal of the History of Sport* 16(4) (1999): 43–45.

22. Andrew Foxall, "Photographing Vladimir Putin: Masculinity, Nationalism and Visuality in Russian Political Culture," *Geopolitics* 18 (2013): 141.

23. Cara A. Finnegan, *Photographic Presidents: Making History from Daguerreotype to Digital* (Champaign: University of Illinois Press, 2021).

24. Ellen Nakashima and Rick Maese, "In Pointed Snub, no U.S. Government Official Will Attend Beijing Winter Olympics," *Washington Post*, December 6, 2021, available at: https://www.washingtonpost.com/national-security/us-beijing-winter-olympics-diplomatic-boycott/2021/12/06/1d2e9920-56b1-11ec-9a18-a506cf3aa31d_story.html; Heather Dichter, "A Boycott of the Olympics Won't Force China to Change," *Washington Post*, December 8, 2021, available at: https://www.washingtonpost.com/outlook/2021/12/08/olympic-boycott.

25. For example, see Cesar R. Torres, "Peronism, International Sport, and Diplomacy," in Heather L. Dichter and Andrew L. Johns (eds.), *Diplomatic Games: Sport, Statecraft, and International Relations Since 1945* (Lexington: University Press of Kentucky, 2014), 151–182; Euclides de Freitas Couto and Alan Castellano Valente, "The World Cup is Ours! The Myth of Brazilianness in Lula's Diplomatic Rhetoric, 2007–2014," in Heather L. Dichter (ed.), *Soccer Diplomacy: International Relations and Football Since 1914* (Lexington: University Press of Kentucky, 2020), 198–220.

26. Doris Pieroth, "Los Angeles 1932," in John E. Findling and Kimberly D. Pelle (eds.), *Encyclopedia of the Modern Olympic Movement* (Westport, CT: Greenwood Press, 2004), 95; John Fea, "Lake Placid

1932," in John E. Findling and Kimberly D. Pelle (eds.), *Encyclopedia of the Modern Olympic Movement* (Westport, CT: Greenwood Press, 2004), 299.

27. "Detroit Delegates Bid for 1968 Olympics Friday," *Traverse City Record-Eagle*, October 15, 1963, 14.

28. Owen Gibson, "President Obama Goes All Out to Push Chicago's Olympic Bid," *The Guardian*, September 28, 2009, available at: https://www.theguardian.com/world/2009/sep/28/chicago-olympics-2016-barack-obama.

29. "Detroit 'Never Had a Chance' for Olympics," *Traverse City Record-Eagle*, October 19, 1963, 1; Telegram 52, Beliard, Chicago to Diplomatie Paris, November 13, 1963, 179QO/75, Centre des Archives diplomatiques de La Courneuve, Paris.

30. Kristi Keck, "Obama, Chicago Come Up Short in Olympics Bid," CNN.com, October 2, 2009, available at: https://edition.cnn.com/2009/POLITICS/10/02/denmark.olympics.obama.

Index